D0119445

Scott's

Last Expedition

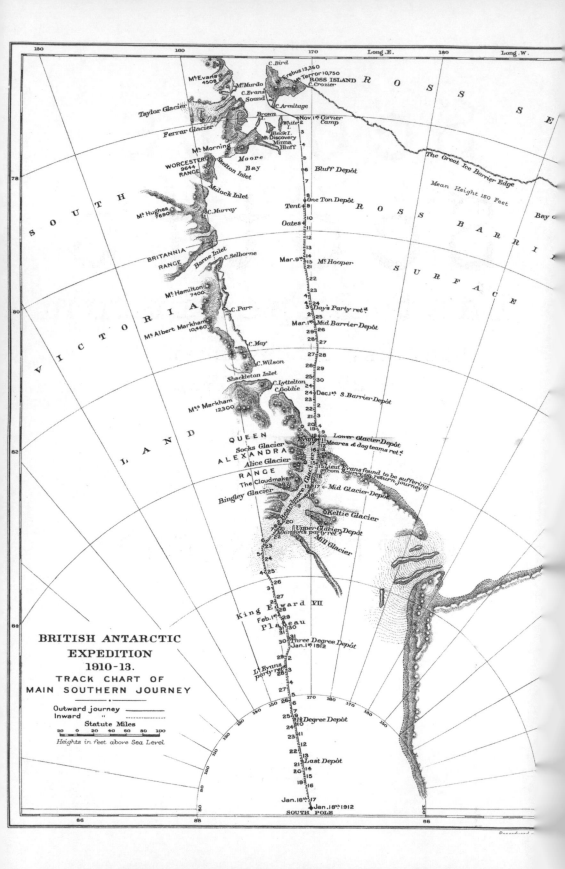

BRITISH ANTARCTIC
EXPEDITION
1910-13.
TRACK CHART OF
MAIN SOUTHERN JOURNEY

Outward journey ———————
Inward   "   ....

Statute Miles

Heights in feet above Sea Level

Scott's
Last Expedition
Diaries, 26 November 1910
– 29 March 1912

CAPTAIN SCOTT

AMBERLEY

This illustrated edition first published 2012

Amberley Publishing
The Hill, Stroud
Gloucestershire, GL5 4EP

www.amberley-books.com

British Library Cataloguing in Publication Data.
A catalogue record for this book is available from the British Library.

ISBN 978 1 4456 0444 2

Typesetting and origination by Amberley Publishing
Printed in Great Britain

CONTENTS

PREFACE TO THE 1913 EDITION

Fourteen years ago Robert Falcon Scott was a rising naval officer, able, accomplished, popular, highly thought of by his superiors, and devoted to his noble profession. It was a serious responsibility to induce him to take up the work of an explorer; yet no man living could be found who was so well fitted to command a great Antarctic Expedition. The undertaking was new and unprecedented. The object was to explore the unknown Antarctic continent by land. Captain Scott entered upon the enterprise with enthusiasm tempered by prudence and sound sense. All had to be learnt by a thorough study of the history of Arctic travelling, combined with experience of different conditions in the Antarctic regions. Scott was the initiator and founder of Antarctic sledge travelling.

His discoveries were of great importance. The survey and soundings along the barrier cliffs, the discovery of King Edward Land, the discovery of Ross Island and the other volcanic islets, the examination of the Barrier surface, the discovery of the Victoria Mountains – a range of great height and many hundreds of miles in length, which had only before been seen from a distance out at sea – and above all the discovery of the great ice cap on which the South Pole is situated, by one of the most remarkable Polar journeys on record. His small but excellent scientific staff worked hard and with trained intelligence, their results being recorded in twelve large quarto volumes.

The great discoverer had no intention of losing touch with his beloved profession though resolved to complete his Antarctic work. The exigencies of the naval service called him to the command of battleships and to confidential work of the Admiralty; so that five years elapsed before he could resume his Antarctic labours.

The object of Captain Scott's second expedition was mainly scientific, to complete and extend his former work in all branches of science. It was his ambition that in his ship there should be the most completely equipped expedition for scientific purposes connected with the Polar regions, both as regards men and material, that ever left these shores. In this he succeeded. He had on board a fuller complement of geologists, one of them especially trained for the study of physiography, biologists, physicists, and surveyors than ever before composed the staff of a Polar expedition. Thus Captain Scott's objects were strictly scientific, including the completion and extension of his former discoveries. Never before, in the Polar regions, have meteorological, magnetic and tidal observations been taken, in one locality, during five years. It was also part of Captain Scott's plan to reach the South Pole by a long and most arduous journey, but here again his intention was, if possible, to achieve scientific results on the way, especially hoping to discover fossils which would throw light on the former history of the great range of mountains which he had made known to science.

The principal aim of this great man – for he rightly has his niche among the Polar *Dii Majores* – was the advancement of knowledge. From all aspects Scott was among the most remarkable men of our time, and the vast number of readers of his journal will be deeply impressed with the beauty of his character. The chief traits which shone forth through his life were conspicuous in the hour of death. There are few events in history to be compared, for grandeur and pathos, with the last closing scene in that silent wilderness of snow. The great leader, with the bodies of his dearest friends beside him, wrote and wrote until the pencil dropped from his dying grasp. There was no thought of himself, only the earnest desire to give comfort and consolation to others in their sorrow. His very last lines were written lest he who induced him to enter upon Antarctic work should now feel regret for what he had done.

'If I cannot write to Sir Clements, tell him I thought much of him, and never regretted his putting me in command of the *Discovery*.'

CLEMENTS R. MARKHAM
September 1913

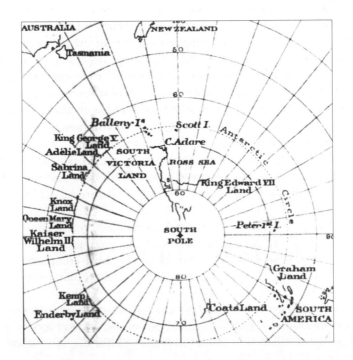

GLOSSARY

Barrier. The immense sheet of ice, over 400 miles wide and of still greater length, which lies south of Ross Island to the west of Victoria Land.

Brash. Small ice fragments from a floe that is breaking up.

Drift. Snow swept from the ground like dust and driven before the wind.

Finnesko. Fur boots.

Flense, flence. To cut the blubber from a skin or carcase.

Frost smoke. A mist of water vapour above the open leads, condensed by the severe cold.

Hoosh. A thick camp soup with a basis of pemmican.

Ice-foot. Properly the low fringe of ice formed about Polar lands by the sea spray. More widely, the banks of ice of varying height which skirt many parts of the Antarctic shores.

Piedmont. Coastwise stretches of the ancient ice sheet which once covered the Antarctic continent, remaining either on the land, or wholly or partially afloat.

Pram. A Norwegian skiff, with a spoon bow.

Primus. A portable stove for cooking.

Ramp. A great embankment of morainic material with ice beneath, once part of the glacier, on the lowest slopes of Erebus at the landward end of C. Evans.

Saennegras. A kind of fine Norwegian hay, used as packing in the finnesko to keep the feet warm and to make the fur boot fit firmly.

Sastrugus. An irregularity formed by the wind on a snow-plain. 'Snow wave' is not completely descriptive, as the sastrugus has often a fantastic shape unlike the ordinary conception of a wave.

Skua. A large gull.

Working crack. An open crack which leaves the ice free to move with the movement of the water beneath.

NOTE TO THE READER

Passages enclosed in inverted commas are taken from home letters of Captain Scott. Some additional notes from the editor of Scott's diaries (Leonard Huxley) have been inserted in square brackets within the diary entries.

I
THROUGH STORMY SEAS:
26 NOVEMBER 1910 – 10 DECEMBER 1910

THE FINAL PREPARATIONS IN NEW ZEALAND

The first three weeks of November have gone with such a rush that I have neglected my diary and can only patch it up from memory.

The dates seem unimportant, but throughout the period the officers and men of the ship have been unremittingly busy.

On arrival the ship was cleared of all the shore party stores, including huts, sledges, etc. Within five days she was in dock. Bowers attacked the ship's stores, surveyed, relisted, and restowed them, saving very much space by unstowing numerous cases and stowing the contents in the lazarette. Meanwhile our good friend Miller attacked the leak and traced it to the stern. We found the false stem split, and in one case a hole bored for a long-stem through-bolt which was much too large for the bolt. Miller made the excellent job in overcoming this difficulty which I expected, and since the ship has been afloat and loaded the leak is found to be enormously reduced. The ship still leaks, but the amount of water entering is little more than one would expect in an old wooden vessel.

The stream which was visible and audible inside the stern has been entirely stopped. Without steam the leak can now be kept under with the hand pump by two daily efforts of a quarter of an hour to twenty minutes. As the ship was, and in her present heavily laden condition, it would certainly have taken three to four hours each day.

Before the ship left dock, Bowers and Wyatt were at work again in the shed with a party of stevedores, sorting and relisting the shore party stores. Everything seems to have gone without a hitch. The various gifts and purchases made in New Zealand were collected – butter, cheese, bacon, hams, some preserved meats, tongues.

Meanwhile the huts were erected on the waste ground beyond the harbour works. Everything was overhauled, sorted, and marked afresh to prevent difficulty in the South. Davies, our excellent carpenter, Forde, Abbott, and Keohane were employed in this work. The large green tent was put up and proper supports made for it.

When the ship came out of dock she presented a scene of great industry. Officers and men of the ship, with a party of stevedores, were busy storing the holds. Miller's men were building horse stalls, caulking the decks, resecuring the deckhouses, putting in bolts and various small fittings. The engine-room staff and Anderson's people on the engines; scientists were stowing their laboratories; the cook refitting his galley, and so forth – not a single spot but had its band of workers.

We prepared to start our stowage much as follows: the main hold contains all the shore party provisions and part of the huts; above this on the main deck is packed in wonderfully close fashion the remainder of the wood of the huts, the sledges, and travelling equipment, and the larger instruments and machines to be employed by the scientific people; this encroaches far on the men's space, but the extent has been determined by their own wish; they have requested, through Evans, that they should not be considered: they were prepared to pig it anyhow, and a few cubic feet of space didn't matter – such is their spirit.

The men's space, such as it is, therefore, extends from the fore hatch to the stem on the main deck.

Under the forecastle are stalls for fifteen ponies, the maximum the space would hold; the narrow irregular space in front is packed tight with fodder.

Immediately behind the forecastle bulkhead is the small booby hatch, the only entrance to the men's mess deck in bad weather. Next comes the foremast, and between that and the fore hatch the galley and winch; on the port side of the fore hatch are stalls for four ponies – a very stout wooden structure.

Abaft the fore hatch is the ice-house. We managed to get 3 tons of ice, 162 carcases of mutton, and three carcases of beef, besides some boxes of sweetbreads and kidneys, into this space. The carcases are stowed in tiers with wooden battens between the tiers – it looks a triumph of orderly stowage, and I have great hope that it will ensure fresh mutton throughout our winter.

On either side of the main hatch and close up to the ice-house are two out of our three motor sledges; the third rests across the break of the poop in a space formerly occupied by a winch.

In front of the break of the poop is a stack of petrol cases; a further stack surmounted with bales of fodder stands between the main hatch and the mainmast, and cases of petrol, paraffin, and alcohol, arranged along either gangway.

We have managed to get 405 tons of coal in bunkers and main hold, 25 tons in a space left in the fore hold, and a little over 30 tons on the upper deck.

The sacks containing this last, added to the goods already mentioned, make a really heavy deck cargo, and one is naturally anxious concerning it; but everything that can be done by lashing and securing has been done.

The appearance of confusion on deck is completed by our thirty-three dogs[1] chained to stanchions and bolts on the ice-house and on the main hatch, between the motor sledges.

With all these stores on board the ship still stood two inches above her load mark. The tanks are filled with compressed forage, except one, which contains 12 tons of fresh water, enough, we hope, to take us to the ice.

Forage. I originally ordered 30 tons of compressed oaten hay from Melbourne. Oates has gradually persuaded us that this is insufficient, and our pony food weight has gone up to 45 tons, besides 3 or 4 tons for immediate use. The extra consists of 5 tons of hay, 5 or 6 tons of oil-cake, 4 or 5 tons of bran, and some crushed oats. We are not taking any corn.

We have managed to wedge in all the dog biscuits, the total weight being about 5 tons; Meares is reluctant to feed the dogs on seal, but I think we ought to do so during the winter.

We stayed with the Kinseys at their house 'Te Han' at Clifton. The house stands at the edge of the cliff, 400 feet above the sea, and looks far over the Christchurch plains and the long northern beach which limits it; close beneath one is the harbour bar and winding estuary of the two small rivers, the Avon and Waimakariri. Far away beyond the plains are the mountains, ever changing their aspect, and yet farther in over this northern sweep of sea can be seen in clear weather the beautiful snow-capped peaks of the Kaikouras. The scene is wholly enchanting, and such a view from some sheltered sunny corner in a garden which blazes with masses of red and golden flowers tends to feelings of inexpressible satisfaction with all things. At night we slept in this garden under peaceful clear skies; by day I was off to my office in Christchurch, then perhaps to the ship or the Island, and so home by the mountain road over the Port Hills. It is a pleasant time to remember in spite of interruptions – and it gave time for many necessary consultations with Kinsey. His interest in the expedition is wonderful, and such interest on the part of a thoroughly shrewd business man is an asset of which I have taken full advantage. Kinsey will act as my agent in Christchurch during my absence; I have given him an ordinary power of attorney, and I think have left him in possession of all facts. His kindness to us was beyond words.

THE VOYAGE OUT

Saturday 26 November We advertised our start at 3 p.m., and at three minutes to that hour the *Terra Nova* pushed off from the jetty. A great mass of people assembled. K. and I lunched with a party in the New Zealand Company's ship *Ruapehu*. Mr. Kinsey, Ainsley, the Arthur and George Rhodes, Sir George Clifford, etc.² K. and I went out in the ship, but left her inside the heads after passing the *Cambrian*, the only naval ship present. We came home in the Harbour Tug; two other tugs followed the ship out and innumerable small boats. Ponting busy with cinematograph. We walked over the hills to Sumner. Saw the *Terra Nova*, a little dot to the S.E.

Monday 28 November Caught 8 o'clock express to Port Chalmers, Kinsey saw us off. Wilson joined train. Rhodes met us Timaru. Telegram to say *Terra Nova* had arrived Sunday night. Arrived Port Chalmers at 4.30. Found all well.

Tuesday 29 November Saw Fenwick re *Central News* agreement – to town. Thanked Glendenning for handsome gift, 130 grey jerseys. To Town Hall to see Mayor. Found all well on board.

We left the wharf at 2.30 – bright sunshine – very gay scene. If anything more craft following us than at Lyttelton – Mrs. Wilson, Mrs. Evans, and K. left at Heads and back in Harbour Tug. Other tugs followed farther with

Volunteer Reserve Gunboat – all left about 4.30. Pennell 'swung' the ship for compass adjustment, then 'away'.

Evening Loom of land and Cape Saunders Light blinking.

Wednesday 30 November Noon no miles. Light breeze from northward all day, freshening towards nightfall and turning to N.W. Bright sunshine. Ship pitching with south-westerly swell. All in good spirits except one or two sick.

We are away, sliding easily and smoothly through the water, but burning coal – 8 tons in 24 hours reported 8 p.m.

Thursday 1 December The month opens well on the whole. During the night the wind increased; we worked up to 8, to 9, and to 9.5 knots. Stiff wind from N.W. and confused sea. Awoke to much motion.

The ship a queer and not altogether cheerful sight under the circumstances.

Below one knows all space is packed as tight as human skill can devise – and on deck! Under the forecastle fifteen ponies close side by side, seven one side, eight the other, heads together and groom between – swaying, swaying continually to the plunging, irregular motion.

One takes a look through a hole in the bulkhead and sees a row of heads with sad, patient eyes come swinging up together from the starboard side, whilst those on the port swing back; then up come the port heads, whilst the starboard recede. It seems a terrible ordeal for these poor beasts to stand this day after day for weeks together, and indeed though they continue to feed well the strain quickly drags down their weight and condition; but nevertheless the trial cannot be gauged from human standards. There are horses which never lie down, and all horses can sleep standing; anatomically they possess a ligament in each leg which takes their weight without strain. Even our poor animals will get rest and sleep in spite of the violent motion. Some 4 or 5 tons of fodder and the ever watchful Anton take up the remainder of the forecastle space. Anton is suffering badly from sea-sickness, but last night he smoked a cigar. He smoked a little, then had an interval of evacuation, and back to his cigar whilst he rubbed his stomach and remarked to Oates 'no good' – gallant little Anton!

There are four ponies outside the forecastle and to leeward of the fore hatch, and on the whole, perhaps, with shielding tarpaulins, they have a rather better time than their comrades. Just behind the ice-house and on either side of the main hatch are two enormous packing-cases containing motor sledges, each 16 × 5 × 4; mounted as they are several inches above the deck they take a formidable amount of space. A third sledge stands across the break of the poop in the space hitherto occupied by the after winch. All these cases are covered with stout tarpaulin and lashed with heavy chain and rope lashings, so that they may be absolutely secure.

The petrol for these sledges is contained in tins and drums protected in stout wooden packing-cases which are ranged across the deck immediately in front of the poop and abreast the motor sledges. The quantity is 2½ tons and the space occupied considerable.

Round and about these packing-cases, stretching from the galley forward to the wheel aft, the deck is stacked with coal bags forming our deck cargo of coal, now rapidly diminishing.

We left Port Chalmers with 462 tons of coal on board, rather a greater quantity than I had hoped for, and yet the load mark was 3 inches above the water. The ship was over 2 feet by the stern, but this will soon be remedied.

Upon the coal sacks, upon and between the motor sledges and upon the ice-house are grouped the dogs, thirty-three in all. They must perforce be chained up and they are given what shelter is afforded on deck, but their position is not enviable. The seas continually break on the weather bulwarks and scatter clouds of heavy spray over the backs of all who must venture into the waist of the ship. The dogs sit with their tails to this invading water, their coats wet and dripping. It is a pathetic attitude, deeply significant of cold and misery; occasionally some poor beast emits a long pathetic whine. The group forms a picture of wretched dejection; such a life is truly hard for these poor creatures.

We manage somehow to find a seat for everyone at our cabin table, although the wardroom contains twenty-four officers. There are generally one or two on watch, which eases matters, but it is a squash. Our meals are simple enough, but it is really remarkable to see the manner in which our two stewards, Hooper and Neald, provide for all requirements, washing up, tidying cabin, and making themselves generally useful in the cheerfullest manner.

With such a large number of hands on board, allowing nine seamen in each watch, the ship is easily worked, and Meares and Oates have their appointed assistants to help them in custody of dogs and ponies, but on such a night as the last with the prospect of dirty weather, the 'after guard' of volunteers is awake and exhibiting its delightful enthusiasm in the cause of safety and comfort – some are ready to lend a hand if there is difficulty with ponies and dogs, others in shortening or trimming sails, and others again in keeping the bunkers filled with the deck coal.

I think Priestley is the most seriously incapacitated by sea-sickness – others who might be as bad have had some experience of the ship and her movement. Ponting cannot face meals but sticks to his work; on the way to Port Chalmers I am told that he posed several groups before the cinematograph, though obliged repeatedly to retire to the ship's side. Yesterday he was developing plates with the developing dish in one hand and an ordinary basin in the other!

We have run 190 miles today: a good start, but inconvenient in one respect – we have been making for Campbell Island, but early this morning it became evident that our rapid progress would bring us to the Island in the middle of the night, instead of tomorrow, as I had anticipated. The delay of waiting for daylight would not be advisable under the circumstances, so we gave up this item of our programme.

Later in the day the wind has veered to the westward, heading us slightly. I trust it will not go further round; we are now more than a point to eastward of our course to the ice, and three points to leeward of that to Campbell Island, so that we should not have fetched the Island anyhow.

Friday 1 December A day of great disaster. From 4 o'clock last night the wind freshened with great rapidity, and very shortly we were under topsails, jib, and staysail only. It blew very hard and the sea got up at once. Soon we were plunging heavily and taking much water over the lee rail. Oates and Atkinson with intermittent assistance from others were busy keeping the ponies on their legs. Cases of petrol, forage, etc., began to break loose on the upper deck; the principal trouble was caused by the loose coal-bags, which were bodily lifted by the seas and swung against the lashed cases. 'You know how carefully everything had been lashed, but no lashings could have withstood the onslaught of these coal sacks for long'; they acted like battering rams. 'There was nothing for it but to grapple with the evil, and nearly all hands were labouring for hours in the waist of the ship, heaving coal sacks overboard and re-lashing the petrol cases, etc., in the best manner possible under such difficult and dangerous circumstances. The seas were continually breaking over these people and now and again they would be completely submerged. At such times they had to cling for dear life to some fixture to prevent themselves being washed overboard, and with coal bags and loose cases washing about, there was every risk of such hold being torn away.

'No sooner was some semblance of order restored than some exceptionally heavy wave would tear away the lashing and the work had to be done all over again.'

The night wore on, the sea and wind ever rising, and the ship ever plunging more distractedly; we shortened sail to main topsail and staysail, stopped engines and hove to, but to little purpose. Tales of ponies down came frequently from forward, where Oates and Atkinson laboured through the entire night. Worse was to follow, much worse – a report from the engine-room that the pumps had choked and the water risen over the gratings.

From this moment, about 4 a.m., the engine-room became the centre of interest. The water gained in spite of every effort. Lashley, to his neck in rushing water, stuck gamely to the work of clearing suctions. For a time, with donkey engine and bilge pump sucking, it looked as though the water would be got under; but the hope was short-lived: five minutes of pumping invariably led to the same result – a general choking of the pumps.

The outlook appeared grim. The amount of water which was being made, with the ship so roughly handled, was most uncertain. 'We knew that normally the ship was not making much water, but we also knew that a considerable part of the water washing over the upper deck must be finding its way below; the decks were leaking in streams. The ship was very deeply laden; it did not need the addition of much water to get her waterlogged, in which condition anything might have happened.' The hand pump produced only a dribble, and its suction could not be got at; as the water crept higher it got in contact with the boiler and grew warmer – so hot at last that no one could work at the suctions. Williams had to confess he was beaten and must draw fires. What was to be done? Things for the moment appeared very black. The sea seemed higher than ever; it came over lee rail and poop, a rush of green water; the ship wallowed in it; a great piece of the bulwark carried clean away. The bilge pump is dependent on the main engine. To use the pump it was necessary to go ahead. It was at such times that the heaviest seas swept in over the lee rail; over and over [again] the rail, from the forerigging to the main, was covered by a solid sheet of curling water which swept aft and high on the poop. On one occasion I was waist deep when standing on the rail of the poop.

The scene on deck was devastating, and in the engine-room the water, though really not great in quantity, rushed over the floor plates and frames in a fashion that gave it a fearful significance.

The afterguard were organised in two parties by Evans to work buckets; the men were kept steadily going on the choked hand pumps – this seemed all that could be done for the moment, and what a measure to count as the sole safeguard of the ship from sinking, practically an attempt to bale her out! Yet strange as it may seem the effort has not been wholly fruitless – the string of buckets which has now been kept going for four hours [It was continued a night and a day], together with the dribble from the pump, has kept the water under – if anything there is a small decrease.

Meanwhile we have been thinking of a way to get at the suction of the pump: a hole is being made in the engine-room bulkhead, the coal between this and the pump shaft will be removed, and a hole made in the shaft. With so much water coming on board, it is impossible to open the hatch over the shaft. We are not out of the wood, but hope dawns, as indeed it should for me, when I find myself so wonderfully served. Officers and men are singing chanties over their arduous work. Williams is working in sweltering heat behind the boiler to get the door made in the bulkhead. Not a single one has lost his good spirits. A dog was drowned last night, one pony is dead and two others in a bad condition – probably they too will go. 'Occasionally a heavy sea would bear one of them away, and he was only saved by his chain. Meares with some helpers had constantly to be rescuing these wretched creatures from hanging, and trying to find them better shelter, an almost hopeless task. One poor beast was found hanging when dead; one was washed away with such force that his chain broke and he disappeared overboard; the next wave miraculously washed him on board again and he is now fit and well.' The gale has exacted heavy toll, but I feel all will be well if we can only cope with the water. Another dog has just been washed overboard – alas! Thank God, the gale is abating. The sea is still mountainously high, but the ship is not labouring so heavily as she was. I pray we may be under sail again before morning.

Saturday 3 December Yesterday the wind slowly fell towards evening; less water was taken on board, therefore less found its way below, and it soon became evident that our baling was gaining on the engine-room. The work was steadily kept going in two-hour shifts. By 10 p.m. the hole in the engine-room bulkhead was completed, and (Lieut.) Evans, wriggling over the coal, found his way to the pump shaft and down it. He soon cleared the suction 'of the coal balls (a mixture of coal and oil) which choked it', and to the joy of all a good stream of water came from the pump for the first time. From this moment it was evident we should get over the difficulty, and though the pump choked again on several occasions the water in the engine-room steadily decreased. It was good to visit that spot this morning and to find that the water no longer swished from side to side. In the forenoon fires were laid and lighted – the hand pump was got into complete order and sucked the bilges almost dry, so that great quantities of coal and ashes could be taken out.

Now all is well again, and we are steaming and sailing steadily south within two points of our course. Campbell and Bowers have been busy relisting everything on the upper deck. This afternoon we got out the two dead ponies through the forecastle skylight. It was a curious proceeding, as the space looked quite inadequate for their passage. We looked into the ice-house and found it in the best order.

Though we are not yet safe, as another gale might have disastrous results, it is wonderful to realise the change which has been wrought in our outlook in twenty-four hours. The others have confessed the gravely serious view of our position which they shared with me yesterday, and now we are all hopeful again.

As far as one can gather, besides the damage to the bulwarks of the ship, we have lost two ponies, one dog, '10 tons of coal', 65 gallons of petrol, and a case of the biologists' spirit – a serious loss enough, but much less than I expected. 'All things considered we have come off lightly, but it was bad luck to strike a gale at such a time.' The third pony which was down in a sling for some time in the gale is again on his feet. He looks a little groggy, but may pull through if we don't have another gale. Osman, our best sledge dog, was very bad this morning, but has been lying warmly in hay all day, and is now much better. 'Several more were in a very bad way and needed nursing back to life.' The sea and wind seem to be increasing again, and there is a heavy southerly swell, but the glass is high; we ought not to have another gale till it falls.[3]

Monday 5 December Lat. 56° 40′ – The barometer has been almost steady since Saturday, the wind rising and falling slightly, but steady in direction from the west. From a point off course we have crept up to the course itself. Everything looks prosperous except the ponies. Up to this morning, in spite of favourable wind and sea, the ship has been pitching heavily to a south-westerly swell. This has tried the animals badly, especially those under the forecastle. We had thought the ponies on the port side to be pretty safe, but two of them seem to me to be groggy, and I doubt if they could stand more heavy weather without a spell of rest. I pray there may be no more gales. We should be nearing the limits of the westerlies, but one cannot be sure for at least two days. There is still a swell from the S.W., though it is not nearly so heavy as yesterday, but I devoutly wish it would vanish altogether. So much depends on fine weather. December ought to be a fine month in the Ross Sea; it always has been, and just now conditions point to fine weather. Well, we must be prepared for anything, but I'm anxious, anxious about these animals of ours.

The dogs have quite recovered since the fine weather – they are quite in good form again.

Our deck cargo is getting reduced; all the coal is off the upper deck and the petrol is re-stored in better fashion; as far as that is concerned we should not mind another blow. Campbell and Bowers have been untiring in getting things straight on deck.

The idea of making our station Cape Crozier has again come on the *tapis*. There would be many advantages: the ease of getting there at an early date, the fact that none of the autumn or summer parties could be cut off, the fact that the main Barrier could be reached without crossing crevasses and that the track to the Pole would be due south from the first: – the mild condition and absence of blizzards at the penguin rookery, the opportunity of studying the Emperor penguin incubation, and the new interest of the geology of Terror, besides minor facilities, such as the getting of ice, stones for shelters, etc. The disadvantages mainly consist in the possible difficulty of landing stores – a swell would make things very unpleasant, and might possibly prevent the landing of the horses and motors. Then again it would be certain that some distance of bare rock would have to be traversed before a good snow surface was reached from the hut, and possibly a climb of 300 or 400 feet would intervene. Again, it might be difficult to handle the ship whilst stores were being landed, owing to current, bergs, and floe ice. It remains to be seen, but the prospect is certainly alluring. At a pinch we could land the ponies in McMurdo Sound and let them walk round.

The sun is shining brightly this afternoon, everything is drying, and I think the swell continues to subside.

Tuesday 6 December Lat. 59° 7'. Long. 177° 51' E. Made good S. 17 E. 153; 457' to Circle. The promise of yesterday has been fulfilled, the swell has continued to subside, and this afternoon we go so steadily that we have much comfort. I am truly thankful mainly for the sake of the ponies; poor things, they look thin and scraggy enough, but generally brighter and fitter. There is no doubt the forecastle is a bad place for them, but in any case some must have gone there. The four midship ponies, which were expected to be subject to the worst conditions, have had a much better time than their fellows. A few ponies have swollen legs, but all are feeding well. The wind failed in the morning watch and later a faint breeze came from the eastward; the barometer has been falling, but not on a steep gradient; it is still above normal. This afternoon it is overcast with a Scotch mist. Another day ought to put us beyond the reach of westerly gales.

We still continue to discuss the project of landing at Cape Crozier, and the prospect grows more fascinating as we realise it. For instance, we ought from such a base to get an excellent idea of the Barrier movement, and of the relative movement amongst the pressure ridges. There is no doubt it would be a tremendous stroke of luck to get safely landed there with all our paraphernalia.

Everyone is very cheerful – one hears laughter and song all day – it's delightful to be with such a merry crew. A week from New Zealand today.

Wednesday 7 December Lat. 61° 22'. Long. 179° 56' W. Made good S. 25 E. 150; Ant. Circle 313'. The barometer descended on a steep regular gradient all night, turning suddenly to an equally steep up grade this morning. With the turn a smart breeze sprang up from the S.W. and forced us three points off our course. The sea has remained calm, seeming to show that the ice is not far off; this afternoon temperature of air and water both 34°, supporting the assumption. The wind has come fair and we are on our course again, going between 7 and 8 knots.

Quantities of whale birds about the ship, the first fulmars and the first McCormick skua seen. Last night saw 'hour glass' dolphins about. Sooty and black-browed albatrosses continue, with Cape chickens. The cold makes people hungry and one gets just a tremor on seeing the marvellous disappearance of consumables when our twenty-four young appetites have to be appeased.

Last night I discussed the Western Geological Party, and explained to Ponting the desirability of his going with it. I had thought he ought to be in charge, as the oldest and most experienced traveller, and mentioned it to him – then to Griffith Taylor. The latter was evidently deeply disappointed. So we three talked the matter out between us, and Ponting at once disclaimed any right, and announced cheerful agreement with Taylor's leadership; it was a satisfactory arrangement, and shows Ponting in a very pleasant light. I'm sure he's a very nice fellow.

I would record here a symptom of the spirit which actuates the men. After the gale the main deck under the forecastle space in which the ponies are stabled leaked badly, and the dirt of the stable leaked through on hammocks and bedding. Not a word has been said; the men living in that part have done their best to fend off the nuisance with oilskins and canvas, but without sign of complaint. Indeed the discomfort throughout the mess deck has been extreme. Everything has been thrown about, water has found its way down in a dozen places. There is no daylight, and air can come only through the small fore hatch; the artificial lamplight has given much trouble. The men have been wetted to the skin repeatedly on deck, and have no chance of drying their clothing. All things considered, their cheerful fortitude is little short of wonderful.

First Ice There was a report of ice at dinner tonight. Evans corroborated Cheetham's statement that there was a berg far away to the west, showing now and again as the sun burst through the clouds.

Thursday 8 December 63° 20'. 177° 22'. S. 31 E. 138'; to Circle 191'. The wind increased in the first watch last night to a moderate gale. The ship close hauled held within two points of her course. Topgallant sails and mainsail were furled, and later in the night the wind gradually crept ahead. At 6 a.m. we were obliged to furl everything, and throughout the day we have been plunging against a stiff breeze and moderate sea. This afternoon by keeping a little to eastward of the course, we have managed to get fore and aft sail filled. The barometer has continued its steady upward path for twenty-four hours; it shows signs of turning, having reached within 1/10th of 30 inches. It was light throughout last night (always a cheerful condition), but this head wind is trying to the patience, more especially as our coal expenditure is more than I estimated. We manage 62 or 63 revolutions on about 9 tons, but have to distil every three days at expense of half a ton, and then there is a weekly half ton for the cook. It is certainly a case of fighting one's way South.

I was much disturbed last night by the motion; the ship was pitching and twisting with short sharp movements on a confused sea, and with every plunge my thoughts flew to our poor ponies. This afternoon they are fairly well, but one knows that they must be getting weaker as time goes on, and one longs to give them a good sound rest with the ship on an even keel. Poor patient beasts! One wonders how far the memory of such fearful discomfort will remain with them – animals so often remember places and conditions where they have encountered difficulties or hurt. Do they only recollect circumstances which are deeply impressed by some shock of fear or sudden pain, and does the remembrance of prolonged strain pass away? Who can tell? But it would seem strangely merciful if nature should blot out these weeks of slow but inevitable torture.

The dogs are in great form again; for them the greatest circumstance of discomfort is to be constantly wet. It was this circumstance prolonged throughout the gale which nearly lost us our splendid leader 'Osman'. In the morning he was discovered utterly exhausted and only feebly trembling; life was very nearly out of him. He was buried in hay, and lay so for twenty-four hours, refusing food – the wonderful hardihood of his species was again shown by the fact that within another twenty-four hours he was to all appearance as fit as ever.

Antarctic petrels have come about us. This afternoon one was caught.

Later, about 7 p.m. Evans saw two icebergs far on the port beam; they could only be seen from the masthead. Whales have been frequently seen – *Balænoptera Sibbaldi* – supposed to be the biggest mammal that has ever existed.[4]

Friday 9 December 65° 8'. 177° 41'. Made good S. 4 W. 109'; Scott Island S. 22 W. 147'. At six this morning bergs and pack were reported ahead; at first we thought the pack might consist only of fragments of the bergs, but on entering a stream we found small worn floes – the ice not more than two or three feet in thickness. 'I had hoped that we should not meet it till we reached latitude 66½ or at least 66'. We decided to work to the south and west as far as the open water would allow, and have met with some success. At 4 p.m., as I write, we are still in open water, having kept a fairly straight course and come through five or six light streams of ice, none more than 300 yards across.

We have passed some very beautiful bergs, mostly tabular. The heights have varied from 60 to 80 feet, and I am getting to think that this part of the Antarctic yields few bergs of greater altitude.

Two bergs deserve some description. One, passed very close on port hand in order that it might be cinematographed, was about 80 feet in height, and tabular. It seemed to have been calved at a comparatively recent date.

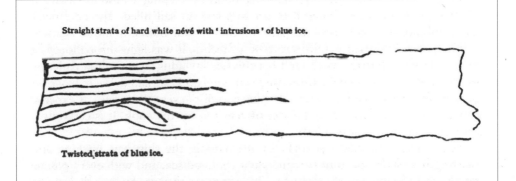

Straight strata of hard white névé with ' intrusions ' of blue ice.

Twisted strata of blue ice.

The picture (on the previous page) shows its peculiarities, and points to the desirability of close examination of other berg faces. There seemed to be a distinct difference of origin between the upper and lower portions of the berg, as though a land glacier had been covered by layer after layer of seasonal snow. Then again, what I have described as 'intrusive layers of blue ice' was a remarkable feature; one could imagine that these layers represent surfaces which have been transformed by regelation under hot sun and wind.

This point required investigation.

The second berg was distinguished by innumerable vertical cracks. These seemed to run criss-cross and to weaken the structure, so that the various séracs formed by them had bent to different angles and shapes, giving a very irregular surface to the berg, and a face scarred with immense vertical fissures.

One imagines that such a berg has come from a region of ice disturbance such as King Edward's Land.

We have seen a good many whales today, rorquals with high black spouts – *Balænoptera Sibbaldi*.

The birds with us: Antarctic and snow petrel – a fulmar – and this morning Cape pigeon.

We have pack ice farther north than expected, and it's impossible to interpret the fact. One hopes that we shall not have anything heavy, but I'm afraid there's not much to build upon.

10 p.m. We have made good progress throughout the day, but the ice streams thicken as we advance, and on either side of us the pack now appears in considerable fields. We still pass quantities of bergs, perhaps nearly one-half the number tabular, but the rest worn and fantastic.

The sky has been wonderful, with every form of cloud in every condition of light and shade; the sun has continually appeared through breaks in the cloudy heavens from time to time, brilliantly illuminating some field of pack, some steep-walled berg, or some patch of bluest sea. So sunlight and shadow have chased each other across our scene. Tonight there is little or no swell – the ship is on an even keel, steady, save for the occasional shocks on striking ice.

It is difficult to express the sense of relief this steadiness gives after our storm-tossed passage. One can only imagine the relief and comfort afforded to the ponies, but the dogs are visibly cheered and the human element is full of gaiety. The voyage seems full of promise in spite of the imminence of delay.

If the pack becomes thick I shall certainly put the fires out and wait for it to open. I do not think it ought to remain close for long in this meridian. Tonight we must be beyond the 66th parallel.

Saturday 10 December Dead Reckoning 66° 38'. Long. 178° 47'. Made good S. 17 W. 94. C. Crozier 688'. Stayed on deck till midnight. The sun just dipped below the southern horizon. The scene was incomparable. The northern sky was gloriously rosy and reflected in the calm sea between the ice, which varied from burnished copper to salmon pink; bergs and pack to the north had a pale greenish hue with deep purple shadows, the sky shaded to saffron and pale green. We gazed long at these beautiful effects. The ship made through leads during the night; morning found us pretty well at the end of the open water. We stopped to water ship from a nice hummocky floe. We made about 8 tons of water. Rennick took a sounding, 1960 fathoms; the tube brought up two small lumps of volcanic lava with the usual globigerina ooze.

Wilson shot a number of Antarctic petrel and snowy petrel. Nelson got some crustaceans and other beasts with a vertical tow net, and got a water sample and temperatures at 400 metres. The water was warmer at that depth. About 1.30 we proceeded at first through fairly easy pack, then in amongst very heavy old floes grouped about a big berg; we shot out of this and made a detour, getting easier going; but though the floes were less formidable as we proceeded south, the pack grew thicker. I noticed large floes of comparatively thin ice very sodden and easily split; these are similar to some we went through in the *Discovery*, but tougher by a month.

At three we stopped and shot four crab-eater seals; tonight we had the livers for dinner – they were excellent.

Tonight we are in very close pack – it is doubtful if it is worth pushing on, but an arch of clear sky which has shown to the southward all day makes me think that there must be clearer water in that direction; perhaps only some 20 miles away – but 20 miles is much under present conditions. As I came below to bed at 11 p.m. Bruce was slogging away, making fair progress, but now and again brought up altogether. I noticed the ice was becoming much smoother and thinner, with occasional signs of pressure, between which the ice was very thin.

'We had been very carefully into all the evidence of former voyages to pick the best meridian to go south on, and I thought and still think that the evidence points to the 178 W. as the best. We entered the pack more or less on this meridian, and have been rewarded by encountering worse conditions than any ship has had before. Worse, in fact, than I imagined would have been possible on any other meridian of those from which we could have chosen.

'To understand the difficulty of the position you must appreciate what the pack is and how little is known of its movements.

'The pack in this part of the world consists (1) of the ice which has formed over the sea on the fringe of the Antarctic continent during the last winter; (2) of very heavy old ice floes which have broken out of bays and inlets during the previous summer, but have not had time to get north before the winter set in; (3) of comparatively heavy ice formed over the Ross Sea early in the last winter; and (4) of comparatively thin ice which has formed over parts of the Ross Sea in middle or towards the end of the last winter.

'Undoubtedly throughout the winter all ice-sheets move and twist, tear apart and press up into ridges, and thousands of bergs charge through these sheets, raising hummocks and lines of pressure and mixing things up; then of course where such rents are made in the winter the sea freezes again, forming a newer and thinner sheet.

'With the coming of summer the northern edge of the sheet decays and the heavy ocean swell penetrates it, gradually breaking it into smaller and smaller fragments. Then the whole body moves to the north and the swell of the Ross Sea attacks the southern edge of the pack.

'This makes it clear why at the northern and southern limits the pieces or ice-floes are comparatively small, whilst in the middle the floes may be two or three miles across; and why the pack may and does consist of various natures of ice-floes in extraordinary confusion.

'Further it will be understood why the belt grows narrower and the floes thinner and smaller as the summer advances.

'We know that where thick pack may be found early in January, open water and a clear sea may be found in February, and broadly that the later the date the easier the chance of getting through.

'A ship going through the pack must either break through the floes, push them aside, or go round them, observing that she cannot push floes which are more than 200 or 300 yards across.

'Whether a ship can get through or not depends on the thickness and nature of the ice, the size of the floes and the closeness with which they are packed together, as well as on her own power.

'The situation of the main bodies of pack and the closeness with which the floes are packed depend almost entirely on the prevailing winds. One cannot tell what winds have prevailed before one's arrival; therefore one cannot know much about the situation or density.

'Within limits the density is changing from day to day and even from hour to hour; such changes depend on the wind, but it may not necessarily be a local wind, so that at times they seem almost mysterious. One sees the floes pressing closely against one another at a given time, and an hour or two afterwards a gap of a foot or more may be seen between each.

'When the floes are pressed together it is difficult and sometimes impossible to force a way through, but when there is release of pressure the sum of many little gaps allows one to take a zigzag path.'

2
IN THE PACK: 11 DECEMBER 1910 –
30 DECEMBER 1910

Sunday 11 December The ice grew closer during the night, and at 6 it seemed hopeless to try and get ahead. The pack here is very regular; the floes about 2 ½ feet thick and very solid. They are pressed closely together, but being irregular in shape, open spaces frequently occur, generally triangular in shape.

It might be noted that such ice as this occupies much greater space than it originally did when it formed a complete sheet – hence if the Ross Sea were wholly frozen over in the spring, the total quantity of pack to the north of it when it breaks out must be immense.

This ice looks as though it must have come from the Ross Sea, and yet one is puzzled to account for the absence of pressure.

We have lain tight in the pack all day; the wind from 6 a.m. strong from W. and N.W., with snow; the wind has eased tonight, and for some hours the glass, which fell rapidly last night, has been stationary. I expect the wind will shift soon; pressure on the pack has eased, but so far it has not opened.

This morning Rennick got a sounding at 2015 fathoms from bottom similar to yesterday, with small pieces of basic lava; these two soundings appear to show a great distribution of this volcanic rock by ice. The line was weighed by hand after the soundings. I read Service in the wardroom.

This afternoon all hands have been away on ski over the floes. It is delightful to get the exercise. I'm much pleased with the ski and ski boots – both are very well adapted to our purposes.

This waiting requires patience, though I suppose it was to be expected at such an early season. It is difficult to know when to try and push on again.

Monday 12 December The pack was a little looser this morning; there was a distinct long swell apparently from N.W. The floes were not apart but barely touching the edges, which were hard pressed yesterday; the wind still holds from N.W., but lighter. Gran, Oates, and Bowers went on ski towards a reported island about which there had been some difference of opinion. I felt certain it was a berg, and it proved to be so; only of a very curious dome shape with very low cliffs all about.

Fires were ordered for 12, and at 11.30 we started steaming with plain sail set. We made, and are making fair progress on the whole, but it is very uneven. We escaped from the heavy floes about us into much thinner pack, then through two water holes, then back to the thinner pack consisting of thin floes of large area fairly easily broken. All went well till we struck heavy floes again, then for half an hour we stopped dead. Then on again, and since alternately bad and good – that is, thin young floes and hoary older ones, occasionally a pressed-up berg, very heavy.

The best news of yesterday was that we drifted 15 miles to the S.E., so that we have not really stopped our progress at all, though it has, of course, been pretty slow.

I really don't know what to think of the pack, or when to hope for open water.

We tried Atkinson's blubber stove this afternoon with great success. The interior of the stove holds a pipe in a single coil pierced with holes on the under side. These holes drip oil on to an asbestos burner. The blubber is placed in a tank suitably built around the chimney; the overflow of oil from this tank leads to the feed pipe in the stove, with a cock to regulate the flow. A very simple device, but as has been shown a very effective one; the stove gives great heat, but, of course, some blubber smell. However, with such stoves in the south one would never lack cooked food or warm hut.

Discussed with Wright the fact that the hummocks on sea-ice always yield fresh water. We agreed that the brine must simply run down out of the ice. It will be interesting to bring up a piece of sea-ice and watch this process. But the fact itself is interesting as showing that the process producing the hummock is really producing fresh water. It may also be noted as phenomenon which makes *all* the difference to the ice navigator.[5]

Truly the getting to our winter quarters is no light task; at first the gales and heavy seas, and now this continuous fight with the pack ice.

8 p.m. We are getting on with much bumping and occasional 'hold ups'.

Tuesday 13 December I was up most of the night. Never have I experienced such rapid and complete changes of prospect. Cheetham in the last dog watch was running the ship through sludgy new ice, making with all sail set four or five knots. Bruce, in the first, took over as we got into heavy ice again; but after a severe tussle got through into better conditions. The ice of yesterday loose with sludgy thin floes between. The middle watch found us making for an open lead, the ice around hard and heavy. We got through, and by sticking to the open water and then to some recently frozen pools made good progress. At the end of the middle watch trouble began again, and during this and the first part of the morning we were wrestling with the worst conditions we have met. Heavy hummocked bay ice, the floes standing 7 or 8 feet out of water, and very deep below. It was just such ice as we encountered at King Edward Land in the *Discovery*. I have never seen anything more formidable. The last part of the morning watch was spent in a long recently frozen lead or pool, and the ship went well ahead again.

These changes sound tame enough, but they are a great strain on one's nerves – one is for ever wondering whether one has done right in trying to come down so far east, and having regard to coal, what ought to be done under the circumstances.

In the first watch came many alterations of opinion; time and again it looks as though we ought to stop when it seemed futile to be pushing and pushing without result; then would come a stretch of easy going and the impression that all was going very well with us. The fact of the matter is, it is difficult not to imagine the conditions in which one finds oneself to be more extensive than they are. It is wearing to have to face new conditions every hour. This morning we met at breakfast in great spirits; the ship has been boring along well for two hours, then Cheetham suddenly ran her into a belt of the worst and we were held up immediately. We can push back again, I think, but meanwhile we have taken advantage of the conditions to water ship. These big floes are very handy for that purpose at any rate. Rennick got a sounding 2124 fathoms, similar bottom *including* volcanic lava.

13 December (cont.) 67° 30' S. 177° 58' W. Made good S. 20 E. 27'. C. Crozier S. 21 W. 644'. We got in several tons of ice, then pushed off and slowly and laboriously worked our way to one of the recently frozen pools. It was not easily crossed, but when we came to its junction with the next part to the S.W. (in which direction I proposed to go) we were quite hung up. A little inspection showed that the big floes were tending to close. It seems as though the tenacity of the 6 or 7 inches of recent ice over the pools is enormously increased by lateral pressure. But whatever the cause, we could not budge.

We have decided to put fires out and remain here till the conditions change altogether for the better. It is sheer waste of coal to make further attempts to break through as things are at present.

We have been set to the east during the past days; is it the normal set in the region, or due to the prevalence of westerly winds? Possibly much depends on this as concerns our date of release. It is annoying, but one must contain one's soul in patience and hope for a brighter outlook in a day or two. Meanwhile we shall sound and do as much biological work as is possible.

The pack is a sunless place as a rule; this morning we had bright sunshine for a few hours, but later the sky clouded over from the north again, and now it is snowing dismally. It is calm.

Wednesday 14 December Position, N. 2', W. ½'. The pack still close around. From the masthead one can see a few patches of open water in different directions, but the main outlook is the same scene of desolate hummocky pack. The wind has come from the S.W., force 2; we have bright sunshine and good sights. The ship has swung to the wind and the floes around are continually moving. They change their relative positions in a slow, furtive, creeping fashion. The temperature is 35°, the water 29.2° to 29.5°. Under such conditions the thin sludgy ice ought to be weakening all the time; a few inches of such stuff should allow us to push through anywhere.

One realises the awful monotony of a long stay in the pack, such as Nansen and others experienced. One can imagine such days as these lengthening into interminable months and years.

For us there is novelty, and everyone has work to do or makes work, so that there is no keen sense of impatience.

Nelson and Lillie were up all night with the current meter; it is not quite satisfactory, but some result has been obtained. They will also get a series of temperatures and samples and use the vertical tow net.

The current is satisfactory. Both days the fixes have been good – it is best that we should go north and west. I had a great fear that we should be drifted east and so away to regions of permanent pack. If we go on in this direction it can only be a question of time before we are freed.

We have all been away on ski on the large floe to which we anchored this morning. Gran is wonderfully good and gives instruction well. It was hot and garments came off one by one – the Soldier [Captain Oates's nickname] and Atkinson were stripped to the waist eventually, and have been sliding round the floe for some time in that condition. Nearly everyone has been wearing goggles; the glare is very bad. Ponting tried to get a colour picture, but unfortunately the ice colours are too delicate for this.

Tonight Campbell, Evans, and I went out over the floe, and each in turn towed the other two; it was fairly easy work – that is, to pull 310 to 320 lbs. One could pull it perhaps more easily on foot, yet it would be impossible to pull such a load on a sledge. What a puzzle this pulling of loads is! If one could think that this captivity was soon to end there would be little reason to regret it; it is giving practice with our deep sea gear, and has made everyone keen to learn the proper use of ski.

The swell has increased considerably, but it is impossible to tell from what direction it comes; one can simply note that the ship and brash ice swing to and fro, bumping into the floe.

We opened the ice-house today, and found the meat in excellent condition – most of it still frozen.

Thursday 15 December 66° 23' S. 177° 59' W. Sit. N. 2', E. 5½'. In the morning the conditions were unaltered. Went for a ski run before breakfast. It makes a wonderful difference to get the blood circulating by a little exercise.

After breakfast we served out ski to the men of the landing party. They are all very keen to learn, and Gran has been out morning and afternoon giving instruction.

Meares got some of his dogs out and a sledge – two lots of seven; those that looked in worst condition (and several are getting very fat) were tried. They were very short of wind; it is difficult to understand how they can get so fat, as they only get two and a half biscuits a day at the most. The ponies are looking very well on the whole, especially those in the outside stalls.

Rennick got a sounding today 1844 fathoms; reversible thermometers were placed close to bottom and 500 fathoms up. We shall get a very good series of temperatures from the bottom up during the wait. Nelson will try to get some more current observations tonight or tomorrow.

It is very trying to find oneself continually drifting north, but one is thankful not to be going east.

Tonight it has fallen calm and the floes have decidedly opened; there is a lot of water about the ship, but it does not look to extend far. Meanwhile the brash and thinner floes are melting; everything of that sort must help – but it's trying to the patience to be delayed like this.

We have seen enough to know that with a north-westerly or westerly wind the floes tend to pack and that they open when it is calm. The question is, will they open more with an easterly or south-easterly wind – that is the hope.

Signs of open water round and about are certainly increasing rather than diminishing.

Friday 16 December The wind sprang up from the N.E. this morning, bringing snow, thin light hail, and finally rain; it grew very thick and has remained so all day.

Early the floe on which we had done so much ski-ing broke up, and we gathered in our ice anchors, then put on head sail, to which she gradually paid off. With a fair wind we set sail on the foremast, and slowly but surely she pushed the heavy floes aside. At lunch time we entered a long lead of open water, and for nearly half an hour we sailed along comfortably in it. Entering the pack again, we found the floes much lighter and again pushed on slowly. In all we may have made as much as three miles.

I have observed for some time some floes of immense area forming a chain of lakes in this pack, and have been most anxious to discover their thickness. They are most certainly the result of the freezing of comparatively recent pools in the winter pack, and it follows that they must be getting weaker day by day. If one could be certain firstly, that these big areas extend to the south, and, secondly, that the ship could go through them, it would be worth getting up steam. We have arrived at the edge of one of these floes, and the ship will not go through under sail, but I'm sure she would do so under steam. Is this a typical floe? And are there more ahead?

One of the ponies got down this afternoon – Oates thinks it was probably asleep and fell, but the incident is alarming; the animals are not too strong. On this account this delay is harassing – otherwise we should not have much to regret.

Saturday 17 December 67° 24'. 177° 34'. Drift for 48 hours S. 82 E. 9.7'. It rained hard and the glass fell rapidly last night with every sign of a coming gale. This morning the wind increased to force 6 from the west with snow. At noon the barograph curve turned up and the wind moderated, the sky gradually clearing.

Tonight it is fairly bright and clear; there is a light south-westerly wind. It seems rather as though the great gales of the Westerlies must begin in these latitudes with such mild disturbances as we have just experienced. I think it is the first time I have known rain beyond the Antarctic circle – it is interesting to speculate on its effect in melting the floes.

We have scarcely moved all day, but bergs which have become quite old friends through the week are on the move, and one has approached and almost circled us. Evidently these bergs are moving about in an irregular fashion, only they must have all travelled a little east in the forty-eight hours as we have done. Another interesting observation tonight is that of the slow passage of a stream of old heavy floes past the ship and the lighter ice in which she is held.

There are signs of water sky to the south, and I'm impatient to be off, but still one feels that waiting may be good policy, and I should certainly contemplate waiting some time longer if it weren't for the ponies.

Everyone is wonderfully cheerful; there is laughter all day long. Nelson finished his series of temperatures and samples today with an observation at 1800 metres.

SERIES OF SEA TEMPERATURES

	Depth Metres	Temp. (uncorrected)
Dec. 14	0	− 1·67
,,	10	− 1·84
,,	20	− 1·86
,,	30	− 1·89
,,	50	− 1·92
,,	75	− 1·93
,,	100	− 1·80
,,	125	− 1·11
,,	150	− 0·63
,,	200	+ 0·24
,,	500	+ 1·18
,,	1500	+ 0·935
Dec. 17	1800	+ 0·61
,,	2300	+ 0·48
Dec. 15	2800	+ 0·28
,,	3220	+ 0·11
,,	3650	− 0·13 no sample
,,	3891	bottom
Dec. 20	2300 (1260 fms.)	+ 0·48° C.
,,	3220 (1760 fms.)	+ 0·11° C.
,,	3300	bottom

A curious point is that the bottom layer is 2/10ths higher on the 20th, remaining in accord with the same depth on the 15th.

Sunday 18 December In the night it fell calm and the floes opened out. There is more open water between the floes around us, yet not a great deal more.

In general what we have observed on the opening of the pack means a very small increase in the open water spaces, but enough to convey the impression that the floes, instead of wishing to rub shoulders and grind against one another, desire to be apart. They touch lightly where they touch at all – such a condition makes much difference to the ship in attempts to force her through, as each floe is freer to move on being struck.

If a pack be taken as an area bounded by open water, it is evident that a small increase of the periphery or a small outward movement of the floes will add much to the open water spaces and create a general freedom.

The opening of this pack was reported at 3 a.m., and orders were given to raise steam. The die is cast, and we must now make a determined push for the open southern sea.

There is a considerable swell from the N.W.; it should help us to get along.

Evening Again extraordinary differences of fortune. At first things looked very bad – it took nearly half an hour to get started, much more than an hour to work away to one of the large area floes to which I have referred; then to my horror the ship refused to look at it. Again by hard fighting we worked away to a crack running across this sheet, and to get through this crack required many stoppages and engine reversals.

Then we had to shoot away south to avoid another unbroken floe of large area, but after we had rounded this things became easier; from 6 o'clock we were almost able to keep a steady course, only occasionally hung up by some thicker floe. The rest of the ice was fairly recent and easily broken. At 7 the leads of recent ice became easier still, and at 8 we entered a long lane of open water. For a time we almost thought we had come to the end of our troubles, and there was much jubilation. But, alas! at the end of the lead we have come again to heavy bay ice. It is undoubtedly this mixture of bay ice which causes the open leads, and I cannot but think that this is the King Edward Land pack. We are making S.W. as best we can.

What an exasperating game this is! One cannot tell what is going to happen in the next half or even quarter of an hour. At one moment everything looks flourishing, the next one begins to doubt if it is possible to get through.

New Fish Just at the end of the open lead tonight we capsized a small floe and thereby jerked a fish out on top of another one. We stopped and picked it up, finding it a beautiful silver grey, genus *Notothenia* – I think a new species.

Snow squalls have been passing at intervals – the wind continues in the N.W. It is comparatively warm.

We saw the first full-grown Emperor penguin tonight.

Monday 19 December On the whole, in spite of many bumps, we made good progress during the night, but the morning (present) outlook is the worst we've had. We seem to be in the midst of a terribly heavy screwed pack; it stretches in all directions as far as the eye can see, and the prospects are alarming from all points of view. I have decided to push west – anything to get out of these terribly heavy floes. Great patience is the only panacea for our ill case. It is bad luck.

We first got amongst the very thick floes at 1 a.m., and jammed through some of the most monstrous I have ever seen. The pressure ridges rose 24 feet above the surface – the ice must have extended at least 30 feet below. The blows given us gave the impression of irresistible solidity. Later in the night we passed out of this into long lanes of water and some of thin brash ice, hence the progress made. I'm afraid we have strained our rudder; it is stiff in one direction. We are in difficult circumstances altogether. This morning we have brilliant sunshine and no wind.

Noon 67° 54.5′ S. 178° 28′ W. Made good S. 34 W. 37′; C. Crozier 606′. Fog has spread up from the south with a very light southerly breeze.

There has been another change of conditions, but I scarcely know whether to call it for the better or the worse. There are fewer heavy old floes; on the other hand, the one year's floes, tremendously screwed and doubtless including old floes in their mass, have now enormously increased in area.

A floe which we have just passed must have been a mile across – this argues lack of swell and from that one might judge the open water to be very far. We made progress in a fairly good direction this morning, but the outlook is bad again – the ice seems to be closing. Again patience, we must go on steadily working through.

At 5.30 We passed two immense bergs in the afternoon watch, the first of an irregular tabular form. The stratified surface had clearly faulted. I suggest that an uneven bottom to such a berg giving unequal buoyancy to parts causes this faulting. The second berg was domed, having a twin peak. These bergs are still a puzzle. I rather cling to my original idea that they become domed when stranded and isolated.

These two bergs had left long tracks of open water in the pack. We came through these making nearly 3 knots, but, alas! only in a direction which carried us a little east of south. It was difficult to get from one tract to another, but the tracts themselves were quite clear of ice. I noticed with rather a sinking that the floes on either side of us were assuming gigantic areas; one or two could not have been less than 2 or 3 miles across. It seemed to point to very distant open water.

But an observation which gave greater satisfaction was a steady reduction in the thickness of the floes. At first they were still much pressed up and screwed. One saw lines and heaps of pressure dotted over the surface of the larger floes, but it was evident from the upturned slopes that the floes had been thin when these disturbances took place.

At about 4.30 we came to a group of six or seven low tabular bergs some 15 or 20 feet in height. It was such as these that we saw in King Edward

Land, and they might very well come from that region. Three of these were beautifully uniform, with flat tops and straight perpendicular sides, and others had overhanging cornices, and some sloped towards the edges.

No more open water was reported on the other side of the bergs, and one wondered what would come next. The conditions have proved a pleasing surprise. There are still large floes on either side of us, but they are not much hummocked; there are pools of water on their surface, and the lanes between are filled with light brash and only an occasional heavy floe. The difference is wonderful. The heavy floes and gigantic pressure ice struck one most alarmingly – it seemed impossible that the ship could win her way through them, and led one to imagine all sorts of possibilities, such as remaining to be drifted north and freed later in the season, and the contrast now that the ice all around is little more than 2 or 3 feet thick is an immense relief. It seems like release from a horrid captivity. Evans has twice suggested stopping and waiting today, and on three occasions I have felt my own decision trembling in the balance. If this condition holds I need not say how glad we shall be that we doggedly pushed on in spite of the apparently hopeless outlook.

In any case, if it holds or not, it will be a great relief to feel that there is this plain of negotiable ice behind one.

Saw two sea leopards this evening, one in the water making short, lazy dives under the floes. It had a beautiful sinuous movement.

I have asked Pennell to prepare a map of the pack; it ought to give some idea of the origin of the various forms of floes, and their general drift. I am much inclined to think that most of the pressure ridges are formed by the passage of bergs through the comparatively young ice. I imagine that when the sea freezes very solid it carries bergs with it, but obviously the enormous mass of a berg would need a great deal of stopping. In support of this view I notice that most of the pressure ridges are formed by pieces of a sheet which did not exceed one or two feet in thickness – also it seems that the screwed ice which we have passed has occurred mostly in the regions of bergs. On one side of the tabular berg passed yesterday pressure was heaped to a height of 15 feet – it was like a ship's bow wave on a large scale. Yesterday there were many bergs and much pressure; last night no bergs and practically no pressure; this morning few bergs and comparatively little pressure. It goes to show that the unconfined pack of these seas would not be likely to give a ship a severe squeeze.

Saw a young Emperor this morning, and whilst trying to capture it one of Wilson's new whales with the sabre dorsal fin rose close to the ship. I estimated this fin to be 4 feet high.

It is pretty to see the snow petrel and Antarctic petrel diving on to the upturned and flooded floes. The wash of water sweeps the Euphausia [a species of shrimp on which the seabirds feed] across such submerged ice. The Antarctic petrel has a pretty crouching attitude.

NOTES ON NICKNAMES

Evans	Teddy
Wilson	Bill, Uncle Bill, Uncle
Simpson	Sunny Jim
Ponting	Ponco
Meares	–
Day	–
Campbell	The Mate, Mr. Mate
Pennell	Penelope
Rennick	Parnie
Bowers	Birdie
Taylor	Griff and Keir Hardy
Nelson	Marie and Brontë
Gran	–
Cherry-Garrard	Cherry
Wright	Silas, Toronto
Priestley	Raymond
Debenham	Deb
Bruce	–
Drake	Francis
Atkinson	Jane, Helmin, Atchison
Oates	Titus, Soldier, 'Farmer Hayseed' (by Bowers)
Levick	Toffarino, the Old Sport
Lillie	Lithley, Hercules, Lithi[6]

Tuesday 20 December Noon 68° 41′ S. 179° 28′ W. Made good S. 36 W. 58; C. Crozier S. 20 W. 563′. The good conditions held up to midnight last night; we went from lead to lead with only occasional small difficulties. At 9 o'clock we passed along the western edge of a big stream of very heavy bay ice – such ice as would come out late in the season from the inner reaches and bays of Victoria Sound, where the snows drift deeply. For a moment one imagined a return to our bad conditions, but we passed this heavy stuff in an hour and came again to the former condition, making our way in leads between floes of great area.

Bowers reported a floe of 12 square miles in the middle watch. We made very fair progress during the night, and an excellent run in the morning watch. Before eight a moderate breeze sprang up from the west and the ice began to close. We have worked our way a mile or two on since, but with much difficulty, so that we have now decided to bank fires and wait for the ice to open again; meanwhile we shall sound and get a haul with tow nets. I'm afraid we are still a long way from the open water; the floes are large, and where we have stopped they seem to be such as must have been formed early last winter. The signs of pressure have increased again. Bergs were very scarce last night, but there are several around us today. One has a number of big humps on top. It is curious to think how these big blocks became perched so high. I imagine the berg must have been calved from a region of hard pressure ridges. [Later] This is a mistake – on closer inspection it is quite clear that the berg has tilted and that a great part of the upper strata, probably 20 feet deep, has slipped off, leaving the humps as islands on top.

It looks as though we must exercise patience again; progress is more difficult than in the worst of our experiences yesterday, but the outlook is very much brighter. This morning there were many dark shades of open water sky to the south; the westerly wind ruffling the water makes these cloud shadows very dark.

The barometer has been very steady for several days and we ought to have fine weather: this morning a lot of low cloud came from the S.W., at one time low enough to become fog – the clouds are rising and dissipating, and we have almost a clear blue sky with sunshine.

Evening The wind has gone from west to W.S.W. and still blows nearly force 6. We are lying very comfortably alongside a floe with open water to windward for 200 or 300 yards. The sky has been clear most of the day, fragments of low stratus occasionally hurry across the sky and a light cirrus is moving with some speed. Evidently it is blowing hard in the upper current. The ice has closed – I trust it will open well when the wind lets up. There is a lot of open water behind us. The berg described this morning has been circling round us, passing within 800 yards; the bearing and distance have altered so un-uniformly that it is evident that the differential movement between the surface water and the berg-driving layers (from 100 to 200 metres down) is very irregular. We had several hours on the floe practising ski running, and thus got some welcome exercise. Coal is now the great anxiety – we are making terrible inroads on our supply – we have come 240 miles since we first entered the pack streams.

The sounding today gave 1804 fathoms – the water bottle didn't work, but temperatures were got at 1300 and bottom. The temperature was down to 20° last night and kept 2 or 3 degrees below freezing all day.

The surface for ski-ing today was very good.

Wednesday 21 December The wind was still strong this morning, but had shifted to the south-west. With an overcast sky it was very cold and raw. The sun is now peeping through, the wind lessening and the weather conditions generally improving. During the night we had been drifting towards two large bergs, and about breakfast time we were becoming uncomfortably close to one of them – the big floes were binding down on one another, but there seemed to be open water to the S.E., if we could work out in that direction.

(*Note* – All directions of wind are given 'true' in this book.)

Noon Position 68° 25′ S. 179° 11′ W. Made good S. 26 E. 2.5′. Set of current N. 32 E. 9.4′. Made good 24 hours – N. 40 E. 8′. We got the steam up and about 9 a.m. commenced to push through. Once or twice we have spent nearly twenty minutes pushing through bad places, but it looks as though we are getting to easier water. It's distressing to have the pack so tight, and the bergs make it impossible to lie comfortably still for any length of time.

Ponting has made some beautiful photographs and Wilson some charming pictures of the pack and bergs; certainly our voyage will be well illustrated. We find quite a lot of sketching talent. Day, Taylor, Debenham, and Wright all contribute to the elaborate record of the bergs and ice features met with.

5 p.m. The wind has settled to a moderate gale from S.W. We went 2½ miles this morning, then became jammed again. The effort has taken us well clear of the threatening bergs. Some others to leeward now are a long way off, but they *are* there and to leeward, robbing our position of its full measure of security. Oh! but it's mighty trying to be delayed and delayed like this, and coal going all the time – also we are drifting N. and E. – the pack has carried us 9′ N. and 6′ E. It really is very distressing. I don't like letting fires go out with these bergs about.

Wilson went over the floe to capture some penguins and lay flat on the surface. We saw the birds run up to him, then turn within a few feet and rush away again. He says that they came towards him when he was singing, and ran away again when he stopped. They were all one-year birds, and seemed exceptionally shy; they appear to be attracted to the ship by a fearful curiosity.[7]

A chain of bergs must form a great obstruction to a field of pack ice, largely preventing its drift and forming lanes of open water. Taken in conjunction with the effect of bergs in forming pressure ridges, it follows that bergs have a great influence on the movement as well as the nature of pack.

Thursday 22 December Noon 68° 26′ 2″ S. 197° 8′ 5″ W. Sit. N. 5 E. 8.5′. – No change. The wind still steady from the S.W., with a clear sky and even barometer. It looks as though it might last any time. This is sheer bad luck. We have let the fires die out; there are bergs to leeward and we must take our chance of clearing them – we cannot go on wasting coal.

There is not a vestige of swell, and with the wind in this direction there certainly ought to be if the open water was reasonably close. No, it looks as though we'd struck a streak of real bad luck; that fortune has determined to put every difficulty in our path. We have less than 300 tons of coal left in a ship that simply eats coal. It's alarming – and then there are the ponies going steadily down-hill in condition. The only encouragement is the persistence of open water to the east and south-east to south; big lanes of open water can be seen in that position, but we cannot get to them in this pressed-up pack.

Atkinson has discovered a new tapeworm in the intestines of the Adélie penguin – a very tiny worm one-eighth of an inch in length with a propeller-shaped head.

A crumb of comfort comes on finding that we have not drifted to the eastward appreciably.

Friday 23 December The wind fell light at about ten last night and the ship swung round. Sail was set on the fore, and she pushed a few hundred yards to the north, but soon became jammed again. This brought us dead to windward of and close to a large berg with the wind steadily increasing. Not a very pleasant position, but also not one that caused much alarm. We set all sail, and with this help the ship slowly carried the pack round, pivoting on the berg until, as the pressure relieved, she slid out into the open water close to the berg. Here it was possible to 'wear ship', and we saw a fair prospect of getting away to the east and afterwards south. Following the leads up we made excellent progress during the morning watch, and early in the forenoon turned south, and then south-west.

We had made 8½′ S. 22 E. and about 5′ S.S.W. by 1 p.m., and could see a long lead of water to the south, cut off only by a broad strip of floe with many water holes in it: a composite floe. There was just a chance of getting through, but we have stuck half-way, advance and retreat equally impossible under sail alone. Steam has been ordered but will not be ready till near midnight. Shall we be out of the pack by Christmas Eve?

The floes today have been larger but thin and very sodden. There are extensive water pools showing in patches on the surface, and one notes some that run in line as though extending from cracks; also here and there close water-free cracks can be seen. Such floes might well be termed '*composite*' floes, since they evidently consist of old floes which have been frozen together – the junction being concealed by more recent snow falls.

A month ago it would probably have been difficult to detect inequalities or differences in the nature of the parts of the floes, but now the younger ice has become waterlogged and is melting rapidly, hence the pools.

I am inclined to think that nearly all the large floes as well as many of the smaller ones are 'composite', and this would seem to show that the cementing of two floes does not necessarily mean a line of weakness, provided the difference in the thickness of the cemented floes is not too great; of course, young ice or even a single season's sea-ice cannot become firmly attached to the thick old bay floes, and hence one finds these isolated even at this season of the year.

Very little can happen in the personal affairs of our company in this comparatively dull time, but it is good to see the steady progress that proceeds unconsciously in cementing the happy relationship that exists between the members of the party. Never could there have been a greater freedom from quarrels and trouble of all sorts. I have not heard a harsh word or seen a black look. A spirit of tolerance and good humour pervades the whole community, and it is glorious to realise that men can live under conditions of hardship, monotony, and danger in such bountiful good comradeship.

Preparations are now being made for Christmas festivities. It is curious to think that we have already passed the longest day in the southern year.

Saw a whale this morning – estimated 25 to 30 feet. Wilson thinks a new species. Find Adélie penguins in batches of twenty or so. Do not remember having seen so many together in the pack.

After midnight Steam was reported ready at 11 p.m. After some pushing to and fro we wriggled out of our ice prison and followed a lead to opener waters.

We have come into a region where the open water exceeds the ice; the former lies in great irregular pools 3 or 4 miles or more across and connecting with many leads. The latter, and the fact is puzzling, still contain floes of enormous dimensions; we have just passed one which is at least 2 miles in diameter. In such a scattered sea we cannot go direct, but often have to make longish detours; but on the whole in calm water and with a favouring wind we make good progress. With the sea even as open as we find it here it is astonishing to find the floes so large, and clearly there cannot be a southerly swell. The floes have water pools as described this afternoon, and none average more than 2 feet in thickness. We have two or three bergs in sight.

Saturday 24 *December, Christmas Eve* 69° 1′ S. 178° 29′ W. S. 22 E. 29′; C. Crozier 551′. Alas! alas! at 7 a.m. this morning we were brought up with a solid sheet of pack extending in all directions, save that from which we had come. I must honestly own that I turned in at three thinking we had come to the end of our troubles; I had a suspicion of anxiety when I thought of the size of the floes, but I didn't for a moment suspect we should get into thick pack again behind those great sheets of open water.

All went well till four, when the white wall again appeared ahead – at five all leads ended and we entered the pack; at seven we were close up to an immense composite floe, about as big as any we've seen. She wouldn't skirt the edge of this and she wouldn't go through it. There was nothing to do but to stop and bank fires. How do we stand? – Any day or hour the floes may open up, leaving a road to further open water to the south, but there is no guarantee that one would not be hung up again and again in this manner as long as these great floes exist. In a fortnight's time the floes will have crumbled somewhat, and in many places the ship will be able to penetrate them.

What to do under these circumstances calls for the most difficult decision. If one lets fires out it means a dead loss of over 2 tons, when the boiler has to be heated again. But this 2 tons would only cover a day under banked fires, so that for anything longer than twenty-four hours it is economy to put the fires out. At each stoppage one is called upon to decide whether it is to be for more or less than twenty-four hours.

Last night we got some five or six hours of good going ahead – but it has to be remembered that this costs 2 tons of coal in addition to that expended in doing the distance.

If one waits one probably drifts north – in all other respects conditions ought to be improving, except that the southern edge of the pack will be steadily augmenting.

Rough Summary of Current in Pack

Dec.	Current	Wind
11–12	S. 48 E. 12′?	N. by W. 3 to 5
13–14	N. 20 W. 2′	N.W. by W. 0–2
14–15	N. 2 E. 5.2′	S.W. 1–2
15–17	apparently little current	variable light
20–21	N. 32 E. 9.4	N.W. to W.S.W. 4 to 6
21–22	N. 5 E. 8.5	West 4 to 5

The above seems to show that the drift is generally with the wind. We have had a predominance of westerly winds in a region where a predominance of easterly might be expected.

Now that we have an easterly, what will be the result?

Sunday 25 December, Christmas Day Dead reckoning 69° 5′ S. 178° 30′ E. The night before last I had bright hopes that this Christmas Day would see us in open water. The scene is altogether too Christmassy. Ice surrounds us, low nimbus clouds intermittently discharging light snow flakes obscure the sky, here and there small pools of open water throw shafts of black shadow on to the cloud – this black predominates in the direction from whence we have come, elsewhere the white haze of ice blink is pervading.

We are captured. We do practically nothing under sail to push through, and could do little under steam, and at each step forward the possibility of advance seems to lessen.

The wind which has persisted from the west for so long fell light last night, and today comes from the N.E. by N., a steady breeze from 2 to 3 in force. Since one must have hope, ours is pinned to the possible effect of a continuance of easterly wind. Again the call is for patience and again patience. Here at least we seem to enjoy full security. The ice is so thin that it could not hurt by pressure – there are no bergs within reasonable distance – indeed the thinness of the ice is one of the most tantalising conditions. In spite of the unpropitious prospect everyone on board is cheerful and one foresees a merry dinner tonight.

The mess is gaily decorated with our various banners. There was full attendance at the Service this morning and a lusty singing of hymns.

Should we now try to go east or west?

I have been trying to go west because the majority of tracks lie that side and no one has encountered such hard conditions as ours – otherwise there is nothing to point to this direction, and all through the last week the prospect to the west has seemed less promising than in other directions; in spite of orders to steer to the S.W. when possible it has been impossible to push in that direction.

An event of Christmas was the production of a family by Crean's rabbit. She gave birth to 17, it is said, and Crean has given away 22!

I don't know what will become of the parent or family; at present they are warm and snug enough, tucked away in the fodder under the forecastle.

Midnight Tonight the air is thick with falling snow; the temperature 28°. It is cold and slushy without.

A merry evening has just concluded. We had an excellent dinner: tomato soup, penguin breast stewed as an entrée, roast beef, plum pudding, and mince pies, asparagus, champagne, port and liqueurs – a festive menu. Dinner began at 6 and ended at 7. For five hours the company has been sitting round the table singing lustily; we haven't much talent, but everyone has contributed more or less, 'and the choruses are deafening. It is rather a surprising circumstance that such an unmusical party should be so keen on singing. On Xmas night it was kept up till 1 a.m., and no work is done without a chanty. I don't know if you have ever heard sea chanties being sung. The merchant sailors have quite a repertoire, and invariably call on it when getting up anchor or hoisting sails. Often as not they are sung in a flat and throaty style, but the effect when a number of men break into the chorus is generally inspiriting.'

The men had dinner at midday – much the same fare, but with beer and some whisky to drink. They seem to have enjoyed themselves much. Evidently the men's deck contains a very merry band.

There are three groups of penguins roosting on the floes quite close to the ship. I made the total number of birds 39. We could easily capture these birds, and so it is evident that food can always be obtained in the pack.

Tonight I noticed a skua gull settle on an upturned block of ice at the edge of the floe on which several penguins were preparing for rest. It is a fact that the latter held a noisy confabulation with the skua as subject – then they advanced as a body towards it; within a few paces the foremost penguin halted and turned, and then the others pushed him on towards the skua. One after another they jibbed at being first to approach their enemy, and it was only with much chattering and mutual support that they gradually edged towards him.

They couldn't reach him as he was perched on a block, but when they got quite close the skua, who up to that time had appeared quite unconcerned, flapped away a few yards and settled close on the other side of the group of penguins. The latter turned and repeated their former tactics until the skua finally flapped away altogether. It really was extraordinarily interesting to watch the timorous protesting movements of the penguins. The frame of mind producing every action could be so easily imagined and put into human sentiments.

On the other side of the ship part of another group of penguins were quarrelling for the possession of a small pressure block which offered only the most insecure foothold. The scrambling antics to secure the point of vantage, the ousting of the bird in possession, and the incontinent loss of balance and position as each bird reached the summit of his ambition was almost as entertaining as the episode of the skua. Truly these little creatures afford much amusement.

Monday 26 December Obs. 69° 9′ S. 178° 13′ W. Made good 48 hours, S. 35 E. 10′. The position tonight is very cheerless. All hope that this easterly wind will open the pack seems to have vanished. We are surrounded with compacted floes of immense area. Openings appear between these floes and we slide crab-like from one to another with long delays between. It is difficult to keep hope alive. There are streaks of water sky over open leads to the north, but everywhere to the south we have the uniform white sky. The day has been overcast and the wind force 3 to 5 from the E.N.E. – snow has fallen from time to time. There could scarcely be a more dreary prospect for the eye to rest upon.

As I lay in my bunk last night I seemed to note a measured crush on the brash ice, and today first it was reported that the floes had become smaller, and then we seemed to note a sort of measured send alongside the ship. There may be a long low swell, but it is not helping us apparently; tonight the floes around are indisputably as large as ever and I see little sign of their breaking or becoming less tightly locked.

It is a very, very trying time.

We have managed to make 2 or 3 miles in a S.W. (?) direction under sail by alternately throwing her aback, then filling sail and pressing through the narrow leads; probably this will scarcely make up for our drift. It's all very disheartening. The bright side is that everyone is prepared to exert himself to the utmost – however poor the result of our labours may show.

Rennick got a sounding again today, 1843 fathoms.

One is much struck by our inability to find a cause for the periodic opening and closing of the floes. One wonders whether there is a reason to be found in tidal movement. In general, however, it seems to show that our conditions are governed by remote causes. Somewhere well north or south of us the wind may be blowing in some other direction, tending to press up or release pressure; then again such sheets of open water as those through which we passed to the north afford space into which bodies of pack can be pushed. The exasperating uncertainty of one's mind in such captivity is due to ignorance of its cause and inability to predict the effect of changes of wind. One can only vaguely comprehend that things are happening far beyond our horizon which directly affect our situation.

Tuesday 27 December Dead reckoning 69° 12′ S. 178° 18′ W. We made nearly 2 miles in the first watch – half push, half drift. Then the ship was again held up. In the middle the ice was close around, even pressing on us, and we didn't move a yard. The wind steadily increased and has been blowing a moderate gale, shifting in direction to E.S.E. We are reduced to lower topsails.

In the morning watch we began to move again, the ice opening out with the usual astonishing absence of reason. We have made a mile or two in a westerly direction in the same manner as yesterday. The floes seem a little smaller, but our outlook is very limited; there is a thick haze, and the only fact that can be known is that there are pools of water at intervals for a mile or two in the direction in which we go.

We commence to move between two floes, make 200 or 300 yards, and are then brought up bows on to a large lump. This may mean a wait of anything from ten minutes to half an hour, whilst the ship swings round, falls away, and drifts to leeward. When clear she forges ahead again and the operation is repeated. Occasionally when she can get a little way on she cracks the obstacle and slowly passes through it. There is a distinct swell – very long, very low. I counted the period as about nine seconds. Everyone says the ice is breaking up. I have not seen any distinct evidence myself, but Wilson saw a large floe which had recently cracked into four pieces in such a position that the ship could not have caused it. The breaking up of the big floes is certainly a hopeful sign.

'I have written quite a lot about the pack ice when under ordinary conditions I should have passed it with few words. But you will scarcely be surprised when I tell you what an obstacle we have found it on this occasion.'

I was thinking during the gale last night that our position might be a great deal worse than it is. We were lying amongst the floes perfectly peacefully whilst the wind howled through the rigging. One felt quite free from anxiety as to the ship, the sails, the bergs or ice pressures. One calmly went below and slept in the greatest comfort. One thought of the ponies, but after all, horses have been carried for all time in small ships, and often enough for very long voyages. The Eastern Party [The party headed by Lieutenant Campbell, which, being unable to disembark on King Edward Land, was ultimately taken by the *Terra Nova* to the north part of Victoria Land, and so came to be known as the Northern Party. The Western Party here mentioned includes all who had their base at Cape Evans: the depots to be laid were for the subsequent expedition to the Pole.] will certainly benefit by any delay we may make; for them the later they get to King Edward Land the better. The depot journey of the Western Party will be curtailed, but even so if we can get landed in January there should be time for a good deal of work. One must confess that things might be a great deal worse and there would be little to disturb one if one's release was certain, say in a week's time.

I'm afraid the ice-house is not going on so well as it might. There is some mould on the mutton and the beef is tainted. There is a distinct smell. The house has been opened by order when the temperature has fallen below 28°. I thought the effect would be to 'harden up' the meat, but apparently we need air circulation. When the temperature goes down tonight we shall probably take the beef out of the house and put a wind sail in to clear the atmosphere. If this does not improve matters we must hang more carcasses in the rigging.

6 p.m. The wind has backed from S.E. to E.S.E. and the swell is going down – this seems to argue open water in the first but not in the second direction and that the course we pursue is a good one on the whole.

The sky is clearing but the wind still gusty, force 4 to 7; the ice has frozen a little and we've made no progress since noon.

9 p.m. One of the ponies went down tonight. He has been down before. It may mean nothing; on the other hand it is not a circumstance of good omen.

Otherwise there is nothing further to record, and I close this volume of my Journal under circumstances which cannot be considered cheerful.

A FRESH MS. BOOK 1910–11
[*On the Flyleaf*]

'And in regions far
Such heroes bring ye forth
As those from whom we came
And plant our name
Under that star
Not known unto our North.'
'To the Virginian Voyage.'
DRAYTON.

'But be the workemen what they may be, let us speake of the worke; that is, the true greatnesse of Kingdom and estates; and the meanes thereof.'
BACON.

STILL IN THE ICE

Wednesday 28 December 1910 Obs. Noon, 69° 17′ S. 179° 42′ W. Made good since 26th S. 74 W. 31′; C. Crozier S. 22 W. 530′. The gale has abated. The sky began to clear in the middle watch; now we have bright, cheerful, warm sunshine (temp. 28°). The wind lulled in the middle watch and has fallen to force 2 to 3. We made 1½ miles in the middle and have added nearly a mile since. This movement has brought us amongst floes of decidedly smaller area and the pack has loosened considerably. A visit to the crow's nest shows great improvement in the conditions. There is ice on all sides, but a large percentage of the floes is quite thin and even the heavier ice appears breakable. It is only possible to be certain of conditions for three miles or so – the limit of observation from the crow's nest; but as far as this limit there is no doubt the ship could work through with ease. Beyond there are vague signs of open water in the southern sky. We have pushed and drifted south and west during the gale and are now near the 180th meridian again. It seems impossible that we can be far from the southern limit of the pack.

On strength of these observations we have decided to raise steam. I trust this effort will carry us through.

The pony which fell last night has now been brought out into the open. The poor beast is in a miserable condition, very thin, very weak on the hind legs, and suffering from a most irritating skin affection which is causing its hair to fall out in great quantities. I think a day or so in the open will help matters; one or two of the other ponies under the forecastle are also in poor condition, but none so bad as this one. Oates is unremitting in his attention and care of the animals, but I don't think he quite realises that whilst in the pack the ship must remain steady and that, therefore, a certain limited scope for movement and exercise is afforded by the open deck on which the sick animal now stands.

If we can get through the ice in the coming effort we may get all the ponies through safely, but there would be no great cause for surprise if we lost two or three more.

These animals are now the great consideration, balanced as they are against the coal expenditure.

This morning a number of penguins were diving for food around and under the ship. It is the first time they have come so close to the ship in the pack, and there can be little doubt that the absence of motion of the propeller has made them bold.

The Adélie penguin on land or ice is almost wholly ludicrous. Whether sleeping, quarrelling, or playing, whether curious, frightened, or angry, its interest is continuously humorous, but the Adélie penguin in the water is another thing; as it darts to and fro a fathom or two below the surface, as it leaps porpoise-like into the air or swims skimmingly over the rippling surface of a pool, it excites nothing but admiration. Its speed probably appears greater than it is, but the ability to twist and turn and the general control of movement is both beautiful and wonderful.

As one looks across the barren stretches of the pack, it is sometimes difficult to realise what teeming life exists immediately beneath its surface.

A tow-net is filled with diatoms in a very short space of time, showing that the floating plant life is many times richer than that of temperate or tropic seas. These diatoms mostly consist of three or four well-known species. Feeding on these diatoms are countless thousands of small shrimps (Euphausia); they can be seen swimming at the edge of every floe and washing about on the overturned pieces. In turn they afford food for creatures great and small: the crab-eater or white seal, the penguins, the Antarctic and snowy petrel, and an unknown number of fish.

These fish must be plentiful, as shown by our capture of one on an overturned floe and the report of several seen two days ago by some men leaning over the counter of the ship. These all exclaimed together, and on inquiry all agreed that they had seen half a dozen or more a foot or so in length swimming away under a floe. Seals and penguins capture these fish, as also, doubtless, the skuas and the petrels.

Coming to the larger mammals, one occasionally sees the long lithe sea leopard, formidably armed with ferocious teeth and doubtless containing a penguin or two and perhaps a young crab-eating seal. The killer whale (*Orca gladiator*), unappeasably voracious, devouring or attempting to devour every smaller animal, is less common in the pack but numerous on the coasts. Finally, we have the great browsing whales of various species, from the vast blue whale (*Balænoptera Sibbaldi*), the largest mammal of all time, to the smaller and less common bottle-nose and such species as have not yet been named. Great numbers of these huge animals are seen, and one realises what a demand they must make on their food supply and therefore how immense a supply of small sea beasts these seas must contain. Beneath the placid ice floes and under the calm water pools the old universal warfare is raging incessantly in the struggle for existence.

Both morning and afternoon we have had brilliant sunshine, and this afternoon all the after-guard lay about on the deck sunning themselves. A happy, care-free group.

10 p.m. We made our start at eight, and so far things look well. We have found the ice comparatively thin, the floes 2 to 3 feet in thickness except where hummocked; amongst them are large sheets from 6 inches to 1 foot in thickness as well as fairly numerous water pools. The ship has pushed on well, covering at least 3 miles an hour, though occasionally almost stopped by a group of hummocked floes. The sky is overcast: stratus clouds come over from the N.N.E. with wind in the same direction soon after we started. This may be an advantage, as the sails give great assistance and the officer of the watch has an easier time when the sun is not shining directly in his eyes. As I write the pack looks a little closer; I hope to heavens it is not generally closing up again – no sign of open water to the south. Alas!

12 p.m. Saw two sea leopards playing in the wake.

Thursday 29 December No sights. At last the change for which I have been so eagerly looking has arrived and we are steaming amongst floes of small area evidently broken by swell, and with edges abraded by contact. The transition was almost sudden. We made very good progress during the night with one or two checks and one or two slices of luck in the way of open water. In one pool we ran clear for an hour, capturing 6 good miles.

This morning we were running through large continuous sheets of ice from 6 inches to 1 foot in thickness, with occasional water holes and groups of heavier floes. This forenoon it is the same tale, except that the sheets of thin ice are broken into comparatively regular figures, none more than 30 yards across. It is the hopefullest sign of the approach to the open sea that I have seen.

The wind remains in the north helping us, the sky is overcast and slight sleety drizzle is falling; the sun has made one or two attempts to break through but without success.

Last night we had a good example of the phenomenon called 'Glazed Frost'. The ship everywhere, on every fibre of rope as well as on her more solid parts, was covered with a thin sheet of ice caused by a fall of light super-cooled rain. The effect was pretty and interesting.

Our passage through the pack has been comparatively uninteresting from the zoologist's point of view, as we have seen so little of the rarer species of animals or of birds in exceptional plumage. We passed dozens of crab-eaters, but have seen no Ross seals nor have we been able to kill a sea leopard. Today we see very few penguins. I'm afraid there can be no observations to give us our position.

RELEASE AFTER TWENTY DAYS IN THE PACK

Friday 30 December Obs. 72° 17′ S. 177° 9′ E. Made good in 48 hours, S. 19 W. 190′; C. Crozier S. 21 W. 334′. We are out of the pack at length and at last; one breathes again and hopes that it will be possible to carry out the main part of our programme, but the coal will need tender nursing.

Yesterday afternoon it became darkly overcast with falling snow. The barometer fell on a very steep gradient and the wind increased to force 6 from the E.N.E. In the evening the snow fell heavily and the glass still galloped down. In any other part of the world one would have felt certain of a coming gale. But here by experience we know that the barometer gives little indication of wind.

Throughout the afternoon and evening the water holes became more frequent and we came along at a fine speed. At the end of the first watch we were passing through occasional streams of ice; the wind had shifted to north and the barometer had ceased to fall. In the middle watch the snow held up, and soon after – 1 a.m. – Bowers steered through the last ice stream.

At six this morning we were well in the open sea, the sky thick and overcast with occasional patches of fog. We passed one small berg on the starboard hand with a group of Antarctic petrels on one side and a group of snow petrels on the other. It is evident that these birds rely on sea and swell to cast their food up on ice ledges – only a few find sustenance in the pack where, though food is plentiful, it is not so easily come by. A flight of Antarctic petrel accompanied the ship for some distance, wheeling to and fro about her rather than following in the wake as do the more northerly sea birds.

It is [good] to escape from the captivity of the pack and to feel that a few days will see us at Cape Crozier, but it is sad to remember the terrible inroad which the fight of the last fortnight has made on our coal supply.

2 p.m. The wind failed in the forenoon. Sails were clewed up, and at eleven we stopped to sound. The sounding showed 1111 fathoms – we appear to be on the edge of the continental shelf. Nelson got some samples and temperatures.

The sun is bursting through the misty sky and warming the air. The snowstorm had covered the ropes with an icy sheet – this is now peeling off and falling with a clatter to the deck, from which the moist slush is rapidly evaporating. In a few hours the ship will be dry – much to our satisfaction; it is very wretched when, as last night, there is slippery wet snow underfoot and on every object one touches.

Our run has exceeded our reckoning by much. I feel confident that our speed during the last two days had been greatly under-estimated and so it has proved. We ought to be off C. Crozier on New Year's Day.

8 p.m. Our calm soon came to an end, the breeze at 3 p.m. coming strong from the S.S.W., dead in our teeth – a regular southern blizzard. We are creeping along a bare 2 knots. I begin to wonder if fortune will ever turn her wheel. On every possible occasion she seems to have decided against us. Of course, the ponies are feeling the motion as we pitch in a short, sharp sea – it's damnable for them and disgusting for us.

SUMMARY OF THE PACK

We may be said to have entered the pack at 4 p.m. on the 9th in latitude 65½ S. We left it at 1 a.m. on 30th in latitude 71½ S. We have taken twenty days and some odd hours to get through, and covered in a direct line over 370 miles – an average of 18 miles a day. We entered the pack with 342 tons of coal and left with 281 tons; we have, therefore, expended 61 tons in forcing our way through – an average of 6 miles to the ton.

These are not pleasant figures to contemplate, but considering the exceptional conditions experienced I suppose one must conclude that things might have been worse.

9th.	Loose streams, steaming.
10th.	Close pack.
11th.	6 a.m. close pack, stopped.
12th.	11.30 a.m. started.
13th.	8 a.m. heavy pack, stopped; 8 p.m. out fires.
14th.	Fires out.
15th.	...
16th.	...
17th.	...
18th.	Noon, heavy pack and leads, steaming.

19th.   Noon, heavy pack and leads, steaming.
20th.   Forenoon, banked fires.
21st.   9 a.m. started. 11 a.m. banked.
22nd.   9 a.m. started. 11 a.m. banked.
23rd.   Midnight, started.
24th.   7 a.m. stopped.
25th.   Fires out.
26th.   Fires out.
27th.   Fires out.
28th.   7.30 p.m. steaming.
29th.   Steaming.
30th.   Steaming.

This column shows that we were steaming for nine out of twenty days. We had two long stops, one of *five* days and one of *four and a half* days. On three other occasions we stopped for short intervals without drawing fires.

I have asked Wright to plot the pack with certain symbols on the chart made by Pennell. It promises to give a very graphic representation of our experiences.

'We hold the record for reaching the northern edge of the pack, whereas three or four times the open Ross Sea has been gained at an earlier date.

'I can imagine few things more trying to the patience than the long wasted days of waiting. Exasperating as it is to see the tons of coal melting away with the smallest mileage to our credit, one has at least the satisfaction of active fighting and the hope of better fortune. To wait idly is the worst of conditions. You can imagine how often and how restlessly we climbed to the crow's nest and studied the outlook. And strangely enough there was generally some change to note. A water lead would mysteriously open up a few miles away or the place where it had been would as mysteriously close. Huge icebergs crept silently towards or past us, and continually we were observing these formidable objects with range finder and compass to determine the relative movement, sometimes with misgiving as to our ability to clear them. Under steam the change of conditions was even more marked. Sometimes we would enter a lead of open water and proceed for a mile or two without hindrance; sometimes we would come to big sheets of thin ice which broke easily as our iron-shod prow struck them, and sometimes even a thin sheet would resist all our attempts to break it; sometimes we would push big floes with comparative ease and sometimes a small floe would bar our passage with such obstinacy that one would almost believe it possessed of an evil spirit; sometimes we passed through acres of sludgy sodden ice which hissed as it swept along the side, and sometimes the hissing ceased seemingly without rhyme or reason, and we found our screw churning the sea without any effect.

'Thus the steaming days passed away in an ever changing environment and are remembered as an unceasing struggle.

'The ship behaved splendidly – no other ship, not even the *Discovery*, would have come through so well. Certainly the *Nimrod* would never have reached the south water had she been caught in such pack. As a result I have grown strangely attached to the *Terra Nova*. As she bumped the floes with mighty shocks, crushing and grinding a way through some, twisting and turning to avoid others, she seemed like a living thing fighting a great fight. If only she had more economical engines she would be suitable in all respects.

'Once or twice we got among floes which stood 7 or 8 feet above water, with hummocks and pinnacles as high as 25 feet. The ship could have stood no chance had such floes pressed against her, and at first we were a little alarmed in such situations. But familiarity breeds contempt; there never was any pressure in the heavy ice, and I'm inclined to think there never would be.

'The weather changed frequently during our journey through the pack. The wind blew strong from the west and from the east; the sky was often darkly overcast; we had snowstorms, flaky snow, and even light rain. In all such circumstances we were better placed in the pack than outside of it. The foulest weather could do us little harm. During quite a large percentage of days, however, we had bright sunshine, which, even with the temperature well below freezing, made everything look bright and cheerful. The sun also brought us wonderful cloud effects, marvellously delicate tints of sky, cloud, and ice, such effects as one might travel far to see. In spite of our impatience we would not willingly have missed many of the beautiful scenes which our sojourn in the pack afforded us. Ponting and Wilson have been busy catching these effects, but no art can reproduce such colours as the deep blue of the icebergs.

'Scientifically we have been able to do something. We have managed to get a line of soundings on our route showing the raising of the bottom from the ocean depths to the shallow water on the continental shelf, and the nature of the bottom. With these soundings we have obtained many interesting observations of the temperature of different layers of water in the sea.

'Then we have added a great deal to the knowledge of life in the pack from observation of the whales, seals, penguins, birds, and fishes as well as of the pelagic beasts which are caught in tow-nets. Life in one form or another is very plentiful in the pack, and the struggle for existence here as elsewhere is a fascinating subject for study.

'We have made a systematic study of the ice also, both the bergs and sea-ice, and have got a good deal of useful information concerning it. Also Pennell has done a little magnetic work.

'But of course this slight list of activity in the cause of science is a very poor showing for the time of our numerous experts; many have had to be idle in regard to their own specialities, though none are idle otherwise. All the scientific people keep night watch when they have no special work to do, and I have never seen a party of men so anxious to be doing work or so cheerful in doing it. When there is anything to be done, such as making or shortening sail, digging ice from floes for the water supply, or heaving up the sounding line, it goes without saying that all the afterguard turn out to do it. There is no hesitation and no distinction. It will be the same when it comes to landing stores or doing any other hard manual labour.

'The spirit of the enterprise is as bright as ever. Every one strives to help every one else, and not a word of complaint or anger has been heard on board. The inner life of our small community is very pleasant to think upon and very wonderful considering the extremely small space in which we are confined.

'The attitude of the men is equally worthy of admiration. In the forecastle as in the wardroom there is a rush to be first when work is to be done, and the same desire to sacrifice selfish consideration to the success of the expedition. It is very good to be able to write in such high praise of one's companions, and I feel that the possession of such support ought to ensure success. Fortune would be in a hard mood indeed if it allowed such a combination of knowledge, experience, ability, and enthusiasm to achieve nothing.'

3
LAND: 31 DECEMBER 1910 –
7 JANUARY 1911

Saturday 31 December, New Year's Eve Obs. 72° 54' S. 174° 55' E. Made good S. 45 W. 55'; C. Crozier S. 17 W. 286'. 'The New Year's Eve found us in the Ross Sea, but not at the end of our misfortunes.' We had a horrible night. In the first watch we kept away 2 points and set fore and aft sail. It did not increase our comfort but gave us greater speed. The night dragged slowly through. I could not sleep thinking of the sore strait for our wretched ponies. In the morning watch the wind and sea increased and the outlook was very distressing, but at six ice was sighted ahead. Under ordinary conditions the safe course would have been to go about and stand to the east. But in our case we must risk trouble to get smoother water for the ponies. We passed a stream of ice over which the sea was breaking heavily and one realised the danger of being amongst loose floes in such a sea. But soon we came to a compacter body of floes, and running behind this we were agreeably surprised to find comparatively smooth water. We ran on for a bit, then stopped and lay to. Now we are lying in a sort of ice bay – there is a mile or so of pack to windward, and two horns which form the bay embracing us. The sea is damped down to a gentle swell, although the wind is as strong as ever. As a result we are lying very comfortably. The ice is drifting a little faster than the ship so that we have occasionally to steam slowly to leeward.

So far so good. From a dangerous position we have achieved one which only directly involved a waste of coal. The question is, which will last longest, the gale or our temporary shelter?

Rennick has just obtained a sounding of 187 fathoms; taken in conjunction with yesterday's 1111 fathoms and Ross's sounding of 180, this is interesting, showing the rapid gradient of the continental shelf. Nelson is going to put over the 8 feet Agassiz trawl.

Unfortunately we could not clear the line for the trawl – it is stowed under the fodder. A light dredge was tried on a small manilla line – very little result. First the weights were insufficient to carry it to the bottom; a second time, with more weight and line, it seems to have touched for a very short time only; there was little of value in the catch, but the biologists are learning the difficulties of the situation.

Evening Our protection grew less as the day advanced but saved us much from the heavy swell. At 8 p.m. we started to steam west to gain fresh protection, there being signs of pack to south and west; the swell is again diminishing. The wind which started south yesterday has gone to S.S.W. (true), the main swell in from S.E. by S. or S.S.E. There seems to be another from south but none from the direction from which the wind is now blowing. The wind has been getting squally: now the squalls are lessening in force, the sky is clearing and we seem to be approaching the end of the blow. I trust it may be so and that the New Year will bring us better fortune than the old.

If so, it will be some pleasure to write 1910 for the last time – Land oh!

At 10 p.m. tonight as the clouds lifted to the west a distant but splendid view of the great mountains was obtained. All were in sunshine; Sabine and Whewell were most conspicuous – the latter from this view is a beautiful sharp peak, as remarkable a landmark as Sabine itself. Mount Sabine was 110 miles away when we saw it. I believe we could have seen it at a distance of 30 or 40 miles farther – such is the wonderful clearness of the atmosphere.

FINIS 1910

1911

Sunday 1 January Obs. 73° 5′ S. 174° 11′ E. Made good S. 48 W. 13.4; C. Crozier S. 15 W. 277′. At 4 a.m. we proceeded, steaming slowly to the S.E. The wind having gone to the S.W. and fallen to force 3 as we cleared the ice, we headed into a short steep swell, and for some hours the ship pitched most uncomfortably.

At 8 a.m. the ship was clear of the ice and headed south with fore and aft sail set. She is lying easier on this course, but there is still a good deal of motion, and would be more if we attempted to increase speed.

Oates reports that the ponies are taking it pretty well.

Soon after 8 a.m. the sky cleared, and we have had brilliant sunshine throughout the day; the wind came from the N.W. this forenoon, but has dropped during the afternoon. We increased to 55 revolutions at 10 a.m. The swell is subsiding but not so quickly as I had expected.

Tonight it is absolutely calm, with glorious bright sunshine. Several people were sunning themselves at 11 o'clock! sitting on deck and reading.

The land is clear tonight. Coulman Island 75 miles west.

Sounding at 7 p.m., 187 fathoms.

Sounding at 4 a.m., 310 fathoms.

Monday 2 January Obs. 75° 3′, 173° 41′. Made good S. 3 W. 119′; C. Crozier S. 22 W. 159′. It has been a glorious night followed by a glorious forenoon; the sun has been shining almost continuously. Several of us drew a bucket of sea water and had a bath with salt water soap on the deck. The water was cold, of course, but it was quite pleasant to dry oneself in the sun. The deck bathing habit has fallen off since we crossed the Antarctic circle, but Bowers has kept going in all weathers.

There is still a good deal of swell – difficult to understand after a day's calm – and less than 200 miles of water to windward.

Wilson saw and sketched the new white stomached whale seen by us in the pack.

At 8.30 we sighted Mount Erebus, distant about 115 miles; the sky is covered with light cumulus and an easterly wind has sprung up, force 2 to 3. With all sail set we are making very good progress.

Tuesday 3 January 10 a.m. – The conditions are very much the same as last night. We are only 24 miles from C. Crozier and the land is showing up well, though Erebus is veiled in stratus cloud.

It looks finer to the south and we may run into sunshine soon, but the wind is alarming and there is a slight swell which has little effect on the ship, but makes all the difference to our landing.

For the moment it doesn't look hopeful. We have been continuing our line of soundings. From the bank we crossed in latitude 71° the water has gradually got deeper, and we are now getting 310 to 350 fathoms against 180 on the bank.

The *Discovery* soundings give depths up to 450 fathoms East of Ross Island.

6 p.m. No good!! Alas! Cape Crozier with all its attractions is denied us.

We came up to the Barrier five miles east of the Cape soon after 1 p.m. The swell from the E.N.E. continued to the end. The Barrier was not more than 60 feet in height. From the crow's nest one could see well over it, and noted that there was a gentle slope for at least a mile towards the edge. The land of Black (or White?) Island could be seen distinctly behind, topping the huge lines of pressure ridges. We plotted the Barrier edge from the point at which we met it to the Crozier cliffs; to the eye it seems scarcely to have changed since *Discovery* days, and Wilson thinks it meets the cliff in the same place.

The Barrier takes a sharp turn back at 2 or 3 miles from the cliffs, runs back for half a mile, then west again with a fairly regular surface until within a few hundred yards of the cliffs; the interval is occupied with a single high-pressure ridge – the evidences of pressure at the edge being less marked than I had expected.

Ponting was very busy with cinematograph and camera. In the angle at the corner near the cliffs Rennick got a sounding of 140 fathoms and Nelson some temperatures and samples. When lowering the water bottle on one occasion the line suddenly became slack at 100 metres, then after a moment's pause began to run out again. We are curious to know the cause, and imagine the bottle struck a seal or whale.

Meanwhile, one of the whale boats was lowered and Wilson, Griffith Taylor, Priestley, Evans, and I were pulled towards the shore. The after-guard are so keen that the proper boat's crew was displaced and the oars manned by Oates, Atkinson, and Cherry-Garrard, the latter catching several crabs.

The swell made it impossible for us to land. I had hoped to see whether there was room to pass between the pressure ridge and the cliff, a route by which Royds once descended to the Emperor rookery; as we approached the corner we saw that a large piece of sea floe ice had been jammed between the Barrier and the cliff and had buckled up till its under surface stood 3 or 4 ft.

above the water. On top of this old floe we saw an old Emperor moulting and a young one shedding its down. (The down had come off the head and flippers and commenced to come off the breast in a vertical line similar to the ordinary moult.) This is an age and stage of development of the Emperor chick of which we have no knowledge, and it would have been a triumph to have secured the chick, but, alas! there was no way to get at it. Another most curious sight was the feet and tails of two chicks and the flipper of an adult bird projecting from the ice on the under side of the jammed floe; they had evidently been frozen in above and were being washed out under the floe.

Finding it impossible to land owing to the swell, we pulled along the cliffs for a short way. These Crozier cliffs are remarkably interesting. The rock, mainly volcanic tuff, includes thick strata of columnar basalt, and one could see beautiful designs of jammed and twisted columns as well as caves with whole and half pillars very much like a miniature Giant's Causeway. Bands of bright yellow occurred in the rich brown of the cliffs, caused, the geologists think, by the action of salts on the brown rock. In places the cliffs overhung. In places, the sea had eaten long low caves deep under them, and continued to break into them over a shelving beach. Icicles hung pendant everywhere, and from one fringe a continuous trickle of thaw water had swollen to a miniature waterfall. It was like a big hose playing over the cliff edge. We noticed a very clear echo as we passed close to a perpendicular rock face. Later we returned to the ship, which had been trying to turn in the bay – she is not very satisfactory in this respect owing to the difficulty of starting the engines either ahead or astern – several minutes often elapse after the telegraph has been put over before there is any movement of the engines.

It makes the position rather alarming when one is feeling one's way into some doubtful corner. When the whaler was hoisted we proceeded round to the penguin rookery; hopes of finding a quiet landing had now almost disappeared.[8]

There were several small grounded bergs close to the rookery; going close to these we got repeated soundings varying from 34 down to 12 fathoms. There is evidently a fairly extensive bank at the foot of the rookery. There is probably good anchorage behind some of the bergs, but none of these afford shelter for landing on the beach, on which the sea is now breaking incessantly; it would have taken weeks to land the ordinary stores and heaven only knows how we could have got the ponies and motor sledges ashore. Reluctantly and sadly we have had to abandon our cherished plan – it is a thousand pities. Every detail of the shore promised well for a wintering party. Comfortable quarters for the hut, ice for water, snow for the animals, good slopes for ski-ing, vast tracks of rock for walks. Proximity to the Barrier and to the rookeries of two types of penguins – easy ascent of Mount Terror – good ground for biological work – good peaks for observation of all sorts – fairly easy approach to the Southern Road, with no chance of being cut off – and so forth. It is a thousand pities to have to abandon such a spot.

On passing the rookery it seemed to me we had been wrong in assuming that all the guano is blown away. I think there must be a pretty good deposit in places. The penguins could be seen very clearly from the ship. On the large rookery they occupy an immense acreage, and one imagines have extended as far as shelter can be found. But on the small rookery they are patchy and there seems ample room for the further extension of the colonies. Such unused spaces would have been ideal for a wintering station if only some easy way could have been found to land stores.

I noted many groups of penguins on the snow slopes overlooking the sea far from the rookeries, and one finds it difficult to understand why they meander away to such places.

A number of killer whales rose close to the ship when we were opposite the rookery. What an excellent time these animals must have with thousands of penguins passing to and fro!

We saw our old *Discovery* post-office pole sticking up as erect as when planted, and we have been comparing all we have seen with old photographs. No change at all seems to have taken place anywhere, and this is very surprising in the case of the Barrier edge.

From the penguin rookeries to the west it is a relentless coast with high ice cliffs and occasional bare patches of rock showing through. Even if landing were possible, the grimmest crevassed snow slopes lie behind to cut one off from the Barrier surface; there is no hope of shelter till we reach Cape Royds.

Meanwhile all hands are employed making a running survey. I give an idea of the programme opposite. Terror cleared itself of cloud some hours ago, and we have had some change in views of it. It is quite certain that the ascent would be easy. The Bay on the north side of Erebus is much deeper than shown on the chart.

The sun has been obstinate all day, peeping out occasionally and then shyly retiring; it makes a great difference to comfort.

Programme
Bruce continually checking speed with hand log.
Bowers taking altitudes of objects as they come abeam.
Nelson noting results.
Pennell taking verge plate bearings on bow and quarter.
Cherry-Garrard noting results.
Evans taking verge plate bearings abeam.
Atkinson noting results.
Campbell taking distances abeam with range finder.
Wright noting results.
Rennick sounding with Thomson machine.
Drake noting results.

Beaufort Island looks very black from the south.

10.30 We find pack off Cape Bird; we have passed through some streams and there is some open water ahead, but I'm afraid we may find the ice pretty thick in the Strait at this date.

Wednesday 4 January 1 a.m. We are around Cape Bird and in sight of our destination, but it is doubtful if the open water extends so far.

We have advanced by following an open water lead close along the land. Cape Bird is a very rounded promontory with many headlands; it is not easy to say which of these is the Cape.

The same grim unattainable ice-clad coast line extends continuously from the Cape Crozier Rookery to Cape Bird. West of C. Bird there is a very extensive expanse of land, and on it one larger and several small penguin rookeries.

On the uniform dark reddish brown of the land can be seen numerous grey spots; these are erratic boulders of granite. Through glasses one could be seen perched on a peak at least 1300 feet above the sea.

Another group of killer whales were idly diving off the penguin rookery; an old one with a very high straight dorsal fin and several youngsters. We watched a small party of penguins leaping through the water towards their enemies. It seemed impossible that they should have failed to see the sinister fins during their frequent jumps into the air, yet they seemed to take no notice whatever – stranger still, the penguins must have actually crossed the whales, yet there was no commotion whatever, and presently the small birds could be seen leaping away on the other side. One can only suppose the whales are satiated.

As we rounded Cape Bird we came in sight of the old well-remembered landmarks – Mount Discovery and the Western Mountains – seen dimly through a hazy atmosphere. It was good to see them again, and perhaps after all we are better this side of the Island. It gives one a homely feeling to see such a familiar scene.

4 a.m. The steep exposed hill sides on the west side of Cape Bird look like high cliffs as one gets south of them and form a most conspicuous landmark. We pushed past these cliffs into streams of heavy bay ice, making fair progress; as we proceeded the lanes became scarcer, the floes heavier, but the latter remain loose. 'Many of us spent the night on deck as we pushed through the pack.' We have passed some very large floes evidently frozen in the strait. This is curious, as all previous evidence has pointed to the clearance of ice sheets north of Cape Royds early in the spring.

I have observed several floes with an entirely new type of surface. They are covered with scales, each scale consisting of a number of little flaky ice sheets superimposed, and all 'dipping' at the same angle. It suggests to me a surface with sastrugi and layers of fine dust on which the snow has taken hold.

We are within 5 miles of Cape Royds and ought to get there.

Wednesday 4 January p.m. This work is full of surprises. At 6 a.m. we came through the last of the Strait pack some three miles north of Cape Royds. We steered for the Cape, fully expecting to find the edge of the pack ice ranging westward from it. To our astonishment we ran on past the Cape with clear water or thin sludge ice on all sides of us. Past Cape Royds, past Cape Barne, past the glacier on its south side, and finally round and past Inaccessible Island, a good 2 miles south of Cape Royds. 'The Cape itself was cut off from the south.'

We could have gone farther, but the last sludge ice seemed to be increasing in thickness, and there was no wintering spot to aim for but Cape Armitage [The extreme S. point of the Island, a dozen miles farther, one of whose headlands, Hut Point, stood the *Discovery* hut]. 'I have never seen the ice of the Sound in such a condition or the land so free from snow. Taking these facts in conjunction with the exceptional warmth of the air, I came to the conclusion that it had been an exceptionally warm summer. At this point it was evident that we had a considerable choice of wintering spots. We could have gone to either of the small islands, to the mainland, the Glacier Tongue, or pretty well anywhere except Hut Point. My main wish was to choose a place that would not be easily cut off from the Barrier, and my eye fell on a cape which we used to call the Skuary a little behind us. It was separated from old *Discovery* quarters by two deep bays on either side of the Glacier Tongue, and I thought that these bays would remain frozen until late in the season, and that when they froze over again the ice would soon become firm.' I called a council and put these propositions. To push on to the Glacier Tongue and winter there; to push west to the 'tombstone' ice and to make our way to an inviting spot to the northward of the cape we used to call 'the Skuary'. I favoured the latter course, and on discussion we found it obviously the best, so we turned back close around Inaccessible Island and steered for the fast ice off the Cape at full speed. After piercing a small fringe of thin ice at the edge of the fast floe the ship's stem struck heavily on hard bay ice about a mile and a half from the shore. Here was a road to the Cape and a solid wharf on which to land our stores. We made fast with ice anchors. Wilson, Evans, and I went to the Cape, which I had now rechristened Cape Evans in honour of our excellent second in command. A glance at the land showed, as we expected, ideal spots for our wintering station. The rock of the Cape consists mainly of volcanic agglomerate with olivine kenyte; it is much weathered and the destruction had formed quantities of coarse sand. We chose a spot for the hut on a beach facing N.W. and well protected by numerous small hills behind. This spot seems to have all the local advantages (which I must detail later) for a winter station, and we realised that at length our luck had turned. The most favourable circumstance of all is the strong chance of communication with Cape Armitage being established at an early date.

It was in connection with this fact that I had had such a strong desire to go to Mount Terror, and such misgivings if we had been forced to go to Cape Royds. It is quite evident that the ice south of Cape Royds does not become secure till late in the season, probably in May. Before that, all evidence seems to show that the part between Cape Royds and Cape Barne is continually going out. How, I ask myself, was our depot party to get back to home quarters? I feel confident we can get to the new spot we have chosen at a comparatively early date; it will probably only be necessary to cross the sea-ice in the deep bays north and south of the Glacier Tongue, and the ice rarely goes out of there after it has first formed. Even if it should, both stages can be seen before the party ventures upon them.

After many frowns fortune has treated us to the kindest smile – for twenty-four hours we have had a calm with brilliant sunshine. Such weather in such a place comes nearer to satisfying my ideal of perfection than any condition that I have ever experienced. The warm glow of the sun with the keen invigorating cold of the air forms a combination which is inexpressibly health-giving and satisfying to me, whilst the golden light on this wonderful scene of mountain and ice satisfies every claim of scenic magnificence. No words of mine can convey the impressiveness of the wonderful panorama displayed to our eyes. Ponting is enraptured and uses expressions which in anyone else and alluding to any other subject might be deemed extravagant.

THE LANDING: A WEEK'S WORK

Whilst we were on shore Campbell was taking the first steps towards landing our stores. Two of the motor sledges were soon hoisted out, and Day with others was quickly unpacking them. Our luck stood again. In spite of all the bad weather and the tons of sea water which had washed over them the sledges and all the accessories appeared as fresh and clean as if they had been packed on the previous day – much credit is due to the officers who protected them with tarpaulins and lashings. After the sledges came the turn of the ponies – there was a good deal of difficulty in getting some of them into the horse box, but Oates rose to the occasion and got most in by persuasion, whilst others were simply lifted in by the sailors. Though all are thin and some few looked pulled down I was agreeably surprised at the evident vitality which they still possessed – some were even skittish. I cannot express the relief when the whole seventeen were safely picketed on the floe. From the moment of getting on the snow they seemed to take a new lease of life, and I haven't a doubt they will pick up very rapidly. It really is a triumph to have got them through safely and as well as they are. Poor brutes, how they must have enjoyed their first roll, and how glad they must be to have freedom to scratch themselves! It is evident all have suffered from skin irritation – one can imagine the horror of suffering from such an ill for weeks without being able to get at the part that itched. I note that now they are picketed together they administer kindly offices to each other; one sees them gnawing away at each other's flanks in most amicable and obliging manner.

Meares and the dogs were out early, and have been running to and fro most of the day with light loads. The great trouble with them has been due to the fatuous conduct of the penguins. Groups of these have been constantly leaping on to our floe. From the moment of landing on their feet their whole attitude expressed devouring curiosity and a pig-headed disregard for their own safety. They waddle forward, poking their heads to and fro in their usually absurd way, in spite of a string of howling dogs straining to get at them. 'Hulloa', they seem to say, 'here's a game – what do all you ridiculous things want?' And they come a few steps nearer. The dogs make a rush as far as their leashes or harness allow. The penguins are not daunted in the least, but their ruffs go up and they squawk with semblance of anger, for all the world as though they were rebuking a rude stranger – their attitude might be imagined to convey 'Oh, that's the sort of animal you are; well, you've come to the wrong place – we aren't going to be bluffed and bounced by you,' and then the final fatal steps forward are taken and they come within reach. There is a spring, a squawk, a horrid red patch on the snow, and the incident is closed. Nothing can stop these silly birds. Members of our party rush to head them off, only to be met with evasions – the penguins squawk and duck as much as to say, 'What's it got to do with you, you silly ass? Let us alone.'

With the first spilling of blood the skua gulls assemble, and soon, for them at least, there is a gruesome satisfaction to be reaped. Oddly enough, they don't seem to excite the dogs; they simply alight within a few feet and wait for their turn in the drama, clamouring and quarrelling amongst themselves when the spoils accrue. Such incidents were happening constantly today, and seriously demoralising the dog teams. Meares was exasperated again and again.

The motor sledges were running by the afternoon, Day managing one and Nelson the other. In spite of a few minor breakdowns they hauled good loads to the shore. It is early to call them a success, but they are certainly extremely promising.

The next thing to be got out of the ship was the hut, and the large quantity of timber comprising it was got out this afternoon.

And so tonight, with the sun still shining, we look on a very different prospect from that of 48 or even 24 hours ago.

I have just come back from the shore.

The site for the hut is levelled and the erecting party is living on shore in our large green tent with a supply of food for eight days. Nearly all the timber, etc., of the hut is on shore, the remainder half-way there. The ponies are picketed in a line on a convenient snow slope so that they cannot eat sand. Oates and Anton are sleeping ashore to watch over them. The dogs are tied to a long length of chain stretched on the sand; they are coiled up after a long day, looking fitter already. Meares and Demetri are sleeping in the green tent to look after them. A supply of food for ponies and dogs as well as for the men has been landed. Two motor sledges in good working order are safely on the beach.

A fine record for our first day's work. All hands start again at 6 a.m. tomorrow.

It's splendid to see at last the effect of all the months of preparation and organisation. There is much snoring about me as I write (2 p.m.) from men tired after a hard day's work and preparing for such another tomorrow. I also must sleep, for I have had none for 48 hours – but it should be to dream happily.

Thursday 5 January All hands were up at 5 this morning and at work at 6. Words cannot express the splendid way in which everyone works and gradually the work gets organised. I was a little late on the scene this morning, and thereby witnessed a most extraordinary scene. Some 6 or 7 killer whales, old and young, were skirting the fast floe edge ahead of the ship; they seemed excited and dived rapidly, almost touching the floe. As we watched, they suddenly appeared astern, raising their snouts out of water. I had heard weird stories of these beasts, but had never associated serious danger with them. Close to the water's edge lay the wire stern rope of the ship, and our two Esquimaux dogs were tethered to this. I did not think of connecting the movements of the whales with this fact, and seeing them so close I shouted to Ponting, who was standing abreast of the ship. He seized his camera and ran towards the floe edge to get a close picture of the beasts, which had momentarily disappeared. The next moment the whole floe under him and the dogs heaved up and split into fragments. One could hear the 'booming' noise as the whales rose under the ice and struck it with their backs. Whale after whale rose under the ice, setting it rocking fiercely; luckily Ponting kept his feet and was able to fly to security. By an extraordinary chance also, the splits had been made around and between the dogs, so that neither of them fell into the water. Then it was clear that the whales shared our astonishment, for one after another their huge hideous heads shot vertically into the air through the cracks which they had made. As they reared them to a height of 6 or 8 feet it was possible to see their tawny head markings, their small glistening eyes, and their terrible array of teeth – by far the largest and most terrifying in the world. There cannot be a doubt that they looked up to see what had happened to Ponting and the dogs.

The latter were horribly frightened and strained to their chains, whining; the head of one killer must certainly have been within 5 feet of one of the dogs.

After this, whether they thought the game insignificant, or whether they missed Ponting is uncertain, but the terrifying creatures passed on to other hunting grounds, and we were able to rescue the dogs, and what was even more important, our petrol – 5 or 6 tons of which was waiting on a piece of ice which was not split away from the main mass.

Of course, we have known well that killer whales continually skirt the edge of the floes and that they would undoubtedly snap up anyone who was unfortunate enough to fall into the water; but the facts that they could display such deliberate cunning, that they were able to break ice of such thickness (at least 2½ feet), and that they could act in unison, were a revelation to us. It is clear that they are endowed with singular intelligence, and in future we shall treat that intelligence with every respect.

NOTES ON THE KILLER OR GRAMPUS (Orca gladiator)

One killed at Greenwich, 31 feet.

Teeth about 2½ inches above jaw; about 3½ inches total length.

'British Quadrupeds' – Bell:

'The fierceness and voracity of the killer, in which it surpasses all other known cetaceans.'

In stomach of a 21 ft. specimen were found remains of 13 porpoises and 14 seals.

A herd of white whales has been seen driven into a bay and literally torn to pieces.

Teeth, large, conical, and slightly recurved, 11 or 12 on each side of either jaw.

'*Mammals*' – *Flower and Lydekker*:
'Distinguished from all their allies by great strength and ferocity.'
'Combine in packs to hunt down and destroy ... full sized whales.'
'*Marine Mammalia*' – *Scammon*:
Adult males average 20 feet; females 15 feet.
Strong sharp conical teeth which interlock. Combines great strength with agility.
Spout 'low and bushy'.
Habits exhibit a boldness and cunning peculiar to their carnivorous propensities.
Three or four do not hesitate to grapple the largest baleen whales, who become paralysed with terror – frequently evince no efforts to escape.
Instances have occurred where a band of orcas laid siege to whales in tow, and although frequently lanced and cut with boat spades, made away with their prey.
Inclined to believe it rarely attacks larger cetaceans.
Possessed of great swiftness.
Sometimes seen peering above the surface with a seal in their bristling jaws, shaking and crushing their victims and swallowing them apparently with gusto.
Tear white whales into pieces.

Ponting has been ravished yesterday by a view of the ship seen from a big cave in an iceberg, and wished to get pictures of it. He succeeded in getting some splendid plates. This forenoon I went to the iceberg with him and agreed that I had rarely seen anything more beautiful than this cave. It was really a sort of crevasse in a tilted berg parallel to the original surface; the strata on either side had bent outwards; through the back the sky could be seen through a screen of beautiful icicles – it looked a royal purple, whether by contrast with the blue of the cavern or whether from optical illusion I do not know. Through the larger entrance could be seen, also partly through icicles, the ship, the Western Mountains, and a lilac sky; a wonderfully beautiful picture.

Ponting is simply entranced with this view of Mt. Erebus, and with the two bergs in the foreground and some volunteers he works up foregrounds to complete his picture of it.

I go to bed very satisfied with the day's work, but hoping for better results with the improved organisation and familiarity with the work.

Today we landed the remainder of the woodwork of the hut, all the petrol, paraffin and oil of all descriptions, and a quantity of oats for the ponies besides odds and ends. The ponies are to begin work tomorrow; they did nothing today, but the motor sledges did well – they are steadying down to their work and made nothing but non-stop runs today. One begins to believe they will be reliable, but I am still fearing that they will not take such heavy loads as we hoped.

Day is very pleased and thinks he's going to do wonders, and Nelson shares his optimism. The dogs find the day work terribly heavy and Meares is going to put them on to night work.

The framework of the hut is nearly up; the hands worked till 1 a.m. this morning and were at it again at 7 a.m. – an instance of the spirit which actuates everyone. The men teams formed of the after-guard brought in good loads, but they are not yet in condition. The hut is about 11 or 12 feet above the water as far as I can judge. I don't think spray can get so high in such a sheltered spot even if we get a northerly gale when the sea is open.

In all other respects the situation is admirable. This work makes one very tired for Diary-writing.

Friday 6 January We got to work at 6 again this morning. Wilson, Atkinson, Cherry-Garrard, and I took each a pony, returned to the ship, and brought a load ashore; we then changed ponies and repeated the process. We each took three ponies in the morning, and I took one in the afternoon.

Bruce, after relief by Rennick, took one in the morning and one in the afternoon – of the remaining five Oates deemed two unfit for work and three requiring some breaking in before getting to serious business.

I was astonished at the strength of the beasts I handled; three out of the four pulled hard the whole time and gave me much exercise. I brought back loads of 700 lbs. and on one occasion over 1000 lbs.

With ponies, motor sledges, dogs, and men parties we have done an excellent day of transporting – another such day should practically finish all the stores and leave only fuel and fodder (60 tons) to complete our landing. So far it has been remarkably expeditious.

The motor sledges are working well, but not very well; the small difficulties will be got over, but I rather fear they will never draw the loads we expect of them. Still they promise to be a help, and they are lively and attractive features of our present scene as they drone along over the floe. At a little distance, without silencers, they sound exactly like threshing machines.

The dogs are getting better, but they only take very light loads still and get back from each journey pretty dead beat. In their present state they don't inspire confidence, but the hot weather is much against them.

The men parties have done splendidly. Campbell and his Eastern Party made eight journeys in the day, a distance over 24 miles. Everyone declares that the ski sticks greatly help pulling; it is surprising that we never thought of using them before.

Atkinson is very bad with snow blindness tonight; also Bruce. Others have a touch of the same disease. It's well for people to get experience of the necessity of safeguarding their eyes.

The only thing which troubles me at present is the wear on our sledges owing to the hard ice. No great harm has been done so far, thanks to the excellent wood of which the runners are made, but we can't afford to have them worn. Wilson carried out a suggestion of his own tonight by covering the runners of a 9-ft. sledge with strips from the skin of a seal which he killed and flensed for the purpose. I shouldn't wonder if this acted well, and if it does we will cover more sledges in a similar manner. We shall also try Day's new under-runners tomorrow. After 48 hours of brilliant sunshine we have a haze over the sky.

List of sledges:
  12 ft. 11 in use, 14 spare
  10 ft. 10 not now used
  9 ft. 10 in use

Today I walked over our peninsula to see what the southern side was like. Hundreds of skuas were nesting and attacked in the usual manner as I passed. They fly round shrieking wildly until they have gained some altitude. They then swoop down with great impetus directly at one's head, lifting again when within a foot of it. The bolder ones actually beat on one's head with their wings as they pass. At first it is alarming, but experience shows that they never strike except with their wings. A skua is nesting on a rock between the ponies and the dogs. People pass every few minutes within a pace or two, yet the old bird has not deserted its chick. In fact, it seems gradually to be getting confidence, for it no longer attempts to swoop at the intruder. Today Ponting went within a few feet, and by dint of patience managed to get some wonderful cinematograph pictures of its movements in feeding and tending its chick, as well as some photographs of these events at critical times.

The main channel for thaw water at Cape Evans is now quite a rushing stream.

Evans, Pennell, and Rennick have got sight for meridian distance; we ought to get a good longitude fix.

Saturday 7 January The sun has returned. Today it seemed better than ever and the glare was blinding. There are quite a number of cases of snow blindness.

We have done splendidly. Tonight all the provisions except some in bottles are ashore and nearly all the working paraphernalia of the scientific people – no light item. There remains some hut furniture, 2½ tons of carbide, some bottled stuff, and some odds and ends which should occupy only part of tomorrow; then we come to the two last and heaviest items – coal and horse fodder.

If we are not through in the week we shall be very near it. Meanwhile the ship is able to lay at the ice edge without steam; a splendid saving.

There has been a steady stream of cases passing along the shore route all day and transport arrangements are hourly improving.

Two parties of four and three officers made ten journeys each, covering over 25 miles and dragging loads one way which averaged 250 to 300 lbs. per man.

The ponies are working well now, but beginning to give some excitement. On the whole they are fairly quiet beasts, but they get restive with their loads, mainly but indirectly owing to the smoothness of the ice. They know perfectly well that the swingle trees and traces are hanging about their hocks and hate it (I imagine it gives them the nervous feeling that they are going to be carried off their feet). This makes it hard to start them, and when going they seem to appreciate the fact that the sledges will overrun them should they hesitate or stop. The result is that they are constantly fretful and the more nervous ones tend to become refractory and unmanageable.

Oates is splendid with them – I do not know what we should do without him.

I did seven journeys with ponies and got off with a bump on the head and some scratches.

One pony got away from Debenham close to the ship, and galloped the whole way in with its load behind; the load capsized just off the shore and the animal and sledge dashed into the station. Oates very wisely took this pony straight back for another load.

Two or three ponies got away as they were being harnessed, and careered up the hill again. In fact there were quite a lot of minor incidents which seemed to endanger life and limb to the animals if not the men, but which all ended safely.

One of Meares' dog teams ran away – one poor dog got turned over at the start and couldn't get up again (Mukáka). He was dragged at a gallop for nearly half a mile; I gave him up as dead, but apparently he was very little hurt.

The ponies are certainly going to keep things lively as time goes on and they get fresher. Even as it is, their condition can't be half as bad as we imagined; the runaway pony wasn't much done even after the extra trip.

The station is beginning to assume the appearance of an orderly camp. We continue to find advantages in the situation; the long level beach has enabled Bowers to arrange his stores in the most systematic manner. Everything will be handy and there will never be a doubt as to the position of a case when it is wanted. The hut is advancing apace – already the matchboarding is being put on. The framework is being clothed. It should be extraordinarily warm and comfortable, for in addition to this double coating of insulation, dry seaweed in quilted sacking, I propose to stack the pony fodder all around it.

I am wondering how we shall stable the ponies in the winter.

The only drawback to the present position is that the ice is getting thin and sludgy in the cracks and on some of the floes. The ponies drop their feet through, but most of them have evidently been accustomed to something of the sort; they make no fuss about it. Everything points to the desirability of the haste which we are making – so we go on tomorrow, Sunday.

A whole host of minor ills besides snow blindness have come upon us. Sore faces and lips, blistered feet, cuts and abrasions; there are few without some troublesome ailment, but, of course, such things are 'part of the business'. The soles of my feet are infernally sore.

'Of course the elements are going to be troublesome, but it is good to know them as the only adversary and to feel there is so small a chance of internal friction.'

Ponting had an alarming adventure about this time. Bent on getting artistic photographs with striking objects, such as hummocked floes or reflecting water, in the foreground, he used to depart with his own small sledge laden with cameras and cinematograph to journey alone to the grounded icebergs. One morning as he tramped along harnessed to his sledge, his snow glasses clouded with the mist of perspiration, he suddenly felt the ice giving under his feet. He describes the sensation as the worst he ever experienced, and one can well believe it; there was no one near to have lent assistance had he gone through. Instinctively he plunged forward, the ice giving at every step and the sledge dragging through water. Providentially the weak area he had struck was very limited, and in a minute or two he pulled out on a firm surface. He remarked that he was perspiring very freely!

Looking back it is easy to see that we were terribly incautious in our treatment of this decaying ice.

4
SETTLING IN: 8 JANUARY 1911 – 23 JANUARY 1911

Sunday 8 January A day of disaster. I stupidly gave permission for the third motor to be got out this morning. This was done first thing and the motor placed on firm ice. Later Campbell told me one of the men had dropped a leg through crossing a sludgy patch some 200 yards from the ship. I didn't consider it very serious, as I imagined the man had only gone through the surface crust. About 7 a.m. I started for the shore with a single man load, leaving Campbell looking about for the best crossing for the motor. I sent Meares and the dogs over with a can of petrol on arrival. After some twenty minutes he returned to tell me the motor had gone through. Soon after Campbell and Day arrived to confirm the dismal tidings. It appears that getting frightened of the state of affairs Campbell got out a line and attached it to the motor – then manning the line well he attempted to rush the machine across the weak place. A man on the rope, Wilkinson, suddenly went through to the shoulders, but was immediately hauled out. During the operation the ice under the motor was seen to give, and suddenly it and the motor disappeared. The men kept hold of the rope, but it cut through the ice towards them with an ever increasing strain, obliging one after another to let go. Half a minute later nothing remained but a big hole. Perhaps it was lucky there was no accident to the men, but it's a sad incident for us in any case. It's a big blow to know that one of the two best motors, on which so much time and trouble have been spent, now lies at the bottom of the sea. The actual spot where the motor disappeared was crossed by its fellow motor with a very heavy load as well as by myself with heavy ponies only yesterday.

Meares took Campbell back and returned with the report that the ice in the vicinity of the accident was hourly getting more dangerous.

It was clear that we were practically cut off, certainly as regards heavy transport. Bowers went back again with Meares and managed to ferry over some wind clothes and odds and ends. Since that no communication has been held; the shore party have been working, but the people on board have had a half-holiday.

At 6 I went to the ice edge farther to the north. I found a place where the ship could come and be near the heavy ice over which sledging is still possible. I went near the ship and semaphored directions for her to get to this place as soon as she could, using steam if necessary. She is at present wedged in with the pack, and I think Pennell hopes to warp her along when the pack loosens.

Meares and I marked the new trail with kerosene tins before returning. So here we are waiting again till fortune is kinder. Meanwhile the hut proceeds; altogether there are four layers of boarding to go on, two of which are nearing completion; it will be some time before the rest and the insulation is on.

It's a big job getting settled in like this and a tantalising one when one is hoping to do some depot work before the season closes.

We had a keen north wind tonight and a haze, but wind is dropping and sun shining brightly again. Today seemed to be the hottest we have yet had; after walking across I was perspiring freely, and later as I sat in the sun after lunch one could almost imagine a warm summer day in England.

This is my first night ashore. I'm writing in one of my new domed tents which makes a very comfortable apartment.

Monday 9 January I didn't poke my nose out of my tent till 6.45, and the first object I saw was the ship, which had not previously been in sight from our camp. She was now working her way along the ice edge with some difficulty. I heard afterwards that she had started at 6.15 and she reached the point I marked yesterday at 8.15. After breakfast I went on board and was delighted to find a good solid road right up to the ship. A flag was hoisted immediately for the ponies to come out, and we commenced a good day's work. All day the sledges have been coming to and fro, but most of the pulling work has been done by the ponies: the track is so good that these little animals haul anything from 12 to 18 cwt. Both dogs and men parties have been a useful addition to the haulage – no party or no single man comes over without a load averaging 300 lbs. per man. The dogs, working five to a team, haul 5 to 6 cwt. and of course they travel much faster than either ponies or men.

In this way we transported a large quantity of miscellaneous stores; first about 3 tons of coal for present use, then 2½ tons of carbide, all the many stores, chimney and ventilators for the hut, all the biologists' gear – a big pile, the remainder of the physicists' gear and medical stores, and many old cases; in fact a general clear up of everything except the two heavy items of forage and fuel. Later in the day we made a start on the first of these, and got 7 tons ashore before ceasing work. We close with a good day to our credit, marred by an unfortunate incident – one of the dogs, a good puller, was seen to cough after a journey; he was evidently trying to bring something up – two minutes later he was dead. Nobody seems to know the reason, but a post-mortem is being held by Atkinson and I suppose the cause of death will be found. We can't afford to lose animals of any sort.

All the ponies except three have now brought loads from the ship. Oates thinks these three are too nervous to work over this slippery surface. However, he tried one of the hardest cases tonight, a very fine pony, and got him in successfully with a big load.

Tomorrow we ought to be running some twelve or thirteen of these animals.

Griffith Taylor's bolted on three occasions, the first two times more or less due to his own fault, but the third owing to the stupidity of one of the sailors. Nevertheless a third occasion couldn't be overlooked by his messmates, who made much merriment of the event. It was still funnier when he brought his final load (an exceptionally heavy one) with a set face and ardent pace, vouchsafing not a word to anyone he passed.

We have achieved fair organisation today. Evans is in charge of the road and periodically goes along searching for bad places and bridging cracks with boards and snow.

Bowers checks every case as it comes on shore and dashes off to the ship to arrange the precedence of different classes of goods. He proves a perfect treasure; there is not a single case he does not know or a single article of any sort which he cannot put his hand on at once.

Rennick and Bruce are working gallantly at the discharge of stores on board.

Williamson and Leese load the sledges and are getting very clever and expeditious. Evans (seaman) is generally superintending the sledging and camp outfit. Forde, Keohane, and Abbott are regularly assisting the carpenter, whilst Day, Lashly, Lillie, and others give intermittent help.

Wilson, Cherry-Garrard, Wright, Griffith Taylor, Debenham, Crean, and Browning have been driving ponies, a task at which I have assisted myself once or twice. There was a report that the ice was getting rotten, but I went over it myself and found it sound throughout. The accident with the motor sledge has made people nervous.

The weather has been very warm and fine on the whole, with occasional gleams of sunshine, but tonight there is a rather chill wind from the south. The hut is progressing famously. In two more working days we ought to have everything necessary on shore.

Tuesday 10 January We have been six days in McMurdo Sound and tonight I can say we are landed. Were it impossible to land another pound we could go on without hitch. Nothing like it has been done before; nothing so expeditious and complete. This morning the main loads were fodder. Sledge after sledge brought the bales, and early in the afternoon the last (except for about a ton stowed with Eastern Party stores) was brought on shore. Some addition to our patent fuel was made in the morning, and later in the afternoon it came in a steady stream. We have more than 12 tons and could make this do if necessity arose.

In addition to this oddments have been arriving all day – instruments, clothing, and personal effects. Our camp is becoming so perfect in its appointments that I am almost suspicious of some drawback hidden by the summer weather.

The hut is progressing apace, and all agree that it should be the most perfectly comfortable habitation. 'It amply repays the time and attention given to the planning.' The sides have double boarding inside and outside the frames, with a layer of our excellent quilted seaweed insulation between each pair of boardings. The roof has a single matchboarding inside, but on the outside is a matchboarding, then a layer of 2-ply 'ruberoid', then a layer of quilted seaweed, then a second matchboarding, and finally a cover of 3-ply 'ruberoid'. The first floor is laid, but over this there will be a quilting, a felt layer, a second boarding, and finally linoleum; as the plenteous volcanic sand can be piled well up on every side it is impossible to imagine that draughts can penetrate into the hut from beneath, and it is equally impossible to imagine great loss of heat by contact or radiation in that direction. To add to the wall insulation the south and east sides of the hut are piled high with compressed forage bales, whilst the north side is being prepared as a winter stable for the ponies. The stable will stand between the wall of the hut and a wall built of forage bales, six bales high and two bales thick. This will be roofed with rafters and tarpaulin, as we cannot find enough boarding. We shall have to take care that too much snow does not collect on the roof, otherwise the place should do excellently well.

Some of the ponies are very troublesome, but all except two have been running today, and until this evening there were no excitements. After tea Oates suggested leading out the two intractable animals behind other sledges; at the same time he brought out the strong, nervous grey pony. I led one of the supposedly safe ponies, and all went well whilst we made our journey; three loads were safely brought in. But whilst one of the sledges was being unpacked the pony tied to it suddenly got scared. Away he dashed with sledge attached; he made straight for the other ponies, but finding the incubus still fast to him he went in wider circles, galloped over hills and boulders, narrowly missing Ponting and his camera, and finally dashed down hill to camp again pretty exhausted – oddly enough neither sledge nor pony was much damaged. Then we departed again in the same order. Half-way over the floe my rear pony got his foreleg foul of his halter, then got frightened, tugged at his halter, and lifted the unladen sledge to which he was tied – then the halter broke and away he went. But by this time the damage was done. My pony snorted wildly and sprang forward as the sledge banged to the ground. I just managed to hold him till Oates came up, then we started again; but he was thoroughly frightened – all my blandishments failed when he reared and plunged a second time, and I was obliged to let go. He galloped back and the party dejectedly returned. At the camp Evans got hold of the pony, but in a moment it was off again, knocking Evans off his legs. Finally he was captured and led forth once more between Oates and Anton. He remained fairly well on the outward journey, but on the homeward grew restive again; Evans, who was now leading him, called for Anton, and both tried to hold him, but to no purpose – he dashed off, upset his load, and came back to camp with the sledge. All these troubles arose after he had made three journeys without a hitch and we had come to regard him as a nice, placid, gritty pony. Now I'm afraid it will take a deal of trouble to get him safe again, and we have three very troublesome beasts instead of two. I have written this in some detail to show the unexpected difficulties that arise with these animals, and the impossibility of knowing exactly where one stands. The majority of our animals seem pretty quiet now, but any one of them may break out in this way if things go awry.

There is no doubt that the bumping of the sledges close at the heels of the animals is the root of the evil.

The weather has the appearance of breaking. We had a strongish northerly breeze at midday with snow and hail storms, and now the wind has turned to the south and the sky is overcast with threatenings of a blizzard. The floe is cracking and pieces may go out – if so the ship will have to get up steam again. The hail at noon made the surface very bad for some hours; the men and dogs felt it most.

The dogs are going well, but Meares says he thinks that several are suffering from snow blindness. I never knew a dog get it before, but Day says that Shackleton's dogs suffered from it. The post-mortem on last night's death revealed nothing to account for it. Atkinson didn't examine the brain, and wonders if the cause lay there. There is a certain satisfaction in believing that there is nothing infectious.

Wednesday 11 January A week here today – it seems quite a month, so much has been crammed into a short space of time.

The threatened blizzard materialised at about four o'clock this morning. The wind increased to force 6 or 7 at the ship, and continued to blow, with drift, throughout the forenoon.

Campbell and his sledging party arrived at the Camp at 8 a.m. bringing a small load: there seemed little object, but I suppose they like the experience of a march in the blizzard. They started to go back, but the ship being blotted out, turned and gave us their company at breakfast. The day was altogether too bad for outside work, so we turned our attention to the hut interior, with the result that tonight all the matchboarding is completed. The floor linoleum is the only thing that remains to be put down; outside, the roof and ends have to be finished. Then there are several days of odd jobs for the carpenter, and all will be finished. It is a first-rate building in an extraordinarily sheltered spot; whilst the wind was raging at the ship this morning we enjoyed comparative peace. Campbell says there was an extraordinary change as he approached the beach.

I sent two or three people to dig into the hard snow drift behind the camp; they got into solid ice immediately, became interested in the job, and have begun the making of a cave which is to be our larder. Already they have tunnelled 6 or 8 feet in and have begun side channels. In a few days they will have made quite a spacious apartment – an ideal place to keep our meat store. We had been speculating as to the origin of this solid drift and attached great antiquity to it, but the diggers came to a patch of earth with skua feathers, which rather knocks our theories on the head.

The wind began to drop at midday, and after lunch I went to the ship. I was very glad to learn that she can hold steam at two hours' notice on an expenditure of 13 cwt. The ice anchors had held well during the blow.

As far as I can see the open water extends to an east and west line which is a little short of the glacier tongue.

Tonight the wind has dropped altogether and we return to the glorious conditions of a week ago. I trust they may last for a few days at least.

Thursday 12 January Bright sun again all day, but in the afternoon a chill wind from the S.S.W. Again we are reminded of the shelter afforded by our position; tonight the anemometers on Observatory Hill show a 20-mile wind – down in our valley we only have mild puffs.

Sledging began as usual this morning; seven ponies and the dog teams were hard at it all the forenoon. I ran six journeys with five dogs, driving them in the Siberian fashion for the first time. It was not difficult, but I kept forgetting the Russian words at critical moments: 'Ki' – 'right'; 'Tchui' – 'left'; 'Itah' – 'right ahead'; [here is a blank in memory and in Diary] – 'get along'; 'Paw' – 'stop'. Even my short experience makes me think that we may have to reorganise this driving to suit our particular requirements. I am inclined for smaller teams and the driver behind the sledge. However, it's early days to decide such matters, and we shall learn much on the depot journey.

Early in the afternoon a message came from the ship to say that all stores had been landed. Nothing remains to be brought but mutton, books and pictures, and the pianola. So at last we really are a self-contained party ready for all emergencies. We are LANDED eight days after our arrival – a very good record.

The hut could be inhabited at this moment, but probably we shall not begin to live in it for a week. Meanwhile the carpenter will go on steadily fitting up the dark room and various other compartments as well as Simpson's Corner [Here were the meteorological instruments].

The grotto party are making headway into the ice for our larder, but it is slow and very arduous work. However, once made it will be admirable in every way.

Tomorrow we begin sending ballast off to the ship; some 30 tons will be sledged off by the ponies. The hut and grotto parties will continue, and the arrangements for the depot journey will be commenced. I discussed these with Bowers this afternoon – he is a perfect treasure, enters into one's ideas at once, and evidently thoroughly understands the principles of the game.

I have arranged to go to Hut Point with Meares and some dogs tomorrow to test the ice and see how the land lies. As things are at present we ought to have little difficulty in getting the depot party away any time before the end of the month, but the ponies will have to cross the Cape [Cape Evans, which lay on the S. side of the new hut] without loads. There is a way down on the south side straight across, and another way round, keeping the land on the north side and getting on ice at the Cape itself. Probably the ship will take the greater part of the loads.

Saturday 14 January The completion of our station is approaching with steady progress. The wind was strong from the S.S.E. yesterday morning, sweeping over the camp; the temperature fell to 15°, the sky became overcast. To the south the land outlines were hazy with drift, so my dog tour was abandoned. In the afternoon, with some moderation of conditions, the ballast party went to work, and wrought so well that more than 10 tons were got off before night. The organisation of this work is extremely good. The loose rocks are pulled up, some 30 or 40 feet up the hillside, placed on our heavy rough sledges and rushed down to the floe on a snow track; here they are laden on pony sledges and transported to the ship. I slept on board the ship and found it colder than the camp – the cabins were below freezing all night and the only warmth existed in the cheery spirit of the company. The cold snap froze the water in the boiler and Williams had to light one of the fires this morning. I shaved and bathed last night (the first time for 10 days) and wrote letters from breakfast till tea time today. Meanwhile the ballast team has been going on merrily, and tonight Pennell must have some 26 tons on board.

It was good to return to the camp and see the progress which had been made even during such a short absence. The grotto has been much enlarged and is, in fact, now big enough to hold all our mutton and a considerable quantity of seal and penguin.

Close by Simpson and Wright have made surprising progress in excavating for the differential magnetic hut. They have already gone in 7 feet and, turning a corner, commenced the chamber, which is to be 13 feet × 5 feet. The hard ice of this slope is a godsend and both grottoes will be ideal for their purposes.

The cooking range and stove have been placed in the hut and now chimneys are being constructed; the porch is almost finished as well as the interior; the various carpenters are busy with odd jobs and it will take them some time to fix up the many small fittings that different people require.

I have been making arrangements for the depot journey, telling off people for ponies and dogs, etc.[9]

Tomorrow is to be our first rest day, but next week everything will be tending towards sledging preparations. I have also been discussing and writing about the provisions of animals to be brought down in the *Terra Nova* next year.

The wind is very persistent from the S.S.E., rising and falling; tonight it has sprung up again, and is rattling the canvas of the tent.

Some of the ponies are not turning out so well as I expected; they are slow walkers and must inevitably impede the faster ones. Two of the best had been told off for Campbell by Oates, but I must alter the arrangement. 'Then I am not quite sure they are going to stand the cold well, and on this first journey they may have to face pretty severe conditions. Then, of course, there is the danger of losing them on thin ice or by injury sustained in rough places. Although we have fifteen now (two having gone for the Eastern Party) it is not at all certain that we shall have such a number when the main journey is undertaken next season. One can only be careful and hope for the best.'

Sunday 15 January We had decided to observe this day as a 'day of rest', and so it has been.

At one time or another the majority have employed their spare hours in writing letters.

We rose late, having breakfast at nine. The morning promised well and the day fulfilled the promise: we had bright sunshine and practically no wind.

At 10 a.m. the men and officers streamed over from the ship, and we all assembled on the beach and I read Divine Service, our first Service at the camp and impressive in the open air. After Service I told Campbell that I should have to cancel his two ponies and give him two others. He took it like the gentleman he is, thoroughly appreciating the reason.

He had asked me previously to be allowed to go to Cape Royds over the glacier and I had given permission. After our talk we went together to explore the route, which we expected to find much crevassed. I only intended to go a short way, but on reaching the snow above the uncovered hills of our Cape I found the surface so promising and so free from cracks that I went quite a long way. Eventually I turned, leaving Campbell, Gran, and Nelson roped together and on ski to make their way onward, but not before I felt certain that the route to Cape Royds would be quite easy. As we topped the last rise we saw Taylor and Wright some way ahead on the slope; they had come up by a different route. Evidently they are bound for the same goal.

I returned to camp, and after lunch Meares and I took a sledge and nine dogs over the Cape to the sea-ice on the south side and started for Hut Point. We took a little provision and a cooker and our sleeping-bags. Meares had found a way over the Cape which was on snow all the way except about 100 yards. The dogs pulled well, and we went towards the Glacier Tongue at a brisk pace; found much of the ice uncovered. Towards the Glacier Tongue there were some heaps of snow much wind-blown. As we rose the glacier we saw the *Nimrod* depot some way to the right and made for it. We found a good deal of compressed fodder and boxes of maize, but no grain crushed as expected. The open water was practically up to the Glacier Tongue.

We descended by an easy slope ¼ mile from the end of the Glacier Tongue, but found ourselves cut off by an open crack some 15 feet across and had to get on the glacier again and go some ½ mile farther in. We came to a second crack, but avoided it by skirting to the west. From this point we had an easy run without difficulty to Hut Point. There was a small pool of open water and a longish crack off Hut Point. I got my feet very wet crossing the latter. We passed hundreds of seals at the various cracks.

On the arrival at the hut to my chagrin we found it filled with snow. Shackleton reported that the door had been forced by the wind, but that he had made an entrance by the window and found shelter inside – other members of his party used it for shelter. But they actually went away and left the window (which they had forced) open; as a result, nearly the whole of the interior of the hut is filled with hard icy snow, and it is now impossible to find shelter inside.

Meares and I were able to clamber over the snow to some extent and to examine the neat pile of cases in the middle, but they will take much digging out. We got some asbestos sheeting from the magnetic hut and made the best shelter we could to boil our cocoa.

There was something too depressing in finding the old hut in such a desolate condition. I had had so much interest in seeing all the old landmarks and the huts apparently intact. To camp outside and feel that all the old comfort and cheer had departed, was dreadfully heartrending. I went to bed thoroughly depressed. It stems a fundamental expression of civilised human sentiment that men who come to such places as this should leave what comfort they can to welcome those who follow.

Monday 16 January We slept badly till the morning and, therefore, late. After breakfast we went up the hills; there was a keen S.E. breeze, but the sun shone and my spirits revived. There was very much less snow everywhere than I had ever seen. The ski run was completely cut through in two places, the Gap and Observation Hill almost bare, a great bare slope on the side of Arrival Heights, and on top of Crater Heights an immense bare table-land. How delighted we should have been to see it like this in the old days! The pond was thawed and the confervæ green in fresh water. The hole which we had dug in the mound in the pond was still there, as Meares discovered by falling into it up to his waist and getting very wet.

On the south side we could see the Pressure Ridges beyond Pram Point as of old – Horseshoe Bay calm and unpressed – the sea-ice pressed on Pram Point and along the Gap ice foot, and a new ridge running around C. Armitage about 2 miles off. We saw Ferrar's old thermometer tubes standing out of the snow slope as though they'd been placed yesterday. Vince's cross might have been placed yesterday – the paint was so fresh and the inscription so legible.

The flagstaff was down, the stays having carried away, but in five minutes it could be put up again. We loaded some asbestos sheeting from the old magnetic hut on our sledges for Simpson, and by standing ¼ mile off Hut Point got a clear run to Glacier Tongue. I had hoped to get across the wide crack by going west, but found that it ran for a great distance and had to get on the glacier at the place at which we had left it. We got to camp about teatime. I found our larder in the grotto completed and stored with mutton and penguins – the temperature inside has never been above 27°, so that it ought to be a fine place for our winter store. Simpson has almost completed the differential magnetic cave next door. The hut stove was burning well and the interior of the building already warm and homelike – a day or two and we shall be occupying it.

I took Ponting out to see some interesting thaw effects on the ice cliffs east of the Camp. I noted that the ice layers were pressing out over thin dirt bands as though the latter made the cleavage lines over which the strata slid.

It has occurred to me that although the sea-ice may freeze in our bays early in March it will be a difficult thing to get ponies across it owing to the cliff edges at the side. We must therefore be prepared to be cut off for a longer time than I anticipated. I heard that all the people who journeyed towards C. Royds yesterday reached their destination in safety. Campbell, Levick, and Priestley had just departed when I returned.[10]

Tuesday 17 January We took up our abode in the hut today and are simply overwhelmed with its comfort. After breakfast this morning I found Bowers making cubicles as I had arranged, but I soon saw these would not fit in, so instructed him to build a bulkhead of cases which shuts off the officers' space from the men's, I am quite sure to the satisfaction of both. The space between my bulkhead and the men's I allotted to five: Bowers, Oates, Atkinson, Meares, and Cherry-Garrard. These five are all special friends and have already made their dormitory very habitable. Simpson and Wright are near the instruments in their corner. Next come Day and Nelson in a space which includes the latter's 'Lab.' near the big window; next to this is a space for three – Debenham, Taylor, and Gran; they also have already made their space part dormitory and part workshop.

It is fine to see the way everyone sets to work to put things straight; in a day or two the hut will become the most comfortable of houses, and in a week or so the whole station, instruments, routine, men and animals, etc., will be in working order.

It is really wonderful to realise the amount of work which has been got through of late.

It will be a *fortnight tomorrow* since we arrived in McMurdo Sound, and here we are absolutely settled down and ready to start on our depot journey directly the ponies have had a proper chance to recover from the effects of the voyage. I had no idea we should be so expeditious.

It snowed hard all last night; there were about three or four inches of soft snow over the camp this morning and Simpson tells me some six inches out by the ship. The camp looks very white. During the day it has been blowing very hard from the south, with a great deal of drift. Here in this camp as usual we do not feel it much, but we see the anemometer racing on the hill and the snow clouds sweeping past the ship. The floe is breaking between the point and the ship, though curiously it remains fast on a direct route to the ship. Now the open water runs parallel to our ship road and only a few hundred yards south of it. Yesterday the whaler was rowed in close to the camp, and if the ship had steam up she could steam round to within a few hundred yards of us. The big wedge of ice to which the ship is holding on the outskirts of the Bay can have very little grip to keep it in and must inevitably go out very soon. I hope this may result in the ship finding a more sheltered and secure position close to us.

A big iceberg sailed past the ship this afternoon. Atkinson declares it was the end of the Cape Barne Glacier. I hope they will know in the ship, as it would be interesting to witness the birth of a glacier in this region.

It is clearing tonight, but still blowing hard. The ponies don't like the wind, but they are all standing the cold wonderfully and all their sores are healed up.

Wednesday 18 January The ship had a poor time last night; steam was ordered, but the floe began breaking up fast at 1 a.m., and the rest of the night was passed in struggling with ice anchors; steam was reported ready just as the ship broke adrift. In the morning she secured to the ice edge on the same line as before but a few hundred yards nearer. After getting things going at the hut, I walked over and suggested that Pennell should come round the corner close in shore. The ice anchors were tripped and we steamed slowly in, making fast to the floe within 200 yards of the ice foot and 400 yards of the hut.

For the present the position is extraordinarily comfortable. With a southerly blow she would simply bind on to the ice, receiving great shelter from the end of the Cape. With a northerly blow she might turn rather close to the shore, where the soundings run to 3 fathoms, but behind such a stretch of ice she could scarcely get a sea or swell without warning. It looks a wonderfully comfortable little nook, but, of course, one can be certain of nothing in this place; one knows from experience how deceptive the appearance of security may be. Pennell is truly excellent in his present position – he's invariably cheerful, unceasingly watchful, and continuously ready for emergencies. I have come to possess implicit confidence in him.

The temperature fell to 4° last night, with a keen S.S.E. breeze; it was very unpleasant outside after breakfast. Later in the forenoon the wind dropped and the sun shone forth. This afternoon it fell almost calm, but the sky clouded over again and now there is a gentle warm southerly breeze with light falling snow and an overcast sky. Rather significant of a blizzard if we had not had such a lot of wind lately. The position of the ship makes the casual transport that still proceeds very easy, but the ice is rather thin at the edge. In the hut all is marching towards the utmost comfort.

Bowers has completed a storeroom on the south side, an excellent place to keep our travelling provisions. Every day he conceives or carries out some plan to benefit the camp. Simpson and Wright are worthy of all admiration: they have been unceasingly active in getting things to the fore and I think will be ready for routine work much earlier than was anticipated. But, indeed, it is hard to specialise praise where everyone is working so indefatigably for the cause.

Each man in his way is a treasure.

Clissold the cook has started splendidly, has served seal, penguin, and skua now, and I can honestly say that I have never met these articles of food in such a pleasing guise; 'this point is of the greatest practical importance, as it means the certainty of good health for any number of years'. Hooper was landed today, much to his joy. He got to work at once, and will be a splendid help, freeing the scientific people of all dirty work. Anton and Demetri are both most anxious to help on all occasions; they are excellent boys.

Thursday 19 January The hut is becoming the most comfortable dwelling-place imaginable. We have made unto ourselves a truly seductive home, within the walls of which peace, quiet, and comfort reign supreme.

Such a noble dwelling transcends the word 'hut', and we pause to give it a more fitting title only from lack of the appropriate suggestion. What shall we call it?

'The word "hut" is misleading. Our residence is really a house of considerable size, in every respect the finest that has ever been erected in the Polar regions; 50 ft. long by 25 wide and 9 ft. to the eaves.

'If you can picture our house nestling below this small hill on a long stretch of black sand, with many tons of provision cases ranged in neat blocks in front of it and the sea lapping the ice-foot below, you will have some idea of our immediate vicinity. As for our wider surroundings it would be difficult to describe their beauty in sufficiently glowing terms. Cape Evans is one of the many spurs of Erebus and the one that stands closest under the mountain, so that always towering above us we have the grand snowy peak with its smoking summit. North and south of us are deep bays, beyond which great glaciers come rippling over the lower slopes to thrust high blue-walled snouts into the sea. The sea is blue before us, dotted with shining bergs or ice floes, whilst far over the Sound, yet so bold and magnificent as to appear near, stand the beautiful Western Mountains with their numerous lofty peaks, their deep glacial valley and clear cut scarps, a vision of mountain scenery that can have few rivals.

'Ponting is the most delighted of men; he declares this is the most beautiful spot he has ever seen and spends all day and most of the night in what he calls "gathering it in" with camera and cinematograph.'

The wind has been boisterous all day, to advantage after the last snow fall, as it has been drifting the loose snow along and hardening the surfaces. The horses don't like it, naturally, but it wouldn't do to pamper them so soon before our journey. I think the hardening process must be good for animals though not for men; nature replies to it in the former by growing a thick coat with wonderful promptitude. It seems to me that the shaggy coats of our ponies are already improving. The dogs seem to feel the cold little so far, but they are not so exposed.

A milder situation might be found for the ponies if only we could picket them off the snow.

Bowers has completed his southern storeroom and brought the wing across the porch on the windward side, connecting the roofing with that of the porch. The improvement is enormous and will make the greatest difference to those who dwell near the door.

The carpenter has been setting up standards and roof beams for the stables, which will be completed in a few days. Internal affairs have been straightening out as rapidly as before, and every hour seems to add some new touch for the better.

This morning I overhauled all the fur sleeping-bags and found them in splendid order – on the whole the skins are excellent. Since that I have been trying to work out sledge details, but my head doesn't seem half as clear on the subject as it ought to be.

I have fixed the 25th as the date for our departure. Evans is to get all the sledges and gear ready whilst Bowers superintends the filling of provision bags.
Griffith Taylor and his companions have been seeking advice as to their Western trip. Wilson, dear chap, has been doing his best to coach them.

Ponting has fitted up his own dark room – doing the carpentering work with extraordinary speed and to everyone's admiration. Tonight he made a window in the dark room in an hour or so.

Meares has become enamoured of the gramophone. We find we have a splendid selection of records. The pianola is being brought in sections, but I'm not at all sure it will be worth the trouble. Oates goes steadily on with the ponies – he is perfectly excellent and untiring in his devotion to the animals.

Day and Nelson, having given much thought to the proper fitting up of their corner, have now begun work. There seems to be little doubt that these ingenious people will make the most of their allotted space.

I have done quite a lot of thinking over the autumn journeys and a lot remains to be done, mainly on account of the prospect of being cut off from our winter quarters; for this reason we must have a great deal of food for animals and men.

Friday 20 January Our house has assumed great proportions. Bowers' annexe is finished, roof and all thoroughly snow-tight; an excellent place for spare clothing, furs, and ready use stores, and its extension affording complete protection to the entrance porch of the hut. The stables are nearly finished – a thoroughly stout well-roofed lean-to on the north side. Nelson has a small extension on the east side and Simpson a prearranged projection on the S.E. corner, so that on all sides the main building has thrown out limbs. Simpson has almost completed his ice cavern, light-tight lining, niches, floor and all. Wright and Forde have almost completed the absolute hut, a patchwork building for which the framework only was brought – but it will be very well adapted for our needs.

Gran has been putting 'record' on the ski runners. Record is a mixture of vegetable tar, paraffin, soft soap, and linseed oil, with some patent addition which prevents freezing – this according to Gran.

P.O. Evans and Crean have been preparing sledges; Evans shows himself wonderfully capable, and I haven't a doubt as to the working of the sledges he has fitted up.

We have been serving out some sledging gear and wintering boots. We are delighted with everything. First the felt boots and felt slippers made by Jaeger and then summer wind clothes and fur mits – nothing could be better than these articles. Finally tonight we have overhauled and served out two pairs of finnesko (fur boots) to each traveller. They are excellent in quality. At first I thought they seemed small, but a stiffness due to cold and dryness misled me – a little stretching and all was well. They are very good indeed. I have an idea to use putties to secure our wind trousers to the finnesko. But indeed the whole time we are thinking of devices to make our travelling work easier.

'We have now tried most of our stores, and so far we have not found a single article that is not perfectly excellent in quality and preservation. We are well repaid for all the trouble which was taken in selecting the food list and the firms from which the various articles could best be obtained, and we are showering blessings on Mr. Wyatt's head for so strictly safeguarding our interests in these particulars.

'Our clothing is as good as good. In fact first and last, running through the whole extent of our outfit, I can say with some pride that there is not a single arrangement which I would have had altered.'

An Emperor penguin was found on the Cape well advanced in moult, a good specimen skin. Atkinson found cysts formed by a tapeworm in the intestines. It seems clear that this parasite is not transferred from another host, and that its history is unlike that of any other known tapeworm – in fact, Atkinson scores a discovery in parasitology of no little importance.

The wind has turned to the north tonight and is blowing quite fresh. I don't much like the position of the ship as the ice is breaking away all the time.

The sky is quite clear and I don't think the wind often lasts long under such conditions.

The pianola has been erected by Rennick. He is a good fellow and one feels for him much at such a time – it must be rather dreadful for him to be returning when he remembers that he was once practically one of the shore party.[11] The pianola has been his special care, and it shows well that he should give so much pains in putting it right for us.

Day has been explaining the manner in which he hopes to be able to cope with the motor sledge difficulty. He is hopeful of getting things right, but I fear it won't do to place more reliance on the machines.

Everything looks hopeful for the depot journey if only we can get our stores and ponies past the Glacier Tongue.

We had some seal rissoles today so extraordinarily well cooked that it was impossible to distinguish them from the best beef rissoles. I told two of the party they were beef, and they made no comment till I enlightened them after they had eaten two each. It is the first time I have tasted seal without being aware of its particular flavour. But even its own flavour is acceptable in our cook's hands – he really is excellent.

Saturday 21 January My anxiety for the ship was not unfounded. Fearing a little trouble I went out of the hut in the middle of the night and saw at once that she was having a bad time – the ice was breaking with a northerly swell and the wind increasing, with the ship on dead lee shore; luckily the ice anchors had been put well in on the floe and some still held. Pennell was getting up steam and his men struggling to replace the anchors.

We got out the men and gave some help. At 6 steam was up, and I was right glad to see the ship back out to windward, leaving us to recover anchors and hawsers.

She stood away to the west, and almost immediately after a large berg drove in and grounded in the place she had occupied.

We spent the day measuring our provisions and fixing up clothing arrangements for our journey; a good deal of progress has been made.

In the afternoon the ship returned to the northern ice edge; the wind was still strong (about N. 30 W.) and loose ice all along the edge – our people went out with the ice anchors and I saw the ship pass west again. Then as I went out on the floe came the report that she was ashore. I ran out to the Cape with Evans and saw that the report was only too true. She looked to be firmly fixed and in a very uncomfortable position. It looked as though she had been trying to get round the Cape, and therefore I argued she must have been going a good pace as the drift was making rapidly to the south. Later Pennell told me he had been trying to look behind the berg and had been going astern some time before he struck.

My heart sank when I looked at her and I sent Evans off in the whaler to sound, recovered the ice anchors again, set the people to work, and walked disconsolately back to the Cape to watch.

Visions of the ship failing to return to New Zealand and of sixty people waiting here arose in my mind with sickening pertinacity, and the only consolation I could draw from such imaginations was the determination that the southern work should go on as before – meanwhile the least ill possible seemed to be an extensive lightening of the ship with boats as the tide was evidently high when she struck – a terribly depressing prospect.

Some three or four of us watched it gloomily from the shore whilst all was bustle on board, the men shifting cargo aft. Pennell tells me they shifted 10 tons in a very short time.

The first ray of hope came when by careful watching one could see that the ship was turning very slowly, then one saw the men running from side to side and knew that an attempt was being made to roll her off. The rolling produced a more rapid turning movement at first and then she seemed to hang again. But only for a short time; the engines had been going astern all the time and presently a slight movement became apparent. But we only knew she was getting clear when we heard cheers on board and more cheers from the whaler.

Then she gathered stern way and was clear. The relief was enormous.

The wind dropped as she came off, and she is now securely moored off the northern ice edge, where I hope the greater number of her people are finding rest. For here and now I must record the splendid manner in which these men are working. I find it difficult to express my admiration for the manner in which the ship is handled and worked under these very trying circumstances.

From Pennell down there is not an officer or man who has not done his job nobly during the past weeks, and it will be a glorious thing to remember the unselfish loyal help they are giving us.

Pennell has been over to tell me all about it tonight; I think I like him more every day.

Campbell and his party returned late this afternoon – I have not heard details.

Meares and Oates went to the Glacier Tongue and satisfied themselves that the ice is good. It only has to remain another three days, and it would be poor luck if it failed in that time.

Sunday 22 January A quiet day with little to record.

The ship lies peacefully in the bay; a brisk northerly breeze in the forenoon died to light airs in the evening – it is warm enough, the temperature in the hut was 63° this evening. We have had a long busy day at clothing – everyone sewing away diligently. The Eastern Party ponies were put on board the ship this morning.

Monday 23 January Placid conditions last for a very short time in these regions. I got up at 5 this morning to find the weather calm and beautiful, but to my astonishment an opening lane of water between the land and the ice in the bay. The latter was going out in a solid mass.

The ship discovered it easily, got up her ice anchors, sent a boat ashore, and put out to sea to dredge. We went on with our preparations, but soon Meares brought word that the ice in the south bay was going in an equally rapid fashion. This proved an exaggeration, but an immense piece of floe had separated from the land. Meares and I walked till we came to the first ice.

Luckily we found that it extends for some 2 miles along the rock of our Cape, and we discovered a possible way to lead ponies down to it. It was plain that only the ponies could go by it – no loads.

Since that everything has been rushed – and a wonderful day's work has resulted; we have got all the forage and food sledges and equipment off to the ship – the dogs will follow in an hour, I hope, with pony harness, etc., that is everything to do with our depot party, except the ponies.

As at present arranged they are to cross the Cape and try to get over the Southern Road tomorrow morning. [The Southern Road was the one feasible line of communication between the new station at C. Evans and the *Discovery* hut at Hut Point, for the rugged mountains and crevassed ice slopes of Ross Island forbade a passage by land. The Road afforded level going below the cliffs of the ice-foot, except where disturbed by the descending glacier, and there it was necessary to cross the body of the glacier itself. It consisted of the more enduring ice in the bays and the sea-ice along the coast, which only stayed fast for the season. Thus it was of the utmost importance to get safely over the precarious part of the Road before the seasonal going-out of the sea-ice. To wait until all the ice should go out and enable the ship to sail to Hut Point would have meant long uncertainty and delay. As it happened, the Road broke up the day after the party had gone by.] One breathes a prayer that the Road holds for the few remaining hours. It goes in one place between a berg in open water and a large pool of the glacier face – it may be weak in that part, and at any moment the narrow isthmus may break away. We are doing it on a very narrow margin.

If all is well I go to the ship tomorrow morning after the ponies have started, and then to Glacier Tongue.

5
DEPOT LAYING TO ONE TON CAMP:
24 JANUARY 1911 – 17 FEBRUARY 1911

Tuesday 24 January People were busy in the hut all last night – we got away at 9 a.m. A boat from the *Terra Nova* fetched the Western Party and myself as the ponies were led out of the camp. Meares and Wilson went ahead of the ponies to test the track. On board the ship I was taken in to see Lillie's catch of sea animals. It was wonderful, quantities of sponges, isopods, pentapods, large shrimps, corals, etc., etc. – but the *pièce de résistance* was the capture of several buckets full of cephalodiscus of which only seven pieces had been previously caught. Lillie is immensely pleased, feeling that it alone repays the whole enterprise.

In the forenoon we skirted the Island, getting 30 and 40 fathoms of water north and west of Inaccessible Island. With a telescope we could see the string of ponies steadily progressing over the sea-ice past the Razor Back Islands. As soon as we saw them well advanced we steamed on to the Glacier Tongue. The open water extended just round the corner and the ship made fast in the narrow angle made by the sea-ice with the glacier, her port side flush with the surface of the latter. I walked over to meet the ponies whilst Campbell went to investigate a broad crack in the sea-ice on the Southern Road. The ponies were got on to the Tongue without much difficulty, then across the glacier, and picketed on the sea-ice close to the ship. Meanwhile Campbell informed me that the big crack was 30 feet across: it was evident we must get past it on the glacier, and I asked Campbell to peg out a road clear of cracks. Oates reported the ponies ready to start again after tea, and they were led along Campbell's road, their loads having already been taken on the floe – all went well until the animals got down on the floe level and Oates led across an old snowed-up crack. His and the next pony got across, but the third made a jump at the edge and sank to its stomach in the middle. It couldn't move, and with such struggles as it made it sank deeper till only its head and forelegs showed above the slush. With some trouble we got ropes on these, and hauling together pulled the poor creature out looking very weak and miserable and trembling much.

We led the other ponies round farther to the west and eventually got all out on the floe, gave them a small feed, and started them off with their loads. The dogs meanwhile gave some excitement. Starting on hard ice with a light load nothing could hold them, and they dashed off over everything – it seemed wonderful that we all reached the floe in safety. Wilson and I drive one team, whilst Evans and Meares drive the other. I withhold my opinion of the dogs in much doubt as to whether they are going to be a real success – but the ponies are going to be real good. They work with such extraordinary steadiness, stepping out briskly and cheerfully, following in each other's tracks. The great drawback is the ease with which they sink in soft snow: they go through in lots of places where the men scarcely make an impression – they struggle pluckily when they sink, but it is trying to watch them. We came with the loads noted below and one bale of fodder (105 lbs.) added to each sledge. We are camped 6 miles from the glacier and 2 from Hut Point – a cold east wind; tonight the temperature 19°.

AUTUMN PARTY TO START 25 JANUARY 1911

12 men [viz. Atkinson and Crean, who were left at Safety Camp; E. Evans, Forde and Keohane, who returned with the weaker ponies on 13 February; Meares and Wilson with the dog teams; and Scott, Bowers, Oates, Cherry-Garrard, and Gran.], 8 ponies, 26 dogs.

First load estimated 5385 lbs., including 14 weeks' food and fuel for men – taken to Cache No. 1.

Ship transports following to Glacier Tongue:

	lbs.
130 Bales compressed fodder	13,650
24 Cases dog biscuit	1,400
10 Sacks of oats	1,600?
	16,650

Teams return to ship to transport this load to Cache No. 1. Dog teams also take on 500 lbs. of biscuit from Hut Point.

PONY SLEDGES

		lbs.
On all sledges	Sledge with straps and tank	52
	Pony furniture	25
	Driver's ski and sleeping-bag, etc.	40
Nos. 1 & 5	Cooker and primus instruments	40
	Tank containing biscuit	172
	Sack of oats	160
	Tent and poles	28
	Alpine rope	5
	1 oil can and spirit can	15
		530

Nos. 2 & 6	Oil	100
	Tank contents: food bags	285
	Ready provision bag	63
	2 picks	20
		576

Nos. 3 & 7	Oil	100
	Tank contents: biscuit	196
	Sack of oats	160
	2 shovels	9
		570

Nos. 4 & 8	Box with tools, etc.	35
	Cookers, etc.	105
	Tank contents food bags	252
	Sack of oats	160
	3 long bamboos and spare gear	15
		567

SPARE GEAR PER MAN
2 pairs under socks
2 pairs outer socks
1 pair hair socks
1 pair night socks
1 pyjama jacket
1 pyjama trousers
1 woollen mits
2 finnesko

Skein	= 10 lbs.	
Books, diaries, tobacco, etc.	2 lbs.	
	12 lbs.	

DRESS

Vest and drawers	Wind Suit
Woollen shirt	Two pairs socks
Jersey	Ski boots.
Balaclava	

DOGS

No. 1.

	lbs.
Sledge straps and tanks	54
Drivers' ski and bags	80
Cooker primus and instruments	50
Tank contents: biscuit	221
Alpine rope	5

Lamps and candles	4
2 shovels	9
Ready provision bag	63
Sledge meter	0
	486

No. 2.

Sledge straps and tanks	54
Drivers' ski and bags	80
Tank contents: food bags	324
Tent and poles	33
	491

10-ft. sledge: men's harness, extra tent.

Thursday 26 January Yesterday I went to the ship with a dog team. All went well till the dogs caught sight of a whale breeching in the 30 ft. lead and promptly made for it! It was all we could do to stop them before we reached the water.

Spent the day writing letters and completing arrangements for the ship – a brisk northerly breeze sprang up in the night and the ship bumped against the glacier until the pack came in as protection from the swell. Ponies and dogs arrived about 1 p.m., and at 5 we all went out for the final start.

A little earlier Pennell had the men aft and I thanked them for their splendid work. They have behaved like bricks and a finer lot of fellows never sailed in a ship. It was good to get their hearty send off. Before we could get away Ponting had his half-hour photographing us, the ponies and the dog teams – I hope he will have made a good thing of it. It was a little sad to say farewell to all these good fellows and Campbell and his men. I do most heartily trust that all will be successful in their ventures, for indeed their unselfishness and their generous high spirit deserves reward. God bless them.

So here we are with all our loads. One wonders what the upshot will be. It will take three days to transport the loads to complete safety; the break-up of the sea-ice ought not to catch us before that. The wind is from the S.E. again tonight.

Friday 27 January – Camp 2. Started at 9.30 and moved a load of fodder 3¾ miles south – returned to camp to lunch – then shifted camp and provisions. Our weights are now divided into three loads: two of food for ponies, one of men's provisions with some ponies' food. It is slow work, but we retreat slowly but surely from the chance of going out on the sea-ice.

We are camped about a mile south of C. Armitage. After camping I went to the east till abreast of Pram Point, finding the ice dangerously thin off C. Armitage. It is evident we must make a considerable detour to avoid danger. The rest of the party went to the *Discovery* hut to see what could be done towards digging it out. The report is unfavourable, as I expected. The drift inside has become very solid – it would take weeks of work to clear it. A great deal of biscuit and some butter, cocoa, etc., was seen, so that we need not have any anxiety about provisions if delayed in returning to Cape Evans.

The dogs are very tired tonight. I have definitely handed the control of the second team to Wilson. He was very eager to have it and will do well I'm sure – but certainly also the dogs will not pull heavy loads – 500 pounds proved a back-breaking load for 11 dogs today – they brought it at a snail's pace. Meares has estimated to give them two-thirds of a pound of biscuit a day. I have felt sure he will find this too little.

The ponies are doing excellently. Their loads run up to 800 and 900 lbs. and they make very light of them. Oates said he could have gone on for some time tonight.

Saturday 28 January Camp 2. The ponies went back for the last load at Camp 1, and I walked south to find a way round the great pressure ridge. The sea-ice south is covered with confused irregular sastrugi well remembered from *Discovery* days. The pressure ridge is new. The broken ice of the ridge ended east of the spot I approached and the pressure was seen only in a huge domed wave, the hollow of which on my left was surrounded with a countless number of seals – these lay about sleeping or apparently gambolling in the shallow water. I imagine the old ice in this hollow has gone well under and that the seals have a pool above it which may be warmer on such a bright day.

It was evident that the ponies could be brought round by this route, and I returned to camp to hear that one of the ponies (Keohane's) had gone lame. The Soldier took a gloomy view of the situation, but he is not an optimist. It looks as though a tendon had been strained, but it is not at all certain. Bowers' pony is also weak in the forelegs, but we knew this before: it is only a question of how long he will last. The pity is that he is an excellently strong pony otherwise. Atkinson has a bad heel and laid up all day – his pony was tied behind another sledge, and went well, a very hopeful sign.

In the afternoon I led the ponies out 2¾ miles south to the crossing of the pressure ridge, then east 1¼ till we struck the barrier edge and ascended it. Going about ½ mile in we dumped the loads – the ponies sank deep just before the loads were dropped, but it looked as though the softness was due to some rise in the surface.

We saw a dark object a quarter of a mile north as we reached the Barrier. I walked over and found it to be the tops of two tents more than half buried – Shackleton's tents we suppose. A moulting Emperor penguin was sleeping between them. The canvas on one tent seemed intact, but half stripped from the other.

The ponies pulled splendidly today, as also the dogs, but we have decided to load both lightly from now on, to march them easily, and to keep as much life as possible in them. There is much to be learnt as to their powers of performance.

Keohane says, 'Come on, lad, you'll be getting to the Pole' by way of cheering his animal – all the party is cheerful, there never were a better set of people.

Sunday 29 January Camp 2. This morning after breakfast I read prayers. Excellent day. The seven good ponies have made two journeys to the Barrier, covering 18 geographical miles, half with good loads – none of them were at all done. Oates' pony, a spirited, nervous creature, got away at start when his head was left for a moment and charged through the camp at a gallop; finally his sledge cannoned into another, the swingle tree broke, and he galloped away, kicking furiously at the dangling trace. Oates fetched him when he had quieted down, and we found that nothing had been hurt or broken but the swingle tree.

Gran tried going on ski with his pony. All went well while he was alongside, but when he came up from the back the swish of the ski frightened the beast, who fled faster than his pursuer – that is, the pony and load were going better than the Norwegian on ski.

Gran is doing very well. He has a lazy pony and a good deal of work to get him along, and does it very cheerfully.

The dogs are doing excellently – getting into better condition every day.

They ran the first load 1 mile 1200 yards past the stores on the Barrier, to the spot chosen for 'Safety Camp', the big home depot.

I don't think that any part of the Barrier is likely to go, but it's just as well to be prepared for everything, and our camp must deserve its distinctive title of 'Safety'.

In the afternoon the dogs ran a second load to the same place – covering over 24 geographical miles in the day – an excellent day's work.[12]

Evans and I took a load out on foot over the pressure ridge. The camp load alone remains to be taken to the Barrier. Once we get to Safety Camp we can stay as long as we like before starting our journey. It is only when we start that we must travel fast.

Most of the day it has been overcast, but tonight it has cleared again. There is very little wind. The temperatures of late have been ranging from 9° at night to 24° in the day. Very easy circumstances for sledging.

Monday 30 January Camp 3. Safety Camp. Bearings: Lat. 77.55; Cape Armitage N. 64 W.; Camel's Hump of Blue Glacier left, extreme; Castle Rock N. 40 W. Called the camp at 7.30. Finally left with ponies at 11.30. There was a good deal to do, which partly accounts for delays, but we shall have to 'buck up' with our camp arrangement. Atkinson had his foot lanced and should be well in a couple of days.

I led the lame pony; his leg is not swelled, but I fear he's developed a permanent defect – there are signs of ring bone and the hoof is split.

A great shock came when we passed the depoted fodder and made for this camp. The ponies sank very deep and only brought on their loads with difficulty, getting pretty hot. The distance was but 1½ miles, but it took more out of them than the rest of the march. We camped and held a council of war after lunch. I unfolded my plan, which is to go forward with five weeks' food for men and animals: to depot a fortnight's supply after twelve or thirteen days and return here. The loads for ponies thus arranged work out a little over 600 lbs., for the dog teams 700 lbs., both apart from sledges. The ponies ought to do it easily if the surface is good enough for them to walk, which is doubtful – the dogs may have to be lightened – such as it is, it is the best we can do under the circumstances!

This afternoon I went forward on ski to see if the conditions changed. In 2 or 3 miles I could see no improvement.

Bowers, Garrard, and the three men went and dug out the *Nimrod* tent. They found a cooker and provisions and remains of a hastily abandoned meal. One tent was half full of hard ice, the result of thaw. The Willesden canvas was rotten except some material used for the doors. The floor cloth could not be freed.

The Soldier doesn't like the idea of fetching up the remainder of the loads to this camp with the ponies. I think we will bring on all we can with the dogs and take the risk of leaving the rest.

The *Nimrod* camp was evidently made by some relief or ship party, and if that has stood fast for so long there should be little fear for our stuff in a single season. Tomorrow we muster stores, build the depot, and pack our sledges.

Tuesday 31 January Camp 3. We have everything ready to start – but this afternoon we tried our one pair of snow-shoes on 'Weary Willy'. The effect was magical. He strolled around as though walking on hard ground in places where he floundered woefully without them. Oates hasn't had any faith in these shoes at all, and I thought that even the quietest pony would need to be practised in their use.

Immediately after our experiment I decided that an effort must be made to get more, and within half an hour Meares and Wilson were on their way to the station more than 20 miles away. There is just the chance that the ice may not have gone out, but it is a very poor one I fear. At present it looks as though we might double our distance with the snow-shoes.

Atkinson is better today, but not by any means well, so that the delay is in his favour. We cannot start on till the dogs return with or without the shoes. The only other hope for this journey is that the Barrier gets harder farther out, but I feel that the prospect of this is not very bright. In any case it is something to have discovered the possibilities of these shoes.

Low temperature at night for first time. Min. 2.4°. Quite warm in tent.

Wednesday 1 February Camp 3. A day of comparative inactivity and some disappointment. Meares and Wilson returned at noon, reporting the ice out beyond the Razor Back Island – no return to Cape Evans – no pony snow-shoes – alas! I have decided to make a start tomorrow without them. Late tonight Atkinson's foot was examined: it is bad and there's no possibility of its getting right for some days. He must be left behind – I've decided to leave Crean with him. Most luckily we now have an extra tent and cooker. How the ponies are to be led is very doubtful. Well, we must do the best that circumstances permit. Poor Atkinson is in very low spirits.

I sent Gran to the *Discovery* hut with our last mail. He went on ski and was nearly 4 hours away, making me rather anxious, as the wind had sprung up and there was a strong surface-drift; he narrowly missed the camp on returning and I am glad to get him back.

Our food allowance seems to be very ample, and if we go on as at present we shall thrive amazingly.

Thursday 2 February Camp 4. Made a start at last. Roused out at 7, left camp about 10.30. Atkinson and Crean remained behind – very hard on the latter. Atkinson suffering much pain and mental distress at his condition – for the latter I fear I cannot have much sympathy, as he ought to have reported his trouble long before. Crean will manage to rescue some more of the forage from the Barrier edge – I am very sorry for him.

On starting with all the ponies (I leading Atkinson's) I saw with some astonishment that the animals were not sinking deeply, and to my pleased surprise we made good progress at once. This lasted for more than an hour, then the surface got comparatively bad again – but still most of the ponies did well with it, making 5 miles. Birdie's [The favourite nickname for Bowers] animal, however, is very heavy and flounders where the others walk fairly easily. He is eager and tries to go faster as he flounders. As a result he was brought in, in a lather. I inquired for our one set of snow-shoes and found they had been left behind. The difference in surface from what was expected makes one wonder whether better conditions may not be expected during the night and in the morning, when the temperatures are low. My suggestion that we should take to night marching has met with general approval. Even if there is no improvement in the surface the ponies will rest better during the warmer hours and march better in the night.

So we are resting in our tents, waiting to start tonight. Gran has gone back for the snow-shoes – he volunteered good-naturedly – certainly his expertness on ski is useful.

Last night the temperature fell to -6° after the wind dropped – today it is warm and calm.

Impressions

The seductive folds of the sleeping-bag.

The hiss of the primus and the fragrant steam of the cooker issuing from the tent ventilator.

The small green tent and the great white road.

The whine of a dog and the neigh of our steeds.

The driving cloud of powdered snow.

The crunch of footsteps which break the surface crust.

The wind-blown furrows.

The blue arch beneath the smoky cloud.

The crisp ring of the ponies' hoofs and the swish of the following sledge.

The droning conversation of the march as driver encourages or chides his horse.

The patter of dog pads.

The gentle flutter of our canvas shelter.

Its deep booming sound under the full force of a blizzard.

The drift snow like finest flour penetrating every hole and corner – flickering up beneath one's head covering, pricking sharply as a sand blast.

The sun with blurred image peeping shyly through the wreathing drift giving pale shadowless light.

The eternal silence of the great white desert. Cloudy columns of snow drift advancing from the south, pale yellow wraiths, heralding the coming storm, blotting out one by one the sharp-cut lines of the land.

The blizzard, Nature's protest – the crevasse, Nature's pitfall – that grim trap for the unwary – no hunter could conceal his snare so perfectly – the light rippled snow bridge gives no hint or sign of the hidden danger, its position unguessable till man or beast is floundering, clawing and struggling for foothold on the brink.

The vast silence broken only by the mellow sounds of the marching column.

Friday 3 February 8 a.m. Camp 5. Roused the camp at 10 p.m. and we started marching at 12.30. At first surface bad, but gradually improving. We had two short spells and set up temporary camp to feed ourselves and ponies at 3.20. Started again at 5 and marched till 7. In all covered 9 miles. Surface seemed to have improved during the last part of the march till just before camping time, when Bowers, who was leading, plunged into soft snow. Several of the others following close on his heels shared his fate, and soon three ponies were plunging and struggling in a drift. Garrard's pony, which has very broad feet, found hard stuff beyond and then my pony got round. Forde and Keohane led round on comparatively hard ground well to the right, and the entangled ponies were unharnessed and led round from patch to patch till firmer ground was reached. Then we camped and the remaining loads were brought in. Then came the *triumph of the snow-shoe* again. We put a set on Bowers' big pony – at first he walked awkwardly (for a few minutes only) then he settled down, was harnessed to his load, brought that in and another also – all over places into which he had been plunging. If we had more of these shoes we could certainly put them on seven out of eight of our ponies – and after a little I think on the eighth, Oates' pony, as certainly the ponies so shod would draw their loads over the soft snow patches without any difficulty. It is trying to feel that so great a help to our work has been left behind at the station.

Impressions

It is pathetic to see the ponies floundering in the soft patches. The first sink is a shock to them and seems to brace them to action. Thus they generally try to rush through when they feel themselves sticking. If the patch is small they land snorting and agitated on the harder surface with much effort. And if the patch is extensive they plunge on gamely until exhausted. Most of them after a bit plunge forward with both forefeet together, making a series of jumps and bringing the sledge behind them with jerks. This is, of course, terribly tiring for them. Now and again they have to stop, and it is horrid to see them half engulfed in the snow, panting and heaving from the strain. Now and again one falls and lies trembling and temporarily exhausted. It must be terribly trying for them, but it is wonderful to see how soon they recover their strength. The quiet, lazy ponies have a much better time than the eager ones when such troubles arise.

The soft snow which gave the trouble is evidently in the hollow of one of the big waves that continue through the pressure ridges at Cape Crozier towards the Bluff. There are probably more of these waves, though we crossed several during the last part of the march – so far it seems that the soft parts are in patches only and do not extend the whole length of the hollow. Our course is to pick a way with the sure-footed beasts and keep the others back till the road has been tested.

What extraordinary uncertainties this work exhibits! Every day some new fact comes to light – some new obstacle which threatens the gravest obstruction. I suppose this is the reason which makes the game so well worth playing.

Impressions

The more I think of our sledging outfit the more certain I am that we have arrived at something near a perfect equipment for civilised man under such conditions.

The border line between necessity and luxury is vague enough.

We might save weight at the expense of comfort, but all possible saving would amount to but a mere fraction of one's loads. Supposing it were a grim struggle for existence and we were forced to drop everything but the barest necessities, the total saving on this three weeks' journey would be:

	lbs.
Fuel for cooking	100
Cooking apparatus	45
Personal clothing, etc., say	100
Tent, say	30
Instruments, etc.	100
	375

This is half of one of ten sledge-loads, or about one-twentieth of the total weight carried. If this is the only part of our weights which under any conceivable circumstances could be included in the category of luxuries, it follows the sacrifice to comfort is negligible. Certainly we could not have increased our mileage by making such a sacrifice.

But beyond this it may be argued that we have an unnecessary amount of food: 32 oz. per day per man is our allowance. I well remember the great strait of hunger to which we were reduced in 1903 after four or five weeks on 26 oz., and am perfectly confident that we were steadily losing stamina at that time. Let it be supposed that 4 oz. per day per man might conceivably be saved. We have then 3 lbs. a day saved in the camp, or 63 lbs. in the three weeks, or 1/100th part of our present loads.

The smallness of the fractions on which the comfort and physical well-being of the men depend is due to the fact of travelling with animals whose needs are proportionately so much greater than those of the men. It follows that it must be sound policy to keep the men of a sledge party keyed up to a high pitch of well-fed physical condition as long as they have animals to drag their loads. The time for short rations, long marches and carefullest scrutiny of detail comes when the men are dependent on their own traction efforts.

6 p.m. It has been blowing from the S.W., but the wind is dying away – the sky is overcast – I write after 9 hours' sleep, the others still peacefully slumbering. Work with animals means long intervals of rest which are not altogether easily occupied. With our present routine the dogs remain behind for an hour or more, trying to hit off their arrival in the new camp soon after the ponies have been picketed. The teams are pulling very well, Meares' especially. The animals are getting a little fierce. Two white dogs in Meares' team have been trained to attack strangers – they were quiet enough on board ship, but now bark fiercely if anyone but their driver approaches the team. They suddenly barked at me as I was pointing out the stopping place to Meares, and Osman, my erstwhile friend, swept round and nipped my leg lightly. I had no stick and there is no doubt that if Meares had not been on the sledge the whole team, following the lead of the white dogs, would have been at me in a moment.

Hunger and fear are the only realities in dog life: an empty stomach makes a fierce dog. There is something almost alarming in the sudden fierce display of natural instinct in a tame creature. Instinct becomes a blind, unreasoning, relentless passion. For instance the dogs are as a rule all very good friends in harness: they pull side by side rubbing shoulders, they walk over each other as they settle to rest, relations seem quite peaceful and quiet. But the moment food is in their thoughts, however, their passions awaken; each dog is suspicious of his neighbour, and the smallest circumstance produces a fight. With like suddenness their rage flares out instantaneously if they get mixed up on the march – a quiet, peaceable team which has been lazily stretching itself with wagging tails one moment will become a set of raging, tearing, fighting devils the next. It is such stern facts that resign one to the sacrifice of animal life in the effort to advance such human projects as this.

The Corner Camp. [Bearings: Obs. Hill < Bluff 86°; Obs. Hill < Knoll 80½°; Mt. Terror N. 4 W.; Obs. Hill N. 69 W.]

Saturday 4 February 1911 8 a.m. Camp 6. A satisfactory night march covering 10 miles and some hundreds of yards.

Roused party at 10, when it was blowing quite hard from the S.E., with temperature below zero. It looked as though we should have a pretty cold start, but by the end of breakfast the wind had dropped and the sun shone forth.

Started on a bad surface – ponies plunging a good deal for 2 miles or so, Bowers' 'Uncle Bill' walking steadily on his snow-shoes. After this the surface improved and the marching became steadier. We camped for lunch after 5 miles. Going still better in the afternoon, except that we crossed several crevasses. Oates' pony dropped his legs into two of these and sank into one – oddly the other ponies escaped and we were the last. Some 2 miles from our present position the cracks appeared to cease, and in the last march we have got on to quite a hard surface on which the ponies drag their loads with great ease. This part seems to be swept by the winds which so continually sweep round Cape Crozier, and therefore it is doubtful if it extends far to the south, but for the present the going should be good. Had bright moonshine for the march, but now the sky has clouded and it looks threatening to the south. I think we may have a blizzard, though the wind is northerly at present.

The ponies are in very good form; 'James Pigg' remarkably recovered from his lameness.

8 p.m. It is blowing a blizzard – wind moderate – temperature mild.

Impressions

The deep, dreamless sleep that follows the long march and the satisfying supper.

The surface crust which breaks with a snap and sinks with a snap, startling men and animals.

Custom robs it of dread but not of interest to the dogs, who come to imagine such sounds as the result of some strange freak of hidden creatures. They become all alert and spring from side to side, hoping to catch the creature. The hope clings in spite of continual disappointment.[13]

A dog must be either eating, asleep, or *interested*. His eagerness to snatch at interest, to chain his attention to something, is almost pathetic. The monotony of marching kills him.

This is the fearfullest difficulty for the dog driver on a snow plain without leading marks or objects in sight. The dog is almost human in its demand for living interest, yet fatally less than human in its inability to foresee.

The dog lives for the day, the hour, even the moment. The human being can live and support discomfort for a future.

Sunday 5 February Corner Camp, No. 6. The blizzard descended on us at about 4 p.m. yesterday; for twenty-four hours it continued with moderate wind, then the wind shifting slightly to the west came with much greater violence. Now it is blowing very hard and our small frail tent is being well tested. One imagines it cannot continue long as at present, but remembers our proximity to Cape Crozier and the length of the blizzards recorded in that region. As usual we sleep and eat, conversing as cheerfully as may be in the intervals. There is scant news of our small outside world – only a report of comfort and a rumour that Bowers' pony has eaten one of its putties!!

11 p.m. Still blowing hard – a real blizzard now with dusty, floury drift – two minutes in the open makes a white figure. What a wonderful shelter our little tent affords! We have just had an excellent meal, a quiet pipe, and fireside conversation within, almost forgetful for the time of the howling tempest without; now, as we lie in our bags warm and comfortable, one can scarcely realise that 'hell' is on the other side of the thin sheet of canvas that protects us.

Monday 6 February 6 p.m. Corner Camp, No. 6. The wind increased in the night. It has been blowing very hard all day. No fun to be out of the tent

– but there are no shirkers with us. Oates has been out regularly to feed the ponies; Meares and Wilson to attend to the dogs – the rest of us as occasion required. The ponies are fairly comfortable, though one sees now what great improvements could be made to the horse clothes. The dogs ought to be quite happy. They are curled snugly under the snow and at meal times issue from steaming warm holes. The temperature is high, luckily. We are comfortable enough in the tent, but it is terribly trying to the patience – over fifty hours already and no sign of the end. The drifts about the camp are very deep – some of the sledges almost covered. It is the old story – eat and sleep, sleep and eat – and it's surprising how much sleep can be put in.

Tuesday 7 February 5 p.m. Corner Camp, No. 6. The wind kept on through the night, commencing to lull at 8 a.m. At 10 a.m. one could see an arch of clear sky to the S.W. and W., White Island, the Bluff, and the Western Mountains clearly defined. The wind had fallen very light and we were able to do some camp work, digging out sledges and making the ponies more comfortable. At 11 a low dark cloud crept over the southern horizon and there could be no doubt the wind was coming upon us again. At 1 p.m. the drift was all about us once more and the sun obscured. One began to feel that fortune was altogether too hard on us – but now as I write the wind has fallen again to a gentle breeze, the sun is bright, and the whole southern horizon clear. A good sign is the freedom of the Bluff from cloud. One feels that we ought to have a little respite for the next week, and now we must do everything possible to tend and protect our ponies. All looks promising for the night march.

Wednesday 8 February No. 7 Camp. Bearings: Lat. 78° 13′; Mt. Terror N. 3 W.; Erebus 23½ Terror 2nd peak from south; Pk. 2 White Island 74 Terror; Castle Rk. 43 Terror. Night march just completed. 10 miles, 200 yards. The ponies were much shaken by the blizzard. One supposes they did not sleep – all look listless and two or three are visibly thinner than before. But the worst case by far is Forde's little pony; he was reduced to a weight little exceeding 400 lbs. on his sledge and caved in altogether on the second part of the march. The load was reduced to 200 lbs., and finally Forde pulled this in, leading the pony. The poor thing is a miserable scarecrow and never ought to have been brought – it is the same pony that did so badly in the ship. Today it is very fine and bright. We are giving a good deal of extra food to the animals, and my hope is that they will soon pick up again – but they cannot stand more blizzards in their present state. I'm afraid we shall not get very far, but at all hazards we must keep the greater number of the ponies alive. The dogs are in fine form – the blizzard has only been a pleasant rest *for them.*

Memo Left No. 7 Camp. 2 bales of fodder.

Thursday 9 February No. 8 Camp. Made good 11 miles. Good night march; surface excellent, but we are carrying very light loads with the exception of one or two ponies. Forde's poor 'Misery' is improving slightly. It is very keen on its feed. Its fate is much in doubt. Keohane's 'Jimmy Pigg' is less lame than yesterday. In fact there is a general buck-up all round.

It was a coldish march with light head wind and temperature 5° or 6° below zero, but it was warm in the sun all yesterday and promises to be warm again today. If such weather would hold there would be nothing to fear for the ponies. We have come to the conclusion that the principal cause of their discomfort is the comparative thinness of their coats.

We get the well-remembered glorious views of the Western Mountains, but now very distant. No crevasses today. I shall be surprised if we pass outside all sign of them.

One begins to see how things ought to be worked next year if the ponies hold out. Ponies and dogs are losing their snow blindness.

Friday 10 February No. 9 Camp. 12 miles 200 yards. Cold march, very chilly wind, overcast sky, difficult to see surface or course.

Noticed sledges, ponies, etc., cast shadows all round.

Surface very good and animals did splendidly.

We came over some undulations during the early part of the march, but the last part appeared quite flat. I think I remember observing the same fact on our former trip.

The wind veers and backs from S. to W. and even to N., coming in gusts. The sastrugi are distinctly S.S.W. There isn't a shadow of doubt that the prevailing wind is along the coast, taking the curve of the deep bay south of the Bluff.

The question now is: Shall we by going due southward keep this hard surface? If so, we should have little difficulty in reaching the Beardmore Glacier next year.

We turn out of our sleeping-bags about 9 p.m. Somewhere about 11.30 I shout to the Soldier 'How are things?' There is a response suggesting readiness, and soon after figures are busy amongst sledges and ponies. It is chilling work for the fingers and not too warm for the feet. The rugs come off the animals, the harness is put on, tents and camp equipment are loaded on the sledges, nosebags filled for the next halt; one by one the animals are taken off the picketing rope and yoked to the sledge. Oates watches his animal warily, reluctant to keep such a nervous creature standing in the traces. If one is prompt one feels impatient and fretful whilst watching one's more tardy fellows. Wilson and Meares hang about ready to help with odds and ends. Still we wait: the picketing lines must be gathered up, a few pony putties need adjustment, a party has been slow striking their tent. With numbed fingers on our horse's bridle and the animal striving to turn its head from the wind one feels resentful. At last all is ready. One says 'All right, Bowers, go ahead,' and Birdie leads his big animal forward, starting, as he continues, at a steady pace. The horses have got cold and at the word they are off, the Soldier's and one or two others with a rush. Finnesko give poor foothold on the slippery sastrugi, and for a minute or two drivers have some difficulty in maintaining the pace on their feet. Movement is warming, and in ten minutes the column has settled itself to steady marching.

The pace is still brisk, the light bad, and at intervals one or another of us suddenly steps on a slippery patch and falls prone. These are the only real incidents of the march – for the rest it passes with a steady tramp and slight variation of formation. The weaker ponies drop a bit but not far, so that they are soon up in line again when the first halt is made. We have come to a single halt in each half march. Last night it was too cold to stop long and a very few minutes found us on the go again.

As the end of the half march approaches I get out my whistle. Then at a shrill blast Bowers wheels slightly to the left, his tent mates lead still farther out to get the distance for the picket lines; Oates and I stop behind Bowers and Evans, the two other sledges of our squad behind the two other of Bowers'. So we are drawn up in camp formation. The picket lines are run across at right angles to the line of advance and secured to the two sledges at each end. In a few minutes ponies are on the lines covered, tents up again and cookers going.

Meanwhile the dog drivers, after a long cold wait at the old camp, have packed the last sledge and come trotting along our tracks. They try to time their arrival in the new camp immediately after our own and generally succeed well. The mid-march halt runs into an hour to an hour and a half, and at the end we pack up and tramp forth again. We generally make our final camp about 8 o'clock, and within an hour and a half most of us are in our sleeping-bags. Such is at present the daily routine. At the long halt we do our best for our animals by building snow walls and improving their rugs, etc.

Saturday 11 *February* No. 10 Camp. Bearings: Lat. 78° 47′. Bluff S. 79 W.; Left extreme Bluff 65°; Bluff A White Island near Sound. 11 miles. Covered 6 and 5 miles between halts. The surface has got a good deal softer. In the next two marches we should know more certainly, but it looks as though the conditions to the south will not be so good as those we have had hitherto.

Blossom, Evans' pony, has very small hoofs and found the going very bad. It is less a question of load than one of walking, and there is no doubt that some form of snow-shoe would help greatly. The question is, what form?

All the ponies were a little done when we stopped, but the weather is favourable for a good rest; there is no doubt this night marching is the best policy.

Even the dogs found the surface more difficult today, but they are pulling very well. Meares has deposed Osman in favour of Rabchick, as the former was getting either very disobedient or very deaf. The change appears excellent. Rabchick leads most obediently.

Memo For next year. A stout male bamboo shod with a spike to sound for crevasses.

Sunday 12 *February* No. 11 Camp. 10 miles. Depot one bale of fodder. Variation 150 E. South True = N. 30 E. by compass. The surface is getting decidedly worse. The ponies sink quite deep every now and again. We marched 6¼ miles before lunch, Blossom dropping considerably behind. He lagged more on the second march and we halted at 9 miles. Evans said he might be dragged for another mile and we went on for that distance and camped.

The sky was overcast: very dark and snowy looking in the south – very difficult to steer a course. Mt. Discovery is in line with the south end of the

Bluff from the camp and we are near the 79th parallel. We must get exact bearings for this is to be called the 'Bluff Camp' and should play an important part in the future. Bearings: Bluff 36° 13′; Black Island Rht. Ex. I have decided to send E. Evans, Forde, and Keohane back with the three weakest ponies which they have been leading. The remaining five ponies which have been improving in condition will go on for a few days at least, and we must see how near we can come to the 80th parallel.

Tonight we have been making all the necessary arrangements for this plan. Cherry-Garrard is to come into our tent.

Monday 13 February No. 12 Camp. 9 miles 150 yds. The wind got up from the south with drift before we started yesterday – all appearance of a blizzard. But we got away at 12.30 and marched through drift for 7 miles. It was exceedingly cold at first. Just at starting the sky cleared in the wonderfully rapid fashion usual in these regions. We saw that our camp had the southern edge of the base rock of the Bluff in line with Mt. Discovery, and White Island well clear of the eastern slope of Mt. Erebus. A fairly easy alignment to pick up.

At lunch time the sky lightened up and the drift temporarily ceased. I thought we were going to get in a good march, but on starting again the drift came thicker than ever and soon the course grew wild. We went on for 2 miles and then I decided to camp. So here we are with a full blizzard blowing. I told Wilson I should camp if it grew thick, and hope he and Meares have stopped where they were. They saw Evans start back from No. 11 Camp before leaving. I trust they have got in something of a march before stopping. This continuous bad weather is exceedingly trying, but our own ponies are quite comfortable this time, I'm glad to say. We have built them extensive snow walls behind which they seem to get quite comfortable shelter. We are five in a tent yet fairly comfortable.

Our ponies' coats are certainly getting thicker and I see no reason why we shouldn't get to the 80th parallel if only the weather would give us a chance.

Bowers is wonderful. Throughout the night he has worn no head-gear but a common green felt hat kept on with a chin stay and affording no cover whatever for the ears. His face and ears remain bright red. The rest of us were glad to have thick Balaclavas and wind helmets. I have never seen anyone so unaffected by the cold. Tonight he remained outside a full hour after the rest of us had got into the tent. He was simply pottering about the camp doing small jobs to the sledges, etc. Cherry-Garrard is remarkable because of his eyes. He can only see through glasses and has to wrestle with all sorts of inconveniences in consequence. Yet one could never guess it – for he manages somehow to do more than his share of the work.

Tuesday 14 February 13 Camp. 7 miles 650 yards. A disappointing day: the weather had cleared, the night was fine though cold, temperature well below zero with a keen S.W. breeze. Soon after the start we struck very bad surface conditions. The ponies sank lower than their hocks frequently and the soft patches of snow left by the blizzard lay in sandy heaps, making great friction for the runners. We struggled on, but found

Gran with Weary Willy dropping to the rear. I consulted Oates as to distance and he cheerfully proposed 15 miles for the day! This piqued me somewhat and I marched till the sledge meter showed 6½ miles. By this time Weary Willy had dropped about three-quarters of a mile and the dog teams were approaching. Suddenly we heard much barking in the distance, and later it was evident that something had gone wrong. Oates and then I hurried back. I met Meares, who told me the dogs of his team had got out of hand and attacked Weary Willy when they saw him fall. Finally they had been beaten off and W.W. was being led without his sledge. W.W. had been much bitten, but luckily I think not seriously: he appears to have made a gallant fight, and bit and shook some of the dogs with his teeth. Gran did his best, breaking his ski stick. Meares broke his dog stick – one way and another the dogs must have had a rocky time, yet they seemed to bear charmed lives when their blood is up, as apparently not one of them has been injured.

After lunch four of us went back and dragged up the load. It taught us the nature of the surface more than many hours of pony leading!! The incident is deplorable and the blame widespread. I find W.W.'s load was much heavier than that of the other ponies.

I blame myself for not supervising these matters more effectively and for allowing W.W. to get so far behind.

We started off again after lunch, but when we had done two-thirds of a mile, W.W.'s condition made it advisable to halt. He has been given a hot feed, a large snow wall, and some extra sacking – the day promises to be quiet and warm for him, and one can only hope that these measures will put him right again. But the whole thing is very annoying.

Memo Arrangements for ponies.

1. Hot bran or oat mashes.
2. Clippers for breaking wires of bales.
3. Pickets for horses.
4. Lighter ponies to take 10 ft. sledges?

The surface is so crusty and friable that the question of snow-shoes again becomes of great importance.

All the sastrugi are from S.W. by S. to S.W. and all the wind that we have experienced in this region – there cannot be a doubt that the wind sweeps up the coast at all seasons.

A point has arisen as to the deposition. David [Professor T. Edgeworth David, C.M.G., F.R.S., of Sydney University, who was the geologist to Shackleton's party] called the crusts seasonal. This must be wrong; they mark blizzards, but after each blizzard fresh crusts are formed only over the patchy heaps left by the blizzard. A blizzard seems to leave heaps which cover anything from one-sixth to one-third of the whole surface – such heaps presumably turn hollows into mounds with fresh hollows between – these are filled in turn by ensuing blizzards. If this is so, the only way to get at the seasonal deposition would be to average the heaps deposited and multiply this by the number of blizzards in the year.

Monday 15 February 14 Camp. 7 miles 775 yards. The surface was wretched today, the two drawbacks of yesterday (the thin crusts which let the ponies through and the sandy heaps which hang on the runners) if anything exaggerated.

Bowers' pony refused work at intervals for the first time. His hind legs sink very deep. Weary Willy is decidedly better. The Soldier takes a gloomy view of everything, but I've come to see that this is a characteristic of him. In spite of it he pays every attention to the weaker horses.

We had frequent halts on the march, but managed 4 miles before lunch and 3½ after.

The temperature was -15° at the lunch camp. It was cold sitting in the tent waiting for the ponies to rest. The thermometer is now -7°, but there is a bright sun and no wind, which makes the air feel quite comfortable: one's socks and finnesko dry well. Our provision allowance is working out very well. In fact all is well with us except the condition of the ponies. The more I see of the matter the more certain I am that we must save all the ponies to get better value out of them next year. It would have been ridiculous to have worked some out this year as the Soldier wished. Even now I feel we went too far with the first three.

One thing is certain. A good snow-shoe would be worth its weight in gold on this surface, and if we can get something really practical we ought to greatly increase our distances next year.

Memo Storage of biscuit next year, lashing cases on sledges.

Look into sledgemeter.

Picket lines for ponies.

Food tanks to be size required.

Two sledges altered to take steel runners.

Stowage of pony food. Enough sacks for ready bags.

Thursday 16 February 6 miles 1450 yards. 15 Camp. The surface a good deal better, but the ponies running out. Three of the five could go on without difficulty. Bowers' pony might go on a bit, but Weary Willy is a good deal done up, and to push him further would be to risk him unduly, so tomorrow we turn. The temperature on the march tonight fell to -21° with a brisk S.W. breeze. Bowers started out as usual in his small felt hat, ears uncovered. Luckily I called a halt after a mile and looked at him. His ears were quite white. Cherry and I nursed them back whilst the patient seemed to feel nothing but intense surprise and disgust at the mere fact of possessing such unruly organs. Oates' nose gave great trouble. I got frostbitten on the cheek lightly, as also did Cherry-Garrard.

Tried to march in light woollen mits to great discomfort.

Friday 17 February Camp 15. Lat. 79° 28½' S. It clouded over yesterday – the temperature rose and some snow fell. Wind from the south, cold and biting, as we turned out. We started to build the depot. I had intended to go on half a march and return to same camp, leaving Weary Willy to rest, but under the circumstances did not like to take risk.

The Great Ice Barrier, looking east from Cape Crozier.
Hut Point, midnight, March 27th, 1911.

A sunset from Hut Point, April 2nd 1911.
Mount Erebus.

Opposite page: Lunar Corona.

Paraselene   Jan. 15. 11.   9.20 p.m.

Opposite page: Paraselene, June 15th, 1911.
Above: Mr. Ponting lecturing on Japan.
Below: Dr. Wilson working up the sketch. All the coloured sketches in this section are drawn by him.

Opposite page: "Birdie" Bowers reading the thermometer on the ramp, June 6th, 1911.
Above: Exercising the ponies.
Below: Iridescent clouds: Looking north from Cape Evans.

Opposite page: Cave in the Barrier, Cape Crozier, Jan. 4th, 1911.
Above: Mount Erebus.
Below: Sledging.

Opposite page: Hut Point from Observation Hill.
Above: Looking West from Cape Evans.

An April sunset from Hut Point, looking West.

Opposite page: The ramp and the slopes of Erebus.
Above: An April after glow. Reproduced form an autochrome photograph by Herbert G. Ponting.

The five explorers at the South Pole Thursday 18 January 1912, after discovering Amundsen had beaten them to it. The agony of failure etched onto their faces. Sitting, left to right, Edgar Evans, Lawrence Oates. Standing, left to right, Henry Bowers, Captain Robert Falcon Scott and Edward Wilson. Bowers pulls the string on the camera. Scott wrote in his diary: 'Well, we have turned our back now on the goal of our ambition and must face our 800 miles of solid dragging - and goodbye to most of the day dreams!'

Captain Oates and ponies on the *Terra Nova*.

Above: Captain Scott in his 'den'.
Right: Lieut. H. R. Bowers – 'Birdie'.

Petty Officer Edgar Evans, R.N.

Stores left in depot:

Lat. 79° 29'. Depot.

	lbs.
7 weeks' full provision bags for 1 unit	245
12 days' provision bags for 1 unit	12
8 weeks' tea	8
6 weeks' extra butter	31
lbs. biscuit (7 weeks' full biscuit)	176
8½ gallons oil (12 weeks' oil for 1 unit)	85
5 sacks of oats	850
4 bales of fodder	424
Tank of dog biscuit	250
2 cases of biscuit	100
	2181

white line 1 skein
breast harness 1 set
Sledges 2 x 12 ft.
2 pair ski, 1 pair ski sticks
1 Minimum Thermometer
1 tin Rowntree cocoa
1 tin matches

With packing we have landed considerably over a ton of stuff. It is a pity we couldn't get to 80°, but as it is we shall have a good leg up for next year and can at least feed the ponies full up to this point.

Our Camp 15 is very well marked, I think. Besides the flagstaff and black flag we have piled biscuit boxes, filled and empty, to act as reflectors – secured tea tins to the sledges, which are planted upright in the snow. The depot cairn is more than 6 ft. above the surface, very solid and large; then there are the pony protection walls; altogether it should show up for many miles.

I forgot to mention that looking back on the 15th we saw a cairn built on a camp 12½ miles behind – it was miraged up.

It seems as though some of our party will find spring journeys pretty trying. Oates' nose is always on the point of being frostbitten; Meares has a refractory toe which gives him much trouble – this is the worst prospect for summit work. I have been wondering how I shall stick the summit again, this cold spell gives ideas. I think I shall be all right, but one must be prepared for a pretty good doing.

6

ADVENTURE & PERIL: 18 FEBRUARY 1911 – 5 MARCH 1911

Saturday 18 February Camp 12. North 22 miles 1996 yards. I scattered some oats 50 yards east of depot [This was done in order to measure on the next visit the results of wind and snow]. The minimum thermometer showed -16° when we left camp: *inform Simpson!*

The ponies started off well, Gran leading my pony with Weary Willy behind, the Soldier leading his with Cherry's behind, and Bowers steering course as before with a light sledge. [Scott, Wilson, Meares and Cherry-Garrard now went back swiftly with the dog teams, to look after the return parties at Safety Camp. Having found all satisfactory, Scott left Wilson and Meares there with the dogs, and marched back with the rest to Corner Camp, taking more stores to the depot and hoping to meet Bowers rearguard party.]

We started half an hour later, soon overtook the ponies, and luckily picked up a small bag of oats which they had dropped. We went on for 10¾ miles and stopped for lunch. After lunch to our astonishment the ponies appeared, going strong. They were making for a camp some miles farther on, and meant to remain there. I'm very glad to have seen them making the pace so well. They don't propose to stop for lunch at all but to march right through 10 or 12 miles a day. I think they will have little difficulty in increasing this distance.

For the dogs the surface has been bad, and one or another of us on either sledge has been running a good part of the time. But we have covered 23 miles: three marches out. We have four days' food for them and ought to get in very easily.

As we camp late the temperature is evidently very low and there is a low drift. Conditions are beginning to be severe on the Barrier and I shall be glad to get the ponies into more comfortable quarters.

Sunday 19 February Started 10 p.m. Camped 6.30. Nearly 26 miles to our credit. The dogs went very well and the surface became excellent after the first 5 or 6 miles. At the Bluff Camp, No. 11, we picked up Evans' track and found that he must have made excellent progress. No. 10 Camp was much snowed up: I should imagine our light blizzard was severely felt along this part of the route. We must look out tomorrow for signs of Evans being 'held up'.

The old tracks show better here than on the softer surface. During this journey both ponies and dogs have had what under ordinary circumstances would have been a good allowance of food, yet both are desperately hungry. Both eat their own excrement. With the ponies it does not seem so horrid, as there must be a good deal of grain, etc., which is not fully digested. It is the worst side of dog driving. All the rest is diverting. The way in which they keep up a steady jog trot for hour after hour is wonderful. Their legs seem steel springs, fatigue unknown – for at the end of a tiring march any unusual incident will arouse them to full vigour. Osman has been restored to leadership. It is curious how these leaders come off and go off, all except old Stareek, who remains as steady as ever.

We are all acting like seasoned sledge travellers now, such is the force of example. Our tent is up and cooker going in the shortest time after halt, and we are able to break camp in exceptionally good time. Cherry-Garrard is cook. He is excellent, and is quickly learning all the tips for looking after himself and his gear.

What a difference such care makes is apparent now, but was more so when he joined the tent with all his footgear iced up, whilst Wilson and I nearly always have dry socks and finnesko to put on. This is only a point amongst many in which experience gives comfort. Every minute spent in keeping one's gear dry and free of snow is very well repaid.

Monday 20 February 29 miles. Lunch. Excellent run on hard wind-swept surface – *covered nearly seventeen miles*. Very cold at starting and during march. Suddenly wind changed and temperature rose so that at the moment of stopping for final halt it appeared quite warm, almost sultry. On stopping found we had covered 29 miles, some 35 statute miles. The dogs are weary but by no means played out – during the last part of the journey they trotted steadily with a wonderfully tireless rhythm. I have been off the sledge a good deal and trotting for a good many miles, so should sleep well. E. Evans has left a bale of forage at Camp 8 and has not taken on the one which he might have taken from the depot – facts which show that his ponies must have been going strong. I hope to find them safe and sound the day after tomorrow.

We had the most wonderfully beautiful sky effects on the march with the sun circling low on the southern horizon. Bright pink clouds hovered overhead on a deep grey-blue background. Gleams of bright sunlit mountains appeared through the stratus.

Here it is most difficult to predict what is going to happen. Sometimes the southern sky looks dark and ominous, but within half an hour all has changed – the land comes and goes as the veil of stratus lifts and falls. It seems as though weather is made here rather than dependent on conditions elsewhere. It is all very interesting.

Tuesday 21 February New Camp about 12 miles from Safety Camp. 15½ miles. We made a start as usual about 10 p.m. The light was good at first, but rapidly grew worse till we could see little of the surface. The dogs showed signs of wearying. About an hour and a half after starting we came on mistily outlined pressure ridges. We were running by the sledges. Suddenly Wilson shouted 'Hold on to the sledge,' and I saw him slip a leg into a crevasse. I jumped to the sledge, but saw nothing. Five minutes after, as the teams were trotting side by side, the middle dogs of our team disappeared. In a moment the whole team were sinking – two by two we lost sight of them, each pair struggling for foothold. Osman the leader exerted all his great strength and kept a foothold – it was wonderful to see him. The sledge stopped and we leapt aside. The situation was clear in another moment. We had been actually travelling along the bridge of a crevasse, the sledge had stopped on it, whilst the dogs hung in their harness in the abyss, suspended between the sledge and the leading dog. Why the sledge and ourselves didn't follow the dogs we shall never know. I think a fraction of a pound of added weight must have taken us down. As soon as we grasped the position, we hauled the sledge clear of the bridge and anchored it. Then we peered into the depths of the crack. The dogs were howling dismally, suspended in all sorts of fantastic positions and evidently terribly frightened. Two had dropped out of their harness, and we could see them indistinctly on a snow bridge far below. The rope at either end of the chain had bitten deep into the snow at the side of the crevasse, and with the weight below, it was impossible to move it. By this time Wilson and Cherry-Garrard, who had seen the accident, had come to our assistance. At first things looked very bad for our poor team, and I saw little prospect of rescuing them. I had luckily inquired about the Alpine rope before starting the march, and now Cherry-Garrard hurriedly brought this most essential aid. It takes one a little time to make plans under such sudden circumstances, and for some minutes our efforts were rather futile. We could get not an inch on the main trace of the sledge or on the leading rope, which was binding Osman to the snow with a throttling pressure. Then thought became clearer. We unloaded our sledge, putting in safety our sleeping-bags with the tent and cooker. Choking sounds from Osman made it clear that the pressure on him must soon be relieved. I seized the lashing off Meares' sleeping-bag, passed the tent poles across the crevasse, and with Meares managed to get a few inches on the leading line; this freed Osman, whose harness was immediately cut.

Then securing the Alpine rope to the main trace we tried to haul up together. One dog came up and was unlashed, but by this time the rope had cut so far back at the edge that it was useless to attempt to get more of it. But we could now unbend the sledge and do that for which we should have aimed from the first, namely, run the sledge across the gap and work from it. We managed to do this, our fingers constantly numbed. Wilson held on to the anchored trace whilst the rest of us laboured at the leader end. The leading rope was very small and I was fearful of its breaking, so Meares was lowered down a foot or two to secure the Alpine rope to the leading end of the trace; this done, the work of rescue proceeded in better order. Two by two we hauled the animals up to the sledge and one by one cut them out of their harness. Strangely the last dogs were the most difficult, as they were close under the lip of the gap, bound in by the snow-covered rope. Finally, with a gasp we got the last poor creature on to firm snow. We had recovered eleven of the thirteen.[13a]

Then I wondered if the last two could not be got, and we paid down the Alpine rope to see if it was long enough to reach the snow bridge on which they were coiled. The rope is 90 feet, and the amount remaining showed that the depth of the bridge was about 65 feet. I made a bowline and the others lowered me down. The bridge was firm and I got hold of both dogs, which were hauled up in turn to the surface. Then I heard dim shouts and howls above. Some of the rescued animals had wandered to the second sledge, and a big fight was in progress. All my rope-tenders had to leave to separate the combatants; but they soon returned, and with some effort I was hauled to the surface.

All is well that ends well, and certainly this was a most surprisingly happy ending to a very serious episode. We felt we must have refreshment, so camped and had a meal, congratulating ourselves on a really miraculous escape. If the sledge had gone down Meares and I *must* have been badly injured, if not killed outright. The dogs are wonderful, but have had a terrible shaking – three of them are passing blood and have more or less serious internal injuries. Many were held up by a thin thong round the stomach, writhing madly to get free. One dog better placed in its harness stretched its legs full before and behind and just managed to claw either side of the gap – it had continued attempts to climb throughout, giving vent to terrified howls. Two of the animals hanging together had been fighting at intervals when they swung into any position which allowed them to bite one another. The crevasse for the time being was an inferno, and the time must have been all too terribly long for the wretched creatures. It was twenty minutes past three when we had completed the rescue work, and the accident must have happened before one-thirty. Some of the animals must have been dangling for over an hour. I had a good opportunity of examining the crack.

The section seemed such as I have shown (on previous page). It narrowed towards the east and widened slightly towards the west. In this direction there were curious curved splinters; below the snow bridge on which I stood the opening continued, but narrowing, so that I think one could not have fallen many more feet without being wedged. Twice I have owed safety to a snow bridge, and it seems to me that the chance of finding some obstruction or some saving fault in the crevasse is a good one, but I am far from thinking that such a chance can be relied upon, and it would be an awful situation to fall beyond the limits of the Alpine rope.

We went on after lunch, and very soon got into soft snow and regular surface where crevasses are most unlikely to occur. We have pushed on with difficulty, for the dogs are badly cooked and the surface tries them. We are all pretty done, but luckily the weather favours us. A sharp storm from the south has been succeeded by ideal sunshine which is flooding the tent as I write. It is the calmest, warmest day we have had since we started sledging. We are only about 12 miles from Safety Camp, and I trust we shall push on without accident tomorrow, but I am anxious about some of the dogs. We shall be lucky indeed if all recover.

My companions today were excellent; Wilson and Cherry-Garrard if anything the most intelligently and readily helpful.

I begin to think that there is no avoiding the line of cracks running from the Bluff to Cape Crozier, but my hope is that the danger does not extend beyond a mile or two, and that the cracks are narrower on the pony road to Corner Camp. If eight ponies can cross without accident I do not think there can be great danger. Certainly we must rigidly adhere to this course on all future journeys. We must try and plot out the danger line. [The party had made a shortcut where in going out with the ponies they had made an elbow, and so had passed within this 'danger line'.] I begin to be a little anxious about the returning ponies.

I rather think the dogs are being underfed – they have weakened badly in the last few days – more than such work ought to entail. Now they are absolutely ravenous.

Meares has very dry feet. Whilst we others perspire freely and our skin remains pink and soft his gets horny and scaly. He amused us greatly tonight by scraping them. The sound suggested the whittling of a hard wood block and the action was curiously like an attempt to shape the feet to fit the finnesko!

Summary of Marches made on the Depôt Journey

Distances in Geographical Miles.   Variation 152 E.

			m.	yds.	
Safety	No. 3 to 4	E.	4	2000	
	4 to 5	S. 64 E.	4	500 ⎫	
		S. 77 E.	1	312 ⎬ 9·359	
		S. 60 E.	3	1575 ⎭	
	5 to 6	S. 48 E.	10	270	Var. 149½ E.
Corner	6 to 7	S.	10	145	
	7 to 8	S.	? 11	198	
	8 to 9	S.	12	325	
	9 to 10	S.	11	118	
Bluff Camp	10 to 11	S.	10	226 ⎰ Var.	
	11 to 12	S.	9	150 ⎱ 152½ E.	
	12 to 13	S.	7	650	
	13 to 14	S.	7	Bowers 775	
	14 to 15	S.	8	1450	
			111	610	
Return 17th–18th 15 to 12		N.	22	1994	
18th–19th 12 to midway					
between 9 & 10		N.	48	1825	
19th–20th Lunch 8 Camp		N.	65	1720	
19th–20th 7 Camp		N.	77	1820	
20th–21st		N. 30 to			
		35 W.	93	950	
21st–22nd Safety Camp		N. & W.	107	1125	

Wednesday 22 February Safety Camp. Got away at 10 again: surface fairly heavy: dogs going badly.

The dogs are as thin as rakes; they are ravenous and very tired. I feel this should not be, and that it is evident that they are underfed. The ration must be increased next year and we *must* have some properly thought out diet. The biscuit alone is not good enough. Meares is excellent to a point, but ignorant of the conditions here. One thing is certain, the dogs will never continue to drag heavy loads with men sitting on the sledges; we must all learn to run with the teams and the Russian custom must be dropped. Meares, I think, rather imagined himself racing to the Pole and back on a dog sledge. This journey has opened his eyes a good deal.

We reached Safety Camp (dist. 14 miles) at 4.30 a.m.; found Evans and his party in excellent health, but, alas! with only *one* pony. As far as I can gather Forde's pony only got 4 miles back from the Bluff Camp; then a blizzard came on, and in spite of the most tender care from Forde the pony sank under it. Evans says that Forde spent hours with the animal trying to keep it going, feeding it, walking it about; at last he returned to the tent to say that the poor creature had fallen; they all tried to get it on its feet again but their efforts were useless. It couldn't stand, and soon after it died.

Then the party marched some 10 miles, but the blizzard had had a bad effect on Blossom – it seemed to have shrivelled him up, and now he was terribly emaciated. After this march he could scarcely move. Evans describes his efforts as pathetic; he got on 100 yards, then stopped with legs outstretched and nose to the ground. They rested him, fed him well, covered him with rugs; but again all efforts were unavailing. The last stages came with painful detail. So Blossom is also left on the Southern Road.

The last pony, James Pigg, as he is called, has thriven amazingly – of course great care has been taken with him and he is now getting full feed and very light work, so he ought to do well. The loss is severe; but they were the two oldest ponies of our team and the two which Oates thought of least use.

Atkinson and Crean have departed, leaving no trace – not even a note.

Crean had carried up a good deal of fodder, and some seal meat was found buried.

After a few hours' sleep we are off for Hut Point.

There are certain points in night marching, if only for the glorious light effects which the coming night exhibits.

Wednesday 22 February 10 p.m. Safety Camp. Turned out at 11 this morning after 4 hours' sleep.

Wilson, Meares, Evans, Cherry-Garrard, and I went to Hut Point. Found a great enigma. The hut was cleared and habitable – but no one was there. A pencil line on the wall said that a bag containing a mail was inside, but no bag could be found. We puzzled much, then finally decided on the true solution, viz. that Atkinson and Crean had gone towards Safety Camp as we went to Hut Point – later we saw their sledge track leading round on the sea-ice. Then we returned towards Safety Camp and endured a very bad hour in which we could see the two bell tents but not the domed. It was an enormous relief to find the dome securely planted, as the ice round Cape Armitage is evidently very weak; I have never seen such enormous water holes off it.

But every incident of the day pales before the startling contents of the mail bag which Atkinson gave me – a letter from Campbell setting out his doings and the finding of Amundsen established in the Bay of Whales.

One thing only fixes itself definitely in my mind. The proper, as well as the wiser, course for us is to proceed exactly as though this had not happened. To go forward and do our best for the honour of the country without fear or panic.

There is no doubt that Amundsen's plan is a very serious menace to ours. He has a shorter distance to the Pole by 60 miles – I never thought he could have got so many dogs safely to the ice. His plan for running them seems excellent. But above and beyond all he can start his journey early in the season – an impossible condition with ponies.

The ice is still in at the Glacier Tongue: a very late date – it looks as though it will not break right back this season, but off Cape Armitage it is so thin that I doubt if the ponies could safely be walked round.

Thursday 23 February Spent the day preparing sledges, etc., for party to meet Bowers at Corner Camp. It was blowing and drifting and generally uncomfortable. Wilson and Meares killed three seals for the dogs.

Friday 24 February Roused out at 6. Started marching at 9. Self, Crean, and Cherry-Garrard one sledge and tent; Evans, Atkinson, Forde, second sledge and tent; Keohane leading his pony. We pulled on ski in the forenoon; the second sledge couldn't keep up, so we changed about for half the march. In the afternoon we pulled on foot. On the whole I thought the labour greater on foot, so did Crean, showing the advantage of experience.

There is no doubt that very long days' work could be done by men in hard condition on ski.

The hanging back of the second sledge was mainly a question of condition, but to some extent due to the sledge. We have a 10 ft., whilst the other party has a 12 ft.; the former is a distinct advantage in this case.

It has been a horrid day. We woke to find a thick covering of sticky ice crystals on everything – a frost rime. I cleared my ski before breakfast and found more on afterwards. There was the suggestion of an early frosty morning at home – such a morning as develops into a beautiful sunshiny day; but in our case, alas! such hopes were shattered: it was almost damp, with temperature near zero and a terribly bad light for travelling. In the afternoon Erebus and Terror showed up for a while. Now it is drifting hard with every sign of a blizzard – a beastly night. This marching is going to be very good for our condition and I shall certainly keep people at it.

Saturday 25 February Fine bright day – easy marching – covered 9 miles and a bit yesterday and the same today. Should reach Corner Camp before lunch tomorrow.

Turned out at 3 a.m. and saw a short black line on the horizon towards White Island. Thought it an odd place for a rock exposure and then observed movement in it. Walked 1½ miles towards it and made certain that it was

Oates, Bowers, and the ponies. They seemed to be going very fast and evidently did not see our camp. Today we have come on their tracks, and I fear there are only four ponies left.

James Pigg, our own pony, limits the length of our marches. The men haulers could go on much longer, and we all like pulling on ski. Everyone must be practised in this.

Sunday 26 February Marched on Corner Camp, but second main party found going very hard and eventually got off their ski and pulled on foot. James Pigg also found the surface bad, so we camped and had lunch after doing 3 miles.

Except for our tent the camp routine is slack. Shall have to tell people that we are out on business, not picnicking. It was another 3 miles to depot after lunch. Found signs of Bowers' party having camped there and glad to see five pony walls. Left six full weeks' provision: 1 bag of oats, ¾ of a bale of fodder. Then Cherry-Garrard, Crean, and I started for home, leaving the others to bring the pony by slow stages. We covered 6¼ miles in direct line, then had some tea and marched another 8. We must be less than 10 miles from Safety Camp. Pitched tent at 10 p.m., very dark for cooking.

Monday 27 February Awoke to find it blowing a howling blizzard – absolutely confined to tent at present – to step outside is to be covered with drift in a minute. We have managed to get our cooking things inside and have had a meal. Very anxious about the ponies – am wondering where they can be. The return party [Bowers, Oates, and Gran, with the five ponies – the two days had after all brought them to Safety Camp] has had two days and may have got them into some shelter – but more probably they were not expecting this blow – I wasn't. The wind is blowing force 8 or 9; heavy gusts straining the tent; the temperature is evidently quite low. This is poor luck.

Tuesday 28 February Safety Camp. Packed up at 6 a.m. and marched into Safety Camp. Found everyone very cold and depressed. Wilson and Meares had had continuous bad weather since we left, Bowers and Oates since their arrival. The blizzard had raged for two days. The animals looked in a sorry condition but all were alive. The wind blew keen and cold from the east. There could be no advantage in waiting here, and soon all arrangements were made for a general shift to Hut Point. Packing took a long time. The snowfall had been prodigious, and parts of the sledges were 3 or 4 feet under drift. About 4 o'clock the two dog teams got safely away. Then the pony party prepared to go. As the clothes were stripped from the ponies the ravages of the blizzard became evident. The animals without exception were terribly emaciated, and Weary Willy was in a pitiable condition.

The plan was for the ponies to follow the dog tracks, our small party to start last and get in front of the ponies on the sea-ice. I was very anxious about the sea-ice passage owing to the spread of the water holes.

The ponies started, but Weary Willy, tethered last without a load, immediately fell down. We tried to get him up and he made efforts, but was too exhausted.

Then we rapidly reorganised. Cherry-Garrard and Crean went on whilst Oates and Gran stayed with me. We made desperate efforts to save the poor creature, got him once more on his legs and gave him a hot oat mash. Then after a wait of an hour Oates led him off, and we packed the sledge and followed on ski; 500 yards away from the camp the poor creature fell again and I felt it was the last effort. We camped, built a snow wall round him, and did all we possibly could to get him on his feet. Every effort was fruitless, though the poor thing made pitiful struggles. Towards midnight we propped him up as comfortably as we could and went to bed.

Wednesday 1 March a.m. Our pony died in the night. It is hard to have got him back so far only for this. It is clear that these blizzards are terrible for the poor animals. Their coats are not good, but even with the best of coats it is certain they would lose condition badly if caught in one, and we cannot afford to lose condition at the beginning of a journey. It makes a late start *necessary for next year*.

Well, we have done our best and bought our experience at a heavy cost. Now every effort must be bent on saving the remaining animals, and it will be good luck if we get four back to Cape Evans, or even three. Jimmy Pigg may have fared badly; Bowers' big pony is in a bad way after that frightful blizzard. I cannot remember such a bad storm in February or March: the temperature was -7°.

BOWERS INCIDENT

I note the events of the night of 1 March whilst they are yet fresh in my memory.

Thursday 2 March a.m. The events of the past 48 hours bid fair to wreck the expedition, and the only one comfort is the miraculous avoidance of loss of life. We turned out early yesterday, Oates, Gran, and I, after the dismal night of our pony's death, and pulled towards the forage depot on ski. [This was at a point on the Barrier, ½ mile from the edge, in a S.S.E. direction from Hut Point.] As we approached, the sky looked black and lowering, and mirage effects of huge broken floes loomed out ahead. At first I thought it one of the strange optical illusions common in this region – but as we neared the depot all doubt was dispelled. The sea was full of broken pieces of Barrier edge. My thoughts flew to the ponies and dogs, and fearful anxieties assailed my mind. We turned to follow the sea edge and suddenly discovered a working crack. We dashed over this and slackened pace again after a quarter of a mile. Then again cracks appeared ahead and we increased pace as much as possible, not slackening again till we were in line between the Safety Camp and Castle Rock. Meanwhile my first thought was to warn Evans. We set up tent, and Gran went to the depot with a note as Oates and I disconsolately thought out the situation. I thought to myself that if either party had reached safety either on the Barrier or at Hut Point they would immediately have sent a warning messenger to Safety Camp. By this time the messenger should have been with us. Some half-hour passed, and suddenly with a 'Thank God!' I made certain that two specks in the direction of Pram Point were human beings. I hastened towards them and found they were Wilson and Meares, who had led the homeward way with the dog teams. They were astonished to see me – they said they feared the ponies were adrift on the sea-ice – they had seen them with glasses from Observation Hill. They thought I was with them. They had hastened out without breakfast: we made them cocoa and discussed the gloomiest situation. Just after cocoa Wilson discovered a figure making rapidly for the depot from the west. Gran was sent off again to intercept. It proved to be Crean – he was exhausted and a little incoherent. The ponies had camped at 2.30 a.m. on the sea-ice well beyond the seal crack on the previous night. In the middle of the night ...

Friday 3 March a.m. I was interrupted when writing yesterday and continue my story this morning ... In the middle of the night at 4.30 Bowers got out of the tent and discovered the ice had broken all round him: a crack ran under the picketing line, and one pony had disappeared. They had packed with great haste and commenced jumping the ponies from floe to floe, then dragging the loads over after – the three men must have worked splendidly and fearlessly. At length they had worked their way to heavier floes lying near the Barrier edge, and at one time thought they could get up, but soon discovered that there were gaps everywhere off the high Barrier face. In this dilemma Crean volunteering was sent off to try to reach me. The sea was like a cauldron at the time of the break up, and killer whales were putting their heads up on all sides. Luckily they did not frighten the ponies.

He travelled a great distance over the sea-ice, leaping from floe to floe, and at last found a thick floe from which with help of ski stick he could climb the Barrier face. It was a desperate venture, but luckily successful.

As soon as I had digested Crean's news I sent Gran back to Hut Point with Wilson and Meares and started with my sledge, Crean, and Oates for the scene of the mishap. We stopped at Safety Camp to load some provisions and oil and then, marching carefully round, approached the ice edge. To my joy I caught sight of the lost party. We got our Alpine rope and with its help dragged the two men to the surface. I pitched camp at a safe distance from the edge and then we all started salvage work. The ice had ceased to drift and lay close and quiet against the Barrier edge. We got the men at 5.30 p.m. and all the sledges and effects on to the Barrier by 4 a.m. As we were getting up the last loads the ice showed signs of drifting off, and we saw it was hopeless to try and move the ponies. The three poor beasts had to be left on their floe for the moment, well fed. None of our party had had sleep the previous night and all were dog tired. I decided we must rest, but turned everyone out at 8.30 yesterday morning. Before breakfast we discovered the ponies had drifted away. We had tried to anchor their floe with the Alpine rope, but the anchors had drawn. It was a sad moment. At breakfast we decided to pack and follow the Barrier edge: this was the position when I last wrote, but the interruption came when Bowers, who had taken the binoculars, announced that he could see the ponies about a mile to the N.W. We packed and went on at once. We found it easy enough to get down to the poor animals and decided to rush them for a last chance of life. Then there was an unfortunate mistake: I went along the Barrier edge and discovered what I thought and what proved to be a practicable way to land a pony, but the others meanwhile, a little overwrought, tried to leap Punch across a gap. The poor beast fell in; eventually we had to kill him – it was awful. I recalled all hands and pointed out my road. Bowers and Oates went out on it with a sledge and worked their way to the remaining ponies, and started back with them on the same track. Meanwhile Cherry and I dug a road at the Barrier edge. We saved one pony; for a time I thought we should get both, but Bowers' poor animal slipped at a jump and plunged into the water: we dragged him out on some brash ice – killer whales all about us in an intense state of excitement. The poor animal couldn't rise, and the only merciful thing was to kill it. These incidents were too terrible.

At 5 p.m. we sadly broke our temporary camp and marched back to the one I had first pitched. Even here it seemed unsafe, so I walked nearly two miles to discover cracks: I could find none, and we turned in about midnight.

So here we are ready to start our sad journey to Hut Point. Everything out of joint with the loss of the ponies, but mercifully with all the party alive and well.

Saturday 4 March a.m. We had a terrible pull at the start yesterday, taking four hours to cover some three miles to march on the line between Safety Camp and Fodder Depot. From there Bowers went to Safety Camp and found my notes to Evans had been taken. We dragged on after lunch to the place where my tent had been pitched when Wilson first met me and where we had left our ski and other loads. All these had gone. We found sledge tracks leading in towards the land and at length marks of a pony's hoofs. We followed these and some ski tracks right into the land, coming at length to the highest of the Pram Point ridges. I decided to camp here, and as we unpacked I saw four figures approaching. They proved to be Evans and his party. They had ascended towards Castle Rock on Friday and found a good camp site on top of the Ridge. They were in good condition. It was a relief to hear they had found a good road up. They went back to their camp later, dragging one of our sledges and a light load. Atkinson is to go to Hut Point this morning to tell Wilson about us. The rest ought to meet us and help us up the hill – just off to march up the hill, hoping to avoid trouble with the pony.[14]

Sunday 5 March a.m. Marched up the hill to Evans' Camp under Castle Rock. Evans' party came to meet us and helped us up with the loads – it was a steep, stiff pull; the pony was led up by Oates. As we camped for lunch Atkinson and Gran appeared, the former having been to Hut Point to carry news of the relief. I sent Gran on to Safety Camp to fetch some sugar and chocolate, left Evans, Oates, and Keohane in camp, and marched on with remaining six to Hut Point. It was calm at Evans' Camp, but blowing hard on the hill and harder at Hut Point. Found the hut in comparative order and slept there.

7
AT DISCOVERY HUT: 6 MARCH 1911 – 16 APRIL 1911

Monday 6 March a.m. Roused the hands at 7.30. Wilson, Bowers, Garrard, and I went out to Castle Rock. We met Evans just short of his camp and found the loads had been dragged up the hill. Oates and Keohane had gone back to lead on the ponies. At the top of the ridge we harnessed men and ponies to the sledges and made rapid progress on a good surface towards the hut. The weather grew very thick towards the end of the march, with all signs of a blizzard. We unharnessed the ponies at the top of Ski slope – Wilson guided them down from rock patch to rock patch; the remainder of us got down a sledge and necessaries over the slope. It is a ticklish business to get the sledge along the ice foot, which is now all blue ice ending in a drop to the sea. One has to be certain that the party has good foothold. All reached the hut in safety. The ponies have admirably comfortable quarters under the verandah.

After some cocoa we fetched in the rest of the dogs from the Gap and another sledge from the hill. It had ceased to snow and the wind had gone down slightly. Turned in with much relief to have all hands and the animals safely housed.

Tuesday 7 March a.m. Yesterday went over to Pram Point with Wilson. We found that the corner of sea-ice in Pram Point Bay had not gone out – it was crowded with seals. We killed a young one and carried a good deal of the meat and some of the blubber back with us.

Meanwhile the remainder of the party had made some progress towards making the hut more comfortable. In the afternoon we all set to in earnest and by supper time had wrought wonders.

We have made a large L-shaped inner apartment with packing-cases, the intervals stopped with felt. An empty kerosene tin and some firebricks have been made into an excellent little stove, which has been connected to the old stove-pipe. The solider fare of our meals is either stewed or fried on this stove whilst the tea or cocoa is being prepared on a primus.

The temperature of the hut is low, of course, but in every other respect we are absolutely comfortable. There is an unlimited quantity of biscuit, and our discovery at Pram Point means an unlimited supply of seal meat. We have heaps of cocoa, coffee, and tea, and a sufficiency of sugar and salt. In addition a small store of luxuries, chocolate, raisins, lentils, oatmeal, sardines, and jams, which will serve to vary the fare. One way and another we shall manage to be very comfortable during our stay here, and already we can regard it as a temporary home.

Thursday 9 March a.m. Yesterday and today very busy about the hut and overcoming difficulties fast. The stove threatened to exhaust our store of firewood. We have redesigned it so that it takes only a few chips of wood to light it and then continues to give great heat with blubber alone. Today there are to be further improvements to regulate the draught and increase the cooking range. We have further housed in the living quarters with our old *Discovery* winter awning, and begin already to retain the heat which is generated inside. We are beginning to eat blubber and find biscuits fried in it to be delicious.

We really have everything necessary for our comfort and only need a little more experience to make the best of our resources. The weather has been wonderfully, perhaps ominously, fine during the last few days. The sea has frozen over and broken up several times already. The warm sun has given a grand opportunity to dry all gear.

Yesterday morning Bowers went with a party to pick up the stores rescued from the floe last week. Evans volunteered to join the party with Meares, Keohane, Atkinson, and Gran. They started from the hut about 10 a.m.; we helped them up the hill, and at 7.30 I saw them reach the camp containing the gear, some 12 miles away. I don't expect them in till tomorrow night.

It is splendid to see the way in which everyone is learning the ropes, and the resource which is being shown. Wilson as usual leads in the making of useful suggestions and in generally providing for our wants. He is a tower of strength in checking the ill-usage of clothes – what I have come to regard as the greatest danger with Englishmen.

Friday 10 March a.m. Went yesterday to Castle Rock with Wilson to see what chance there might be of getting to Cape Evans [i.e. by land, now that the sea-ice was out]. The day was bright and it was quite warm walking in the sun. There is no doubt the route to Cape Evans lies over the worst corner of Erebus. From this distance the whole mountain side looks a mass of crevasses, but a route might be found at a level of 3,000 or 4,000 ft.

The hut is getting warmer and more comfortable. We have very excellent nights; it is cold only in the early morning. The outside temperatures range from 8° or so in the day to 2° at night. Today there is a strong S.E. wind with drift. We are going to fetch more blubber for the stove.

Saturday 11 March a.m. Went yesterday morning to Pram Point to fetch in blubber – wind very strong to Gap but very little on Pram Point side.

In the evening went half-way to Castle Rock; strong bitter cold wind on summit. Could not see the sledge party, but after supper they arrived, having had very hard pulling. They had had no wind at all till they approached the hut. Their temperatures had fallen to -10° and -15°, but with bright clear sunshine in the daytime. They had thoroughly enjoyed their trip and the pulling on ski.

Life in the hut is much improved, but if things go too fast there will be all too little to think about and give occupation in the hut.

It is astonishing how the miscellaneous assortment of articles remaining in and about the hut have been put to useful purpose.

This deserves description.[15]

Monday 13 March a.m. The weather grew bad on Saturday night and we had a mild blizzard yesterday. The wind went to the south and increased in force last night, and this morning there was quite a heavy sea breaking over the ice foot. The spray came almost up to the dogs. It reminds us of the gale in which we drove ashore in the *Discovery*. We have had some trouble with our blubber stove and got the hut very full of smoke on Saturday night. As a result we are all as black as sweeps and our various garments are covered with oily soot. We look a fearful gang of ruffians. The blizzard has delayed our plans and everyone's attention is bent on the stove, the cooking, and the various internal arrangements. Nothing is done without a great amount of advice received from all quarters, and consequently things are pretty well done. The hut has a pungent odour of blubber and blubber smoke. We have grown accustomed to it, but imagine that ourselves and our clothes will be given a wide berth when we return to Cape Evans.

Wednesday 15 March a.m. It was blowing continuously from the south throughout Sunday, Monday, and Tuesday – I never remember such a persistent southerly wind.

Both Monday and Tuesday I went up Crater Hill. I feared that our floe at Pram Point would go, but yesterday it still remained, though the cracks are getting more open. We should be in a hole if it went [because the seals would cease to come up].

As I came down the hill yesterday I saw a strange figure advancing and found it belonged to Griffith Taylor. He and his party had returned safely. They were very full of their adventures. The main part of their work seems to be rediscovery of many facts which were noted but perhaps passed over too lightly in the *Discovery* – but it is certain that the lessons taught by the physiographical and ice features will now be thoroughly explained. A very interesting fact lies in the continuous bright sunshiny weather which the party enjoyed during the first four weeks of their work. They seem to have avoided all our stormy winds and blizzards.

But I must leave Griffith Taylor to tell his own story, which will certainly be a lengthy one. The party gives Evans [P.O.] a very high character.

Today we have a large seal-killing party. I hope to get in a good fortnight's allowance of blubber as well as meat, and pray that our floe will remain.

Friday 17 March a.m. We killed eleven seals at Pram Point on Wednesday, had lunch on the Point, and carried some half ton of the blubber and meat back to camp – it was a stiff pull up the hill.

Yesterday the last Corner Party started: Evans, Wright, Crean, and Forde in one team; Bowers, Oates, Cherry-Garrard, and Atkinson in the other. It was very sporting of Wright to join in after only a day's rest. He is evidently a splendid puller.

Debenham has become principal cook, and evidently enjoys the task.

Taylor is full of good spirits and anecdote, an addition to the party.

Yesterday after a beautifully fine morning we got a strong northerly wind which blew till the middle of the night, crowding the young ice up the Strait. Then the wind suddenly shifted to the south, and I thought we were in for a blizzard; but this morning the wind has gone to the S.E. – the stratus cloud formed by the north wind is dissipating, and the damp snow deposited in the night is drifting. It looks like a fine evening.

Steadily we are increasing the comforts of the hut. The stove has been improved out of all recognition; with extra stove-pipes we get no back draughts, no smoke inside, whilst the economy of fuel is much increased.

Insulation inside and out is the subject we are now attacking.

The young ice is going to and fro, but the sea refuses to freeze over so far – except in the region of Pram Point, where a bay has remained for some four days holding some pieces of Barrier in its grip. These pieces have come from the edge of the Barrier and some are crumbling already, showing a deep and rapid surface deposit of snow and therefore the probability that they are drifted sea-ice not more than a year or two old, the depth of the drift being due to proximity to an old Barrier edge.

I have just taken to pyjama trousers and shall don an extra shirt – I have been astonished at the warmth which I have felt throughout in light clothing. So far I have had nothing more than a singlet and jersey under pyjama jacket and a single pair of drawers under wind trousers. A hole in the drawers of ancient date means that one place has had no covering but the wind trousers, yet I have never felt cold about the body.

In spite of all little activities I am impatient of our wait here. But I shall be impatient also in the main hut. It is ill to sit still and contemplate the ruin which has assailed our transport. The scheme of advance must be very different from that which I first contemplated. The Pole is a very long way off, alas!

Bit by bit I am losing all faith in the dogs – I'm afraid they will never go the pace we look for.

Saturday 18 March a.m. Still blowing and drifting. It seems as though there can be no peace at this spot till the sea is properly frozen over. It blew very hard from the S.E. yesterday – I could scarcely walk against the wind. In the night it fell calm; the moon shone brightly at midnight. Then the sky became overcast and the temperature rose to +11. Now the wind is coming in spurts from the south – all indications of a blizzard.

With the north wind of Friday the ice must have pressed up on Hut Point. A considerable floe of pressed up young ice is grounded under the point, and this morning we found a seal on this. Just as the party started out to kill it, it slid off into the water – it had evidently finished its sleep – but it is encouraging to have had a chance to capture a seal so close to the hut.

Monday 20 March On Saturday night it blew hard from the south, thick overhead, low stratus and drift. The sea spray again came over the ice foot and flung up almost to the dogs; by Sunday morning the wind had veered to the S.E., and all yesterday it blew with great violence and temperature down to -11° and -12°.

We were confined to the hut and its immediate environs. Last night the wind dropped, and for a few hours this morning we had light airs only, the temperature rising to -2°.

The continuous bad weather is very serious for the dogs. We have strained every nerve to get them comfortable, but the changes of wind made it impossible to afford shelter in all directions. Some five or six dogs are running loose, but we dare not allow the stronger animals such liberty. They suffer much from the cold, but they don't get worse.

The small white dog which fell into the crevasse on our home journey died yesterday. Under the best circumstances I doubt if it could have lived, as there had evidently been internal injury and an external sore had grown gangrenous. Three other animals are in a poor way, but may pull through with luck.

We had a stroke of luck today. The young ice pressed up off Hut Point has remained fast – a small convenient platform jutting out from the point. We found two seals on it today and killed them – thus getting a good supply of meat for the dogs and some more blubber for our fire. Other seals came up as the first two were being skinned, so that one may now hope to keep up all future supplies on this side of the ridge.

As I write the wind is blowing up again and looks like returning to the south. The only comfort is that these strong cold winds with no sun must go far to cool the waters of the Sound.

The continuous bad weather is trying to the spirits, but we are fairly comfortable in the hut and only suffer from lack of exercise to work off the heavy meals our appetites demand.

Tuesday 21 March The wind returned to the south at 8 last night. It gradually increased in force until 2 a.m., when it was blowing from the S.S.W., force 9 to 10. The sea was breaking constantly and heavily on the ice foot. The spray carried right over the Point – covering all things and raining on the roof of the hut. Poor Vince's cross, some 30 feet above the water, was enveloped in it.

Of course the dogs had a very poor time, and we went and released two or three, getting covered in spray during the operation – our wind clothes very wet.

This is the third gale from the south since our arrival here. Any one of these would have rendered the Bay impossible for a ship, and therefore it is extraordinary that we should have entirely escaped such a blow when the *Discovery* was in it in 1902.

The effects of this gale are evident and show that it is a most unusual occurrence. The rippled snow surface of the ice foot is furrowed in all directions and covered with briny deposit – a condition we have never seen before. The ice foot at the S.W. corner of the bay is broken down, bare rock appearing for the first time.

The sledges, magnetic huts, and in fact every exposed object on the Point are thickly covered with brine. Our seal floe has gone, so it is good-bye to seals on this side for some time.

The dogs are the main sufferers by this continuance of phenomenally terrible weather. At least four are in a bad state; some six or seven others are by no means fit and well, but oddly enough some ten or a dozen animals are as fit as they can be. Whether constitutionally harder or whether better fitted by nature or chance to protect themselves it is impossible to say – Osman, Czigane, Krisravitsa, Hohol, and some others are in first-rate condition, whilst Lappa is better than he has ever been before.

It is so impossible to keep the dogs comfortable in the traces and so laborious to be continually attempting it, that we have decided to let the majority run loose. It will be wonderful if we can avoid one or two murders, but on the other hand probably more would die if we kept them in leash.

We shall try and keep the quarrelsome dogs chained up.

The main trouble that seems to come on the poor wretches is the icing up of their hindquarters; once the ice gets thoroughly into the coat the hind legs get half paralysed with cold. The hope is that the animals will free themselves of this by running about.

Well, well, fortune is not being very kind to us. This month will have sad memories. Still I suppose things might be worse; the ponies are well housed and are doing exceedingly well, though we have slightly increased their food allowance.

Yesterday afternoon we climbed Observation Hill to see some examples of spheroidal weathering – Wilson knew of them and guided. The geologists state that they indicate a columnar structure, the tops of the columns being weathered out.

The specimens we saw were very perfect. Had some interesting instruction in geology in the evening. I should not regret a stay here with our two geologists if only the weather would allow us to get about.

This morning the wind moderated and went to the S.E.; the sea naturally fell quickly. The temperature this morning was +17°; minimum +11°. But now the wind is increasing from the S.E. and it is momentarily getting colder.

Thursday 23 March a.m. No signs of depot party, which tonight will have been a week absent. On Tuesday afternoon we went up to the Big Boulder above Ski slope. The geologists were interested, and we others learnt something of olivines, green in crystal form or oxidised to bright red, granites or granulites or quartzites, hornblende and feldspars, ferrous and ferric oxides of lava acid, basic, plutonic, igneous, eruptive – schists, basalts, etc. All such things I must get clearer in my mind. [As a step towards 'getting these things clearer' in his mind two spare pages of the diary are filled with neat tables, showing the main classes into which rocks are divided, and their natural subdivisions – the sedimentary, according to mode of deposition, chemical, organic, or aqueous; the metamorphic, according to the kind of rock altered by heat; the igneous, according to their chemical composition.]

Tuesday afternoon a cold S.E. wind commenced and blew all night.

Yesterday morning it was calm and I went up Crater Hill. The sea of stratus cloud hung curtain-like over the Strait – blue sky east and south of it and the Western Mountains bathed in sunshine, sharp, clear, distinct, a glorious glimpse of grandeur on which the curtain gradually descended. In the morning it looked as though great pieces of Barrier were drifting out. From the hill one found these to be but small fragments which the late gale had dislodged, leaving in places a blue wall very easily distinguished from the general white of the older fractures. The old floe and a good extent of new ice had remained fast in Pram Point Bay. Great numbers of seals up as usual. The temperature was up to +20° at noon. In the afternoon a very chill wind from the east, temperature rapidly dropping till zero in the evening. The Strait obstinately refuses to freeze.

We are scoring another success in the manufacture of blubber lamps, which relieves anxiety as to lighting as the hours of darkness increase.

The young ice in Pram Point Bay is already being pressed up.

Friday 24 March a.m. Skuas still about, a few – very shy – very dark in colour after moulting.

Went along Arrival Heights yesterday with very keen over-ridge wind – it was difficult to get shelter. In the evening it fell calm and has remained all night with temperature up to +18°. This morning it is snowing with fairly large flakes.

Yesterday for the first time saw the ice foot on the south side of the bay, a wall some 5 or 6 ft. above water and 12 or 14 ft. below; the sea bottom quite clear with the white wall resting on it. This must be typical of the ice foot all along the coast, and the wasting of caves at sea level alone gives the idea of an overhanging mass. Very curious and interesting erosion of surface of the ice foot by waves during recent gale.

The depot party returned yesterday morning. They had thick weather on the outward march and missed the track, finally doing 30 miles between Safety Camp and Corner Camp. They had a hard blow up to force 8 on the night of our gale. Started N.W. and strongest S.S.E.

The sea wants to freeze – a thin coating of ice formed directly the wind dropped; but the high temperature does not tend to thicken it rapidly and the tide makes many an open lead. We have been counting our resources and arranging for another twenty days' stay.

Saturday 25 March a.m. We have had two days of surprisingly warm weather, the sky overcast, snow falling, wind only in light airs. Last night the sky was clearing, with a southerly wind, and this morning the sea was open all about us. It is disappointing to find the ice so reluctant to hold; at the same time one supposes that the cooling of the water is proceeding and therefore that each day makes it easier for the ice to form – the sun seems to have lost all power, but I imagine its rays still tend to warm the surface water about the noon hours. It is only a week now to the date which I thought would see us all at Cape Evans.

The warmth of the air has produced a comparatively uncomfortable state of affairs in the hut. The ice on the inner roof is melting fast, dripping on the floor and streaming down the sides. The increasing cold is checking the evil even as I write. Comfort could only be ensured in the hut either by making a clean sweep of all the ceiling ice or by keeping the interior at a critical temperature little above freezing-point.

Sunday 26 March p.m. Yesterday morning went along Arrival Heights in very cold wind. Afternoon to east side Observation Hill. As afternoon advanced, wind fell. Glorious evening – absolutely calm, smoke ascending straight. Sea frozen over – looked very much like final freezing, but in night wind came from S.E., producing open water all along shore. Wind continued this morning with drift, slackened in afternoon; walked over Gap and back by Crater Heights to Arrival Heights.

Sea east of Cape Armitage pretty well covered with ice; some open pools – sea off shore west of the Cape frozen in pools, open lanes close to shore as far as Castle Rock. Bays either side of Glacier Tongue *look* fairly well frozen. Hut still dropping water badly.

Held Service in hut this morning, read Litany. *One* skua seen today.

Monday 27 March p.m. Strong easterly wind on ridge today rushing down over slopes on western side.

Ice holding south from about Hut Point, but cleared ½ to ¾ mile from shore to northward. Cleared in patches also, I am told, on both sides of Glacier Tongue, which is annoying. A regular local wind. The Barrier edge can be seen clearly all along, showing there is little or no drift. Have been out over the Gap for walk. Glad to say majority of people seem anxious to get exercise, but one or two like the fire better.

The dogs are getting fitter each day, and all save one or two have excellent coats. I was very pleased to find one or two of the animals voluntarily accompanying us on our walk. It is good to see them trotting against a strong drift.

Tuesday 28 March Slowly but surely the sea is freezing over. The ice holds and thickens south of Hut Point in spite of strong easterly wind and in spite of isolated water holes which obstinately remain open. It is difficult to account for these – one wonders if the air currents shoot downward on such places; but even so it is strange that they do not gradually diminish in extent. A great deal of ice seems to have remained in and about the northern islets, but it is too far to be sure that there is a continuous sheet.

We are building stabling to accommodate four more ponies under the eastern verandah. When this is complete we shall be able to shelter seven animals, and this should be enough for winter and spring operations.

Thursday 30 March The ice holds south of Hut Point, though not thickening rapidly – yesterday was calm and the same ice conditions seemed to obtain on both sides of the Glacier Tongue. It looks as though the last part of the road to become safe will be the stretch from Hut Point to Turtleback Island. Here the sea seems disinclined to freeze even in calm weather. Today there is more strong wind from the east. White horse all along under the ridge.

The period of our stay here seems to promise to lengthen. It is trying – trying – but we can live, which is something. I should not be greatly surprised if we had to wait till May. Several skuas were about the camp yesterday. I have seen none today.

Two rorquals were rising close to Hut Point this morning – although the ice is nowhere thick it was strange to see them making for the open leads and thin places to blow.

Friday 31 March I studied the wind blowing along the ridge yesterday and came to the conclusion that a comparatively thin shaft of air was moving along the ridge from Erebus. On either side of the ridge it seemed to pour down from the ridge itself – there was practically no wind on the sea-ice off Pram Point, and to the westward of Hut Point the frost smoke was drifting to the N.W. The temperature ranges about zero. It seems to be almost certain that the perpetual wind is due to the open winter. Meanwhile the sea refuses to freeze over.

Wright pointed out the very critical point which zero temperature represents in the freezing of salt water, being the freezing temperature of concentrated brine – a very few degrees above or below zero would make all the difference to the rate of increase of the ice thickness.

Yesterday the ice was 8 inches in places east of Cape Armitage and 6 inches in our Bay: it was said to be fast to the south of the Glacier Tongue well beyond Turtleback Island and to the north out of the Islands, except for a strip of water immediately north of the Tongue.

We are good for another week in pretty well every commodity and shall then have to reduce luxuries. But we have plenty of seal meat, blubber and biscuit, and can therefore remain for a much longer period if needs be. Meanwhile the days are growing shorter and the weather colder.

Saturday 1 April The wind yesterday was blowing across the Ridge from the top down on the sea to the west: very little wind on the eastern slopes and practically none at Pram Point. A seal came up in our Bay and was killed. Taylor found a number of fish frozen into the sea-ice – he says there are several in a small area.

The pressure ridges in Pram Point Bay are estimated by Wright to have set up about 3 feet. This ice has been 'in' about ten days. It is now safe to work pretty well anywhere south of Hut Point.

Went to Third Crater (next Castle Rock) yesterday. The ice seems to be holding in the near Bay from a point near Hulton Rocks to Glacier; also in the whole of the North Bay except for a tongue of open water immediately north of the Glacier.

The wind is the same today as yesterday, and the open water apparently not reduced by a square yard. I'm feeling impatient.

Sunday 2 April a.m. Went round Cape Armitage to Pram Point on sea-ice for first time yesterday afternoon. Ice solid everywhere, except off the Cape, where there are numerous open pools. Can only imagine layers of comparatively warm water brought to the surface by shallows. The ice between the pools is fairly shallow. One Emperor killed off the Cape. Several skuas seen – three seals up in our Bay – several off Pram Point in the shelter of Horse Shoe Bay. A great many fish on sea-ice – mostly small, but a second species 5 or 6 inches long: imagine they are chased by seals and caught in brashy ice where they are unable to escape. Came back over hill: glorious sunset, brilliant crimson clouds in west.

Returned to find wind dropping, the first time for three days. It turned to north in the evening. Splendid aurora in the night; a bright band of light from S.S.W. to E.N.E. passing within 10° of the zenith with two waving spirals at the summit. This morning sea to north covered with ice. Min. temp, for night -5°, but I think most of the ice was brought in by the wind. Things look more hopeful. Ice now continuous to Cape Evans, but very thin as far as Glacier Tongue; three or four days of calm or light winds should make everything firm.

Wednesday 5 April a.m. The east wind has continued with a short break on Sunday for five days, increasing in violence and gradually becoming colder and more charged with snow until yesterday, when we had a thick overcast day with falling and driving snow and temperature down to -11°.

Went beyond Castle Rock on Sunday and Monday mornings with Griffith Taylor.

Think the wind fairly local and that the Strait has frozen over to the north, as streams of drift snow and ice crystals (off the cliffs) were building up the ice sheet towards the wind. Monday we could see the approaching white sheet – yesterday it was visibly closer to land, though the wind had not decreased. Walking was little pleasure on either day: yesterday climbed about hills to see all possible. No one else left the hut. In the evening the wind fell and freezing continued during night (min. -17°). This morning there is ice everywhere. I cannot help thinking it has come to stay. In Arrival Bay it is 6 to 7 inches thick, but the new pools beyond have only 1 inch of the regular elastic sludgy new ice. The sky cleared last night, and this morning we have sunshine for the first time for many days. If this weather holds for a day we shall be all right. We are getting towards the end of our luxuries, so that it is quite time we made a move – we are very near the end of the sugar.

The skuas seem to have gone, the last was seen on Sunday. These birds were very shy towards the end of their stay, also very dark in plumage; they did not seem hungry, and yet it must have been difficult for them to get food.

The seals are coming up in our Bay – five last night. Luckily the dogs have not yet discovered them or the fact that the sea-ice will bear them.

Had an interesting talk with Taylor on agglomerate and basaltic dykes of Castle Rock. The perfection of the small cone craters below Castle Rock seem to support the theory we have come to, that there have been volcanic disturbances since the recession of the greater ice sheet.

It is a great thing having Wright to fog out the ice problems, and he has had a good opportunity of observing many interesting things here. He is keeping notes of ice changes and a keen eye on ice phenomena; we have many discussions.

Yesterday Wilson prepared a fry of seal meat with penguin blubber. It had a flavour like cod-liver oil and was not much appreciated – some ate their share, and I think all would have done so if we had had sledging appetites – shades of *Discovery* days!![16]

This Emperor weighed anything from 88 to 96 lbs., and therefore approximated to or exceeded the record.

The dogs are doing pretty well with one or two exceptions. Deek is the worst, but I begin to think all will pull through.

Thursday 6 April a.m. The weather continued fine and clear yesterday – one of the very few fine days we have had since our arrival at the hut.

The sun shone continuously from early morning till it set behind the northern hills about 5 p.m. The sea froze completely, but with only a thin sheet to the north. A fairly strong northerly wind sprang up, causing this thin ice to override and to leave several open leads near the land. In the forenoon I went to the edge of the new ice with Wright. It looked at the limit of safety and we did not venture far. The overriding is interesting: the edge of one sheet splits as it rises and slides over the other sheet in long tongues which creep onward impressively. Whilst motion lasts there is continuous music, a medley of high pitched but tuneful notes – one might imagine small birds chirping in a wood. The ice sings, we say.

p.m. In the afternoon went nearly two miles to the north over the young ice; found it about 3½ inches thick. At supper arranged programme for shift to Cape Evans – men to go on Saturday – dogs Sunday – ponies Monday – all subject to maintenance of good weather of course.

Friday 7 April Went north over ice with Atkinson, Bowers, Taylor, Cherry-Garrard; found the thickness nearly 5 inches everywhere except in open water leads, which remain open in many places. As we got away from the land we got on an interesting surface of small pancakes, much capped and pressed up, a sort of mosaic. This is the ice which was built up from lee side of the Strait, spreading across to windward against the strong winds of Monday and Tuesday.

Another point of interest was the manner in which the overriding ice sheets had scraped the under floes.

Taylor fell in when rather foolishly trying to cross a thinly covered lead – he had a very scared face for a moment or two whilst we hurried to the rescue, but hauled himself out with his ice axe without our help and walked back with Cherry.

The remainder of us went on till abreast of the sulphur cones under Castle Rock, when we made for the shore, and with a little mutual help climbed the cliff and returned by land.

As far as one can see all should be well for our return tomorrow, but the sky is clouding tonight and a change of weather seems imminent. Three successive fine days seem near the limit in this region.

We have picked up quite a number of fish frozen in the ice – the larger ones about the size of a herring and the smaller of a minnow. We imagined both had been driven into the slushy ice by seals, but today Gran found a large fish frozen in the act of swallowing a small one. It looks as though both small and large are caught when one is chasing the other.

We have achieved such great comfort here that one is half sorry to leave – it is a fine healthy existence with many hours spent in the open and generally some interesting object for our walks abroad. The hill climbing gives excellent exercise – we shall miss much of it at Cape Evans. But I am anxious to get back and see that all is well at the latter, as for a long time I have been wondering how our beach has withstood the shocks of northerly winds. The thought that the hut may have been damaged by the sea in one of the heavy storms will not be banished.

A SKETCH OF THE LIFE AT HUT POINT

We gather around the fire seated on packing-cases, with a hunk of bread and butter and a steaming pannikin of tea, and life is well worth living. After lunch we are out and about again; there is little to tempt a long stay indoors and exercise keeps us all the fitter.

The falling light and approach of supper drives us home again with good appetites about 5 or 6 o'clock, and then the cooks rival one another in preparing succulent dishes of fried seal liver. A single dish may not seem to offer much opportunity of variation, but a lot can be done with a little flour, a handful of raisins, a spoonful of curry powder, or the addition of a little boiled pea meal. Be this as it may, we never tire of our dish and exclamations of satisfaction can be heard every night – or nearly every night, for two nights ago [4 April] Wilson, who has proved a genius in the invention of 'plats', almost ruined his reputation. He proposed to fry the seal liver in penguin blubber, suggesting that the latter could be freed from all rankness. The blubber was obtained and rendered down with great care, the result appeared as delightfully pure fat free from smell; but appearances were deceptive; the 'fry' proved redolent of penguin, a concentrated essence of that peculiar flavour which faintly lingers in the meat and should not be emphasised. Three heroes got through their pannikins, but the rest of us decided to be contented with cocoa and biscuit after tasting the first mouthful. After supper we have an hour or so of smoking and conversation – a cheering, pleasant hour – in which reminiscences are exchanged by a company which has very literally had world-wide experience. There is scarce a country under the sun which one or another of us has not travelled in, so diverse are our origins and occupations. An hour or so after supper we tail off one by one, spread out our sleeping-bags, take off our shoes and creep into comfort, for our reindeer bags are really warm and comfortable now that they have had a chance of drying, and the hut retains some of the heat generated in it. Thanks to the success of the blubber lamps and to a fair supply of candles, we can muster ample light to read for another hour or two, and so tucked up in our furs we study the social and political questions of the past decade.

We muster no less than sixteen. Seven of us pretty well cover the floor of one wing of the L-shaped enclosure, four sleep in the other wing, which also holds the store, whilst the remaining five occupy the annexe and affect to find the colder temperature more salubrious. Everyone can manage eight or nine hours' sleep without a break, and not a few would have little difficulty in sleeping the clock round, which goes to show that our extremely simple life is an exceedingly healthy one, though with faces and hands blackened with smoke, appearances might not lead an outsider to suppose it.

Sunday 9 April a.m. On Friday night it grew overcast and the wind went to the south. During the whole of yesterday and last night it blew a moderate blizzard – the temperature at highest +5°, a relatively small amount of drift. On Friday night the ice in the Strait went out from a line meeting the shore ¾ mile north of Hut Point. A crack off Hut Point and curving to N.W. opened to about 15 or 20 feet, the opening continuing on the north side of the Point. It is strange that the ice thus opened should have remained.

Ice cleared out to the north directly wind commenced – it didn't wait a single instant, showing that our journey over it earlier in the day was a very risky proceeding – the uncertainty of these conditions is beyond words, but there shall be no more of this foolish venturing on young ice. This decision seems to put off the return of the ponies to a comparatively late date.

Yesterday went to the second crater, Arrival Heights, hoping to see the condition of the northerly bays, but could see little or nothing owing to drift. A white line dimly seen on the horizon seemed to indicate that the ice drifted out has not gone far.

Some skuas were seen yesterday, a very late date. The seals disinclined to come on the ice; one can be seen at Cape Armitage this morning, but it is two or three days since there was one up in our Bay. It will certainly be some time before the ponies can be got back.

Monday 10 April p.m. Intended to make for Cape Evans this morning. Called hands early, but when we were ready for departure after breakfast, the sky became more overcast and snow began to fall. It continued off and on all day, only clearing as the sun set. It would have been the worst condition possible for our attempt, as we could not have been more than 100 yards.

Conditions look very unfavourable for the continued freezing of the Strait.

Thursday 13 April Started from Hut Point 9 a.m. Tuesday. Party consisted of self, Bowers, P.O. Evans, Taylor, one tent; Evans, Gran, Crean, Debenham, and Wright, second tent. Left Wilson in charge at Hut Point with Meares, Forde, Keohane, Oates, Atkinson, and Cherry-Garrard. All gave us a pull up the ski slope; it had become a point of honour to take this slope without a 'breather'. I find such an effort trying in the early morning, but had to go through with it.

Weather fine; we marched past Castle Rock, east of it; the snow was soft on the slopes, showing the shelter afforded – continued to traverse the ridge for the first time – found quite good surface much wind-swept – passed both cones on the ridge on the west side. Caught a glimpse of fast ice in the Bays either side of Glacier as expected, but in the near Bay its extent was very small. Evidently we should have to go well along the ridge before descending, and then the problem would be how to get down over the cliffs. On to Hulton Rocks 7½ miles from the start – here it was very icy and wind-swept, inhospitable – the wind got up and light became bad just at the critical moment, so we camped and had some tea at 2 p.m. A clearance half an hour later allowed us to see a possible descent to the ice cliffs, but between Hulton Rocks and Erebus all the slope was much cracked and crevassed. We chose a clear track to the edge of the cliffs, but could find no low place in these, the lowest part being 24 feet sheer drop. Arriving here the wind increased, the snow drifting off the ridge – we had to decide quickly; I got myself to the edge and made standing places to work the rope; dug away at the cornice, well situated for such work in harness. Got three people lowered by the Alpine rope – Evans, Bowers, and Taylor – then sent down the sledges, which went down in fine style, fully packed – then the remainder of the party. For the last three, drove a stake hard down in the snow and used the rope round it, the men being lowered by people below – came down last myself. Quite a neat and speedy bit of work and all done in 20 minutes without serious frostbite – quite pleased with the result.

We found pulling to Glacier Tongue very heavy over the surface of ice covered with salt crystals, and reached Glacier Tongue about 5.30; found a low place and got the sledges up the 6 ft. wall pretty easily. Stiff incline, but easy pulling on hard surface – the light was failing and the surface criss-crossed with innumerable cracks; several of us fell in these with risk of strain, but the north side was well snow-covered and easy, with a good valley leading to a low ice cliff – here a broken piece afforded easy descent. I decided to push on for Cape Evans, so camped for tea at 6. At 6.30 found darkness suddenly arrived; it was very difficult to see anything – we got down on the sea-ice, very heavy pulling, but plodded on for some hours; at 10 arrived close under little Razor Back Island, and not being able to see anything ahead, decided to camp and got to sleep at 11.30 in no very comfortable circumstances.

The wind commenced to rise during night. We found a roaring blizzard in the morning. We had many alarms for the safety of the ice on which the camp was pitched. Bowers and Taylor climbed the island; reported wind terrific on the summit – sweeping on either side but comparatively calm immediately to windward and to leeward. Waited all day in hopes of a lull; at 3 I went round the island myself with Bowers, and found a little ice platform close under the weather side; resolved to shift camp here. It took two very cold hours, but we gained great shelter, the cliffs rising almost sheer from the tents. Only now and again a whirling wind current eddied down on the tents, which were well secured, but the noise of the wind sweeping over the rocky ridge above our heads was deafening; we could scarcely hear ourselves speak. Settled down for our second night with little comfort, and slept better, knowing we could not be swept out to sea, but provisions were left only for one more meal.

During the night the wind moderated and we could just see outline of land.

I roused the party at 7 a.m. and we were soon under weigh, with a desperately cold and stiff breeze and frozen clothes; it was very heavy pulling, but the distance only two miles. Arrived off the point about ten and found sea-ice continued around it. It was a very great relief to see the hut on rounding it and to hear that all was well.

Another pony, Hackenschmidt, and one dog reported dead, but this certainly is not worse than expected. All the other animals are in good form.

Delighted with everything I see in the hut. Simpson has done wonders, but indeed so has everyone else, and I must leave description to a future occasion.

Friday 14 April Good Friday. Peaceful day. Wind continuing 20 to 30 miles per hour.

Had Divine Service.

Saturday 15 April Weather continuing thoroughly bad. Wind blowing from 30 to 40 miles an hour all day; drift bad, and tonight snow falling. I am waiting to get back to Hut Point with relief stores. Tonight sent up signal light to inform them there of our safe arrival – an answering flare was shown.

Sunday 16 April Same wind as yesterday up to 6 o'clock, when it fell calm with gusts from the north.

Have exercised the ponies today and got my first good look at them. I scarcely like to express the mixed feelings with which I am able to regard this remnant.

FREEZING OF BAYS. CAPE EVANS

15 March General young ice formed.

19 March Bay cleared except strip inside Inaccessible and Razor Back Islands to Corner Turk's Head.

20 March Everything cleared.

25 March Sea froze over inside Islands for good.

28 March Sea frozen as far as seen.

30 March Remaining only inside Islands.

1 April Limit Cape to Island.

6 April Present limit freezing in Strait and in North Bay.

9 April Strait cleared except former limit and *some* ice in North Bay likely to remain.

8
HOME IMPRESSIONS & AN EXCURSION: 17 APRIL 1911 – 22 APRIL 1911

IMPRESSIONS ON RETURNING TO THE HUT, 13 APRIL 1911
In choosing the site of the hut on our Home Beach I had thought of the possibility of northerly winds bringing a swell, but had argued, firstly, that no heavy northerly swell had ever been recorded in the Sound; secondly, that a strong northerly wind was bound to bring pack which would damp the swell; thirdly, that the locality was excellently protected by the Barne Glacier, and finally, that the beach itself showed no signs of having been swept by the sea, the rock fragments composing it being completely angular.

When the hut was erected and I found that its foundation was only 11 feet above the level of the sea-ice, I had a slight misgiving, but reassured myself again by reconsidering the circumstances that afforded shelter to the beach.

The fact that such question had been considered makes it easier to understand the attitude of mind that readmitted doubt in the face of phenomenal conditions.

The event has justified my original arguments, but I must confess a sense of having assumed security without sufficient proof in a case where an error of judgment might have had dire consequences.

It was not until I found all safe at the Home Station that I realised how anxious I had been concerning it. In a normal season no thought of its having been in danger would have occurred to me, but since the loss of the ponies and the breaking of the Glacier Tongue I could not rid myself of the fear that misfortune was in the air and that some abnormal swell had swept the beach; gloomy thoughts of the havoc that might have been wrought by such an event would arise in spite of the sound reasons which had originally led me to choose the site of the hut as a safe one.

The late freezing of the sea, the terrible continuance of wind and the abnormalities to which I have referred had gradually strengthened the profound distrust with which I had been forced to regard our mysterious Antarctic climate until my imagination conjured up many forms of disaster as possibly falling on those from whom I had parted for so long.

We marched towards Cape Evans under the usually miserable conditions which attend the breaking of camp in a cold wind after a heavy blizzard. The outlook was dreary in the grey light of early morning, our clothes were frozen stiff and our fingers, wet and cold in the tent, had been frostbitten in packing the sledges.

A few comforting signs of life appeared as we approached the Cape; some old footprints in the snow, a long silk thread from the meteorologist's balloon; but we saw nothing more as we neared the rocks of the promontory and the many grounded bergs which were scattered off it.

To my surprise the fast ice extended past the Cape and we were able to round it into the North Bay. Here we saw the weather screen on Wind Vane Hill, and a moment later turned a small headland and brought the hut in full view. It was intact – stables, outhouses and all; evidently the sea had left it undisturbed. I breathed a huge sigh of relief. We watched two figures at work near the stables and wondered when they would see us. In a moment or two they did so, and fled inside the hut to carry the news of our arrival. Three minutes later all nine occupants [viz. Simpson, Nelson, Day, Ponting, Lashly, Clissold, Hooper, Anton, and Demetri] were streaming over the floe towards us with shouts of welcome. There were eager inquiries as to mutual welfare and it took but a minute to learn the most important events of the quiet station life which had been led since our departure. These under the circumstances might well be considered the deaths of one pony and one dog. The pony was that which had been nicknamed Hackenschmidt from his vicious habit of using both fore and hind legs in attacking those who came near him. He had been obviously of different breed from the other ponies, being of lighter and handsomer shape, suggestive of a strain of Arab blood. From no cause which could be discovered either by the symptoms of his illness or the post-mortem held by Nelson could a reason be found for his death. In spite of the best feeding and every care he had gradually sickened until he was too weak to stand, and in this condition there had been no option but to put him out of misery. Anton considers the death of Hackenschmidt to have been an act of 'cussedness' – the result of a determination to do no work for the Expedition!! Although the loss is serious I remember doubts which I had as to whether this animal could be anything but a source of trouble to us. He had been most difficult to handle all through, showing a vicious, intractable temper. I had foreseen great difficulties with him, especially during the early part of any journey on which he was taken, and this consideration softened the news of his death. The dog had been left behind in a very sick condition, and this loss was not a great surprise.

These items were the worst of the small budget of news that awaited me; for the rest, the hut arrangements had worked out in the most satisfactory manner possible and the scientific routine of observations was in full swing. After our primitive life at Cape Armitage it was wonderful to enter the precincts of our warm, dry Cape Evans home. The interior space seemed palatial, the light resplendent, and the comfort luxurious. It was very good to eat in civilised fashion, to enjoy the first bath for three months, and have contact with clean, dry clothing. Such fleeting hours of comfort (for custom soon banished their delight) are the treasured remembrance of every Polar traveller. They throw into sharpest contrast the hardships of the past and the comforts of the present, and for the time he revels in the unaccustomed physical contentment that results.

I was not many hours or even minutes in the hut before I was haled round to observe in detail the transformation which had taken place during my absence, and in which a very proper pride was taken by those who had wrought it.

Simpson's Corner was the first visited. Here the eye travelled over numerous shelves laden with a profusion of self-recording instruments, electric batteries and switchboards, whilst the ear caught the ticking of many clocks, the gentle whir of a motor and occasionally the trembling note of an electric bell. But such sights and sounds conveyed only an impression of the delicate methodical means by which the daily and hourly variations of our weather conditions were being recorded – a mere glimpse of the intricate arrangements of a first-class meteorological station – the one and only station of that order which has been established in Polar regions. It took me days and even months to realise fully the aims of our meteorologist and the scientific accuracy with which he was achieving them. When I did so to an adequate extent I wrote some description of his work which will be found in the following pages of this volume [see Chapter 10]. The first impression which I am here describing was more confused; I appreciated only that by going to 'Simpson's Corner' one could ascertain at a glance how hard the wind was blowing and had been blowing, how the barometer was varying, to what degree of cold the thermometer had descended; if one were still more inquisitive he could further inform himself as to the electrical tension of the atmosphere and other matters of like import. That such knowledge could be gleaned without a visit to the open air was an obvious advantage to those who were clothing themselves to face it, whilst the ability to study the variation of a storm without exposure savoured of no light victory of mind over matter.

The dark room stands next to the parasitologist's side of the bench which flanks Sunny Jim's Corner – an involved sentence. To be more exact, the physicists adjust their instruments and write up books at a bench which projects at right angles to the end wall of the hut; the opposite side of this bench is allotted to Atkinson, who is to write with his back to the dark room. Atkinson being still absent his corner was unfurnished, and my attention was next claimed by the occupant of the dark room beyond Atkinson's limit. The art of photography has never been so well housed within the Polar regions and rarely without them. Such a palatial chamber for the development of negatives and prints can only be justified by the quality of the work produced in it, and is only justified in our case by the possession of such an artist as Ponting. He was eager to show me the results of his summer work, and meanwhile my eye took in the neat shelves with their array of cameras, etc., the porcelain sink and automatic water tap, the two acetylene gas burners with their shading screens, and the general obviousness of all conveniences of the photographic art. Here, indeed, was encouragement for the best results, and to the photographer be all praise, for it is mainly his hand which has executed the designs which his brain conceived. In this may be clearly seen the advantage of a traveller's experience. Ponting has had to fend for himself under primitive conditions in a new land; the result is a 'handy man' with every form of tool and in any circumstances. Thus, when building operations were to the fore and mechanical labour scarce, Ponting returned to the shell of his apartment with only the raw material for completing it. In the shortest possible space of time shelves and tanks were erected, doors hung and windows framed, and all in a workmanlike manner commanding the admiration of all beholders. It was well that speed could be commanded for such work, since the fleeting hours of the summer season had been altogether too few to be spared from the immediate service of photography. Ponting's nervous temperament allowed no waste of time – for him fine weather meant no sleep; he decided that lost opportunities should be as rare as circumstances would permit.

This attitude was now manifested in the many yards of cinematograph film remaining on hand and yet greater number recorded as having been sent back in the ship, in the boxes of negatives lying on the shelves and a well-filled album of prints.

Of the many admirable points in this work perhaps the most notable are Ponting's eye for a picture and the mastery he has acquired of ice subjects; the composition of most of his pictures is extraordinarily good, he seems to know by instinct the exact value of foreground and middle distance and of the introduction of 'life', whilst with more technical skill in the manipulation of screens and exposures he emphasises the subtle shadows of the snow and reproduces its wondrously transparent texture. He is an artist in love with his work, and it was good to hear his enthusiasm for results of the past and plans of the future.

Long before I could gaze my fill at the contents of the dark room I was led to the biologists' cubicle; Nelson and Day had from the first decided to camp together, each having a habit of methodical neatness; both were greatly relieved when the arrangement was approved, and they were freed from the chance of an untidy companion. No attempt had been made to furnish this cubicle before our departure on the autumn journey, but now on my return I found it an example of the best utilisation of space. The prevailing note was neatness; the biologist's microscope stood on a neat bench surrounded by enamel dishes, vessels, and books neatly arranged; behind him, when seated, rose two neat bunks with neat, closely curtained drawers for clothing and neat reflecting sconces for candles; overhead was a neat arrangement for drying socks with several nets, neatly bestowed. The carpentering to produce this effect had been of quite a high order, and was in very marked contrast with that exhibited for the hasty erections in other cubicles. The pillars and boarding of the bunks had carefully finished edges and were stained to mahogany brown. Nelson's bench is situated very conveniently under the largest of the hut windows, and had also an acetylene lamp, so that both in summer and winter he has all conveniences for his indoor work.

Day appeared to have been unceasingly busy during my absence. Everyone paid tribute to his mechanical skill and expressed gratitude for the help he had given in adjusting instruments and generally helping forward the scientific work. He was entirely responsible for the heating, lighting, and ventilating arrangements, and as all these appear satisfactory he deserved much praise. Particulars concerning these arrangements I shall give later; as a first impression it is sufficient to note that the warmth and lighting of the hut seemed as good as could be desired, whilst for our comfort the air seemed fresh and pure. Day had also to report some progress with the motor sledges, but this matter also I leave for future consideration.

My attention was very naturally turned from the heating arrangements to the cooking stove and its custodian, Clissold. I had already heard much of the surpassingly satisfactory meals which his art had produced, and had indeed already a first experience of them. Now I was introduced to the cook's corner with its range and ovens, its pots and pans, its side tables and well-covered shelves. Much was to be gathered therefrom, although a good meal by no means depends only on kitchen conveniences. It was gratifying to learn that the stove had proved itself economical and the patent fuel blocks a most convenient and efficient substitute for coal. Save for the thickness of the furnace cheeks and the size of the oven Clissold declared himself wholly satisfied. He feared that the oven would prove too small to keep up a constant supply of bread for all hands; nevertheless he introduced me to this oven with an air of pride which I soon found to be fully justified. For connected therewith was a contrivance for which he was entirely responsible, and which in its ingenuity rivalled any of which the hut could boast. The interior of the oven was so arranged that the 'rising' of the bread completed an electric circuit, thereby ringing a bell and switching on a red lamp. Clissold had realised that the continuous ringing of the bell would not be soothing to the nerves of our party, nor the continuous burning of the lamp calculated to prolong its life, and he had therefore added the clockwork mechanism which automatically broke the circuit after a short interval of time; further, this clockwork mechanism could be made to control the emersion of the same warning signals at intervals of time varied according to the desire of the operator; thus because, when in bed, he would desire a signal at short periods, but if absent from the hut he would wish to know at a glance what had happened when he returned. Judged by any standard it was a remarkably pretty little device, but when I learnt that it had been made from odds and ends, such as a cog-wheel or spring here and a cell or magnet there, begged from other departments, I began to realise that we had a very exceptional cook. Later when I found that Clissold was called in to consult on the ailments of Simpson's motor and that he was capable of constructing a dog sledge out of packing cases, I was less surprised, because I knew by this time that he had had considerable training in mechanical work before he turned his attention to pots and pans.

My first impressions include matters to which I was naturally eager to give an early half-hour, namely the housing of our animals. I found herein that praise was as justly due to our Russian boys as to my fellow Englishmen.

Anton with Lashly's help had completed the furnishing of the stables. Neat stalls occupied the whole length of the 'lean to', the sides so boarded that sprawling legs could not be entangled beneath and the front well covered with tin sheet to defeat the 'cribbers'. I could but sigh again to think of the stalls that must now remain empty, whilst appreciating that there was ample room for the safe harbourage of the ten beasts that remain, be the winter never so cold or the winds so wild.

Later we have been able to give double space to all but two or three of our animals, in which they can lie down if they are so inclined.

The ponies look fairly fit considering the low diet on which they have been kept; their coats were surprisingly long and woolly in contrast with those of the animals I had left at Hut Point. At this time they were being exercised by Lashly, Anton, Demetri, Hooper, and Clissold, and as a rule were ridden, the sea having only recently frozen. The exercise ground had lain on the boulder-strewn sand of the home beach and extending towards the Skua lake; and across these stretches I soon saw barebacked figures dashing at speed, and not a few amusing incidents in which horse and rider parted with abrupt lack of ceremony. I didn't think this quite the most desirable form of exercise for the beasts, but decided to leave matters as they were till our pony manager returned.

Demetri had only five or six dogs left in charge, but these looked fairly fit, all things considered, and it was evident the boy was bent on taking every care of them, for he had not only provided shelters, but had built a small 'lean to' which would serve as a hospital for any animal whose stomach or coat needed nursing.

Such were in broad outline the impressions I received on my first return to our home station; they were almost wholly pleasant and, as I have shown, in happy contrast with the fears that had assailed me on the homeward route. As the days went by I was able to fill in the detail in equally pleasant fashion, to watch the development of fresh arrangements and the improvement of old ones. Finally, in this way I was brought to realise what an extensive and intricate but eminently satisfactory organisation I had made myself responsible for.

A FRESH MS. BOOK
[*On the Flyleaf*]

Genus Homo, Species Sapiens!

FLOTSAM

Wm. Barents' house in Novaya Zemlya built 1596. Found by Capt. Carlsen 1871 (275 years later) intact, everything inside as left! What of this hut?

The ocean girt continent.

'Might have seemed almost heroic if any higher end than excessive love of gain and traffic had animated the design.' – MILTON.

'He is not worthy to live at all, who, for fear and danger of death shunneth his country's service or his own honour, since death is inevitable and the fame of virtue immortal.' – SIR HUMPHREY GILBERT.

There is no part of the world that *can* not be reached by man. When the 'can be' is turned to 'has been' the Geographical Society will have altered its status.

'At the whirring loom of time unawed

I weave the living garment of God.' – GOETHE.

By all means think yourself big but don't think everyone else small!

The man who knows everyone's job isn't much good at his own.

'When you are attacked unjustly avoid the appearance of evil, but avoid also the appearance of being too good!' 'A man can't be too good, but he can appear too good.'

Monday 17 April Started from C. Evans with two 10 ft. sledges.

Party 1. Self, Lashly, Day, Demetri.

Party 2. Bowers, Nelson, Crean, Hooper.

We left at 8 a.m., taking our personal equipment, a week's provision of sledging food, and butter, oatmeal, flour, lard, chocolate, etc., for the hut.

Two of the ponies hauled the sledges to within a mile of the Glacier Tongue; the wind, which had been north, here suddenly shifted to S.E., very biting. (The wind remained north at C. Evans during the afternoon, the ponies walked back into it.) Sky overcast, very bad light. Found the place to get on the glacier, but then lost the track – crossed more or less direct, getting amongst many cracks. Came down in bay near the open water – stumbled over the edge to an easy drift. More than once on these trips I as leader have suddenly disappeared from the sight of the others, affording some consternation till they got close enough to see what has happened. The pull over sea-ice was very heavy and in face of strong wind and drift. Every member of the party was frostbitten about the face, several with very cold feet. Pushed on after repairs. Found drift streaming off the ice cliff, a new cornice formed and our rope buried at both ends. The party getting cold, I decided to camp, have tea, and shift foot gear. Whilst tea was preparing, Bowers and I went south, then north, along the cliffs to find a place to ascend – nearly everywhere ascent seemed impossible in the vicinity of Hulton Rocks or north, but eventually we found an overhanging cornice close to our rope.

After lunch we unloaded a sledge, which, held high on end by four men, just reached the edge of the cornice. Clambering up over backs and up sledge I used an ice-axe to cut steps over the cornice and thus managed to get on top, then cut steps and surmounted the edge of the cornice. Helped Bowers up with the rope; others followed – then the gear was hauled up piecemeal. For Crean, the last man up, we lowered the sledge over the cornice and used a bowline in the other end of the rope on top of it. He came up grinning with delight, and we all thought the ascent rather a cunning piece of work. It was fearfully cold work, but everyone working with rare intelligence, we eventually got everything up and repacked the sledge; glad to get in harness again. Then a heavy pull up a steep slope in wretched light, making detour to left to avoid crevasses. We reached the top and plodded on past the craters as nearly as possible as on the outward route. The party was pretty exhausted and very wet with perspiration. Approaching Castle Rock the weather and light improved. Camped on Barrier Slope north of Castle Rock about 9 p.m. Night cold but calm, -38° during night; slept pretty well.

Tuesday 18 April Hut Point. Good moonlight at 7 a.m. – had breakfast. Broke camp very quickly – Lashly splendid at camp work as of old – very heavy pull up to Castle Rock, sweated much. This sweating in cold temperature is a serious drawback. Reached Hut Point 1 p.m. Found all well in excellent spirits – didn't seem to want us much!!

Party reported very bad weather since we left, cold blizzard, then continuous S.W. wind with -20° and below. The open water was right up to Hut Point, wind absolutely preventing all freezing along shore. Wilson reported skua gull seen Monday.

Found party much shorter of blubber than I had expected – they were only just keeping themselves supplied with a seal killed two days before and one as we arrived.

Actually less fast ice than when we left!

Wednesday 19 April Hut Point. Calm during night, sea froze over at noon, 4½ inches thick off Hut Point, showing how easily the sea will freeze when the chance is given.

Three seals reported on the ice; all hands out after breakfast and the liver and blubber of all three seals were brought in. This relieves one of a little anxiety, leaving a twelve days' stock, in which time other seals ought to be coming up. I am making arrangements to start back tomorrow, but at present it is overcast and wind coming up from the south. This afternoon, all ice frozen last night went out quietly; the sea tried to freeze behind it, but the wind freshened soon. The ponies were exercised yesterday and today; they look pretty fit, but their coats are not so good as those in winter quarters – they want fatty foods.

Am preparing to start tomorrow, satisfied that the *Discovery* Hut is very comfortable and life very liveable in it. The dogs are much the same, all looking pretty fit except Vaida and Rabchick – neither of which seem to get good coats. I am greatly struck with the advantages of experience in Crean and Lashly for all work about camps.

Thursday 20 April Hut Point. Everything ready for starting this morning, but of course it 'blizzed'. Weather impossible – much wind and drift from south. Wind turned to S.E. in afternoon – temperatures low. Went for walk to Cape Armitage, but it is really very unpleasant. The wind blowing round the Cape is absolutely blighting, force 7 and temperature below -30°. Sea a black cauldron covered with dark frost smoke. No ice can form in such weather.

Friday 21 April Started homeward at 10.30.

Left Meares in charge of station with Demetri to help with dogs, Lashly and Keohane to look out for ponies, Nelson and Day and Forde to get some idea of the life and experience. Homeward party, therefore:

Self	Bowers
Wilson	Oates
Atkinson	Cherry-Garrard
Crean	Hooper

As usual all hands pulled up Ski slope, which we took without a halt. Lashly and Demetri came nearly to Castle Rock – very cold side wind and some frostbites. We reached the last downward slope about 2.30; at the cliff edge found the cornice gone – heavy wind and drift worse than before, if anything. We bustled things, and after tantalising delays with the rope got Bowers and some others on the floe, then lowered the sledges packed; three men, including Crean and myself, slid down last on the Alpine rope – doubled and taken round an ash stave, so that we were able to unreeve the end and recover the rope – we recovered also most of the old Alpine rope, all except a piece buried in snow on the sea-ice and dragged down under the slush, just like the *Discovery* boats; I could not have supposed this could happen in so short a time.[17]

By the time all stores were on the floe, with swirling drift about us, everyone was really badly cold – one of those moments for quick action. We harnessed and dashed for the shelter of the cliffs; up tents, and hot tea as quick as possible; after this and some shift of foot gear all were much better. Heavy plod over the sea-ice, starting at 4.30 – very bad light on the glacier, and we lost our way as usual, stumbling into many crevasses, but finally descended in the old place; by this time sweating much. Crean reported our sledge pulling much more heavily than the other one. Marched on to Little Razor Back Island without halt, our own sledge dragging fearfully. Crean said there was great difference in the sledges, though loads were equal. Bowers politely assented when I voiced this sentiment, but I'm sure he and his party thought it the plea of tired men. However there was nothing like proof, and he readily assented to change sledges. The difference was really extraordinary; we felt the new sledge a featherweight compared with the old, and set up a great pace for the home quarters regardless of how much we perspired. We arrived at the hut (two miles away) ten minutes ahead of the others, who by this time were quite convinced as to the difference in the sledges.

The difference was only marked when pulling over the salt-covered sea-ice; on snow the sledges seemed pretty much the same. It is due to the grain of the wood in the runners and is worth looking into.

We all arrived bathed in sweat – our garments were soaked through, and as we took off our wind clothes showers of ice fell on the floor. The accumulation was almost incredible and shows the whole trouble of sledging in cold weather. It would have been very uncomfortable to have camped in the open under such conditions, and assuredly a winter and spring party cannot afford to get so hot if they wish to retain any semblance of comfort.

Our excellent cook had just the right meal prepared for us – an enormous dish of rice and figs, and cocoa in a bucket! The hut party were all very delighted to see us, and the fittings and comforts of the hut are amazing to the newcomers.

Saturday 22 *April* Cape Evans, Winter Quarters. The sledging season is at an end. It's good to be back in spite of all the losses we have sustained.

Today we enjoy a very exceptional calm. The sea is freezing over of course, but unfortunately our view from Observatory Hill is very limited. Oates and the rest are exercising the ponies. I have been sorting my papers and getting ready for the winter work.

9

THE WORK & THE WORKERS: 23 APRIL 1911 – 14 MAY 1911

Sunday 23 April Winter Quarters. The last day of the sun and a very glorious view of its golden light over the Barne Glacier. We could not see the sun itself on account of the Glacier, the fine ice cliffs of which were in deep shadow under the rosy rays.

Impression The long mild twilight which like a silver clasp unites today with yesterday; when morning and evening sit together hand in hand beneath the starless sky of midnight.

It blew hard last night and most of the young ice has gone as expected. Patches seem to be remaining south of the Glacier Tongue and the Island and off our own bay. In this very queer season it appears as though the final freezing is to be reached by gradual increments to the firmly established ice.

Had Divine Service. Have only seven hymn-books, those brought on shore for our first Service being very stupidly taken back to the ship.

I begin to think we are *too* comfortable in the hut and hope it will not make us slack; but it is good to see everyone in such excellent spirits – so far not a rift in the social arrangements.

Monday 24 April A night watchman has been instituted mainly for the purpose of observing the aurora, of which the displays have been feeble so far. The observer is to look round every hour or oftener if there is aught to be seen. He is allowed cocoa and sardines with bread and butter – the cocoa can be made over an acetylene Bunsen burner, part of Simpson's outfit. I took the first turn last night; the remainder of the afterguard follow in rotation. The long night hours give time to finish up a number of small tasks – the hut remains quite warm though the fires are out.

Simpson has been practising with balloons during our absence. This morning he sent one up for trial. The balloon is of silk and has a capacity of 1 cubic metre. It is filled with hydrogen gas, which is made in a special generator. The generation is a simple process. A vessel filled with water has an inverted vessel within it; a pipe is led to the balloon from the latter and a tube of india-rubber is attached which contains calcium hydrate. By tipping the tube the amount of calcium hydrate required can be poured into the generator. As the gas is made it passes into the balloon or is collected in the inner vessel, which acts as a bell jar if the stop cock to the balloon is closed.

The arrangements for utilising the balloon are very pretty.

An instrument weighing only 2¼ oz. and recording the temperature and pressure is attached beneath a small flag and hung 10 to 15 ft. below the balloon with balloon silk thread; this silk thread is of such fine quality that 5 miles of it only weighs 4 ozs., whilst its breaking strain is 1¼ lbs. The lower part of the instrument is again attached to the silk thread, which is cunningly wound on coned bobbins from which the balloon unwinds it without hitch or friction as it ascends.

In order to spare the silk any jerk as the balloon is released two pieces of string united with a slow match carry the strain between the instrument and the balloon until the slow match is consumed.

The balloon takes about a quarter of an hour to inflate; the slow match is then lit, and the balloon released; with a weight of 8 oz. and a lifting power of 2½ lbs. it rises rapidly. After it is lost to ordinary vision it can be followed with glasses as mile after mile of thread runs out. Theoretically, if strain is put on the silk thread it should break between the instrument and the balloon, leaving the former free to drop, when the thread can be followed up and the instrument with its record recovered.

Today this was tried with a dummy instrument, but the thread broke close to the bobbins. In the afternoon a double thread was tried, and this acted successfully.

Today I allotted the ponies for exercise. Bowers, Cherry-Garrard, Hooper, Clissold, P.O. Evans, and Crean take animals, besides Anton and Oates. I have had to warn people that they will not necessarily lead the ponies which they now tend.

Wilson is very busy making sketches.

Tuesday 25 April It was comparatively calm all day yesterday and last night, and there have been light airs only from the south today. The temperature, at first comparatively high at -5°, has gradually fallen to -13°; as a result the Strait has frozen over at last and it looks as though the Hut Point party should be with us before very long. If the blizzards hold off for another three days the crossing should be perfectly safe, but I don't expect Meares to hurry.

Although we had very good sunset effects at Hut Point, Ponting and others were much disappointed with the absence of such effects at Cape Evans. This was probably due to the continual interference of frost smoke; since our return here and especially yesterday and today the sky and sea have been glorious in the afternoon.

Ponting has taken some coloured pictures, but the result is not very satisfactory and the plates are much spotted; Wilson is very busy with pencil and brush.

Atkinson is unpacking and setting up his sterilisers and incubators. Wright is wrestling with the electrical instruments. Evans is busy surveying the Cape and its vicinity. Oates is reorganising the stable, making bigger stalls, etc. Cherry-Garrard is building a stone house for taxidermy and with a view to getting hints for making a shelter at Cape Crozier during the winter. Debenham and Taylor are taking advantage of the last of the light to examine the topography of the peninsula. In fact, everyone is extraordinarily busy.

I came back with the impression that we should not find our winter walks so interesting as those at Hut Point, but I'm rapidly altering my opinion; we may miss the hill climbing here, but in every direction there is abundance of interest. Today I walked round the shores of the North Bay examining the kenyte cliffs and great masses of morainic material of the Barne Glacier, then on under the huge blue ice cliffs of the Glacier itself. With the sunset lights, deep shadows, the black islands and white bergs it was all very beautiful.

Simpson and Bowers sent up a balloon today with a double thread and instrument attached; the line was checked at about 3 miles, and soon after the instrument was seen to disengage. The balloon at first went north with a light southerly breeze till it reached 300 or 400 ft., then it turned to the south but did not travel rapidly; when 2 miles of thread had gone it seemed to be going north again or rising straight upward.

In the afternoon Simpson and Bowers went to recover their treasure, but somewhere south of Inaccessible Island they found the thread broken and the light was not good enough to continue the search.

The sides of the galley fire have caved in – there should have been cheeks to prevent this; we got some fire clay cement today and plastered up the sides. I hope this will get over the difficulty, but have some doubt.

Wednesday 26 April Calm. Went round Cape Evans – remarkable effects of icicles on the ice foot, formed by spray of southerly gales.

Thursday 27 April The fourth day in succession without wind, but overcast. Light snow has fallen during the day – tonight the wind comes from the north.

We should have our party back soon. The temperature remains about -5° and the ice should be getting thicker with rapidity.

Went round the bergs off Cape Evans – they are very beautiful, especially one which is pierced to form a huge arch. It will be interesting to climb around these monsters as the winter proceeds.

Today I have organised a series of lectures for the winter; the people seem keen and it ought to be exceedingly interesting to discuss so many diverse subjects with experts.

We have an extraordinary diversity of talent and training in our people; it would be difficult to imagine a company composed of experiences which differed so completely. We find one hut contains an experience of every country and every clime! What an assemblage of motley knowledge!

Friday 28 April Another comparatively calm day – temp. -12°, clear sky. Went to ice caves on glacier S. of Cape; these are really very wonderful. Ponting took some photographs with long exposure and Wright got some very fine ice crystals. The Glacier Tongue comes close around a high bluff headland of kenyte; it is much cracked and curiously composed of a broad wedge of white névé over blue ice. The faults in the dust strata in these surfaces are very mysterious and should be instructive in the explanation of certain ice problems.

It looks as though the sea had frozen over for good. If no further blizzard clears the Strait it can be said for this season that:

The Bays froze over on 25 March.

The Strait froze over on 22 April.

The Strait dissipated 29 April.

The Strait froze over on 30 April.

Later. The Hut Point record of freezing is:

Night 24th–25th. Ice forming mid-day 25th, opened with leads.

26th. Ice all out, sound apparently open.

27th. Strait apparently freezing.

Early 28th. Ice over whole Strait.

29th. All ice gone.

30th. Freezing over.

4th May. Broad lead opened along land to Castle Rock, 300 to 400 yds. wide. Party intended to start on 11th, if weather fine.

Very fine display of aurora tonight, one of the brightest I have ever seen – over Erebus; it is conceded that a red tinge is seen after the movement of light.

Saturday 29 April Went to Inaccessible Island with Wilson. The agglomerates, kenytes, and lavas are much the same as those at Cape Evans. The Island is 540 ft. high, and it is a steep climb to reach the summit over very loose sand and boulders. From the summit one has an excellent view of our surroundings and the ice in the Strait, which seemed to extend far beyond Cape Royds, but had some ominous cracks beyond the Island.

We climbed round the ice foot after descending the hill and found it much broken up on the south side; the sea spray had washed far up on it.

It is curious to find that all the heavy seas come from the south and that it is from this direction that protection is most needed.

There is some curious weathering on the ice blocks on the N. side; also the snow drifts show interesting dirt bands. The island had a good sprinkling of snow, which will all be gone, I expect, tonight. For as we reached the summit we saw a storm approaching from the south; it had blotted out the Bluff, and we watched it covering Black Island, then Hut Point and Castle Rock. By the time we started homeward it was upon us, making a harsh chatter as it struck the high rocks and sweeping along the drift on the floe.

The blow seems to have passed over tonight and the sky is clear again, but I much fear the ice has gone out in the Strait. There is an ominous black look to the westward.

Sunday 30 April As I feared last night, the morning light revealed the havoc made in the ice by yesterday's gale. From Wind Vane Hill (66 feet) it appeared that the Strait had not opened beyond the island, but after church I went up the Ramp with Wilson and steadily climbed over the Glacier ice to a height of about 650 feet. From this elevation one could see that a broad belt of sea-ice had been pushed bodily to seaward, and it was evident that last night the whole stretch of water from Hut Point to Turtle Island must have been open – so that our poor people at Hut Point are just where they were.

The only comfort is that the Strait is already frozen again; but what is to happen if every blow clears the sea like this?

Had an interesting walk. One can go at least a mile up the glacier slope before coming to crevasses, and it does not appear that these would be serious for a good way farther. The view is magnificent, and on a clear day like this, one still enjoys some hours of daylight, or rather twilight, when it is possible to see everything clearly.

Have had talks of the curious cones which are such a feature of the Ramp – they are certainly partly produced by ice and partly by weathering. The ponds and various forms of ice grains interest us.

Tonight have been naming all the small land features of our vicinity.

Tuesday 2 May It was calm yesterday. A balloon was sent up in the morning, but only reached a mile in height before the instrument was detached (by slow match).

In the afternoon went out with Bowers and his pony to pick up instrument, which was close to the shore in the South Bay. Went on past Inaccessible Island. The ice outside the bergs has grown very thick, 14 inches or more, but there were freshly frozen pools beyond the Island.

In the evening Wilson opened the lecture series with a paper on 'Antarctic Flying Birds'. Considering the limits of the subject the discussion was interesting. The most attractive point raised was that of pigmentation. Does the absence of pigment suggest absence of reserve energy? Does it increase the insulating properties of the hair or feathers? Or does the animal clothed in white radiate less of his internal heat? The most interesting example of Polar colouring here is the increased proportion of albinos amongst the giant petrels found in high latitudes.

Today have had our first game of football; a harassing southerly wind sprang up, which helped my own side to the extent of three goals.

This same wind came with a clear sky and jumped up and down in force throughout the afternoon, but has died away tonight. In the afternoon I saw an ominous lead outside the Island which appeared to extend a long way south. I'm much afraid it may go across our pony track from Hut Point. I am getting anxious to have the hut party back, and begin to wonder if the ice to the south will ever hold in permanently now that the Glacier Tongue has gone.

Wednesday 3 May Another calm day, very beautiful and clear. Wilson and Bowers took our few dogs for a run in a sledge. Walked myself out over ice in North Bay – there are a good many cracks and pressures with varying thickness of ice, showing how tide and wind shift the thin sheets – the newest leads held young ice of 4 inches.

The temperature remains high, the lowest yesterday -13°; it should be much lower with such calm weather and clear skies. A strange fact is now very commonly noticed: in calm weather there is usually a difference of 4° or 5° between the temperature at the hut and that on Wind Vane Hill (64 feet), the latter being the higher. This shows an inverted temperature.

As I returned from my walk the southern sky seemed to grow darker, and later stratus cloud was undoubtedly spreading up from that direction – this at about 5 p.m. About 7 a moderate north wind sprang up. This seemed to indicate a southerly blow, and at about 9 the wind shifted to that quarter and blew gustily, 25 to 35 m.p.h. One cannot see the result on the Strait, but I fear it means that the ice has gone out again in places. The wind dropped as suddenly as it had arisen soon after midnight.

In the evening Simpson gave us his first meteorological lecture – the subject, 'Coronas, Halos, Rainbows, and Auroras'. He has a remarkable power of exposition and taught me more of these phenomena in the hour than I had learnt by all previous interested inquiries concerning them.

I note one or two points concerning each phenomenon.

Corona White to brown inside ring called Aureola – outside are sometimes seen two or three rings of prismatic light in addition. Caused by diffraction of light round drops of water or ice crystals; diameter of rings inversely proportionate to size of drops or crystals – mixed sizes of ditto causes aureola without rings.

Halos Caused by refraction and reflection through and from ice crystals. In this connection the hexagonal, tetrahedonal type of crystallisation is first to be noted; then the infinite number of forms in which this can be modified together with result of fractures: two forms predominate, the plate and the needle; these forms falling through air assume definite position – the plate falls horizontally swaying to and fro, the needle turns rapidly about its longer axis, which remains horizontal. Simpson showed excellent experiments to illustrate; consideration of these facts and refraction of light striking crystals clearly leads to explanation of various complicated halo phenomena such as recorded and such as seen by us on the Great Barrier, and draws attention to the critical refraction angles of $32°$ and $46°$, the radius of inner and outer rings, the position of mock suns, contra suns, zenith circles, etc.

Further measurements are needed; for instance of streamers from mock suns and examination of ice crystals. (Record of ice crystals seen on Barrier Surface.)

Rainbows Caused by reflection and refraction from and through *drops of water* – colours vary with size of drops, the smaller the drop the lighter the colours and nearer to the violet end of the spectrum – hence white rainbow as seen on the Barrier, very small drops.

Double Bows Diameters must be $84°$ and $100°$ – again from laws of refraction – colours: inner, red outside; outer, red inside – i.e. reds come together.

Wanted to see more rainbows on Barrier. In this connection a good rainbow was seen to N.W. in February from winter quarters. Reports should note colours and relative width of bands of colour.

Iridescent Clouds Not yet understood; observations required, especially angular distance from the sun.

Auroras Clearly most frequent and intense in years of maximum sun spots; this argues connection with the sun.

Points noticed requiring confirmation:

Arch: centre of arch in magnetic meridian.

Shafts: take direction of dipping needle.

Bands and Curtains with convolutions – not understood.

Corona: shafts meeting to form.

Notes required on movement and direction of movement – colours seen – supposed red and possibly green rays preceding or accompanying movement. Auroras are sometimes accompanied by magnetic storms, but not always, and *vice versa* – in general significant signs of some connection – possible common dependants on a third factor. The phenomenon further connects itself in form with lines of magnetic force about the earth. (Curious apparent connection between spectrum of aurora and that of a heavy gas, 'argon'. May be coincidence.)

Two theories enunciated:

Arrhenius Bombardments of minute charged particles from the sun gathered into the magnetic field of the earth.

Birkeland Bombardment of free negative electrons gathered into the magnetic field of the earth.

It is experimentally shown that minute drops of water are deflected by light.

It is experimentally shown that ions are given off by dried calcium, which the sun contains.

Professor Störmer has collected much material showing connection of the phenomenon with lines of magnetic force.

Thursday 4 May From the small height of Wind Vane Hill (64 feet) it was impossible to say if the ice in the Strait had been out after yesterday's wind. The sea was frozen, but after twelve hours' calm it would be in any case. The dark appearance of the ice is noticeable, but this has been the case of late since the light is poor; little snow has fallen or drifted and the ice flowers are very sparse and scattered.

We had an excellent game of football again today – the exercise is delightful and we get very warm. Atkinson is by far the best player, but Hooper, P.O. Evans, and Crean are also quite good. It has been calm all day again.

Went over the sea-ice beyond the Arch berg; the ice half a mile beyond is only 4 inches. I think this must have been formed since the blow of yesterday, that is, in sixteen hours or less.

Such rapid freezing is a hopeful sign, but the prompt dissipation of the floe under a southerly wind is distinctly the reverse.

I am anxious to get our people back from Hut Point, mainly on account of the two ponies; with so much calm weather there should have been no difficulty for the party in keeping up its supply of blubber; an absence of which is the only circumstance likely to discomfort it.

The new ice over which I walked is extraordinarily slippery and free from efflorescence. I think this must be a further sign of rapid formation.

Friday 5 May Another calm day following a quiet night. Once or twice in the night a light northerly wind, soon dying away. The temperature down to -12°. What is the meaning of this comparative warmth? As usual in calms the Wind Vane Hill temperature is 3° or 4° higher. It is delightful to contemplate the amount of work which is being done at the station. No one is idle – all hands are full, and one cannot doubt that the labour will be productive of remarkable result.

I do not think there can be any life quite so demonstrative of character as that which we had on these expeditions. One sees a remarkable reassortment of values. Under ordinary conditions it is so easy to carry a point with a little bounce; self-assertion is a mask which covers many a weakness. As a rule we have neither the time nor the desire to look beneath it, and so it is that commonly we accept people on their own valuation. Here the outward show is nothing, it is the inward purpose that counts. So the 'gods' dwindle and the humble supplant them. Pretence is useless.

One sees Wilson busy with pencil and colour box, rapidly and steadily adding to his portfolio of charming sketches and at intervals filling the gaps in his zoological work of *Discovery* times; withal ready and willing to give advice and assistance to others at all times; his sound judgment appreciated and therefore a constant referee.

Simpson, master of his craft, untiringly attentive to the working of his numerous self-recording instruments, observing all changes with scientific acumen, doing the work of two observers at least and yet ever seeking to correlate an expanded scope. So the current meteorological and magnetic observations are taken as never before by Polar expeditions.

Wright, good-hearted, strong, keen, striving to saturate his mind with the ice problems of this wonderful region. He has taken the electrical work in hand with all its modern interest of association with radioactivity.

Evans, with a clear-minded zeal in his own work, does it with all the success of result which comes from the taking of pains. Therefrom we derive a singularly exact preservation of time – an important consideration to all, but especially necessary for the physical work. Therefrom also, and including more labour, we have an accurate survey of our immediate surroundings and can trust to possess the correctly mapped results of all surveying data obtained. He has Gran for assistant.

Taylor's intellect is omnivorous and versatile – his mind is unceasingly active, his grasp wide. Whatever he writes will be of interest – his pen flows well.

Debenham's is clearer. Here we have a well-trained, sturdy worker, with a quiet meaning that carries conviction; he realises the conceptions of thoroughness and conscientiousness.

To Bowers' practical genius is owed much of the smooth working of our station. He has a natural method in line with which all arrangements fall, so that expenditure is easily and exactly adjusted to supply, and I have the inestimable advantage of knowing the length of time which each of our possessions will last us and the assurance that there can be no waste. Active mind and active body were never more happily blended. It is a restless activity, admitting no idle moments and ever budding into new forms.

So we see the balloons ascending under his guidance and anon he is away over the floe tracking the silk thread which held it. Such a task completed, he is away to exercise his pony, and later out again with the dogs, the last typically self-suggested, because for the moment there is no one else to care for these animals. Now in a similar manner he is spreading thermometer screens to get comparative readings with the home station. He is for the open air, seemingly incapable of realising any discomfort from it, and yet his hours within doors spent with equal profit. For he is intent on tracking the problems of sledging food and clothing to their innermost bearings and is becoming an authority on past records. This will be no small help to me and one which others never could have given.

Adjacent to the physicists' corner of the hut Atkinson is quietly pursuing the subject of parasites. Already he is in a new world. The laying out of the fish trap was his action and the catches are his field of labour. Constantly he comes to ask if I would like to see some new form and I am taken to see some protozoa or ascidian isolated on the slide plate of his microscope. The fishes themselves are comparatively new to science; it is strange that their parasites should have been under investigation so soon.

Atkinson's bench with its array of microscopes, test-tubes, spirit lamps, etc., is next the dark room in which Ponting spends the greater part of his life. I would describe him as sustained by artistic enthusiasm. This world of ours is a different one to him than it is to the rest of us – he gauges it by its picturesqueness – his joy is to reproduce its pictures artistically, his grief to fail to do so. No attitude could be happier for the work which he has undertaken, and one cannot doubt its productiveness. I would not imply that he is out of sympathy with the works of others, which is far from being the case, but that his energies centre devotedly on the minutiae of his business.

Cherry-Garrard is another of the open-air, self-effacing, quiet workers; his whole heart is in the life, with profound eagerness to help everyone. 'One has caught glimpses of him in tight places; sound all through and pretty hard also.' Indoors he is editing our Polar journal, out of doors he is busy making trial stone huts and blubber stoves, primarily with a view to the winter journey to Cape Crozier, but incidentally these are instructive experiments for any party which may get into difficulty by being cut off from the home station. It is very well to know how best to use the scant resources that nature provides in these regions. In this connection I have been studying our Arctic library to get details concerning snow hut building and the implements used for it.

Oates' whole heart is in the ponies. He is really devoted to their care, and I believe will produce them in the best possible form for the sledging season. Opening out the stores, installing a blubber stove, etc., has kept *him* busy, whilst his satellite, Anton, is ever at work in the stables – an excellent little man.

Evans and Crean are repairing sleeping-bags, covering felt boots, and generally working on sledging kit. In fact there is no one idle, and no one who has the least prospect of idleness.

Saturday 6 May Two more days of calm, interrupted with occasional gusts.

Yesterday, Friday evening, Taylor gave an introductory lecture on his remarkably fascinating subject – modern physiography.

These modern physiographers set out to explain the forms of land erosion on broad common-sense lines, heedless of geological support. They must, in consequence, have their special language. River courses, they say, are not temporary – in the main they are archaic. In conjunction with land elevations they have worked through *geographical cycles*, perhaps many. In each geographical cycle they have advanced from *infantile* V-shaped forms; the courses broaden and deepen, the bank slopes reduce in angle as maturer stages are reached until the level of sea surface is more and more nearly approximated. In *senile* stages the river is a broad sluggish stream flowing over a plain with little inequality of level. The cycle has formed a *Peneplain*. Subsequently, with fresh elevation, a new cycle is commenced. So much for the simple case, but in fact nearly all cases are modified by unequal elevations due to landslips, by variation in hardness of rock, etc. Hence modification in positions of river courses and the fact of different parts of a single river being in different stages of cycle.

Taylor illustrated his explanations with examples: The Red River, Canada – Plain flat though elevated, water lies in pools, river flows in 'V' 'infantile' form.

The Rhine Valley – The gorgeous scenery from Mainz down due to infantile form in recently elevated region.

The Russian Plains – Examples of 'senility'.

Greater complexity in the Blue Mountains – these are undoubted earth folds; the Nepean River flows through an offshoot of a fold, the valley being made as the fold was elevated – curious valleys made by erosion of hard rock overlying soft.

River *piracy* – *Domestic*, the short circuiting of a *meander*, such as at Coo in the Ardennes; *Foreign*, such as Shoalhaven River, Australia – stream has captured river.

Landslips have caused the isolation of Lake George and altered the watershed of the whole country to the south.

Later on Taylor will deal with the effects of ice and lead us to the formation of the scenery of our own region, and so we shall have much to discuss.

Sunday 7 May Daylight now is very short. One wonders why the Hut Point party does not come. Bowers and Cherry-Garrard have set up a thermometer screen containing maximum thermometers and thermographs on the sea floe about ¾' N.W. of the hut. Another smaller one is to go on top of the Ramp. They took the screen out on one of Day's bicycle wheel carriages and found it ran very easily over the salty ice where the sledges give so much trouble. This vehicle is not easily turned, but may be very useful before there is much snowfall.

Yesterday a balloon was sent up and reached a very good height (probably 2 to 3 miles) before the instrument disengaged; the balloon went almost straight up and the silk fell in festoons over the rocky part of the Cape, affording a very difficult clue to follow; but whilst Bowers was following it, Atkinson observed the instrument fall a few hundred yards out on the Bay – it was recovered and gives the first important record of upper air temperature.

Atkinson and Crean put out the fish trap in about 3 fathoms of water off the west beach; both yesterday morning and yesterday evening when the trap was raised it contained over forty fish, whilst this morning and this evening the catches in the same spot have been from twenty to twenty-five. We had fish for breakfast this morning, but an even more satisfactory result of the catches has been revealed by Atkinson's microscope. He had discovered quite a number of new parasites and found work to last quite a long time.

Last night it came to my turn to do night watchman again, so that I shall be glad to have a good sleep tonight.

Yesterday we had a game of football; it is pleasant to mess about, but the light is failing.

Clissold is still producing food novelties; tonight we had galantine of seal – it was *excellent*.

Monday 8 May – Tuesday 9 May As one of the series of lectures I gave an outline of my plans for next season on Monday evening. Everyone was interested naturally. I could not but hint that in my opinion the problem of reaching the Pole can best be solved by relying on the ponies and man haulage. With this sentiment the whole company appeared to be in sympathy. Everyone seems to distrust the dogs when it comes to glacier and summit. I have asked everyone to give thought to the problem, to freely discuss it, and bring suggestions to my notice. It's going to be a tough job; that is better realised the more one dives into it.

Today (Tuesday) Debenham has been showing me his photographs taken west. With Wright's and Taylor's these will make an extremely interesting series – the ice forms especially in the region of the Koettlitz glacier are unique.

The Strait has been frozen over a week. I cannot understand why the Hut Point party doesn't return. The weather continues wonderfully calm though now looking a little unsettled. Perhaps the unsettled look stops the party, or perhaps it waits for the moon, which will be bright in a day or two.

Any way I wish it would return, and shall not be free from anxiety till it does.

Cherry-Garrard is experimenting in stone huts and with blubber fires – all with a view to prolonging the stay at Cape Crozier.

Bowers has placed one thermometer screen on the floe about ¾' out, and another smaller one above the Ramp. Oddly, the floe temperature seems to agree with that on Wind Vane Hill, whilst the hut temperature is always 4° or 5° colder in calm weather. To complete the records a thermometer is to be placed in South Bay.

Science – the rock foundation of all effort!!

Wednesday 10 May It has been blowing from the South 12 to 20 miles per hour since last night; the ice remains fast. The temperature -12° to -19°. The party does not come. I went well beyond Inaccessible Island till Hut Point and Castle Rock appeared beyond Tent Island, that is, well out on the space which was last seen as open water. The ice is 9 inches thick, not much for eight or nine days' freezing; but it is very solid – the surface wet but very slippery. I suppose Meares waits for 12 inches in thickness, or fears the floe is too slippery for the ponies.

Yet I wish he would come.

I took a thermometer on my walk today; the temperature was -12° inside Inaccessible Island, but only -8° on the sea-ice outside – the wind seemed less outside. Coming in under lee of Island and bergs I was reminded of the difficulty of finding shelter in these regions. The weather side of hills seems to afford better shelter than the lee side, as I have remarked elsewhere. May it be in part because all lee sides tend to be filled by drift snow, blown and weathered rock debris? There was a good lee under one of the bergs; in one corner the ice sloped out over me and on either side, forming a sort of grotto; here the air was absolutely still.

Ponting gave us an interesting lecture on Burmah, illustrated with fine slides. His descriptive language is florid, but shows the artistic temperament. Bowers and Simpson were able to give personal reminiscences of this land of pagodas, and the discussion led to interesting statements on the religion, art, and education of its people, their philosophic idleness, etc. Our lectures are a real success.

Friday 12 May Yesterday morning was quiet. Played football in the morning; wind got up in the afternoon and evening.

All day it has been blowing hard, 30 to 60 miles an hour; it has never looked very dark overhead, but a watery cirrus has been in evidence for some time, causing well marked paraselene.

I have not been far from the hut, but had a great fear on one occasion that the ice had gone out in the Strait.

The wind is dropping this evening, and I have been up to Wind Vane Hill. I now think the ice has remained fast.

There has been astonishingly little drift with the wind, probably due to the fact that there has been so very little snowfall of late.

Atkinson is pretty certain that he has isolated a very motile bacterium in the snow. It is probably air borne, and though no bacteria have been found in the air, this may be carried in upper currents and brought down by the snow. If correct it is an interesting discovery.

Tonight Debenham gave a geological lecture. It was elementary. He gave little more than the rough origin and classification of rocks with a view to making his further lectures better understood.

Saturday 13 May The wind dropped about 10 last night. This morning it was calm and clear save for a light misty veil of ice crystals through which the moon shone with scarce clouded brilliancy, surrounded with bright cruciform halo and white paraselene. Mock moons with prismatic patches of colour appeared in the radiant ring, echoes of the main source of light. Wilson has a charming sketch of the phenomenon.

I went to Inaccessible Island, and climbing some way up the steep western face, reassured myself concerning the ice. It was evident that there had been no movement in consequence of yesterday's blow.

In climbing I had to scramble up some pretty steep rock faces and screens, and held on only in anticipation of gaining the top of the Island and an easy descent. Instead of this I came to an impossible overhanging cliff of lava, and was forced to descend as I had come up. It was no easy task, and I was glad to get down with only one slip, when I brought myself up with my ice-axe in the nick of time to prevent a fall over a cliff. This Island is very steep on all sides. There is only one known place of ascent; it will be interesting to try and find others.

After tea Atkinson came in with the glad tidings that the dog team were returning from Hut Point. We were soon on the floe to welcome the last remnant of our wintering party. Meares reported everything well and the ponies not far behind.

The dogs were unharnessed and tied up to the chains; they are all looking remarkably fit – apparently they have given no trouble at all of late; there have not even been any fights.

Half an hour later Day, Lashly, Nelson, Forde, and Keohane arrived with the two ponies – men and animals in good form.

It is a great comfort to have the men and dogs back, and a greater to contemplate all the ten ponies comfortably stabled for the winter. Everything seems to depend on these animals.

I have not seen the meteorological record brought back, but it appears that the party had had very fine calm weather since we left them, except during the last three days when wind has been very strong. It is curious that we should only have got one day with wind.

I am promised the sea-freezing record tomorrow. Four seals were got on 22 April, the day after we left, and others have been killed since, so that there is a plentiful supply of blubber and seal meat at the hut – the rest of the supplies seem to have been pretty well run out. Some more forage had been fetched in from the depot. A young sea leopard had been killed on the sea-ice near Castle Rock three days ago, this being the second only found in the Sound.

It is a strange fact that none of the returning party seem to greatly appreciate the food luxuries they have had since their return. It would have been the same with us had we not had a day or two in tents before our return. It seems more and more certain that a very simple fare is all that is needed here – plenty of seal meat, flour, and fat, with tea, cocoa, and sugar; these are the only real requirements for comfortable existence.

The temperatures at Hut Point have not been as low as I expected. There seems to have been an extraordinary heat wave during the spell of calm recorded since we left – the thermometer registering little below zero until the wind came, when it fell to -20°. Thus as an exception we have had a fall instead of a rise of temperature with wind.

[The exact inventory of stores at Hut Point here recorded has no immediate bearing on the history of the expedition, but may be noted as illustrating the care and thoroughness with which all operations were conducted. Other details as to the carbide consumed in making acetylene gas may be briefly quoted. The first tin was opened on 1 February, the second on 26 March. The seventh on 20 May, the next eight at the average interval of 9½ days.]

Sunday 14 May Grey and dull in the morning.

Exercised the ponies and held the usual service. This morning I gave Wright some notes containing speculations on the amount of ice on the Antarctic continent and on the effects of winter movements in the sea-ice. I want to get into his head the larger bearing of the problems which our physical investigations involve. He needs two years here to fully realise these things, and with all his intelligence and energy will produce little unless he has that extended experience.

The sky cleared at noon, and this afternoon I walked over the North Bay to the ice cliffs – such a very beautiful afternoon and evening – the scene bathed in moonlight, so bright and pure as to be almost golden, a very wonderful scene. At such times the Bay seems strangely homely, especially when the eye rests on our camp with the hut and lighted windows.

I am very much impressed with the extraordinary and general cordiality of the relations which exist amongst our people. I do not suppose that a statement of the real truth, namely, that there is no friction at all, will be credited – it is so generally thought that the many rubs of such a life as this are quietly and purposely sunk in oblivion. With me there is no need to draw a veil; there is nothing to cover. There are no strained relations in this hut, and nothing more emphatically evident than the universally amicable spirit which is shown on all occasions.

Such a state of affairs would be delightfully surprising under any conditions, but it is much more so when one remembers the diverse assortment of our company.

This theme is worthy of expansion. Tonight Oates, captain in a smart cavalry regiment, has been 'scrapping' over chairs and tables with Debenham, a young Australian student.

It is a triumph to have collected such men.

The temperature has been down to -23°, the lowest yet recorded here – doubtless we shall soon get lower, for I find an extraordinary difference between this season as far as it has gone and those of 1902–03.

10
IN WINTER QUARTERS, MODERN STYLE:
15 MAY 1911 – 31 MAY 1911

Monday 15 May The wind has been strong from the north all day – about 30 miles an hour. A bank of stratus cloud about 6000 or 7000 feet (measured by Erebus) has been passing rapidly overhead *towards* the north; it is nothing new to find the overlying layers of air moving in opposite directions, but it is strange that the phenomenon is so persistent. Simpson has frequently remarked as a great feature of weather conditions here the seeming reluctance of the air to 'mix' – the fact seems to be the explanation of many curious fluctuations of temperature.

Went for a short walk, but it was not pleasant. Wilson gave an interesting lecture on penguins. He explained the primitive characteristics in the arrangement of feathers on wings and body, the absence of primaries and secondaries or bare tracts; the modification of the muscles of the wings and in the structure of the feet (the metatarsal joint). He pointed out (and the subsequent discussion seemed to support him) that these birds probably branched at a very early stage of bird life – coming pretty directly from the lizard bird Archaeopteryx of the Jurassic age. Fossils of giant penguins of Eocene and Miocene ages show that there has been extremely little development since.

He passed on to the classification and habitat of different genera, nest-making habits, eggs, etc. Then to a brief account of the habits of the Emperors and Adelies, which was of course less novel ground for the old hands.

Of special points of interest I recall his explanation of the desirability of embryonic study of the Emperor to throw further light on the development of the species in the loss of teeth, etc.; and Ponting's contribution and observation of adult Adélies teaching their young to swim – this point has been obscure. It has been said that the old birds push the young into the water, and, *per contra*, that they leave them deserted in the rookery – both statements seemed unlikely. It would not be strange if the young Adélie had to learn to swim (it is a well-known requirement of the Northern fur seal – sea bear), but it will be interesting to see in how far the adult birds lay themselves out to instruct their progeny.

During our trip to the ice and sledge journey one of our dogs, Vaida, was especially distinguished for his savage temper and generally uncouth manners.

He became a bad wreck with his poor coat at Hut Point, and in this condition I used to massage him; at first the operation was mistrusted and only continued to the accompaniment of much growling, but later he evidently grew to like the warming effect and sidled up to me whenever I came out of the hut, though still with some suspicion. On returning here he seemed to know me at once, and now comes and buries his head in my legs whenever I go out of doors; he allows me to rub him and push him about without the slightest protest and scampers about me as I walk abroad. He is a strange beast – I imagine so unused to kindness that it took him time to appreciate it.

Tuesday 16 May The north wind continued all night but dropped this forenoon. Conveniently it became calm at noon and we had a capital game of football. The light is good enough, but not much more than good enough, for this game.

Had some instruction from Wright this morning on the electrical instruments.

Later went into our carbide expenditure with Day: am glad to find it sufficient for two years, but am not making this generally known as there are few things in which economy is less studied than light if regulations allow of waste.

ELECTRICAL INSTRUMENTS

For measuring the ordinary potential gradient we have two self-recording quadrant electrometers. The principle of this instrument is the same as that of the old Kelvin instrument; the clockwork attached to it unrolls a strip of paper wound on a roller; at intervals the needle of the instrument is depressed by an electromagnet and makes a dot on the moving paper. The relative position of these dots forms the record. One of our instruments is adjusted to give only 1/10th the refinement of measurement of the other by means of reduction in the length of the quartz fibre. The object of this is to continue the record in snowstorms, etc., when the potential difference of air and earth is very great. The instruments are kept charged with batteries of small Daniels cells. The clocks are controlled by a master clock.

The instrument available for radioactivity measurements is a modified type of the old gold-leaf electroscope. The measurement is made by the mutual repulsion of quartz fibres acting against a spring – the extent of the repulsion is very clearly shown against a scale magnified by a telescope.

The measurements to be made with instrument are various:

The *ionization of the air*. A length of wire charged with 2000 volts (negative) is exposed to the air for several hours. It is then coiled on a frame and its rate of discharge measured by the electroscope.

The *radioactivity of the various rocks* of our neighbourhood; this by direct measurement of the rock.

The *conductivity of the air*, that is, the relative movement of ions in the air; by movement of air past charged surface. Rate of absorption of + and - ions is measured, the negative ion travelling faster than the positive.

Wednesday 17 May For the first time this season we have a rise of temperature with a southerly wind. The wind force has been about 30 since yesterday evening; the air is fairly full of snow and the temperature has risen to -6° from -18°.

I heard one of the dogs barking in the middle of the night, and on inquiry learned that it was one of the 'Serais' [the white dogs], that he seemed to have something wrong with his hind leg, and that he had been put under shelter. This morning the poor brute was found dead.

I'm afraid we can place but little reliance on our dog teams and reflect ruefully on the misplaced confidence with which I regarded the provision of our transport. Well, one must suffer for errors of judgment.

This afternoon Wilson held a post-mortem on the dog; he could find no sufficient cause of death. This is the third animal that has died at winter quarters without apparent cause. Wilson, who is nettled, proposes to examine the brain of this animal tomorrow.

Went up the Ramp this morning. There was light enough to see our camp, and it looked homely, as it does from all sides. Somehow we loom larger here than at Cape Armitage. We seem to be more significant. It must be from contrast of size; the larger hills tend to dwarf the petty human element.

Tonight the wind has gone back to the north and is now blowing fresh.

This sudden and continued complete change of direction is new to our experience.

Oates has just given us an excellent little lecture on the management of horses.

He explained his plan of feeding our animals 'soft' during the winter, and hardening them up during the spring. He pointed out that the horse's natural food being grass and hay, he would naturally employ a great number of hours in the day filling a stomach of small capacity with food from which he could derive only a small percentage of nutriment.

Hence it is desirable to feed horses often and light. His present routine is as follows:

Morning – Chaff.

Noon, after exercise – Snow. Chaff and either oats or oil-cake alternate days.

Evening, 5 p.m. – Snow. Hot bran mash with oil-cake or boiled oats and chaff; finally a small quantity of hay. This sort of food should be causing the animals to put on flesh, but is not preparing them for work. In October he proposes to give 'hard' food, all cold, and to increase the exercising hours.

As concerning the food we possess he thinks:

The *chaff* made of young wheat and hay is doubtful; there does not seem to be any grain with it – and would farmers cut young wheat? There does not seem to be any 'fat' in this food, but it is very well for ordinary winter purposes.

N.B. – It seems to me this ought to be inquired into. *Bran* much discussed, but good because it causes horses to chew the oats with which mixed.

Oil-cake, greasy, producing energy – excellent for horses to work on.

Oats, of which we have two qualities, also very good working food – our white quality much better than the brown.

Our trainer went on to explain the value of training horses, of getting them 'balanced' to pull with less effort. He owns it is very difficult when one is walking horses only for exercise, but thinks something can be done by walking them fast and occasionally making them step backwards.

Oates referred to the deeds that had been done with horses by foreigners in shows and with polo ponies by Englishmen when the animals were trained; it is, he said, a sort of gymnastic training.

The discussion was very instructive and I have only noted the salient points.

Thursday 18 May The wind dropped in the night; today it is calm, with slight snowfall. We have had an excellent football match – the only outdoor game possible in this light.

I think our winter routine very good, I suppose every leader of a party has thought that, since he has the power of altering it. On the other hand, routine in this connection must take into consideration the facilities of work and play afforded by the preliminary preparations for the expedition. The winter occupations of most of our party depend on the instruments and implements, the clothing and sledging outfit, provided by forethought, and the routine is adapted to these occupations.

The busy winter routine of our party may therefore be excusably held as a subject for self-congratulation.

Friday 19 May Wind from the north in the morning, temperature comparatively high (about -6°). We played football during the noon hour – the game gets better as we improve our football condition and skill.

In the afternoon the wind came from the north, dying away again late at night.

In the evening Wright lectured on 'Ice Problems'. He had a difficult subject and was nervous. He is young and has never done original work; is only beginning to see the importance of his task.

He started on the crystallisation of ice, and explained with very good illustrations the various forms of crystals, the manner of their growth under different conditions and different temperatures. This was instructive. Passing to the freezing of salt water, he was not very clear. Then on to glaciers and their movements, theories for same and observations in these regions.

There was a good deal of disconnected information – silt bands, crevasses were mentioned. Finally he put the problems of larger aspect.

The upshot of the discussion was a decision to devote another evening to the larger problems such as the Great Ice Barrier and the interior ice sheet. I think I will write the paper to be discussed on this occasion.

I note with much satisfaction that the talks on ice problems and the interest shown in them has had the effect of making Wright devote the whole of his time to them. That may mean a great deal, for he is a hard and conscientious worker.

Atkinson has a new hole for his fish trap in 15 fathoms; yesterday morning he got a record catch of forty-three fish, but oddly enough yesterday evening there were only two caught.

Saturday 20 May Blowing hard from the south, with some snow and very cold. Few of us went far; Wilson and Bowers went to the top of the Ramp and found the wind there force 6 to 7, temperature -24°; as a consequence they got frostbitten. There was lively cheering when they reappeared in this condition, such is the sympathy which is here displayed for affliction; but with Wilson much of the amusement arises from his peculiarly scant headgear and the confessed jealousy of those of us who cannot face the weather with so little face protection.

The wind dropped at night.

Sunday 21 May Observed as usual. It blew from the north in the morning. Had an idea to go to Cape Royds this evening, but it was reported that the open water reached to the Barne Glacier, and last night my own observation seemed to confirm this.

This afternoon I started out for the open water. I found the ice solid off the Barne Glacier tongue, but always ahead of me a dark horizon as though I was within a very short distance of its edge. I held on with this appearance still holding up to C. Barne itself and then past that Cape and half way between it and C. Royds. This was far enough to make it evident that the ice was continuous to C. Royds, and has been so for a long time. Under these circumstances the continual appearance of open water to the north is most extraordinary and quite inexplicable.

Have had some very interesting discussions with Wilson, Wright, and Taylor on the ice formations to the west. How to account for the marine organisms found on the weathered glacier ice north of the Koettlitz Glacier? We have been elaborating a theory under which this ice had once a negative buoyancy due to the morainic material on top and in the lower layers of the ice mass, and had subsequently floated when the greater amount of this material had weathered out.

Have arranged to go to C. Royds tomorrow.

The temperatures have sunk very steadily this year; for a long time they hung about zero, then for a considerable interval remained about -10°; now they are down in the minus twenties, with signs of falling (today -24°).

Bowers' meteorological stations have been amusingly named Archibald, Bertram, Clarence – they are entered by the initial letter, but spoken of by full title.

Tonight we had a glorious auroral display – quite the most brilliant I have seen. At one time the sky from N.N.W. to S.S.E. as high as the zenith was massed with arches, band, and curtains, always in rapid movement. The waving curtains were especially fascinating – a wave of bright light would start at one end and run along to the other, or a patch of brighter light would spread as if to reinforce the failing light of the curtain.

AURORAL NOTES

The auroral light is of a palish green colour, but we now see distinctly a red flush preceding the motion of any bright part.

The green ghostly light seems suddenly to spring to life with rosy blushes. There is infinite suggestion in this phenomenon, and in that lies its charm;

the suggestion of life, form, colour and movement never less than evanescent, mysterious – no reality. It is the language of mystic signs and portents – the inspiration of the gods – wholly spiritual – divine signalling. Remindful of superstition, provocative of imagination. Might not the inhabitants of some other world (Mars) controlling mighty forces thus surround our globe with fiery symbols, a golden writing which we have not the key to decipher?

There is argument on the confession of Ponting's inability to obtain photographs of the aurora. Professor Störmer of Norway seems to have been successful. Simpson made notes of his method, which seems to depend merely on the rapidity of lens and plate. Ponting claims to have greater rapidity in both, yet gets no result even with long exposure. It is not only a question of aurora; the stars are equally reluctant to show themselves on Ponting's plate. Even with five seconds' exposure the stars become short lines of light on the plate of a fixed camera. Störmer's stars are points and therefore his exposure must have been short, yet there is detail in some of his pictures which it seems impossible could have been got with a short exposure. It is all very puzzling.

Monday 22 May Wilson, Bowers, Atkinson, Evans (P.O.), Clissold, and self went to C. Royds with a 'go cart' carrying our sleeping-bags, a cooker, and a small quantity of provision.

The 'go cart' consists of a framework of steel tubing supported on four bicycle wheels.

The surface of the floes carries 1 to 2 inches of snow, barely covering the salt ice flowers, and for this condition this vehicle of Day's is excellent. The advantage is that it meets the case where the salt crystals form a heavy frictional surface for wood runners. I'm inclined to think that there are great numbers of cases when wheels would be more efficient than runners on the sea-ice.

We reached Cape Royds in 2½ hours, killing an Emperor penguin in the bay beyond C. Barne. This bird was in splendid plumage, the breast reflecting the dim northern light like a mirror.

It was fairly dark when we stumbled over the rocks and dropped on to Shackleton's Hut. Clissold started the cooking-range, Wilson and I walked over to the Black Beach and round back by Blue Lake.

The temperature was down at -31° and the interior of the hut was very cold.

Tuesday 23 May We spent the morning mustering the stores within and without the hut, after a cold night which we passed very comfortably in our bags.

We found a good quantity of flour and Danish butter and a fair amount of paraffin, with smaller supplies of assorted articles – the whole sufficient to afford provision for such a party as ours for about six or eight months if well administered. In case of necessity this would undoubtedly be a very useful reserve to fall back upon. These stores are somewhat scattered, and the hut has a dilapidated, comfortless appearance due to its tenantless condition; but even so it seemed to me much less inviting than our old *Discovery* hut at C. Armitage.

After a cup of cocoa there was nothing to detain us, and we started back, the only useful articles added to our weights being a scrap or two of leather and *five hymn-books*. Hitherto we have been only able to muster seven copies; this increase will improve our Sunday Services.

Wednesday 24 May A quiet day with northerly wind; the temperature rose gradually to zero. Having the night duty, did not go out. The moon has gone and there is little to attract one out of doors.

Atkinson gave us an interesting little discourse on parasitology, with a brief account of the life history of some ecto- and some endo-parasites – Nematodes, Trematodes. He pointed out how that in nearly every case there was a secondary host, how in some cases disease was caused, and in others the presence of the parasite was even helpful. He acknowledged the small progress that had been made in this study. He mentioned ankylostomiasis, blood-sucking worms, Bilhartsia (Trematode) attacking bladder (Egypt), Filaria (round tapeworm), Guinea worm, Trichina (pork), and others, pointing to disease caused.

From worms he went to Protozoa-Trypanosomes, sleeping sickness, host tsetse-fly – showed life history comparatively, propagated in secondary host or encysting in primary host – similarly malarial germs spread by Anopheles mosquitoes – all very interesting.

In the discussion following Wilson gave some account of the grouse disease worm, and especially of the interest in finding free living species almost identical; also part of the life of disease worm is free living. Here we approached a point pressed by Nelson concerning the degeneration consequent on adoption of the parasitic habit. All parasites seem to have descended from free living beasts. One asks 'what is degeneration?' without receiving a very satisfactory answer. After all, such terms must be empirical.

Thursday 25 May It has been blowing from south with heavy gusts and snow, temperature extraordinarily high, -6°. This has been a heavy gale. The weather conditions are certainly very interesting; Simpson has again called attention to the wind in February, March, and April at Cape Evans – the record shows an extraordinary large percentage of gales. It is quite certain that we scarcely got a fraction of the wind on the Barrier and doubtful if we got as much at Hut Point.

Friday 26 May A calm and clear day – a nice change from recent weather. It makes an enormous difference to the enjoyment of this life if one is able to get out and stretch one's legs every day. This morning I went up the Ramp. No sign of open water, so that my fears for a broken highway in the coming season are now at rest. In future gales can only be a temporary annoyance – anxiety as to their result is finally allayed.

This afternoon I searched out ski and ski sticks and went for a short run over the floe. The surface is quite good since the recent snowfall and wind. This is satisfactory, as sledging can now be conducted on ordinary lines, and if convenient our parties can pull on ski. The young ice troubles of April and May have passed away. It is curious that circumstances caused us to miss them altogether during our stay in the *Discovery*.

We are living extraordinarily well. At dinner last night we had some excellent thick seal soup, very much like thick hare soup; this was followed by an equally tasty seal steak and kidney pie and a fruit jelly. The smell of frying greeted us on awaking this morning, and at breakfast each of us had two of our nutty little *Notothenia* fish after our bowl of porridge. These little fish have an extraordinarily sweet taste – bread and butter and marmalade finished the meal. At the midday meal we had bread and butter, cheese, and cake, and tonight I smell mutton in the preparation. Under the circumstances it would be difficult to conceive more appetising repasts or a regime which is likely to produce scorbutic symptoms. I cannot think we shall get scurvy.

Nelson lectured to us tonight, giving a very able little elementary sketch of the objects of the biologist. A fact struck one in his explanation of the rates of elimination. Two of the offspring of two parents alone survive, speaking broadly; this the same of the human species or the 'ling', with 24 million eggs in the roe of each female! He talked much of evolution, adaptation, etc. Mendelism became the most debated point of the discussion; the transmission of characters has a wonderful fascination for the human mind. There was also a point striking deep in the debate on Professor Loeb's experiments with sea urchins; how far had he succeeded in reproducing the species without the male spermatozoa? Not very far, it seemed, when all was said.

A theme for a pen would be the expansion of interest in polar affairs; compare the interests of a winter spent by the old Arctic voyagers with our own, and look into the causes. The aspect of everything changes as our knowledge expands.

The expansion of human interest in rude surroundings may perhaps best be illustrated by comparisons. It will serve to recall such a simple case as the fact that our ancestors applied the terms horrid, frightful, to mountain crags which in our own day are more justly admired as lofty, grand, and beautiful.

The poetic conception of this natural phenomenon has followed not so much an inherent change of sentiment as the intimacy of wider knowledge and the death of superstitious influence. One is much struck by the importance of realising limits.

Saturday 27 May A very unpleasant, cold, windy day. Annoyed with the conditions, so did not go out.

In the evening Bowers gave his lecture on sledging diets. He has shown great courage in undertaking the task, great perseverance in unearthing facts from books, and a considerable practical skill in stringing these together. It is a thankless task to search Polar literature for dietary facts and still more difficult to attach due weight to varying statements. Some authors omit discussion of this important item altogether, others fail to note alterations made in practice or additions afforded by circumstances, others again forget to describe the nature of various food stuffs.

Our lecturer was both entertaining and instructive when he dealt with old-time rations; but he naturally grew weak in approaching the physiological aspect of the question. He went through with it manfully and with a touch of humour much appreciated; whereas, for instance, he deduced facts from 'the equivalent of Mr. Joule, a gentleman whose statements he had no reason to doubt'.

Wilson was the mainstay of the subsequent discussion and put all doubtful matters in a clearer light. 'Increase your fats (carbohydrate)' is what science seems to say, and practice with conservativism is inclined to step cautiously in response to this urgency. I shall, of course, go into the whole question as thoroughly as available information and experience permits. Meanwhile it is useful to have had a discussion which aired the popular opinions.

Feeling went deepest on the subject of tea versus cocoa; admitting all that can be said concerning stimulation and reaction, I am inclined to see much in favour of tea. Why should not one be mildly stimulated during the marching hours if one can cope with reaction by profounder rest during the hours of inaction?

Sunday 28 May Quite an excitement last night. One of the ponies (the grey which I led last year and salved from the floe) either fell or tried to lie down in his stall, his head being lashed up to the stanchions on either side. In this condition he struggled and kicked till his body was twisted right round and his attitude extremely uncomfortable. Very luckily his struggles were heard almost at once, and his head ropes being cut, Oates got him on his feet again. He looked a good deal distressed at the time, but is now quite well again and has been out for his usual exercise.

Held Service as usual.

This afternoon went on ski around the bay and back across. Little or no wind; sky clear, temperature -25°. It was wonderfully mild considering the temperature – this sounds paradoxical, but the sensation of cold does not conform to the thermometer – it is obviously dependent on the wind and less obviously on the humidity of the air and the ice crystals floating in it. I cannot very clearly account for this effect, but as a matter of fact I have certainly felt colder in still air at -10° than I did today when the thermometer was down to -25°, other conditions apparently equal.

The amazing circumstance is that by no means can we measure the humidity, or indeed the precipitation or evaporation. I have just been discussing with Simpson the insuperable difficulties that stand in the way of experiment in this direction, since cold air can only hold the smallest quantities of moisture, and saturation covers an extremely small range of temperature.

Monday 29 May Another beautiful calm day. Went out both before and after the mid-day meal. This morning with Wilson and Bowers towards the thermometer off Inaccessible Island. On the way my companionable dog was heard barking and dimly seen – we went towards him and found that he was worrying a young sea leopard. This is the second found in the Strait this season. We had to secure it as a specimen, but it was sad to have to kill. The long lithe body of this seal makes it almost beautiful in comparison with our stout, bloated Weddells. This poor beast turned swiftly from side to side as we strove to stun it with a blow on the nose. As it turned it gaped its jaws wide, but oddly enough not a sound came forth, not even a hiss.

After lunch a sledge was taken out to secure the prize, which had been photographed by flashlight.

Ponting has been making great advances in flashlight work, and has opened up quite a new field in which artistic results can be obtained in the winter.

Lecture – Japan. Tonight Ponting gave us a charming lecture on Japan with wonderful illustrations of his own. He is happiest in his descriptions of the artistic side of the people, with which he is in fullest sympathy. So he took us to see the flower pageants. The joyful festivals of the cherry blossom, the wistaria, the iris and chrysanthemum, the sombre colours of the beech blossom and the paths about the lotus gardens, where mankind meditated in solemn mood. We had pictures, too, of Nikko and its beauties, of Temples and great Buddhas. Then in more touristy strain of volcanoes and their craters, waterfalls and river gorges, tiny tree-clad islets, that feature of Japan – baths and their bathers, Ainos, and so on. His descriptions were well given and we all of us thoroughly enjoyed our evening.

Tuesday 30 May Am busy with my physiological investigations [i.e. in relation to a sledging ration]. Atkinson reported a sea leopard at the tide crack; it proved to be a crab-eater, young and very active. In curious contrast to the sea leopard of yesterday in snapping round it uttered considerable noise, a gasping throaty growl.

Went out to the outer berg, where there was quite a collection of people, mostly in connection with Ponting, who had brought camera and flashlight.

It was beautifully calm and comparatively warm. It was good to hear the gay chatter and laughter, and see ponies and their leaders come up out of the gloom to add liveliness to the scene. The sky was extraordinarily clear at noon and to the north very bright.

We have had an exceptionally large tidal range during the last three days – it has upset the tide gauge arrangements and brought a little doubt on the method. Day is going into the question, which we thoroughly discussed today. Tidal measurements will be worse than useless unless we can be sure of the accuracy of our methods. Pools of salt water have formed over the beach floes in consequence of the high tide, and in the chase of the crab eater today very brilliant flashes of phosphorescent light appeared in these pools. We think it due to a small copepod. I have just found a reference to the same phenomena in Nordenskiöld's 'Vega'. He, and apparently Bellot before him, noted the phenomenon. An interesting instance of bi-polarity.

Another interesting phenomenon observed today was a cirrus cloud lit by sunlight. It was seen by Wilson and Bowers 5° above the northern horizon – the sun is 9° below our horizon, and without refraction we calculate a cloud could be seen which was 12 miles high. Allowing refraction the phenomenon appears very possible.

Wednesday 31 May The sky was overcast this morning and the temperature up to -13°. Went out after lunch to 'Land's End'. The surface of snow was sticky for ski, except where drifts were deep. There was an oppressive feel in the air and I got very hot, coming in with head and hands bare.

At 5, from dead calm the wind suddenly sprang up from the south, force 40 miles per hour, and since that it has been blowing a blizzard; wind very gusty, from 20 to 60 miles. I have never known a storm come on so suddenly, and it shows what possibility there is of individuals becoming lost even if they only go a short way from the hut.

Tonight Wilson has given us a very interesting lecture on sketching. He started by explaining his methods of rough sketch and written colour record, and explained its suitability to this climate as opposed to coloured chalks, etc. – a very practical method for cold fingers and one that becomes more accurate with practice in observation. His theme then became the extreme importance of accuracy, his mode of expression and explanation frankly Ruskinesque. Don't put in meaningless lines – every line should be from observation. So with contrast of light and shade – fine shading, subtle distinction, everything – impossible without care, patience, and trained attention.

He raised a smile by generalising failures in sketches of others of our party which had been brought to him for criticism. He pointed out how much had been put in from preconceived notion. 'He will draw a berg faithfully as it is now and he studies it, but he leaves sea and sky to be put in afterwards, as he thinks they must be like sea and sky everywhere else, and he is content to try and remember how these *should* be done.' Nature's harmonies cannot be guessed at.

He quoted much from Ruskin, leading on a little deeper to 'Composition', paying a hearty tribute to Ponting.

The lecture was delivered in the author's usual modest strain, but unconsciously it was expressive of himself and his whole-hearted thoroughness. He stands very high in the scale of human beings – how high I scarcely knew till the experience of the past few months.

There is no member of our party so universally esteemed; only tonight I realise how patiently and consistently he has given time and attention to help the efforts of the other sketchers, and so it is all through; he has had a hand in almost every lecture given, and has been consulted in almost every effort which has been made towards the solution of the practical or theoretical problems of our Polar world.

The achievement of a great result by patient work is the best possible object lesson for struggling humanity, for the results of genius, however admirable, can rarely be instructive. The chief of the Scientific Staff sets an example which is more potent than any other factor in maintaining that bond of good fellowship which is the marked and beneficent characteristic of our community.

11
TO MIDWINTER DAY:
1 JUNE 1911 – 22 JUNE 1911

Thursday 1 June The wind blew hard all night, gusts arising to 72 m.p.h.; the anemometer choked five times – temperature +9°. It is still blowing this morning. Incidentally we have found that these heavy winds react very conveniently on our ventilating system. A fire is always a good ventilator, ensuring the circulation of inside air and the indraught of fresh air; its defect as a ventilator lies in the low level at which it extracts inside air. Our ventilating system utilises the normal fire draught, but also by suitable holes in the funnelling causes the same draught to extract foul air at higher levels. I think this is the first time such a system has been used. It is a bold step to make holes in the funnelling as obviously any uncertainty of draught might fill the hut with smoke. Since this does not happen with us it follows that there is always strong suction through our stovepipes, and this is achieved by their exceptionally large dimensions and by the length of the outer chimney pipe.

With wind this draught is greatly increased and with high winds the draught would be too great for the stoves if it were not for the relief of the ventilating holes.

In these circumstances, therefore, the rate of extraction of air automatically rises, and since high wind is usually accompanied with marked rise of temperature, the rise occurs at the most convenient season, when the interior of the hut would otherwise tend to become oppressively warm. The practical result of the system is that in spite of the numbers of people living in the hut, the cooking, and the smoking, the inside air is nearly always warm, sweet, and fresh.

There is usually a drawback to the best of arrangements, and I have said 'nearly' always. The exceptions in this connection occur when the outside air is calm and warm and the galley fire, as in the early morning, needs to be worked up; it is necessary under these conditions to temporarily close the ventilating holes, and if at this time the cook is intent on preparing our breakfast with a frying-pan we are quickly made aware of his intentions. A combination of this sort is rare and lasts only for a very short time, for directly the fire is aglow the ventilator can be opened again and the relief is almost instantaneous.

This very satisfactory condition of inside air must be a highly important factor in the preservation of health.

I have today regularised the pony 'nicknames'; I must leave it to Drake to pull out the relation to the 'proper' names according to our school contracts! [Officially the ponies were named after the several schools which had subscribed for their purchase: but sailors are inveterate nicknamers, and the unofficial humour prevailed.[18]]

The nicknames are as follows:

James Pigg	Keohane
Bones	Crean
Michael	Clissold
Snatcher	Evans (P.O.)
Jehu	–
China	–
Christopher	Hooper
Victor	Bowers
Snippets (windsucker)	–
Nobby	Lashly

Friday 2 June The wind still high. The drift ceased at an early hour yesterday; it is difficult to account for the fact. At night the sky cleared; then and this morning we had a fair display of aurora streamers to the N. and a faint arch east. Curiously enough the temperature still remains high, about +7°.

The meteorological conditions are very puzzling.

Saturday 3 June The wind dropped last night, but at 4 a.m. suddenly sprang up from a dead calm to 30 miles an hour. Almost instantaneously, certainly within the space of one minute, there was a temperature rise of nine degrees. It is the most extraordinary and interesting example of a rise of temperature with a southerly wind that I can remember. It is certainly difficult to account for unless we imagine that during the calm the surface layer of cold air is extremely thin and that there is a steep inverted gradient. When the wind arose the sky overhead was clearer than I ever remember to have seen it, the constellations brilliant, and the Milky Way like a bright auroral streamer.

The wind has continued all day, making it unpleasant out of doors. I went for a walk over the land; it was dark, the rock very black, very little snow lying; old footprints in the soft, sandy soil were filled with snow, showing quite white on a black ground. Have been digging away at food statistics.

Simpson has just given us a discourse, in the ordinary lecture series, on his instruments. Having already described these instruments, there is little to comment upon; he is excellently lucid in his explanations.

As an analogy to the attempt to make a scientific observation when the condition under consideration is affected by the means employed, he rather quaintly cited the impossibility of discovering the length of trousers by bending over to see!

The following are the instruments described:

	Features
The outside (bimetallic) thermograph.	
The inside thermograph (alcohol)	Alcohol in spiral, small lead pipe – float vessel.
The electrically recording anemometer	Cam device with contact on wheel; slowing arrangement, inertia of wheel.
The Dynes anemometer	Parabola on immersed float.
The recording wind vane	Metallic pen.
The magnetometer	Horizontal force measured in two directions – vertical force in one – timing arrangement.
The high and low potential apparatus of the balloon thermograph	Spotting arrangement and difference, see *ante*.

Simpson is admirable as a worker, admirable as a scientist, and admirable as a lecturer.

Sunday 4 June A calm and beautiful day. The account of this, a typical Sunday, would run as follows: Breakfast. A half-hour or so selecting hymns and preparing for Service whilst the hut is being cleared up. The Service: a hymn; Morning Prayer to the Psalms; another hymn; prayers from Communion Service and Litany; a final hymn and our special prayer. Wilson strikes the note on which the hymn is to start and I try to hit it after with doubtful success! After church the men go out with their ponies.

Today Wilson, Bowers, Cherry-Garrard, Lashly, and I went to start the building of our first 'igloo'. There is a good deal of difference of opinion as to the best implement with which to cut snow blocks. Cherry-Garrard had a knife which I designed and Lashly made, Wilson a saw, and Bowers a large trowel. I'm inclined to think the knife will prove most effective, but the others don't acknowledge it *yet*. As far as one can see at present this knife should have a longer handle and much coarser teeth in the saw edge – perhaps also the blade should be thinner.

We must go on with this hut building till we get good at it. I'm sure it's going to be a useful art.

We only did three courses of blocks when tea-time arrived, and light was not good enough to proceed after tea.

Sunday afternoon for the men means a 'stretch of the land'.

I went over the floe on ski. The best possible surface after the late winds as far as Inaccessible Island. Here, and doubtless in most places along the shore, this, the first week of June, may be noted as the date by which the wet, sticky salt crystals become covered and the surface possible for wood runners. Beyond the island the snow is still very thin, barely covering the ice flowers, and the surface is still bad.

There has been quite a small landslide on the S. side of the Island; seven or eight blocks of rock, one or two tons in weight, have dropped on to the floe, an interesting instance of the possibility of transport by sea-ice.

Ponting has been out to the bergs photographing by flashlight. As I passed south of the Island with its whole mass between myself and the photographer I saw the flashes of magnesium light, having all the appearance of lightning. The light illuminated the sky and apparently objects at a great distance from the camera. It is evident that there may be very great possibilities in the use of this light for signalling purposes and I propose to have some experiments.

N.B. – Magnesium flashlight as signalling apparatus in the summer.

Another crab-eater seal was secured today; he had come up by the bergs.

Monday 5 June The wind has been S. all day, sky overcast and air misty with snow crystals. The temperature has gone steadily up and tonight rose to +16°. Everything seems to threaten a blizzard which cometh not. But what is to be made of this extraordinary high temperature heaven only knows. Went for a walk over the rocks and found it very warm and muggy.

Taylor gave us a paper on the Beardmore Glacier. He has taken pains to work up available information; on the ice side he showed the very gradual gradient as compared with the Ferrar. If crevasses are as plentiful as reported, the motion of glacier must be very considerable. There seem to be three badly crevassed parts where the glacier is constricted and the fall is heavier.

Geologically he explained the rocks found and the problems unsolved. The basement rocks, as to the north, appear to be reddish and grey granites and altered slate (possibly bearing fossils). The Cloudmaker appears to be diorite; Mt. Buckley sedimentary. The suggested formation is of several layers of coal with sandstone above and below; interesting to find if it is so and investigate coal. Wood fossil conifer appears to have come from this – better to get leaves – wrap fossils up for protection.

Mt. Dawson described as pinkish limestone, with a wedge of dark rock; this very doubtful! Limestone is of great interest owing to chance of finding Cambrian fossils (Archeocyathus).

He mentioned the interest of finding here, as in Dry Valley, volcanic cones of recent date (later than the recession of the ice). As points to be looked to in Geology and Physiography:

1. Hope Island shape.
2. Character of wall facets.
3. Type of tributary glaciers – cliff or curtain, broken.
4. Do tributaries enter 'at grade'?
5. Lateral gullies pinnacled, etc., shape and size of slope.
6. Do tributaries cut out gullies – empty unoccupied cirques, hangers, etc.
7. Do upland moraines show tesselation?
8. Arrangement of strata, inclusion of.
9. Types of moraines, distance of blocks.
10. Weathering of glaciers. Types of surface. (Thrust mark? Rippled, snow stool, glass house, coral reef, honeycomb, ploughshare, bastions, piecrust.)
11. Amount of water silt bands, stratified, or irregular folded or broken.

12. Cross section, of valleys 35° slopes?

13. Weather slopes debris covered, height to which.

14. Nunataks, height of rounded, height of any angle in profile, erratics.

15. Evidence of order in glacier delta.

Debenham in discussion mentioned usefulness of small chips of rock – many chips from several places are more valuable than few larger specimens.

We had an interesting little discussion.

I must enter a protest against the use made of the word 'glaciated' by Geologists and Physiographers.

To them a 'glaciated land' is one which appears to have been shaped by former ice action.

The meaning I attach to the phrase, and one which I believe is more commonly current, is that it describes a land at present wholly or partly covered with ice and snow.

I hold the latter is the obvious meaning and the former results from a piracy committed in very recent times.

The alternative terms descriptive of the different meanings are ice covered and ice eroded.

Today I have been helping the Soldier to design pony rugs; the great thing, I think, is to get something which will completely cover the hindquarters.

Tuesday 6 June The temperature has been as high as +19° today; the south wind persisted until the evening with clear sky except for fine effects of torn cloud round about the mountain. Tonight the moon has emerged from behind the mountain and sails across the cloudless northern sky; the wind has fallen and the scene is glorious.

It is my birthday, a fact I might easily have forgotten, but my kind people did not. At lunch an immense birthday cake made its appearance and we were photographed assembled about it. Clissold had decorated its sugared top with various devices in chocolate and crystallised fruit, flags and photographs of myself.

After my walk I discovered that great preparations were in progress for a special dinner, and when the hour for that meal arrived we sat down to a sumptuous spread with our sledge banners hung about us. Clissold's especially excellent seal soup, roast mutton and red currant jelly, fruit salad, asparagus and chocolate – such was our menu. For drink we had cider cup, a mystery not yet fathomed, some sherry and a liqueur.

After this luxurious meal everyone was very festive and amiably argumentative. As I write there is a group in the dark room discussing political progress with large discussions – another at one corner of the dinner table airing its views on the origin of matter and the probability of its ultimate discovery, and yet another debating military problems. The scraps that reach me from the various groups sometimes piece together in ludicrous fashion. Perhaps these arguments are practically unprofitable, but they give a great deal of pleasure to the participants. It's delightful to hear the ring of triumph in some voice when the owner imagines he has delivered himself of a well-rounded period or a clinching statement concerning the point under discussion. They are boys, all of them, but such excellent good-natured ones; there has been no sign of sharpness or anger, no jarring note, in all these wordy contests; all end with a laugh.

Nelson has offered Taylor a pair of socks to teach him some geology! This lulls me to sleep!

Wednesday 7 June A very beautiful day. In the afternoon went well out over the floe to the south, looking up Nelson at his icehole and picking up Bowers at his thermometer. The surface was polished and beautifully smooth for ski, the scene brightly illuminated with moonlight, the air still and crisp, and the thermometer at -10°. Perfect conditions for a winter walk.

In the evening I read a paper on 'The Ice Barrier and Inland Ice'. I have strung together a good many new points and the interest taken in the discussion was very genuine – so keen, in fact, that we did not break up till close on midnight. I am keeping this paper, which makes a very good basis for all future work on these subjects.

SHELTERS TO ICEHOLES

Time out of number one is coming across rediscoveries. Of such a nature is the building of shelters for iceholes.

We knew a good deal about it in the *Discovery*, but unfortunately did not make notes of our experiences. I sketched the figures (below and on next page) for Nelson, and found on going to the hole that the drift accorded with my sketch. The sketches explain themselves. I think wall 'b' should be higher than wall 'a'.

My night on duty. The silent hours passed rapidly and comfortably. To bed 7 a.m.

Thursday 8 June Did not turn out till 1 p.m., then with a bad head, an inevitable sequel to a night of vigil. Walked out to and around the bergs, bright moonlight, but clouds rapidly spreading up from south.

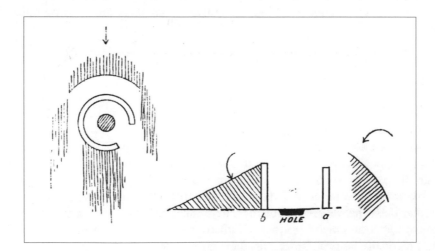

Tried the snow knife, which is developing. Debenham and Gran went off to Hut Point this morning; they should return tomorrow.

Friday 9 June No wind came with the clouds of yesterday, but the sky has not been clear since they spread over it except for about two hours in the middle of the night when the moonlight was so bright that one might have imagined the day returned.

Otherwise the web of stratus which hangs over us thickens and thins, rises and falls with very bewildering uncertainty. We want theories for these mysterious weather conditions; meanwhile it is annoying to lose the advantages of the moonlight.

This morning had some discussion with Nelson and Wright regarding the action of sea water in melting barrier and sea-ice. The discussion was useful to me in drawing attention to the equilibrium of layers of sea water.

In the afternoon I went round the Razor Back Islands on ski, a run of 5 or 6 miles; the surface was good but in places still irregular with the pressures formed when the ice was 'young'.

The snow is astonishingly soft on the south side of both islands. It is clear that in the heaviest blizzard one could escape the wind altogether by camping to windward of the larger island. One sees more and more clearly what shelter is afforded on the weather side of steep-sided objects.

Passed three seals asleep on the ice. Two others were killed near the bergs.

Saturday 10 June The impending blizzard has come; the wind came with a burst at 9.30 this morning.

Simpson spent the night turning over a theory to account for the phenomenon, and delivered himself of it this morning. It seems a good basis for the reference of future observations. He imagines the atmosphere A C in potential equilibrium with large margin of stability, i.e. the difference of temperature between A and C being much less than the adiabatic gradient.

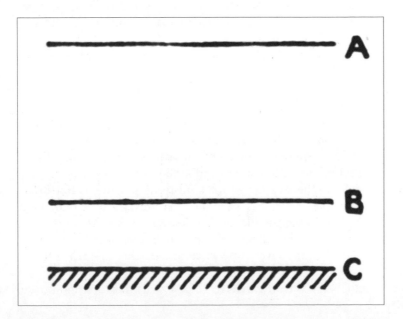

In this condition there is a tendency to cool by radiation until some critical layer, B, reaches its due point. A stratus cloud is thus formed at B; from this moment A B continues to cool, but B C is protected from radiating, whilst heated by radiation from snow and possibly by release of latent heat due to cloud formation.

The condition now rapidly approaches unstable equilibrium, B C tending to rise, A B to descend.

Owing to lack of sun heat the effect will be more rapid in south than north and therefore the upset will commence first in the south. After the first start the upset will rapidly spread north, bringing the blizzard. The facts supporting the theory are the actual formation of a stratus cloud before a blizzard, the snow and warm temperature of the blizzard and its gusty nature.

It is a pretty starting-point, but, of course, there are weak spots.

Atkinson has found a trypanosome in the fish – it has been stained, photographed and drawn – an interesting discovery having regard to the few species that have been found. A trypanosome is the cause of 'sleeping sickness'.

The blizzard has continued all day with a good deal of drift. I went for a walk, but the conditions were not inviting.

We have begun to consider details of next season's travelling equipment. The crampons, repair of finnesko with sealskin, and an idea for a double tent have been discussed today. P.O. Evans and Lashly are delightfully intelligent in carrying out instructions.

Sunday 11 June A fine clear morning, the moon now revolving well aloft and with full face. For exercise a run on ski to the South Bay in the morning and a dash up the Ramp before dinner. Wind and drift arose in the middle of the day, but it is now nearly calm again.

At our morning service Cherry-Garrard, good fellow, vamped the accompaniment of two hymns; he received encouraging thanks and will cope with all three hymns next Sunday.

Day by day news grows scant in this midwinter season; all events seem to compress into a small record, yet a little reflection shows that this is not the case. For instance, I have had at least three important discussions on weather and ice conditions today, concerning which many notes might be made, and quite a number of small arrangements have been made.

If a diary can be so inadequate here, how difficult must be the task of making a faithful record of a day's events in ordinary civilised life! I think this is why I have found it so difficult to keep a diary at home.

Monday 12 June The weather is not kind to us. There has not been much wind today, but the moon has been hid behind stratus cloud. One feels horribly cheated in losing the pleasure of its light. I scarcely know what the Crozier party can do if they don't get better luck next month.

Debenham and Gran have not yet returned; this is their fifth day of absence.

Bowers and Cherry-Garrard went to Cape Royds this afternoon to stay the night. Taylor and Wright walked there and back after breakfast this morning. They returned shortly after lunch.

Went for a short spin on ski this morning and again this afternoon. This evening Evans has given us a lecture on surveying. He was shy and slow, but very painstaking, taking a deal of trouble in preparing pictures, etc.

I took the opportunity to note hurriedly the few points to which I want attention especially directed. No doubt others will occur to me presently. I think I now understand very well how and why the old surveyors (like Belcher) failed in the early Arctic work.

1. Every officer who takes part in the Southern Journey ought to have in his memory the approximate variation of the compass at various stages of the journey and to know how to apply it to obtain a true course from the compass. The variation changes very slowly so that no great effort of memory is required.

2. He ought to know what the true course is to reach one depot from another.

3. He should be able to take an observation with the theodolite.

4. He should be able to work out a meridian altitude observation.

5. He could advantageously add to his knowledge the ability to work out a longitude observation or an ex-meridian altitude.

6. He should know how to read the sledgemeter.

7. He should note and remember the error of the watch he carries and the rate which is ascertained for it from time to time.

8. He should assist the surveyor by noting the coincidences of objects, the opening out of valleys, the observation of new peaks, etc.[19]

Tuesday 13 June A very beautiful day. We revelled in the calm clear moonlight; the temperature has fallen to -26°. The surface of the floe perfect for ski – had a run to South Bay in forenoon and was away on a long circuit around Inaccessible Island in the afternoon. In such weather the cold splendour of the scene is beyond description; everything is satisfying, from the deep purple of the starry sky to the gleaming bergs and the sparkle of the crystals under foot.

Some very brilliant patches of aurora over the southern shoulder of the mountain. Observed an exceedingly bright meteor shoot across the sky to the northward.

On my return found Debenham and Gran back from Cape Armitage. They had intended to start back on Sunday, but were prevented by bad weather; they seemed to have had stronger winds than we.

On arrival at the hut they found poor little 'Mukaka' coiled up outside the door, looking pitifully thin and weak, but with enough energy to bark at them.

This dog was run over and dragged for a long way under the sledge runners whilst we were landing stores in January (the 7th). He has never been worth much since, but remained lively in spite of all the hardships of sledging work. At Hut Point he looked a miserable object, as the hair refused to grow on his hindquarters. It seemed as though he could scarcely continue in such a condition, and when the party came back to Cape Evans he was allowed to run free alongside the sledge.

On the arrival of the party I especially asked after the little animal and was told by Demetri that he had returned, but later it transpired that this was a mistake – that he had been missed on the journey and had not turned up again later as was supposed.

I learned this fact only a few days ago and had quite given up the hope of ever seeing the poor little beast again. It is extraordinary to realise that this poor, lame, half-clad animal has lived for a whole month by himself. He had blood on his mouth when found, implying the capture of a seal, but how he managed to kill it and then get through its skin is beyond comprehension. Hunger drives hard.

Wednesday 14 June Storms are giving us little rest. We found a thin stratus over the sky this morning, foreboding ill. The wind came, as usual with a rush, just after lunch. At first there was much drift – now the drift has gone but the gusts run up to 65 m.p.h.

Had a comfortless stroll around the hut; how rapidly things change when one thinks of the delights of yesterday! Paid a visit to Wright's ice cave; the pendulum is installed and will soon be ready for observation. Wright anticipates the possibility of difficulty with ice crystals on the agate planes.

He tells me that he has seen some remarkably interesting examples of the growth of ice crystals on the walls of the cave and has observed the same unaccountable confusion of the size of grains in the ice, showing how little history can be gathered from the structure of ice.

This evening Nelson gave us his second biological lecture, starting with a brief reference to the scientific classification of the organism into Kingdom, Phylum, Group, Class, Order, Genus, Species; he stated the justification of a biologist in such an expedition, as being 'To determine the condition under which organic substances exist in the sea.'

He proceeded to draw divisions between the bottom organisms without power of motion, benthon, the nekton motile life in mid-water, and the plankton or floating life. Then he led very prettily on to the importance of the tiny vegetable organisms as the basis of all life.

In the killer whale may be found a seal, in the seal a fish, in the fish a smaller fish, in the smaller fish a copepod, and in the copepod a diatom. If this be regular feeding throughout, the diatom or vegetable is essentially the base of all.

Light is the essential of vegetable growth or metabolism, and light quickly vanishes in depth of water, so that all ocean life must ultimately depend on the phyto-plankton. To discover the conditions of this life is therefore to go to the root of matters.

At this point came an interlude – descriptive of the various biological implements in use in the ship and on shore. The otter trawl, the Agassiz trawl, the 'D' net, and the ordinary dredger.

A word or two on the using of 'D' nets and then explanation of sieves for classifying the bottom, its nature causing variation in the organisms living on it.

From this he took us amongst the tow-nets with their beautiful silk fabrics, meshes running 180 to the inch and materials costing 2 guineas the yard – to the German tow-nets for quantitative measurements, the object of the latter and its doubtful accuracy, young fish trawls.

From this to the chemical composition of sea water, the total salt about 3.5 per cent, but variable: the proportions of the various salts do not appear to differ, thus the chlorine test detects the salinity quantitatively. Physically plankton life must depend on this salinity and also on temperature, pressure, light, and movement. (If plankton only inhabits surface waters, then density, temperatures, etc., of surface waters must be the important factors. Why should biologists strive for deeper layers? Why should not deep sea life be maintained by dead vegetable matter?)

Here again the lecturer branched off into descriptions of water bottles, deep sea thermometers, and current-meters, the which I think have already received some notice in this diary. To what depth light may extend is the difficult problem and we had some speculation, especially in the debate on this question. Simpson suggested that laboratory experiment should easily determine. Atkinson suggested growth of bacteria on a scratched plate. The idea seems to be that vegetable life cannot exist without red rays, which probably do not extend beyond 7 feet or so. Against this is an extraordinary recovery of *Holosphera Viridis* by German expedition from 2000 fathoms; this seems to have been confirmed. Bowers caused much amusement by demanding to know 'If the pycnogs (pycnogonids) were more nearly related to the arachnids (spiders) or crustaceans.' As a matter of fact a very sensible question, but it caused amusement because of its sudden display of long names. Nelson is an exceedingly capable lecturer; he makes his subject very clear and is never too technical.

Thursday 15 June Keen cold wind overcast sky till 5.30 p.m. Spent an idle day.

Jimmy Pigg had an attack of colic in the stable this afternoon. He was taken out and doctored on the floe, which seemed to improve matters, but on return to the stable he was off his feed.

This evening the Soldier tells me he has eaten his food, so I hope all be well again.

Friday 16 June Overcast again – little wind but also little moonlight. Jimmy Pigg quite recovered.

Went round the bergs in the afternoon. A great deal of ice has fallen from the irregular ones, showing that a great deal of weathering of bergs goes on during the winter and hence that the life of a berg is very limited, even if it remains in the high latitudes.

Tonight Debenham lectured on volcanoes. His matter is very good, but his voice a little monotonous, so that there were signs of slumber in the audience, but all woke up for a warm and amusing discussion succeeding the lecture.

The lecturer first showed a world chart showing distribution of volcanoes, showing general tendency of eruptive explosions to occur in lines. After following these lines in other parts of the world he showed difficulty of finding symmetrical linear distribution near McMurdo Sound. He pointed out incidentally the important inference which could be drawn from the discovery of altered sandstones in the Erebus region. He went to the shapes of volcanoes:

The massive type formed by very fluid lavas – Mauna Loa (Hawaii), Vesuvius, examples.

The more perfect cones formed by ash talus – Fujiama, Discovery.

The explosive type with parasitic cones – Erebus, Morning, Etna.

Fissure eruption – historic only in Iceland, but best prehistoric examples Deccan (India) and Oregon (U.S.).

There is small ground for supposing relation between adjacent volcanoes – activity in one is rarely accompanied by activity in the other. It seems most likely that vent tubes are entirely separate.

Products of volcanoes The lecturer mentioned the escape of quantities of free hydrogen – there was some discussion on this point afterwards; that water is broken up is easily understood, but what becomes of the oxygen? Simpson suggests the presence of much oxidizable material.

CO_2 as a noxious gas also mentioned and discussed – causes mythical 'upas' tree – sulphurous fumes attend final stages.

Practically little or no heat escapes through sides of a volcano.

There was argument over physical conditions influencing explosions – especially as to barometric influence. There was a good deal of disjointed information on lavas, ropy or rapid flowing and viscous – also on spatter cones and caverns.

In all cases lavas cool slowly – heat has been found close to the surface after 87 years. On Etna there is lava over ice. The lecturer finally reviewed the volcanicity of our own neighbourhood. He described various vents of Erebus, thinks Castle Rock a 'plug' – here some discussion – Observation Hill part of old volcano, nothing in common with Crater Hill. Inaccessible Island seems to have no connection with Erebus.

Finally we had a few words on the origin of volcanicity and afterwards some discussion on an old point – the relation to the sea. Why are volcanoes close to sea? Debenham thinks not cause and effect, but two effects resulting from same cause.

Great argument as to whether effect of barometric changes on Erebus vapour can be observed. Not much was said about the theory of volcanoes, but Debenham touched on American theories – the melting out from internal magma.

There was nothing much to catch hold of throughout, but discussion of such a subject sorts one's ideas.

Saturday 17 June Northerly wind, temperature changeable, dropping to -16°.

Wind doubtful in the afternoon. Moon still obscured – it is very trying. Feeling dull in spirit today.

Sunday 18 June Another blizzard – the weather is distressing. It ought to settle down soon, but unfortunately the moon is passing.

Held the usual Morning Service. Hymns not quite successful today.

Tonight Atkinson has taken the usual monthly measurement. I don't think there has been much change.

Monday 19 June A pleasant change to find the air calm and the sky clear – temperature down to -28°. At 1.30 the moon vanished behind the western mountains, after which, in spite of the clear sky, it was very dark on the floe. Went out on ski across the bay, then round about the cape, and so home, facing a keen northerly wind on return.

Atkinson is making a new fish trap hole; from one cause and another, the breaking of the trap, and the freezing of the hole, no catch has been made for some time. I don't think we shall get good catches during the dark season, but Atkinson's own requirements are small, and the fish, though nice enough, are not such a luxury as to be greatly missed from our 'menu'.

Our daily routine has possessed a settled regularity for a long time. Clissold is up about 7 a.m. to start the breakfast. At 7.30 Hooper starts sweeping the floor and setting the table. Between 8 and 8.30 the men are out and about, fetching ice for melting, etc. Anton is off to feed the ponies, Demetri to see the dogs; Hooper bursts on the slumberers with repeated announcements of the time, usually a quarter of an hour ahead of the clock. There is a stretching of limbs and an interchange of morning greetings, garnished with sleepy humour. Wilson and Bowers meet in a state of nature beside a washing basin filled with snow and proceed to rub glistening limbs with this chilling substance. A little later with less hardihood some others may be seen making the most of a meagre allowance of water. Soon after 8.30 I manage to drag myself from a very comfortable bed and make my toilet with a bare pint of water. By about ten minutes to 9 my clothes are on, my bed is made, and I sit down to my bowl of porridge; most of the others are gathered about the table by this time, but there are a few laggards who run the nine o'clock rule very close. The rule is instituted to prevent delay in the day's work, and it has needed a little pressure to keep one or two up to its observance. By 9.20 breakfast is finished, and before the half-hour has struck the table has been cleared. From 9.30 to 1.30 the men are steadily employed on a programme of preparation for sledging, which seems likely to occupy the greater part of the winter. The repair of sleeping-bags and the alteration of tents have already been done, but there are many other tasks uncompleted or not yet begun, such as the manufacture of provision bags, crampons, sealskin soles, pony clothes, etc.

Hooper has another good sweep up the hut after breakfast, washes the mess traps, and generally tidies things. I think it a good thing that in these matters the officers need not wait on themselves; it gives long unbroken days of scientific work and must, therefore, be an economy of brain in the long run.

We meet for our mid-day meal at 1.30 or 1.45, and spend a very cheerful half-hour over it. Afterwards the ponies are exercised, weather permitting; this employs all the men and a few of the officers for an hour or more – the rest of us generally take exercise in some form at the same time. After this the officers go on steadily with their work, whilst the men do odd jobs to while away the time. The evening meal, our dinner, comes at 6.30, and is finished within the hour. Afterwards people read, write, or play games, or occasionally finish some piece of work. The gramophone is usually started by some kindly disposed person, and on three nights of the week the lectures to which I have referred are given. These lectures still command full audiences and lively discussions.

At 11 p.m. the acetylene lights are put out, and those who wish to remain up or to read in bed must depend on candle-light. The majority of candles are extinguished by midnight, and the night watchman alone remains awake to keep his vigil by the light of an oil lamp.

Day after day passes in this fashion. It is not a very active life perhaps, but certainly not an idle one. Few of us sleep more than eight hours out of the twenty-four.

On Saturday afternoon or Sunday morning some extra bathing takes place; chins are shaven, and perhaps clean garments donned. Such signs, with the regular Service on Sunday, mark the passage of the weeks.

Tonight Day has given us a lecture on his motor sledge. He seems very hopeful of success, but I fear is rather more sanguine in temperament than his sledge is reliable in action. I wish I could have more confidence in his preparations, as he is certainly a delightful companion.

Tuesday 20 June Last night the temperature fell to -36°, the lowest we have had this year. On the Ramp the minimum was -31°, not the first indication of a reversed temperature gradient. We have had a calm day, as is usual with a low thermometer.

It was very beautiful out of doors this morning; as the crescent moon was sinking in the west, Erebus showed a heavy vapour cloud, showing that the quantity is affected by temperature rather than pressure.

I'm glad to have had a good run on ski.

The Cape Crozier party are preparing for departure, and heads have been put together to provide as much comfort as the strenuous circumstances will permit. I came across a hint as to the value of a double tent in Sverdrup's book, 'New Land', and (P.O.) Evans has made a lining for one of the tents; it is secured on the inner side of the poles and provides an air space inside the tent. I think it is going to be a great success, and that it will go far to obviate the necessity of considering the question of snow huts – though we shall continue our efforts in this direction also.

Another new departure is the decision to carry eiderdown sleeping-bags inside the reindeer ones.

With such an arrangement the early part of the journey is bound to be comfortable, but when the bags get iced difficulties are pretty certain to arise.

Day has been devoting his energies to the creation of a blubber stove, much assisted of course by the experience gained at Hut Point.

The blubber is placed in an annular vessel, A. The oil from it passes through a pipe, B, and spreads out on the surface of a plate, C, with a containing flange; *d d* are raised points which serve as heat conductors; *e e* is a tin chimney for flame with air holes at its base.

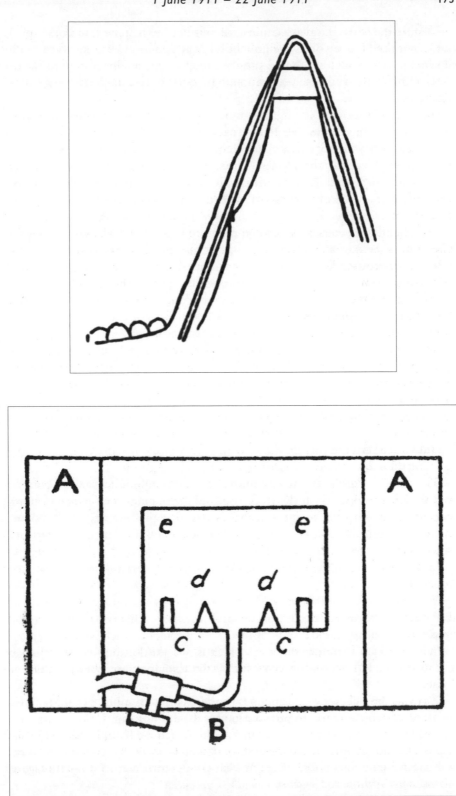

To start the stove the plate C must be warmed with spirit lamp or primus, but when the blubber oil is well alight its heat is quite sufficient to melt the blubber in A and keep up the oil supply – the heat gradually rises until the oil issues from B in a vaporised condition, when, of course, the heat given off by the stove is intense.

This stove was got going this morning in five minutes in the outer temperature with the blubber hard frozen. It will make a great difference to the Crozier Party if they can manage to build a hut, and the experience gained will be everything for the Western Party in the summer. With a satisfactory blubber stove it would never be necessary to carry fuel on a coast journey, and we shall deserve well of posterity if we can perfect one.

The Crozier journey is to be made to serve a good many trial ends. As I have already mentioned, each man is to go on a different food scale, with a view to determining the desirable proportion of fats and carbohydrates. Wilson is also to try the effect of a double wind-proof suit instead of extra woollen clothing.

If two suits of wind-proof will keep one as warm in the spring as a single suit does in the summer, it is evident that we can face the summit of Victoria Land with a very slight increase of weight.

I think the new crampons, which will also be tried on this journey, are going to be a great success. We have returned to the last *Discovery* type with improvements; the magnalium sole plates of our own crampons are retained but shod with ½-inch steel spikes; these plates are riveted through canvas to an inner leather sole, and the canvas is brought up on all sides to form a covering to the 'finnesko' over which it is laced – they are less than half the weight of an ordinary ski boot, go on very easily, and secure very neatly.

Midwinter Day, the turn of the season, is very close; it will be good to have light for the more active preparations for the coming year.

Wednesday 21 June The temperature low again, falling to -36°. A curious hazy look in the sky, very little wind. The cold is bringing some minor troubles with the clockwork instruments in the open and with the acetylene gas plant – no insuperable difficulties. Went for a ski run round the bergs; found it very dark and uninteresting.

The temperature remained low during night and Taylor reported a very fine display of Aurora.

Thursday 22 June, Midwinter The sun reached its maximum depression at about 2.30 p.m. on the 22nd, Greenwich Mean Time: this is 2.30 a.m. on the 23rd according to the local time of the 180th meridian which we are keeping. Dinner tonight is therefore the meal which is nearest the sun's critical change of course, and has been observed with all the festivity customary at Xmas at home.

At tea we broached an enormous Buzzard cake, with much gratitude to its provider, Cherry-Garrard. In preparation for the evening our 'Union Jacks' and sledge flags were hung about the large table, which itself was laid with glass and a plentiful supply of champagne bottles instead of the customary mugs and enamel lime-juice jugs. At seven o'clock we sat down to an extravagant bill of fare as compared with our usual simple diet.

Beginning on seal soup, by common consent the best decoction that our cook produces, we went on to roast beef with Yorkshire pudding, fried potatoes and Brussels sprouts. Then followed a flaming plum-pudding and excellent mince pies, and thereafter a dainty savoury of anchovy and cod's roe. A wondrous attractive meal even in so far as judged by our simple lights, but with its garnishments a positive feast, for withal the table was strewn with dishes of burnt almonds, crystallised fruits, chocolates and such toothsome kickshaws, whilst the unstinted supply of champagne which accompanied the courses was succeeded by a noble array of liqueur bottles from which choice could be made in the drinking of toasts.

I screwed myself up to a little speech which drew attention to the nature of the celebration as a half-way mark not only in our winter but in the plans of the Expedition as originally published. (I fear there are some who don't realise how rapidly time passes and who have barely begun work which by this time ought to be in full swing.)

We had come through a summer season and half a winter, and had before us half a winter and a second summer. We ought to know how we stood in every respect; we did know how we stood in regard to stores and transport, and I especially thanked the officer in charge of stores and the custodians of the animals. I said that as regards the future, chance must play a part, but that experience showed me that it would have been impossible to have chosen people more fitted to support me in the enterprise to the South than those who were to start in that direction in the spring. I thanked them all for having put their shoulders to the wheel and given me this confidence.

We drank to the Success of the Expedition.

Then everyone was called on to speak, starting on my left and working round the table; the result was very characteristic of the various individuals – one seemed to know so well the style of utterance to which each would commit himself.

Needless to say, all were entirely modest and brief; unexpectedly, all had exceedingly kind things to say of me – in fact I was obliged to request the omission of compliments at an early stage. Nevertheless it was gratifying to have a really genuine recognition of my attitude towards the scientific workers of the Expedition, and I felt very warmly towards all these kind, good fellows for expressing it.

If good will and happy fellowship count towards success, very surely shall we deserve to succeed. It was matter for comment, much applauded, that there had not been a single disagreement between any two members of our party from the beginning. By the end of dinner a very cheerful spirit prevailed, and the room was cleared for Ponting and his lantern, whilst the gramophone gave forth its most lively airs.

When the table was upended, its legs removed, and chairs arranged in rows, we had quite a roomy lecture hall. Ponting had cleverly chosen this opportunity to display a series of slides made from his own local negatives. I have never so fully realised his work as on seeing these beautiful pictures; they so easily outclass anything of their kind previously taken in these regions. Our audience cheered vociferously.

After this show the table was restored for snapdragon, and a brew of milk punch was prepared in which we drank the health of Campbell's party and of our good friends in the *Terra Nova*. Then the table was again removed and a set of lancers formed.

By this time the effect of stimulating liquid refreshment on men so long accustomed to a simple life became apparent. Our biologist had retired to bed, the silent Soldier bubbled with humour and insisted on dancing with Anton. Evans, P.O., was imparting confidences in heavy whispers. 'Pat' Keohane had grown intensely Irish and desirous of political argument, whilst Clissold sat with a constant expansive smile and punctuated the babble of conversation with an occasional 'Whoop' of delight or disjointed witticism. Other bright-eyed individuals merely reached the capacity to enjoy that which under ordinary circumstances might have passed without evoking a smile.

In the midst of the revelry Bowers suddenly appeared, followed by some satellites bearing an enormous Christmas Tree whose branches bore flaming candles, gaudy crackers, and little presents for all. The presents, I learnt, had been prepared with kindly thought by Miss Souper (Mrs. Wilson's sister) and the tree had been made by Bowers of pieces of stick and string with coloured paper to clothe its branches; the whole erection was remarkably creditable and the distribution of the presents caused much amusement.

Whilst revelry was the order of the day within our hut, the elements without seemed desirous of celebrating the occasion with equal emphasis and greater decorum. The eastern sky was massed with swaying auroral light, the most vivid and beautiful display that I had ever seen – fold on fold the arches and curtains of vibrating luminosity rose and spread across the sky, to slowly fade and yet again spring to glowing life.

The brighter light seemed to flow, now to mass itself in wreathing folds in one quarter, from which lustrous streamers shot upward, and anon to run in waves through the system of some dimmer figure as if to infuse new life within it.

It is impossible to witness such a beautiful phenomenon without a sense of awe, and yet this sentiment is not inspired by its brilliancy but rather by its delicacy in light and colour, its transparency, and above all by its tremulous evanescence of form. There is no glittering splendour to dazzle the eye, as has been too often described; rather the appeal is to the imagination by the suggestion of something wholly spiritual, something instinct with a fluttering ethereal life, serenely confident yet restlessly mobile.

One wonders why history does not tell us of 'aurora' worshippers, so easily could the phenomenon be considered the manifestation of 'god' or 'demon'. To the little silent group which stood at gaze before such enchantment it seemed profane to return to the mental and physical atmosphere of our house. Finally when I stepped within, I was glad to find that there had been a general movement bedwards, and in the next half-hour the last of the roysterers had succumbed to slumber.

Thus, except for a few bad heads in the morning, ended the High Festival of Midwinter.

There is little to be said for the artificial uplifting of animal spirits, yet few could take great exception to so rare an outburst in a long run of quiet days.

After all we celebrated the birth of a season which for weal or woe must be numbered amongst the greatest in our lives.

12
AWAITING THE CROZIER PARTY:
23 JUNE 1911 – 2 AUGUST 1911

Friday 23 June – Saturday 24 June Two quiet, uneventful days and a complete return to routine.

Sunday 25 June I find I have made no mention of Cherry-Garrard's first number of the revived *South Polar Times*, presented to me on Midwinter Day.

It is a very good little volume, bound by Day in a really charming cover of carved venesta wood and sealskin. The contributors are anonymous, but I have succeeded in guessing the identity of the greater number.

The Editor has taken a statistical paper of my own on the plans for the Southern Journey and a well-written serious article on the Geological History of our region by Taylor. Except for editorial and meteorological notes the rest is conceived in the lighter vein. The verse is mediocre except perhaps for a quaint play of words in an amusing little skit on the sleeping-bag argument; but an article entitled 'Valhalla' appears to me to be altogether on a different level. It purports to describe the arrival of some of our party at the gates proverbially guarded by St. Peter; the humour is really delicious and nowhere at all forced. In the jokes of a small community it is rare to recognise one which would appeal to an outsider, but some of the happier witticisms of this article seem to me fit for wider circulation than our journal enjoys at present. Above all there is distinct literary merit in it – a polish which leaves you unable to suggest the betterment of a word anywhere.

I unhesitatingly attribute this effort to Taylor, but Wilson and Garrard make Meares responsible for it. If they are right I shall have to own that my judgment of attributes is very much at fault. I must find out. [Captain Scott's judgment was not at fault.]

A quiet day. Read Church Service as usual; in afternoon walked up the Ramp with Wilson to have a quiet talk before he departs. I wanted to get his ideas as to the scientific work done.

We agreed as to the exceptionally happy organisation of our party.

I took the opportunity to warn Wilson concerning the desirability of complete understanding with Ponting and Taylor with respect to their photographs and records on their return to civilisation.

The weather has been very mysterious of late; on the 23rd and 24th it continuously threatened a blizzard, but now the sky is clearing again with all signs of fine weather.

Monday 26 June With a clear sky it was quite twilighty at noon today. Already such signs of day are inspiriting. In the afternoon the wind arose with drift and again the prophets predicted a blizzard. After an hour or two the wind fell and we had a calm, clear evening and night. The blizzards proper seem to be always preceded by an overcast sky in accordance with Simpson's theory.

Taylor gave a most interesting lecture on the physiographic features of the region traversed by his party in the autumn. His mind is very luminous and clear and he treated the subject with a breadth of view which was delightful. The illustrative slides were made from Debenham's photographs, and many of them were quite beautiful. Ponting tells me that Debenham knows quite a lot about photography and goes to work in quite the right way.

The lecture being a précis of Taylor's report there is no need to recapitulate its matter. With the pictures it was startling to realise the very different extent to which tributary glaciers have carved the channels in which they lie. The Canadian Glacier lies dead, but at 'grade' it has cut a very deep channel. The 'double curtain' hangs at an angle of 25°, with practically no channel. Mention was made of the difference of water found in Lake Bonney by me in December 1903 and the Western Party in February 1911. It seems certain that water must go on accumulating in the lake during the two or three summer months, and it is hard to imagine that all can be lost again by the winter's evaporation. If it does, 'evaporation' becomes a matter of primary importance.

There was an excellent picture showing the find of sponges on the Koettlitz Glacier. Heaps of large sponges were found containing corals and some shells, all representative of present-day fauna. How on earth did they get to the place where found? There was a good deal of discussion on the point and no very satisfactory solution offered. Cannot help thinking that there is something in the thought that the glacier may have been weighted down with rubble which finally disengaged itself and allowed the ice to rise. Such speculations are interesting.

Preparations for the start of the Crozier Party are now completed, and the people will have to drag 253 lbs. per man – a big weight.

Day has made an excellent little blubber lamp for lighting; it has an annular wick and talc chimney; a small circular plate over the wick conducts the heat down and raises the temperature of combustion, so that the result is a clear white flame.

We are certainly within measurable distance of using blubber in the most effective way for both heating and lighting, and this is an advance which is of very high importance to the future of Antarctic Exploration.

Tuesday 27 June The Crozier Party departed this morning in good spirits – their heavy load was distributed on two 9-feet sledges. Ponting photographed them by flashlight and attempted to get a cinematograph picture by means of a flash candle. But when the candle was ignited it was evident that the light would not be sufficient for the purpose and there was not much surprise when the film proved a failure. The three travellers found they could pull their load fairly easily on the sea-ice when the rest of us stood aside for the trial. I'm afraid they will find much more difficulty on the Barrier, but there was nothing now to prevent them starting, and off they went.

With helping contingent I went round the Cape. Taylor and Nelson left at the Razor Back Island and report all well. Simpson, Meares and Gran continued and have not yet returned.

Gran just back on ski; left party at 5¼ miles. Says Meares and Simpson are returning on foot. Reports a bad bit of surface between Tent Island and Glacier Tongue. It was well that the party had assistance to cross this.

This winter travel is a new and bold venture, but the right men have gone to attempt it. All good luck go with them!

COAL CONSUMPTION

Bowers reports that present consumption (midwinter) = 4 blocks per day (100 lbs.).

An occasional block is required for the absolute magnetic hut.

He reports 8½ tons used since landing.

This is in excess of 4 blocks per day as follows:

      8½ tons in 150 days   = 127 lbs. per diem.

                             = 889 lbs. per week, or nearly 8 cwt.

                             = 20 ½ tons per year.

Report 4 August

Used to date = 9 tons = 20,160 lbs.

Say 190 days at 106 lbs. per day.

Coal remaining 20½ tons.

Estimate 8 tons to return of ship.

Total estimate for year, 17 tons. We should have 13 or 14 tons for next year.

A FRESH MS. BOOK.
[*On the Flyleaf*]

'Where the (Queen's) Law does not carry it is irrational to exact an observance of other and weaker rules.' – RUDYARD KIPLING.

Confident of his good intentions but doubtful of his fortitude.

'So far as I can venture to offer an opinion on such a matter, the purpose of our being in existence, the highest object that human beings can set before themselves is not the pursuit of any such chimera as the annihilation of the unknown; but it is simply the unwearied endeavour to remove its boundaries a little further from our little sphere of action.' – HUXLEY.

Wednesday 28 June The temperature has been hovering around -30° with a clear sky – at midday it was exceptionally light, and even two hours after noon I was able to pick my way amongst the boulders of the Ramp. We miss the Crozier Party. Lectures have ceased during its absence, so that our life is very quiet.

Thursday 29 June It seemed rather stuffy in the hut last night – I found it difficult to sleep, and noticed a good many others in like case. I found the temperature was only 50°, but that the small uptake on the stove pipe was closed. I think it would be good to have a renewal of air at bed time, but don't quite know how to manage this.

It was calm all night and when I left the hut at 8.30. At 9 the wind suddenly rose to 40 m.p.h. and at the same moment the temperature rose 10°. The wind and temperature curves show this sudden simultaneous change more clearly than usual. The curious circumstance is that this blow comes out of a clear sky. This will be disturbing to our theories unless the wind drops again very soon.

The wind fell within an hour almost as suddenly as it had arisen; the temperature followed, only a little more gradually. One may well wonder how such a phenomenon is possible. In the middle of a period of placid calm and out of a clear sky there suddenly rushed upon one this volume of comparatively warm air; it has come and gone like the whirlwind.

Whence comes it and whither goeth?

Went round the bergs after lunch on ski – splendid surface and quite a good light.

We are now getting good records with the tide gauge after a great deal of trouble. Day has given much of his time to the matter, and after a good deal of discussion has pretty well mastered the principles. We brought a self-recording instrument from New Zealand, but this was passed over to Campbell. It has not been an easy matter to manufacture one for our own use. The wire from the bottom weight is led through a tube filled with paraffin as in *Discovery* days, and kept tight by a counter weight after passage through a block on a stanchion rising 6 feet above the floe.

In his first instrument Day arranged for this wire to pass around a pulley, the revolution of which actuated the pen of the recording drum. This should have been successful but for the difficulty of making good mechanical connection between the recorder and the pulley. Backlash caused an unreliable record, and this arrangement had to be abandoned. The motion of the wire was then made to actuate the recorder through a hinged lever, and this arrangement holds, but days and even weeks have been lost in grappling the difficulties of adjustment between the limits of the tide and those of the recording drum; then when all seemed well we found that the floe was not rising uniformly with the water. It is hung up by the beach ice. When we were considering the question of removing the whole apparatus to a more distant point, a fresh crack appeared between it and the shore, and on this 'hinge' the floe seems to be moving more freely.

Friday 30 June 1911 The temperature is steadily falling; we are descending the scale of negative thirties and today reached its limit, -39°. Day has manufactured a current vane, a simple arrangement: up to the present he has used this near the Cape. There is little doubt, however, that the water movement is erratic and irregular inside the islands, and I have been anxious to get observations which will indicate the movement in the 'Strait'. I went with him today to find a crack which I thought must run to the north from Inaccessible Island. We discovered it about 2 to 2½ miles out and found it to be an ideal place for such work, a fracture in the ice sheet which is constantly opening and therefore always edged with thin ice. Have told Day that I think a bottle weighted so as to give it a small negative buoyancy, and attached to a fine line, should give as good results as his vane and would be much handier. He now proposes to go one better and put an electric light in the bottle.

We found that our loose dogs had been attacking a seal, and then came across a dead seal which had evidently been worried to death some time ago. It appears Demetri saw more seal further to the north, and this afternoon Meares has killed a large one as well as the one which was worried this morning.

It is good to find the seals so close, but very annoying to find that the dogs have discovered their resting-place.

The long spell of fine weather is very satisfactory.

Saturday 1 July 1911 We have designed new ski boots and I think they are going to be a success. My object is to stick to the Huitfeldt binding for sledging if possible. One must wear finnesko on the Barrier, and with finnesko alone a loose binding is necessary. For this we brought 'Finon' bindings, consisting of leather toe straps and thong heel binding. With this arrangement one does not have good control of his ski and stands the chance of a chafe on the 'tendon Achillis'. Owing to the last consideration many had decided to go with toe strap alone as we did in the *Discovery*. This brought into my mind the possibility of using the iron cross bar and snap heel strap of the Huitfeldt on a suitable overshoe.

Evans, P.O., has arisen well to the occasion as a boot maker, and has just completed a pair of shoes which are very nearly what we require.

The soles have two thicknesses of seal skin cured with alum, stiffened at the foot with a layer of venesta board, and raised at the heel on a block of wood. The upper part is large enough to contain a finnesko and is secured by a simple strap. A shoe weighs 13 oz. against 2 lbs. for a single ski boot – so that shoe and finnesko together are less weight than a boot.

If we can perfect this arrangement it should be of the greatest use to us.

Wright has been swinging the pendulum in his cavern. Prodigious trouble has been taken to keep the time, and this object has been immensely helped by the telephone communication between the cavern, the transit instrument, and the interior of the hut. The timekeeper is perfectly placed. Wright tells me that his ice platform proves to be five times as solid as the fixed piece of masonry used at Potsdam. The only difficulty is the low temperature, which freezes his breath on the glass window of the protecting dome. I feel sure these gravity results are going to be very good.

The temperature has been hanging in the minus thirties all day with calm and clear sky, but this evening a wind has sprung up without rise of temperature. It is now -32°, with a wind of 25 m.p.h. – a pretty stiff condition to face outside!

Sunday 2 July There was wind last night, but this morning found a settled calm again, with temperature as usual about -35°. The moon is rising again;

it came over the shoulder of Erebus about 5 p.m., in second quarter. It will cross the meridian at night, worse luck, but such days as this will be pleasant even with a low moon; one is very glad to think the Crozier Party are having such a peaceful time.

Sunday routine and nothing much to record.

Monday 3 July Another quiet day, the sky more suspicious in appearance. Thin stratus cloud forming and dissipating overhead, curling stratus clouds over Erebus. Wind at Cape Crozier seemed a possibility.

Our people have been far out on the floe. It is cheerful to see the twinkling light of some worker at a water hole or hear the ring of distant voices or swish of ski.

Tuesday 4 July A day of blizzard and adventure.

The wind arose last night, and although the temperature advanced a few degrees it remained at a very low point considering the strength of the wind.

This forenoon it was blowing 40 to 45 m.p.h. with a temperature -25° to -28°. No weather to be in the open.

In the afternoon the wind modified slightly. Taylor and Atkinson went up to the Ramp thermometer screen. After this, entirely without my knowledge, two adventurous spirits, Atkinson and Gran, decided to start off over the floe, making respectively for the north and south Bay thermometers, 'Archibald' and 'Clarence'. This was at 5.30; Gran was back by dinner at 6.45, and it was only later that I learned that he had gone no more than 200 or 300 yards from the land and that it had taken him nearly an hour to get back again.

Atkinson's continued absence passed unnoticed until dinner was nearly over at 7.15, although I had heard that the wind had dropped at the beginning of dinner and that it remained very thick all round, with light snow falling.

Although I felt somewhat annoyed, I had no serious anxiety at this time, and as several members came out of the hut I despatched them short distances to shout and show lanterns and arranged to have a paraffin flare lit on Wind Vane Hill.

Evans, P.O., Crean and Keohane, being anxious for a walk, were sent to the north with a lantern. Whilst this desultory search proceeded the wind sprang up again from the south, but with no great force, and meanwhile the sky showed signs of clearing and the moon appeared dimly through the drifting clouds. With such a guide we momentarily looked for the return of our wanderer, and with his continued absence our anxiety grew. At 9.30 Evans, P.O., and his party returned without news of him, and at last there was no denying the possibility of a serious accident. Between 9.30 and 10 proper search parties were organised, and I give the details to show the thoroughness which I thought necessary to meet the gravity of the situation. I had by this time learnt that Atkinson had left with comparatively light clothing and, still worse, with leather ski boots on his feet; fortunately he had wind clothing.

P.O. Evans was away first with Crean, Keohane, and Demetri, a light sledge, a sleeping-bag, and a flask of brandy. His orders were to search the edge of the land and glacier through the sweep of the Bay to the Barne Glacier and to Cape Barne beyond, then to turn east along an open crack and follow it to Inaccessible Island. Evans (Lieut.), with Nelson, Forde, and Hooper, left shortly after, similarly equipped, to follow the shore of the South Bay in similar fashion, then turn out to the Razor Back and search there. Next Wright, Gran, and Lashly set out for the bergs to look thoroughly about them and from thence pass round and examine Inaccessible Island. After these parties got away, Meares and Debenham started with a lantern to search to and fro over the surface of our promontory. Simpson and Oates went out in a direct line over the Northern floe to the 'Archibald' thermometer, whilst Ponting and Taylor re-examined the tide crack towards the Barne Glacier. Meanwhile Day went to and fro Wind Vane Hill to light at intervals upon its crest bundles of tow well soaked in petrol. At length Clissold and I were left alone in the hut, and as the hours went by I grew ever more alarmed. It was impossible for me to conceive how an able man could have failed to return to the hut before this or by any means found shelter in such clothing in such weather. Atkinson had started for a point a little more than a mile away; at 10.30 he had been five hours away; what conclusion could be drawn? And yet I felt it most difficult to imagine an accident on open floe with no worse pitfall than a shallow crack or steep-sided snow drift. At least I could feel that every spot which was likely to be the scene of such an accident would be searched. Thus 11 o'clock came without change, then 11.30 with its 6 hours of absence. But at 11.45 I heard voices from the Cape, and presently the adventure ended to my extreme relief when Meares and Debenham led our wanderer home. He was badly frostbitten in the hand and less seriously on the face, and though a good deal confused, as men always are on such occasions, he was otherwise well.

His tale is confused, but as far as one can gather he did not go more than a quarter of a mile in the direction of the thermometer screen before he decided to turn back. He then tried to walk with the wind a little on one side on the bearing he had originally observed, and after some time stumbled on an old fish trap hole, which he knew to be 200 yards from the Cape. He made this 200 yards in the direction he supposed correct, and found nothing. In such a situation had he turned east he must have hit the land somewhere close to the hut and so found his way to it. The fact that he did not, but attempted to wander straight on, is clear evidence of the mental condition caused by that situation. There can be no doubt that in a blizzard a man has not only to safeguard the circulation in his limbs, but must struggle with a sluggishness of brain and an absence of reasoning power which is far more likely to undo him.

In fact Atkinson has really no very clear idea of what happened to him after he missed the Cape. He seems to have wandered aimlessly up wind till he hit an island; he walked all round this; says he couldn't see a yard at this time; fell often into the tide crack; finally stopped under the lee of some rocks; here got his hand frostbitten owing to difficulty of getting frozen mit on again, finally got it on; started to dig a hole to wait in. Saw something of the moon and left the island; lost the moon and wanted to go back; could find nothing; finally stumbled on another island, perhaps the same one; waited again, again saw the moon, now clearing; shaped some sort of course by it – then saw flare on Cape and came on rapidly – says he shouted to someone on Cape quite close to him, greatly surprised not to get an answer. It is a rambling tale tonight and a half-thawed brain. It is impossible to listen to such a tale without appreciating that it has been a close escape or that there would have been no escape had the blizzard continued. The thought that it would return after a short lull was amongst the worst with me during the hours of waiting.

2 a.m. The search parties have returned and all is well again, but we must have no more of these very unnecessary escapades. Yet it is impossible not to realise that this bit of experience has done more than all the talking I could have ever accomplished to bring home to our people the dangers of a blizzard.

Wednesday 5 July Atkinson has a bad hand today, immense blisters on every finger giving them the appearance of sausages. Tonight Ponting has photographed the hand.

As I expected, some amendment of Atkinson's tale as written last night is necessary, partly due to some lack of coherency in the tale as first told and partly a reconsideration of the circumstances by Atkinson himself.

It appears he first hit Inaccessible Island, and got his hand frostbitten before he reached it. It was only on arrival in its lee that he discovered the frostbite. He must have waited there some time, then groped his way to the western end thinking he was near the Ramp. Then wandering away in a swirl of drift to clear some irregularities at the ice foot, he completely lost the island when he could only have been a few yards from it.

He seems in this predicament to have clung to the old idea of walking up wind, and it must be considered wholly providential that on this course he next struck Tent Island. It was round this island that he walked, finally digging himself a shelter on its lee side under the impression that it was Inaccessible Island. When the moon appeared he seems to have judged its bearing well, and as he travelled homeward he was much surprised to see the real Inaccessible Island appear on his left. The distance of Tent Island, 4 to 5 miles, partly accounts for the time he took in returning. Everything goes to confirm the fact that he had a very close shave of being lost altogether.

For some time past some of the ponies have had great irritation of the skin. I felt sure it was due to some parasite, though the Soldier thought the food responsible and changed it.

Today a tiny body louse was revealed under Atkinson's microscope after capture from 'Snatcher's' coat. A dilute solution of carbolic is expected to rid the poor beasts of their pests, but meanwhile one or two of them have rubbed off patches of hair which they can ill afford to spare in this climate. I hope we shall get over the trouble quickly.

The day has been gloriously fine again, with bright moonlight all the afternoon. It was a wondrous sight to see Erebus emerge from soft filmy clouds of mist as though some thin veiling had been withdrawn with infinite delicacy to reveal the pure outline of this moonlit mountain.

Thursday 6 July, continued The temperature has taken a plunge to -46° last night. It is now -45°, with a ten-mile breeze from the south. Frostbiting weather!

Went for a short run on foot this forenoon and a longer one on ski this afternoon. The surface is bad after the recent snowfall. A new pair of sealskin overshoes for ski made by Evans seem to be a complete success. He has modified the shape of the toe to fit the ski irons better. I am very pleased with this arrangement.

I find it exceedingly difficult to settle down to solid work just at present and keep putting off the tasks which I have set myself.

The sun has not yet risen a degree of the 11° below our horizon which it was at noon on Midwinter Day, and yet today there was a distinct red in the northern sky. Perhaps such sunset colours have something to do with this cold snap.

Friday 7 July The temperature fell to -49° last night – our record so far, and likely to remain so, one would think. This morning it was fine and calm, temperature -45°. But this afternoon a 30-mile wind sprang up from the S.E., and the temperature only gradually rose to -30°, never passing above that point. I thought it a little too strenuous and so was robbed of my walk.

The dogs' coats are getting pretty thick, and they seem to take matters pretty comfortably. The ponies are better, I think, but I shall be glad when we are sure of having rid them of their pest.

I was the victim of a very curious illusion today. On our small heating stove stands a cylindrical ice melter which keeps up the supply of water necessary for the dark room and other scientific instruments. This iron container naturally becomes warm if it is not fed with ice, and it is generally hung around with socks and mits which require drying. I put my hand on the cylindrical vessel this afternoon and withdrew it sharply with the sensation of heat. To verify the impression I repeated the action two or three times, when it became so strong that I loudly warned the owners of the socks, etc., of the peril of burning to which they were exposed. Upon this Meares said, 'But they filled the melter with ice a few minutes ago,' and then, coming over to feel the surface himself, added, 'Why, it's cold, sir.' And indeed so it was. The slightly damp chilled surface of the iron had conveyed to me the impression of excessive heat.

There is nothing intrinsically new in this observation; it has often been noticed that metal surfaces at low temperatures give a sensation of burning to the bare touch, but none the less it is an interesting variant of the common fact.

Apropos. Atkinson is suffering a good deal from his hand: the frostbite was deeper than I thought; fortunately he can now feel all his fingers, though it was twenty-four hours before sensation returned to one of them.

Monday 10 July We have had the worst gale I have ever known in these regions and have not yet done with it.

The wind started at about mid-day on Friday, and increasing in violence reached an average of 60 miles for one hour on Saturday, the gusts at this time exceeding 70 m.p.h. This force of wind, although exceptional, has not been without parallel earlier in the year, but the extraordinary feature of this gale was the long continuance of a very cold temperature. On Friday night the thermometer registered -39°. Throughout Saturday and the greater part of Sunday it did not rise above -35°. Late yesterday it was in the minus twenties, and today at length it has risen to zero.

Needless to say no one has been far from the hut. It was my turn for duty on Saturday night, and on the occasions when I had to step out of doors I was struck with the impossibility of enduring such conditions for any length of time. One seemed to be robbed of breath as they burst on one – the fine snow beat in behind the wind guard, and ten paces against the wind were sufficient to reduce one's face to the verge of frostbite. To clear the anemometer vane it is necessary to go to the other end of the hut and climb a ladder. Twice whilst engaged in this task I had literally to lean against the wind with head bent and face averted and so stagger crab-like on my course. In those two days of really terrible weather our thoughts often turned to absentees at Cape Crozier with the devout hope that they may be safely housed.

They are certain to have been caught by this gale, but I trust before it reached them they had managed to get up some sort of shelter. Sometimes I have imagined them getting much more wind than we do, yet at others it seems difficult to believe that the Emperor penguins have chosen an excessively wind-swept area for their rookery.

Today with the temperature at zero one can walk about outside without inconvenience in spite of a 50-mile wind. Although I am loath to believe it there must be some measure of acclimatisation, for it is certain we should have felt today's wind severely when we first arrived in McMurdo Sound.

Tuesday 11 July Never was such persistent bad weather. Today the temperature is up to 5° to 7°, the wind 40 to 50 m.p.h., the air thick with snow, and the moon a vague blue. This is the fourth day of gale; if one reflects on the quantity of transported air (nearly 4000 miles) one gets a conception of the transference which such a gale effects and must conclude that potentially warm upper currents are pouring into our Polar area from more temperate sources.

The dogs are very gay and happy in the comparative warmth. I have been going to and fro on the home beach and about the rocky knolls in its environment – in spite of the wind it was very warm. I dug myself a hole in a drift in the shelter of a large boulder and lay down in it, and covered my legs with loose snow. It was so warm that I could have slept very comfortably.

I have been amused and pleased lately in observing the manners and customs of the persons in charge of our stores; quite a number of secret caches exist in which articles of value are hidden from public knowledge so that they may escape use until a real necessity arises. The policy of every storekeeper is to have something up his sleeve for a rainy day. For instance, Evans (P.O.), after thoroughly examining the purpose of some individual who is pleading for a piece of canvas, will admit that he may have a small piece somewhere which could be used for it, when, as a matter of fact, he possesses quite a number of rolls of that material.

Tools, metal material, leather, straps and dozens of items are administered with the same spirit of jealous guardianship by Day, Lashly, Oates and

Meares, while our main storekeeper Bowers even affects to bemoan imaginary shortages. Such parsimony is the best guarantee that we are prepared to face any serious call.

Wednesday 12 July All night and today wild gusts of wind shaking the hut; long, ragged, twisted wind-cloud in the middle heights. A watery moon shining through a filmy cirro-stratus – the outlook wonderfully desolate with its ghostly illumination and patchy clouds of flying snow drift. It would be hardly possible for a tearing, raging wind to make itself more visible. At Wind Vane Hill the anemometer has registered 68 miles between 9 and 10 a.m. – a record. The gusts at the hut frequently exceed 70 m.p.h. – luckily the temperature is up to 5°, so that there is no hardship for the workers outside.

Thursday 13 July The wind continued to blow throughout the night, with squalls of even greater violence than before; a new record was created by a gust of 77 m.p.h. shown by the anemometer.

The snow is so hard blown that only the fiercest gusts raise the drifting particles – it is interesting to note the balance of nature whereby one evil is eliminated by the excess of another.

For an hour after lunch yesterday the gale showed signs of moderation and the ponies had a short walk over the floe. Out for exercise at this time I was obliged to lean against the wind, my light overall clothes flapping wildly and almost dragged from me; later when the wind rose again it was quite an effort to stagger back to the hut against it.

This morning the gale still rages, but the sky is much clearer; the only definite clouds are those which hang to the southward of Erebus summit, but the moon, though bright, still exhibits a watery appearance, showing that there is still a thin stratus above us.

The work goes on very steadily – the men are making crampons and ski boots of the new style. Evans is constructing plans of the Dry Valley and Koettlitz Glacier with the help of the Western Party. The physicists are busy always, Meares is making dog harness, Oates ridding the ponies of their parasites, and Ponting printing from his negatives.

Science cannot be served by 'dilettante' methods, but demands a mind spurred by ambition or the satisfaction of ideals.

Our most popular game for evening recreation is chess; so many players have developed that our two sets of chessmen are inadequate.

Friday 14 July We have had a horrible fright and are not yet out of the wood.

At noon yesterday one of the best ponies, 'Bones', suddenly went off his feed – soon after it was evident that he was distressed and there could be no doubt that he was suffering from colic. Oates called my attention to it, but we were neither much alarmed, remembering the speedy recovery of 'Jimmy Pigg' under similar circumstances. Later the pony was sent out for exercise with Crean. I passed him twice and seemed to gather that things were well, but Crean afterwards told me that he had had considerable trouble. Every few minutes the poor beast had been seized with a spasm of pain, had first dashed forward as though to escape it and then endeavoured to lie down. Crean had

had much difficulty in keeping him in, and on his legs, for he is a powerful beast. When he returned to the stable he was evidently worse, and Oates and Anton patiently dragged a sack to and fro under his stomach. Every now and again he attempted to lie down, and Oates eventually thought it wiser to let him do so. Once down, his head gradually drooped until he lay at length, every now and again twitching very horribly with the pain and from time to time raising his head and even scrambling to his legs when it grew intense. I don't think I ever realised before how pathetic a horse could be under such conditions; no sound escapes him, his misery can only be indicated by those distressing spasms and by dumb movements of the head turned with a patient expression always suggestive of appeal. Although alarmed by this time, remembering the care with which the animals are being fed I could not picture anything but a passing indisposition. But as hour after hour passed without improvement, it was impossible not to realise that the poor beast was dangerously ill. Oates administered an opium pill and later on a second, sacks were heated in the oven and placed on the poor beast; beyond this nothing could be done except to watch – Oates and Crean never left the patient. As the evening wore on I visited the stable again and again, but only to hear the same tale – no improvement. Towards midnight I felt very downcast. It is so very certain that we cannot afford to lose a single pony – the margin of safety has already been far overstepped, we are reduced to face the circumstance that we must keep all the animals alive or greatly risk failure.

So far everything has gone so well with them that my fears of a loss had been lulled in a growing hope that all would be well – therefore at midnight, when poor 'Bones' had continued in pain for twelve hours and showed little sign of improvement, I felt my fleeting sense of security rudely shattered.

It was shortly after midnight when I was told that the animal seemed a little easier. At 2.30 I was again in the stable and found the improvement had been maintained; the horse still lay on its side with outstretched head, but the spasms had ceased, its eye looked less distressed, and its ears pricked to occasional noises. As I stood looking it suddenly raised its head and rose without effort to its legs; then in a moment, as though some bad dream had passed, it began to nose at some hay and at its neighbour. Within three minutes it had drunk a bucket of water and had started to feed.

I went to bed at 3 with much relief. At noon today the immediate cause of the trouble and an indication that there is still risk were disclosed in a small ball of semi-fermented hay covered with mucus and containing tape worms; so far not very serious, but unfortunately attached to this mass was a strip of the lining of the intestine.

Atkinson, from a humanly comparative point of view, does not think this is serious if great care is taken with the food for a week or so, and so one can hope for the best.

Meanwhile we have had much discussion as to the first cause of the difficulty. The circumstances possibly contributing are as follows: fermentation of the hay, insufficiency of water, overheated stable, a chill from exercise after the gale – I think all these may have had a bearing on the case. It can scarcely be coincidence that the two ponies which have suffered so far are those which are nearest the stove end of the stable. In future the stove will be used more sparingly, a large ventilating hole is to be made near it and an allowance of water is to be added to the snow hitherto given to the animals. In the food line we can only exercise such precautions as are possible, but one way or another we ought to be able to prevent any more danger of this description.

Saturday 15 July There was strong wind with snow this morning and the wind remained keen and cold in the afternoon, but tonight it has fallen calm with a promising clear sky outlook. Have been up the Ramp, clambering about in my sealskin overshoes, which seem extraordinarily satisfactory.

Oates thinks a good few of the ponies have got worms and we are considering means of ridding them. 'Bones' seems to be getting on well, though not yet quite so buckish as he was before his trouble. A good big ventilator has been fitted in the stable. It is not easy to get over the alarm of Thursday night – the situation is altogether too critical.

Sunday 16 July Another slight alarm this morning. The pony 'China' went off his feed at breakfast time and lay down twice. He was up and well again in half an hour; but what on earth is it that is disturbing these poor beasts?

Usual Sunday routine. Quiet day except for a good deal of wind off and on. The Crozier Party must be having a wretched time.

Monday 17 July The weather still very unsettled – the wind comes up with a rush to fade in an hour or two. Clouds chase over the sky in similar fashion: the moon has dipped during daylight hours, and so one way and another there is little to attract one out of doors.

Yet we are only nine days off the 'light value' of the day when we left off football – I hope we shall be able to recommence the game in that time.

I am glad that the light is coming for more than one reason. The gale and consequent inaction not only affected the ponies, Ponting is not very fit as a consequence – his nervous temperament is of the quality to take this wintering experience badly – Atkinson has some difficulty in persuading him to take exercise – he managed only by dragging him out to his own work, digging holes in the ice. Taylor is another backslider in the exercise line and is not looking well. If we can get these people to run about at football all will be well. Anyway the return of the light should cure all ailments physical and mental.

Tuesday 18 July A very brilliant red sky at noon today and enough light to see one's way about.

This fleeting hour of light is very pleasant, but of course dependent on a clear sky, very rare. Went round the outer berg in the afternoon; it was all I could do to keep up with 'Snatcher' on the homeward round – speaking well for his walking powers.

Wednesday 19 July Again calm and pleasant. The temperature is gradually falling down to -35°. Went out to the old working crack [i.e. a crack which leaves the ice free to move with the movements of the sea beneath] north of Inaccessible Island – Nelson and Evans had had great difficulty in rescuing their sounding sledge, which had been left near here before the gale. The course of events is not very clear, but it looks as though the gale pressed up the crack, raising broken pieces of the thin ice formed after recent opening movements. These raised pieces had become nuclei of heavy snow drifts, which in turn weighing down the floe had allowed water to flow in over the sledge level. It is surprising to find such a big disturbance from what appears to be a simple cause. This crack is now joined, and the contraction is taking on a new one which has opened much nearer to us and seems to run to C. Barne.

We have noticed a very curious appearance of heavenly bodies when setting in a north-westerly direction. About the time of midwinter the moon observed in this position appeared in a much distorted shape of blood red colour. It might have been a red flare or distant bonfire, but could not have been guessed for the moon. Yesterday the planet Venus appeared under similar circumstances as a ship's side-light or Japanese lantern. In both cases there was a flickering in the light and a change of colour from deep orange yellow to blood red, but the latter was dominant.

Thursday 20 July, Friday 21 July, Saturday 22 July There is very little to record – the horses are going on well, all are in good form, at least for the moment. They drink a good deal of water in the morning.

Saturday 22 July, continued This and the better ventilation of the stable make for improvement we think – perhaps the increase of salt allowance is also beneficial.

Today we have another raging blizzard – the wind running up to 72 m.p.h. in gusts – one way and another the Crozier Party must have had a pretty poor time. [This was the gale that tore away the roofing of their hut, and left them with only their sleeping-bags for shelter.] I am thankful to remember that the light will be coming on apace now.

Monday 24 July The blizzard continued throughout yesterday (Sunday), in the evening reaching a record force of 82 m.p.h. The vane of our anemometer is somewhat sheltered: Simpson finds the hill readings 20 per cent higher. Hence in such gusts as this the free wind must reach nearly 100 m.p.h. – a hurricane force. Today Nelson found that his sounding sledge had been turned over. We passed a quiet Sunday with the usual Service to break the week-day routine. During my night watch last night I could observe the rapid falling of the wind, which on dying away left a still atmosphere almost oppressively warm at 7°. The temperature has remained comparatively high today. I went to see the crack at which soundings were taken a week ago – then it was several feet open with thin ice between – now it is pressed up into a sharp ridge 3 to 4 feet high: the edge pressed up shows an 18 inch thickness – this is of course an effect of the warm weather.

Tuesday 25 July, Wednesday 26 July There is really very little to be recorded in these days, life proceeds very calmly if somewhat monotonously. Everyone seems fit, there is no sign of depression. To all outward appearance the ponies are in better form than they have ever been; the same may be said of the dogs with one or two exceptions.

The light comes on apace. Today (Wednesday) it was very beautiful at noon: the air was very clear and the detail of the Western Mountains was revealed in infinitely delicate contrasts of light.

Thursday 27 July, Friday 28 July Calmer days: the sky rosier: the light visibly advancing. We have never suffered from low spirits, so that the presence of day raises us above a normal cheerfulness to the realm of high spirits.

The light, merry humour of our company has never been eclipsed, the good-natured, kindly chaff has never ceased since those early days of enthusiasm which inspired them – they have survived the winter days of stress and already renew themselves with the coming of spring. If pessimistic moments had foreseen the growth of rifts in the bond forged by these amenities, they stand prophetically falsified; there is no longer room for doubt that we shall come to our work with a unity of purpose and a disposition for mutual support which have never been equalled in these paths of activity. Such a spirit should tide us [over] all minor difficulties. It is a good omen.

Saturday 29 July, Sunday 30 July Two quiet days, temperature low in the minus thirties – an occasional rush of wind lasting for but a few minutes.

One of our best sledge dogs, 'Julick', has disappeared. I'm afraid he's been set on by the others at some distant spot and we shall see nothing more but his stiffened carcass when the light returns. Meares thinks the others would not have attacked him and imagines he has fallen into the water in some seal hole or crack. In either case I'm afraid we must be resigned to another loss. It's an awful nuisance.

Gran went to C. Royds today. I asked him to report on the open water, and so he went on past the Cape. As far as I can gather he got half-way to C. Bird before he came to thin ice; for at least 5 or 6 miles past C. Royds the ice is old and covered with wind-swept snow. This is very unexpected. In the *Discovery* first year the ice continually broke back to the Glacier Tongue: in the second year it must have gone out to C. Royds very early in the spring if it did not go out in the winter, and in the *Nimrod* year it was rarely fast beyond C. Royds. It is very strange, especially as this has been the windiest year recorded so far. Simpson says the average has exceeded 20 m.p.h. since the instruments were set up, and this figure has for comparison 9 and 12 m.p.h. for the two *Discovery* years. There remains a possibility that we have chosen an especially wind-swept spot for our station. Yet I can scarcely believe that there is generally more wind here than at Hut Point.

I was out for two hours this morning – it was amazingly pleasant to be able to see the inequalities of one's path, and the familiar landmarks bathed in violet light. An hour after noon the northern sky was intensely red.

Monday 31 July It was overcast today and the light not quite so good, but this is the last day of another month, and August means the sun.

One begins to wonder what the Crozier Party is doing. It has been away five weeks.

The ponies are getting buckish. Chinaman squeals and kicks in the stable, Nobby kicks without squealing, but with even more purpose – last night he knocked down a part of his stall. The noise of these animals is rather trying

The Crew of the *Terra Nova*. front row: Skelton, McLeod, Bailey, Forde, Lesse. Second row: Stoker McDonald, Seaman McDonald, Burton, McGillon, Anton, Clissold, Mather, Davies. Third row: Horton, Brissenden, Parsons, McKenzie, Heald, Balson. Back row: Neale, McCarthy.

Ponting cinematographs the bow of the *Terra Nova* breaking through the ice-floes.

Christmas Eve (1910) in the pack.

In the pack – a lead opening up.

The *Terra Nova* in McMurdo Sound.

The midnight sun in McMurdo Sound.

Furling sail in the pack.

A berg breaking up in the pack.

A lead in the pack. From a drawing by Dr. Edward A. Wilson.

Top left: 'Vaida' top right: 'Krisravitsa' above: 'Stareek' malingering.

Above left: Manning the pumps.
Above right: Dr. Wilson and Dr. Atkinson loading the harpoon gun.

Above left: A. B. Cheetham (The boatswain of the *Terra Nova*).
Above right: Lieutenant Evans in the Crow's Nest.

Ponies tethered out on the sea ice.

Disembarking the ponies.

Lieut. Rennick and a friendly penguin.

Above left: The point of the Barne Glacier.
Above right: Lieut. H. E. DE P. Rennick.

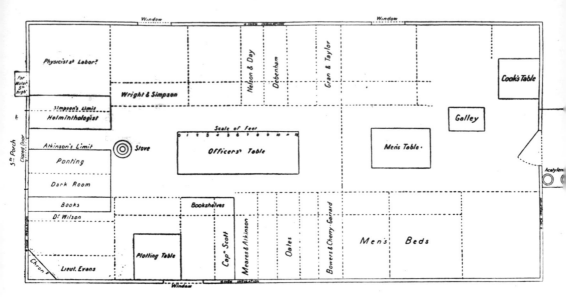

Plan of Hut.

Above left: Winter quarters at Cape Evans.
Above right: Lieut. Tryggve Gran.

Lillie and Dr. Levick sorting a trawl catch.

Seals basking on newly formed pancake ice off Cape Evans.

Landing a motor-sledge.

Lieut. Evans and Nelson cutting a cave for cold storage.

The condition of affairs a week after landing.
The Tenements (Cherry-Garrard, Bowers, Oates, Meares, Atkinson).

The Arch Berg from within.

The Arch Berg from without.

Left: Captain Scott on ski.
Above: Summer time – the ice opening up.

Spray ridges of ice after a blizzard.

Ponting developing a plate in the dark room.

The depot laying and western parties on their return to Cape Evans. Left to right Taylor, Wright, Evans, Bowers, Scott, Debenham, Gran, P.O. Evans, Crean.

Captain Scott's last birthday dinner (Left to right – Atkinson, Meares, Cherry-Garrard, Oates (standing), Taylor, Nelson, Evans, Scott, Wilson, Simpson, Bowers, Gran (standing), Wright, Debenham, Day).

Dr. Wilson and Lieut. Bowers reading the ramp thermometer in the winter night, -40 degrees Fahr. (A flashlight photograph).

Petty Officer Evans binding up Dr. Atkinson's hand. (The marks on Atkinson's face are frost-bites).

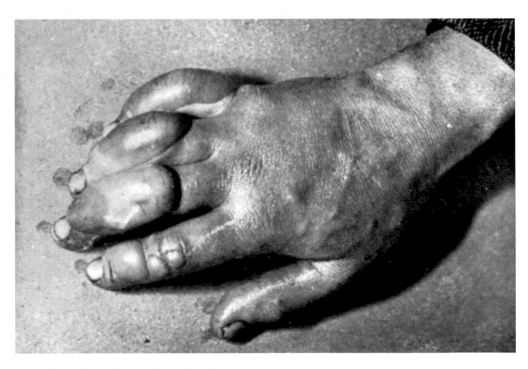

Dr. Atkinson's frost-bitten hand.

The Hut and the Western Mountains from the top of the ramp.

Cape Royds, looking north.

The Castle Berg.

Dr. Atkinson in his laboratory.

Dr. Simpson at the Unifilar Magnetometer.

Winter work. Left to right Debenham – Cherry-Garrard, Bowers, Evans, Taylor.

Dr. Atkinson and Clissold hauling up the fish-trap (Photographed in the midst of the long winter night by flashlight, in a temperature 40 degrees below zero Fah.)

The stables in winter (the figure is Captain Oates).

Left: Pony takes whisky.
Above: Oates and Meares at the blubber-stove in the stables.

Above left: Oates and Meares out ski-ing in the night.
Above right: Petty Officers Crean and Evans exercising their ponies in the winter.
Below: Remarkable Cirrus clouds over the Barne Glacier.

Mount Erebus over a water-worn iceberg.

Above: Cherry-Garrard giving his pony
'Michael' a roll in the snow.
Left: Dr. Wilson and pony 'Nobby'.

Surveying party's tent after a blizzard.

Top: Dogs with stores about to leave Hut Point. Middle: Dogs galloping towards the Barrier. Bottom: Meares and Demetri with their dog teams leaving Hut Point.

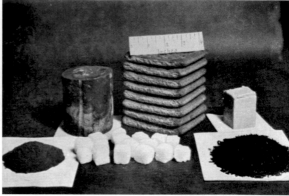

Left: Dr. Simpson sending up a balloon.
Above: The polar party's sledging ration (Pemmican, biscuits, butter, cocoa, sugar and tea).

Above left: An ice grotto – Tent Island in distance (Captain Scott and Wright).
Above right: C. H. Meares and 'Osman', the leader of the dogs.

The main party at Cape Evans after the winter, 1911. Front row: Lieut. Bowers, Mr. Meares, Mr. Debenham, Dr. Wilson, Dr. Simpson, Seaman Evans, Crean. Second row: Mr. Taylor, Garrard, Mr. Nelson, Evans, Oates, Capt. Scott, Wright, Keohane, Lashly, Hooper, Anton, Demetri. Back row: Mr. Cherry, Mr. Day, Lieut. Capt. Dr. Atkinson, Mr. Lieut. Gran, Forde.

Meares and Demetri at *Discovery* hut.

Dr. Simpson in the hut at the other end of the telephone timing the observation.

Lieut. Evans observing an occultation of Jupiter.

Left: Captain L. E. G. Oates by the stable door.
Above: Nelson and his Gear.

Debenham, Gran, and Taylor in their cubicle.

Left: Dr. Wilson.
Above: Preparing sledges for the polar journey (Crean, Forde, Lashly, P.O. Evans).

Day's motor under way.

One of the motor sledges.

at night – one imagines all sorts of dreadful things happening, but when the watchman visits the stables its occupants blink at him with a sleepy air as though the disturbance could not possibly have been there!

There was a glorious northern sky today; the horizon was clear and the flood of red light illuminated the under side of the broken stratus cloud above, producing very beautiful bands of violet light. Simpson predicts a blizzard within twenty-four hours – we are interested to watch results.

Tuesday 1 August The month has opened with a very beautiful day. This morning I took a circuitous walk over our land 'estate', winding to and fro in gulleys filled with smooth ice patches or loose sandy soil, with a twofold object. I thought I might find the remains of poor Julick – in this I was unsuccessful; but I wished further to test our new crampons, and with these I am immensely pleased – they possess every virtue in a footwear designed for marching over smooth ice – lightness, warmth, comfort, and ease in the putting on and off.

The light was especially good today; the sun was directly reflected by a single twisted iridescent cloud in the north, a brilliant and most beautiful object. The air was still, and it was very pleasant to hear the crisp sounds of our workers abroad. The tones of voices, the swish of ski or the chipping of an ice pick carry two or three miles on such days – more than once today we could hear the notes of some blithe singer – happily signalling the coming of the spring and the sun.

This afternoon as I sit in the hut I find it worthy of record that two telephones are in use: the one keeping time for Wright who works at the transit instrument, and the other bringing messages from Nelson at his ice hole three-quarters of a mile away. This last connection is made with a bare aluminium wire and earth return, and shows that we should have little difficulty in completing our circuit to Hut Point as is contemplated.

ACCOUNT OF THE WINTER JOURNEY

Wednesday 2 August The Crozier Party returned last night after enduring for five weeks the hardest conditions on record. They looked more weather-worn than anyone I have yet seen. Their faces were scarred and wrinkled, their eyes dull, their hands whitened and creased with the constant exposure to damp and cold, yet the scars of frostbite were very few and this evil had never seriously assailed them. The main part of their afflictions arose, and very obviously arose, from sheer lack of sleep, and today after a night's rest our travellers are very different in appearance and mental capacity.

The story of a very wonderful performance must be told by the actors. It is for me now to give but an outline of the journey and to note more particularly the effects of the strain which they have imposed on themselves and the lessons which their experiences teach for our future guidance.

Wilson is very thin, but this morning very much his keen, wiry self – Bowers is quite himself today. Cherry-Garrard is slightly puffy in the face and still looks worn. It is evident that he has suffered most severely – but Wilson tells me that his spirit never wavered for a moment. Bowers has come through best, all things considered, and I believe he is the hardest traveller that ever undertook a Polar journey, as well as one of the most undaunted; more by hint than direct statement I gather his value to the party, his untiring energy and the astonishing physique which enables him to continue to work under conditions which are absolutely paralysing to others. Never was such a sturdy, active, undefeatable little man.

So far as one can gather, the story of this journey in brief is much as follows: The party reached the Barrier two days after leaving C. Evans, still pulling their full load of 250 lbs. per man; the snow surface then changed completely and grew worse and worse as they advanced. For one day they struggled on as before, covering 4 miles, but from this onward they were forced to relay, and found the half load heavier than the whole one had been on the sea-ice. Meanwhile the temperature had been falling, and now for more than a week the thermometer fell below -60°. On one night the minimum showed -71°, and on the next -77°, 109° of frost. Although in this truly fearful cold the air was comparatively still, every now and again little puffs of wind came eddying across the snow plain with blighting effect. No civilised being has ever encountered such conditions before with only a tent of thin canvas to rely on for shelter. We have been looking up the records today and find that Amundsen on a journey to the N. magnetic pole in March encountered temperatures similar in degree and recorded a minimum of 79°; but he was with Esquimaux who built him an igloo shelter nightly; he had a good measure of daylight; the temperatures given are probably 'unscreened' from radiation, and finally, he turned homeward and regained his ship after five days' absence. Our party went outward and remained absent for *five weeks*.

It took the best part of a fortnight to cross the coldest region, and then rounding C. Mackay they entered the wind-swept area. Blizzard followed blizzard, the sky was constantly overcast and they staggered on in a light which was little better than complete darkness; sometimes they found themselves high on the slopes of Terror on the left of their track, and sometimes diving into the pressure ridges on the right amidst crevasses and confused ice disturbance. Reaching the foothills near C. Crozier, they ascended 800 feet, then packed their belongings over a moraine ridge and started to build a hut. It took three days to build the stone walls and complete the roof with the canvas brought for the purpose. Then at last they could attend to the object of the journey.

The scant twilight at midday was so short that they must start in the dark and be prepared for the risk of missing their way in returning without light. On the first day in which they set forth under these conditions it took them two hours to reach the pressure ridges, and to clamber over them roped together occupied nearly the same time; finally they reached a place above the rookery where they could hear the birds squawking, but from which they were quite unable to find a way down. The poor light was failing and they returned to camp. Starting again on the following day they wound their way through frightful ice disturbances under the high basalt cliffs; in places the rock overhung, and at one spot they had to creep through a small channel hollowed in the ice. At last they reached the sea-ice, but now the light was so far spent they were obliged to rush everything. Instead of the 2000 or 3000 nesting birds which had been seen here in *Discovery* days, they could now only count about 100; they hastily killed and skinned three to get blubber for their stove, and collecting six eggs, three of which alone survived, they dashed for camp.

It is possible the birds are deserting this rookery, but it is also possible that this early date found only a small minority of the birds which will be collected at a later one. The eggs, which have not yet been examined, should throw light on this point. Wilson observed yet another proof of the strength of the nursing instinct in these birds. In searching for eggs both he and Bowers picked up rounded pieces of ice which these ridiculous creatures had been cherishing with fond hope.

The light had failed entirely by the time the party were clear of the pressure ridges on their return, and it was only by good luck they regained their camp.

That night a blizzard commenced, increasing in fury from moment to moment. They now found that the place chosen for the hut for shelter was worse than useless. They had far better have built in the open, for the fierce wind, instead of striking them directly, was deflected on to them in furious whirling gusts. Heavy blocks of snow and rock placed on the roof were whirled away and the canvas ballooned up, tearing and straining at its securings – its disappearance could only be a question of time. They had erected their tent with some valuables inside close to the hut; it had been well spread and more than amply secured with snow and boulders, but one terrific gust tore it up and whirled it away. Inside the hut they waited for the roof to vanish, wondering what they could do if it went, and vainly endeavouring to make it secure. After fourteen hours it went, as they were trying to pin down one corner. The smother of snow was on them, and they could only dive for their sleeping-bags with a gasp. Bowers put his head out once and said, 'We're all right,' in as near his ordinary tones as he could compass. The others replied 'Yes, we're all right,' and all were silent for a night and half a day whilst the wind howled on; the snow entered every chink and crevice of the sleeping-bags, and the occupants shivered and wondered how it would all end.

This gale was the same (23 July) in which we registered our maximum wind force, and it seems probable that it fell on C. Crozier even more violently than on us.

The wind fell at noon the following day; the forlorn travellers crept from their icy nests, made shift to spread their floorcloth overhead, and lit their primus. They tasted their first food for forty-eight hours and began to plan a means to build a shelter on the homeward route. They decided that they must dig a large pit nightly and cover it as best they could with their floorcloth. But now fortune befriended them; a search to the north revealed the tent lying amongst boulders a quarter of a mile away, and, strange to relate, practically uninjured, a fine testimonial for the material used in its construction. On the following day they started homeward, and immediately another blizzard fell on them, holding them prisoners for two days. By this time the miserable condition of their effects was beyond description. The sleeping-bags were far too stiff to be rolled up, in fact they were so hard frozen that attempts to bend them actually split the skins; the eiderdown bags inside Wilson's and C.-G.'s reindeer covers served but to fitfully stop the gaps made by such rents. All socks, finnesko, and mits had long been coated with ice; placed in breast pockets or inside vests at night they did not even show signs of thawing, much less of drying. It sometimes took C.-G. three-quarters of an hour to get into his sleeping-bag, so flat did it freeze and so difficult was it to open. It is scarcely possible to realise the horrible discomforts of the forlorn travellers as they plodded back across the Barrier with the temperature again constantly below -60°. In this fashion they reached Hut Point and on the following night our home quarters.

Wilson is disappointed at seeing so little of the penguins, but to me and to everyone who has remained here the result of this effort is the appeal it makes to our imagination as one of the most gallant stories in Polar History. That men should wander forth in the depth of a Polar night to face the most dismal cold and the fiercest gales in darkness is something new; that they should have persisted in this effort in spite of every adversity for five full weeks is heroic. It makes a tale for our generation which I hope may not be lost in the telling.

Moreover the material results are by no means despicable. We shall know now when that extraordinary bird the Emperor penguin lays its eggs, and under what conditions; but even if our information remains meagre concerning its embryology, our party has shown the nature of the conditions which exist on the Great Barrier in winter. Hitherto we have only imagined their severity; now we have proof, and a positive light is thrown on the local climatology of our Strait.

EXPERIENCE OF SLEDGING RATIONS AND EQUIPMENT

For our future sledge work several points have been most satisfactorily settled. The party went on a very simple food ration in different and extreme proportions; they took pemmican, butter, biscuit and tea only. After a short experience they found that Wilson, who had arranged for the greatest quantity of fat, had too much of it, and C.-G., who had gone for biscuit, had more than he could eat. A middle course was struck which gave a general proportion agreeable to all, and at the same time suited the total quantities of the various articles carried. In this way we have arrived at a simple and suitable ration for the inland plateau. The only change suggested is the addition of cocoa for the evening meal. The party contented themselves with hot water, deeming that tea might rob them of their slender chance of sleep.

On sleeping-bags little new can be said – the eiderdown bag may be a useful addition for a short time on a spring journey, but they soon get iced up.

Bowers did not use an eiderdown bag throughout, and in some miraculous manner he managed to turn his reindeer bag two or three times during the journey. The following are the weights of sleeping-bags before and after:

	Starting Weight	Final Weight
Wilson, reindeer and eiderdown	17	40
Bowers, reindeer only	17	33
C.-Garrard, reindeer and eiderdown	18	45

This gives some idea of the ice collected.

The double tent has been reported an immense success. It weighed about 35 lbs. at starting and 60 lbs. on return: the ice mainly collected on the inner tent.

The crampons are much praised, except by Bowers, who has an eccentric attachment to our older form. We have discovered a hundred details of clothes, mits, and footwear: there seems no solution to the difficulties which attach to these articles in extreme cold; all Wilson can say, speaking broadly, is 'the gear is excellent, excellent'. One continues to wonder as to the possibilities of fur clothing as made by the Esquimaux, with a sneaking feeling that it may outclass our more civilised garb. For us this can only be a matter of speculation, as it would have been quite impossible to have obtained such articles. With the exception of this radically different alternative, I feel sure we are as near perfection as experience can direct.

At any rate we can now hold that our system of clothing has come through a severer test than any other, fur included.

Effect of Journey Wilson lost 3½ lbs.; Bowers lost 2½ lbs.; C.-Garrard lost 1 lb.

13
THE RETURN OF THE SUN:
3 AUGUST 1911 – 31 AUGUST 1911

Thursday 3 August We have had such a long spell of fine clear weather without especially low temperatures that one can scarcely grumble at the change which we found on waking this morning, when the canopy of stratus cloud spread over us and the wind came in those fitful gusts which promise a gale. All day the wind force has been slowly increasing, whilst the temperature has risen to -15°, but there is no snow falling or drifting as yet. The steam cloud of Erebus was streaming away to the N.W. this morning; now it is hidden.

Our expectations have been falsified so often that we feel ourselves wholly incapable as weather prophets – therefore one scarce dares to predict a blizzard even in face of such disturbance as exists. A paper handed to Simpson by David [Prof. T. Edgeworth David, of Sydney University, who accompanied Shackleton's expedition as geologist], and purporting to contain a description of approaching signs, together with the cause and effect of our blizzards, proves equally hopeless. We have not obtained a single scrap of evidence to verify its statements, and a great number of our observations definitely contradict them. The plain fact is that no two of our storms have been heralded by the same signs.

The low Barrier temperatures experienced by the Crozier Party has naturally led to speculation on the situation of Amundsen and his Norwegians. If his thermometers continuously show temperatures below -60°, the party will have a pretty bad winter and it is difficult to see how he will keep his dogs alive. I should feel anxious if Campbell was in that quarter.

Saturday 5 August The sky has continued to wear a disturbed appearance, but so far nothing has come of it. A good deal of light snow has been falling today; a brisk northerly breeze is drifting it along, giving a very strange yet beautiful effect in the north, where the strong red twilight filters through the haze.

The Crozier Party tell a good story of Bowers, who on their return journey with their recovered tent fitted what he called a 'tent downhaul' and secured it round his sleeping-bag and himself. If the tent went again, he determined to go with it.

Our lecture programme has been renewed. Last night Simpson gave a capital lecture on general meteorology. He started on the general question of insolation, giving various tables to show proportion of sun's heat received at the polar and equatorial regions. Broadly, in latitude 80° one would expect about 22 per cent of the heat received at a spot on the equator.

He dealt with the temperature question by showing interesting tabular comparisons between northern and southern temperatures at given latitudes. So far as these tables go they show the South Polar summer to be 15° colder than the North Polar, but the South Polar winter 3° warmer than the North Polar, but of course this last figure would be completely altered if the observer were to winter on the Barrier. I fancy Amundsen will not concede those 3°!!

From temperatures our lecturer turned to pressures and the upward turn of the gradient in high southern latitudes, as shown by the *Discovery* Expedition. This bears of course on the theory which places an anticyclone in the South Polar region. Lockyer's theories came under discussion; a good many facts appear to support them. The westerly winds of the Roaring Forties are generally understood to be a succession of cyclones. Lockyer's hypothesis supposes that there are some eight or ten cyclones continually revolving at a rate of about 10° of longitude a day, and he imagines them to extend from the 40th parallel to beyond the 60th, thus giving the strong westerly winds in the forties and easterly and southerly in 60° to 70°. Beyond 70° there appears to be generally an irregular outpouring of cold air from the Polar area, with an easterly component significant of anticyclone conditions.

Simpson evolved a new blizzard theory on this. He supposes the surface air intensely cooled over the continental and Barrier areas, and the edge of this cold region lapped by warmer air from the southern limits of Lockyer's cyclones. This would produce a condition of unstable equilibrium, with great potentiality for movement. Since, as we have found, volumes of cold air at different temperatures are very loath to mix, the condition could not be relieved by any gradual process, but continues until the stream is released by some minor cause, when, the ball once started, a huge disturbance results. It seems to be generally held that warm air is passing polewards from the equator continuously at the high levels. It is this potentially warm air which, mixed by the disturbance with the cold air of the interior, gives to our winds so high a temperature.

Such is this theory – like its predecessor it is put up for cockshies, and doubtless by our balloon work or by some other observations it will be upset or modified. Meanwhile it is well to keep one's mind alive with such problems, which mark the road of advance.

Sunday 6 August Sunday with its usual routine. Hymn singing has become a point on which we begin to take some pride to ourselves. With our full attendance of singers we now get a grand volume of sound.

The day started overcast. Chalky is an excellent adjective to describe the appearance of our outlook when the light is much diffused and shadows poor; the scene is dull and flat.

In the afternoon the sky cleared, the moon over Erebus gave a straw colour to the dissipating clouds. This evening the air is full of ice crystals and a stratus forms again. This alternation of clouded and clear skies has been the routine for some time now and is accompanied by the absence of wind which is delightfully novel.

The blood of the Crozier Party, tested by Atkinson, shows a very slight increase of acidity – such was to be expected, and it is pleasing to note that there is no sign of scurvy. If the preserved foods had tended to promote the disease, the length of time and severity of conditions would certainly have brought it out. I think we should be safe on the long journey.

I have had several little chats with Wilson on the happenings of the journey. He says there is no doubt Cherry-Garrard felt the conditions most severely, though he was not only without complaint, but continuously anxious to help others.

Apropos, we both conclude that it is the younger people that have the worst time; Gran, our youngest member (23), is a very clear example, and now Cherry-Garrard at 26.

Wilson (39) says he never felt cold less than he does now; I suppose that between 30 and 40 is the best all-round age. Bowers is a wonder of course. He is 29. When past the forties it is encouraging to remember that Peary was 52!!

Thursday 10 August There has been very little to record of late and my pen has been busy on past records.

The weather has been moderately good and as before wholly incomprehensible. Wind has come from a clear sky and from a clouded one; we had a small blow on Tuesday but it never reached gale force; it came without warning, and every sign which we have regarded as a warning has proved a bogey. The fact is, one must always be prepared for wind and never expect it.

The daylight advances in strides. Day has fitted an extra sash to our window and the light admitted for the first time through triple glass. With this device little ice collects inside.

The ponies are very fit but inclined to be troublesome: the quiet beasts develop tricks without rhyme or reason. Chinaman still kicks and squeals at night. Anton's theory is that he does it to warm himself, and perhaps there is something in it. When eating snow he habitually takes too large a mouthful and swallows it; it is comic to watch him, because when the snow chills his inside he shuffles about with all four legs and wears a most fretful, aggrieved expression: but no sooner has the snow melted than he seizes another mouthful. Other ponies take small mouthfuls or melt a large one on their tongues – this act also produces an amusing expression. Victor and Snippets are confirmed wind suckers. They are at it all the time when the manger board is in place, but it is taken down immediately after feeding time, and then they can only seek vainly for something to catch hold of with their teeth. 'Bones' has taken to kicking at night for no imaginable reason. He hammers away at the back of his stall merrily; we have covered the boards with several layers of sacking, so that the noise is cured, if not the habit. The annoying part of these tricks is that they hold the possibility of damage to the pony. I am glad to say all the lice have disappeared; the final conquest was effected with a very simple remedy – the infected ponies were washed with water in which tobacco had been steeped. Oates had seen this decoction used effectively with troop horses. The result is the greater relief, since we had run out of all the chemicals which had been used for the same purpose.

I have now definitely told off the ponies for the Southern Journey, and the new masters will take charge on 1 September. They will continually exercise the animals so as to get to know them as well as possible. The arrangement has many obvious advantages. The following is the order:

Bowers	Victor	Evans (P.O.)	Snatcher
Wilson	Nobby	Crean	Bones
Atkinson	Jehu	Keohane	Jimmy Pigg
Wright	Chinaman	Oates	Christopher
Cherry-Garrard	Michael	Myself & Oates	Snippets

The first balloon of the season was sent up yesterday by Bowers and Simpson. It rose on a southerly wind, but remained in it for 100 feet or less, then for 300 or 400 feet it went straight up, and after that directly south over Razor Back Island. Everything seemed to go well, the thread, on being held, tightened and then fell slack as it should do. It was followed for two miles or more running in a straight line for Razor Back, but within a few hundred yards of the Island it came to an end. The searchers went round the Island to try and recover the clue, but without result. Almost identically the same thing happened after the last ascent made, and we are much puzzled to find the cause.

The continued proximity of the south moving air currents above is very interesting.

The Crozier Party are not right yet, their feet are exceedingly sore, and there are other indications of strain. I must almost except Bowers, who, whatever his feelings, went off as gaily as usual on the search for the balloon.

Saw a very beautiful effect on my afternoon walk yesterday: the full moon was shining brightly from a quarter exactly opposite to the fading twilight and the icebergs were lit on one side by the yellow lunar light and on the other by the paler white daylight. The first seemed to be gilded, while the diffused light of day gave to the other a deep, cold, greenish-blue colour – the contrast was strikingly beautiful.

Friday 11 August The long-expected blizzard came in the night; it is still blowing hard with drift.

Yesterday evening Oates gave his second lecture on 'Horse management'. He was brief and a good deal to the point. 'Not born but made' was his verdict on the good manager of animals. 'The horse has no reasoning power at all, but an excellent memory'; sights and sounds recall circumstances under which they were previously seen or heard. It is no use shouting at a horse: ten to one he will associate the noise with some form of trouble, and getting excited, will set out to make it. It is ridiculous for the rider of a bucking horse to shout 'Whoa!' – 'I know,' said the Soldier, 'because I have done it.' Also it is to be remembered that loud talk to one horse may disturb other horses. The great thing is to be firm and quiet.

A horse's memory, explained the Soldier, warns it of events to come. He gave instances of hunters and race-horses which go off their feed and show great excitement in other ways before events for which they are prepared; for this reason every effort should be made to keep the animals quiet in camp. Rugs should be put on directly after a halt and not removed till the last moment before a march.

After a few hints on leading, the lecturer talked of possible improvements in our wintering arrangements. A loose box for each animal would be an advantage, and a small amount of litter on which he could lie down. Some of our ponies lie down, but rarely for more than 10 minutes – the Soldier thinks they find the ground too cold. He thinks it would be wise to clip animals before the winter sets in. He is in doubt as to the advisability of grooming. He passed to the improvements preparing for the coming journey – the nose bags, picketing lines, and rugs. He proposes to bandage the legs of all ponies. Finally he dealt with the difficult subjects of snow blindness and soft surfaces: for the first he suggested dyeing the forelocks, which have now grown quite long. Oates indulges a pleasant conceit in finishing his discourses with a merry tale. Last night's tale evoked shouts of laughter, but, alas! it is quite unprintable! Our discussion hinged altogether on the final subjects of the lecture as concerning snow blindness – the dyed forelocks seem inadequate, and the best suggestion seems the addition of a sun bonnet rather than blinkers, or, better still, a peak over the eyes attached to the headstall. I doubt if this question will be difficult to settle, but the snow-shoe problem is much more serious. This has been much in our minds of late, and Petty Officer Evans has been making trial shoes for Snatcher on vague ideas of our remembrance of the shoes worn for lawn mowing.

Besides the problem of the form of the shoes, comes the question of the means of attachment. All sorts of suggestions were made last night as to both points, and the discussion cleared the air a good deal. I think that with slight modification our present pony snow-shoes made on the grating or racquet principle may prove best after all. The only drawback is that they are made for very soft snow and unnecessarily large for the Barrier; this would make them liable to be strained on hard patches. The alternative seems to be to perfect the principle of the lawn mowing shoe, which is little more than a stiff bag over the hoof.

Perhaps we shall come to both kinds: the first for the quiet animals and the last for the more excitable. I am confident the matter is of first importance.

Monday 14 August Since the comparatively short storm of Friday, in which we had a temperature of -30° with a 50 m.p.h. wind, we have had two delightfully calm days, and today there is every promise of the completion of a third. On such days the light is quite good for three to four hours at midday and has a cheering effect on man and beast.

The ponies are so pleased that they seize the slightest opportunity to part company with their leaders and gallop off with tail and heels flung high. The dogs are equally festive and are getting more exercise than could be given in the dark. The two Esquimaux dogs have been taken in hand by Clissold, as I have noted before. He now takes them out with a leader borrowed from Meares, usually little 'Noogis'. On Saturday the sledge capsized at the tide crack; Clissold was left on the snow whilst the team disappeared in the distance. Noogis returned later, having eaten through his harness, and the others were eventually found some two miles away, 'foul' of an ice hummock. Yesterday Clissold took the same team to Cape Royds; they brought back a load of 100 lbs. a dog in about two hours. It would have been a good performance for the best dogs in the time, and considering that Meares pronounced these two dogs useless, Clissold deserves a great deal of credit.

Yesterday we had a really successful balloon ascent: the balloon ran out four miles of thread before it was released, and the instrument fell without a parachute. The searchers followed the clue about 2½ miles to the north, when it turned and came back parallel to itself, and only about 30 yards distant from it. The instrument was found undamaged and with the record properly scratched.

Nelson has been out a good deal more of late. He has got a good little run of serial temperatures with water samples, and however meagre his results, they may be counted as exceedingly accurate; his methods include the great scientific care which is now considered necessary for this work, and one realises that he is one of the few people who have been trained in it. Yesterday he got his first net haul from the bottom, with the assistance of Atkinson and Cherry-Garrard.

Atkinson has some personal interest in the work. He has been getting remarkable results himself and has discovered a host of new parasites in the seals; he has been trying to correlate these with like discoveries in the fishes, in hope of working out complete life histories in both primary and secondary hosts.

But the joint hosts of the fishes may be the mollusca or other creatures on which they feed, and hence the new fields for Atkinson in Nelson's catches. There is a relative simplicity in the round of life in its higher forms in these regions that would seem especially hopeful for the parasitologist.

My afternoon walk has become a pleasure; everything is beautiful in this half light and the northern sky grows redder as the light wanes.

Tuesday 15 August The instrument recovered from the balloon shows an ascent of 2½ miles, and the temperature at that height only 5° or 6° C. below that at the surface. If, as one must suppose, this layer extends over the Barrier, it would there be at a considerably higher temperature than the surface. Simpson has imagined a very cold surface layer on the Barrier.

The acetylene has suddenly failed, and I find myself at this moment writing by daylight for the first time.

The first addition to our colony came last night, when 'Lassie' produced six or seven puppies – we are keeping the family very quiet and as warm as possible in the stable.

It is very pleasant to note the excellent relations which our young Russians have established with other folk; they both work very hard, Anton having most to do. Demetri is the more intelligent and begins to talk English fairly well. Both are on the best terms with their mess-mates, and it was amusing last night to see little Anton jamming a felt hat over P.O. Evans' head in high good humour.

Wright lectured on 'Radium' last night.

The transformation of the radioactive elements suggestive of the transmutation of metals was perhaps the most interesting idea suggested, but the discussion ranged mainly round the effect which the discovery of radioactivity has had on physics and chemistry in its bearing on the origin of matter, on geology as bearing on the internal heat of the earth, and on medicine in its curative powers. The geologists and doctors admitted little virtue to it, but of course the physicists boomed their own wares, which enlivened the debate.

Thursday 17 August The weather has been extremely kind to us of late; we haven't a single grumble against it. The temperature hovers pretty constantly at about -35°, there is very little wind and the sky is clear and bright. In such weather one sees well for more than three hours before and after noon, the landscape unfolds itself, and the sky colours are always delicate and beautiful. At noon today there was bright sunlight on the tops of the Western Peaks and on the summit and steam of Erebus – of late the vapour cloud of Erebus has been exceptionally heavy and fantastic in form.

The balloon has become a daily institution. Yesterday the instrument was recovered in triumph, but today the threads carried the searchers in amongst the icebergs and soared aloft over their crests – anon the clue was recovered beyond, and led towards Tent Island, then towards Inaccessible, then back to the bergs. Never was such an elusive thread. Darkness descended with the searchers on a strong scent for the Razor Backs: Bowers returned full of hope.

The wretched Lassie has killed every one of her litter. She is mother for the first time, and possibly that accounts for it. When the poor little mites were alive she constantly left them, and when taken back she either trod on them or lay on them, till not one was left alive. It is extremely annoying.

As the daylight comes, people are busier than ever. It does one good to see so much work going on.

Friday 18 August Atkinson lectured on 'Scurvy' last night. He spoke clearly and slowly, but the disease is anything but precise. He gave a little summary of its history afloat and the remedies long in use in the Navy.

He described the symptoms with some detail. Mental depression, debility, syncope, petechiæ, livid patches, spongy gums, lesions, swellings, and so on to things that are worse. He passed to some of the theories held and remedies tried in accordance with them. Ralph came nearest the truth in discovering decrease of chlorine and alkalinity of urine. Sir Almroth Wright has hit the truth, he thinks, in finding increased acidity of blood – acid intoxication – by methods only possible in recent years.

This acid condition is due to two salts, sodium hydrogen carbonate and sodium hydrogen phosphate; these cause the symptoms observed and infiltration of fat in organs, leading to feebleness of heart action. The method of securing and testing serum of patient was described (titration, a colorimetric method of measuring the percentage of substances in solution), and the test by litmus paper of normal or super-normal solution. In this test the ordinary healthy man shows normal 30 to 50: the scurvy patient normal 90.

Lactate of sodium increases alkalinity of blood, but only within narrow limits, and is the only chemical remedy suggested.

So far for diagnosis, but it does not bring us much closer to the cause, preventives, or remedies. Practically we are much as we were before, but the lecturer proceeded to deal with the practical side.

In brief, he holds the first cause to be tainted food, but secondary or contributory causes may be even more potent in developing the disease. Damp, cold, over-exertion, bad air, bad light, in fact any condition exceptional to normal healthy existence. Remedies are merely to change these conditions for the better. Dietetically, fresh vegetables are the best curatives – the lecturer was doubtful of fresh meat, but admitted its possibility in Polar climate; lime juice only useful if regularly taken. He discussed lightly the relative values of vegetable stuffs, doubtful of those containing abundance of phosphates such as lentils. He touched theory again in continuing the cause of acidity to bacterial action – and the possibility of infection in epidemic form. Wilson is evidently slow to accept the 'acid intoxication' theory; his attitude is rather 'non proven'. His remarks were extremely sound and practical as usual. He proved the value of fresh meat in Polar regions.

Scurvy seems very far away from us this time, yet after our *Discovery* experience, one feels that no trouble can be too great or no precaution too small to be adopted to keep it at bay. Therefore such an evening as last was well spent.

It is certain we shall not have the disease here, but one cannot foresee equally certain avoidance in the southern journey to come. All one can do is to take every possible precaution.

Ran over to Tent Island this afternoon and climbed to the top – I have not been there since 1903. Was struck with great amount of loose sand; it seemed to get smaller in grain from S. to N. Fine view from top of island: one specially notices the gap left by the breaking up of the Glacier Tongue.

The distance to the top of the island and back is between 7 and 8 statute miles, and the run in this weather is fine healthy exercise. Standing on the island today with a glorious view of mountains, islands, and glaciers, I thought how very different must be the outlook of the Norwegians. A dreary white plain of Barrier behind and an uninviting stretch of sea-ice in front. With no landmarks, nothing to guide if the light fails, it is probable that they venture but a very short distance from their hut.

The prospects of such a situation do not smile on us.

The weather remains fine – this is the sixth day without wind.

Sunday 20 August The long-expected blizzard came yesterday – a good honest blow, the drift vanishing long before the wind. This and the rise of temperature (to 2°) has smoothed and polished all ice or snow surfaces. A few days ago I could walk anywhere in my soft finnesko with sealskin soles; today it needed great caution to prevent tumbles. I think there has been a good deal of ablation.

The sky is clear today, but the wind still strong though warm. I went along the shore of the North Bay and climbed to the glacier over one of the drifted faults in the ice face. It is steep and slippery, but by this way one can arrive above the Ramp without touching rock and thus avoid cutting soft footwear.

The ice problems in our neighbourhood become more fascinating and elusive as one re-examines them by the returning light; some will be solved.

Monday 21 August Weights and measurements last evening. We have remained surprisingly constant. There seems to have been improvement in lung power and grip is shown by spirometer and dynamometer, but weights have altered very little. I have gone up nearly 3 lbs. in winter, but the increase has occurred during the last month, when I have been taking more exercise. Certainly there is every reason to be satisfied with the general state of health.

The ponies are becoming a handful. Three of the four exercised today so far have run away – Christopher and Snippets broke away from Oates and Victor from Bowers. Nothing but high spirits, there is no vice in these animals; but I fear we are going to have trouble with sledges and snow-shoes. At present the Soldier dare not issue oats or the animals would become quite unmanageable. Bran is running low; he wishes he had more of it.

Tuesday 22 August I am renewing study of glacier problems; the face of the ice cliff 300 yards east of the homestead is full of enigmas. Yesterday evening Ponting gave us a lecture on his Indian travels. He is very frank in acknowledging his debt to guide-books for information, nevertheless he tells his story well and his slides are wonderful. In personal reminiscence he is distinctly dramatic – he thrilled us a good deal last night with a vivid description of a sunrise in the sacred city of Benares. In the first dim light the waiting, praying multitude of bathers, the wonderful ritual and its incessant performance; then, as the sun approaches, the hush – the effect of thousands of worshippers waiting in silence – a silence to be felt. Finally, as the first rays appear, the swelling roar of a single word from tens of thousands of throats: 'Ambah!' It was artistic to follow this picture of life with the gruesome horrors of the ghat. This impressionist style of lecturing is very attractive and must essentially cover a great deal of ground. So we saw Jeypore, Udaipore, Darjeeling, and a confusing number of places – temples, monuments and tombs in profusion, with remarkable pictures of the wonderful Taj Mahal – horses, elephants, alligators, wild boars, and flamingoes – warriors, fakirs, and nautch girls – an impression here and an impression there.

It is worth remembering how attractive this style can be – in lecturing one is inclined to give too much attention to connecting links which join one episode to another. A lecture need not be a connected story; perhaps it is better it should not be.

It was my night on duty last night and I watched the oncoming of a blizzard with exceptional beginnings. The sky became very gradually overcast between 1 and 4 a.m. About 2.30 the temperature rose on a steep grade from -20° to -3°; the barometer was falling, rapidly for these regions. Soon after 4 the wind came with a rush, but without snow or drift. For a time it was more gusty than has ever yet been recorded even in this region. In one gust the wind rose from 4 to 68 m.p.h. and fell again to 20 m.p.h. within a minute; another reached 80 m.p.h., but not from such a low point of origin. The effect in the hut was curious; for a space all would be quiet, then a shattering blast would descend with a clatter and rattle past ventilator and chimneys, so sudden, so threatening, that it was comforting to remember the solid structure of our building. The suction of such a gust is so heavy that even the heavy snow-covered roof of the stable, completely sheltered on the lee side of the main building, is violently shaken – one could well imagine the plight of our adventurers at C. Crozier when their roof was destroyed. The snow which came at 6 lessened the gustiness and brought the ordinary phenomena of a blizzard. It is blowing hard today, with broken windy clouds and roving bodies of drift. A wild day for the return of the sun. Had it been fine today we should have seen the sun for the first time; yesterday it shone on the lower foothills to the west, but today we see nothing but gilded drift clouds. Yet it is grand to have daylight rushing at one.

Wednesday 23 August We toasted the sun in champagne last night, coupling Victor Campbell's name as his birthday coincides. The return of the sun could not be appreciated as we have not had a glimpse of it, and the taste of the champagne went wholly unappreciated; it was a very mild revel. Meanwhile the gale continues. Its full force broke last night with an average of nearly 70 m.p.h. for some hours: the temperature has been up to 10° and the snowfall heavy. At seven this morning the air was thicker with whirling drift than it has ever been.

It seems as though the violence of the storms which succeed our rare spells of fine weather is in proportion to the duration of the spells.

Thursday 24 August Another night and day of furious wind and drift, and still no sign of the end. The temperature has been as high as 16°. Now and again the snow ceases and then the drift rapidly diminishes, but such an interval is soon followed by fresh clouds of snow. It is quite warm outside, one can go about with head uncovered – which leads me to suppose that one does get hardened to cold to some extent – for I suppose one would not wish to remain uncovered in a storm in England if the temperature showed 16 degrees of frost. This is the third day of confinement to the hut: it grows tedious, but there is no help, as it is too thick to see more than a few yards out of doors.

Friday 25 August The gale continued all night and it blows hard this morning, but the sky is clear, the drift has ceased, and the few whale-back clouds about Erebus carry a promise of improving conditions.

Last night there was an intensely black cloud low on the northern horizon – but for earlier experience of the winter one would have sworn to it as a water sky; but I think the phenomenon is due to the shadow of retreating drift clouds. This morning the sky is clear to the north, so that the sea-ice cannot have broken out in the Sound.

During snowy gales it is almost necessary to dress oneself in wind clothes if one ventures outside for the briefest periods – exposed woollen or cloth materials become heavy with powdery crystals in a minute or two, and when brought into the warmth of the hut are soon wringing wet. Where there is no drift it is quicker and easier to slip on an overcoat.

It is not often I have a sentimental attachment for articles of clothing, but I must confess an affection for my veteran uniform overcoat, inspired by its persistent utility. I find that it is twenty-three years of age and can testify to its strenuous existence. It has been spared neither rain, wind, nor salt sea spray, tropic heat nor Arctic cold; it has outlived many sets of buttons, from their glittering gilded youth to green old age, and it supports its four-stripe shoulder straps as gaily as the single lace ring of the early days which proclaimed it the possession of a humble sub-lieutenant. Withal it is still a very long way from the fate of the 'one-horse shay'.

Taylor gave us his final physiographical lecture last night. It was completely illustrated with slides made from our own negatives, Ponting's Alpine work, and the choicest illustrations of certain scientific books. The preparation of the slides had involved a good deal of work for Ponting as well as for the lecturer. The lecture dealt with ice erosion, and the pictures made it easy to follow the comparison of our own mountain forms and glacial contours with those that have received so much attention elsewhere. Noticeable differences are the absence of moraine material on the lower surfaces of our glaciers, their relatively insignificant movement, their steep sides, etc. It is difficult to convey the bearing of the difference or similarity of various features common to the pictures under comparison without their aid. It is sufficient to note that the points to which the lecturer called attention were pretty obvious and that the lecture was exceedingly instructive. The origin of 'cirques' or 'cwms', of which we have remarkably fine examples, is still a little mysterious – one notes also the requirement of observation which might throw light on the erosion of previous ages.

After Taylor's effort Ponting showed a number of very beautiful slides of Alpine scenery – not a few are triumphs of the photographer's art. As a wind-up Ponting took a flashlight photograph of our hut converted into a lecture hall: a certain amount of faking will be required, but I think this is very allowable under the circumstances.

Oates tells me that one of the ponies, 'Snippets', will eat blubber! the possible uses of such an animal are remarkable!

The gravel on the north side of the hut against which the stable is built has been slowly but surely worn down, leaving gaps under the boarding. Through these gaps and our floor we get an unpleasantly strong stable effluvium, especially when the wind is strong. We are trying to stuff the holes up, but have not had much success so far.

Saturday 26 August A dying wind and clear sky yesterday, and almost calm today. The noon sun is cut off by the long low foot slope of Erebus which runs to Cape Royds. Went up the Ramp at noon yesterday and found no advantage – one should go over the floe to get the earliest sight, and yesterday afternoon Evans caught a last glimpse of the upper limb from that situation, whilst Simpson saw the same from Wind Vane Hill.

The ponies are very buckish and can scarcely be held in at exercise; it seems certain that they feel the return of daylight. They were out in morning and afternoon yesterday. Oates and Anton took out Christopher and Snippets rather later. Both ponies broke away within 50 yards of the stable and galloped away over the floe. It was nearly an hour before they could be rounded up. Such escapades are the result of high spirits; there is no vice in the animals.

We have had comparatively little aurora of late, but last night was an exception; there was a good display at 3 a.m.

p.m. Just before lunch the sunshine could be seen gilding the floe, and Ponting and I walked out to the bergs. The nearest one has been overturned and is easily climbed. From the top we could see the sun clear over the rugged outline of C. Barne. It was glorious to stand bathed in brilliant sunshine once more. We felt very young, sang and cheered – we were reminded of a bright frosty morning in England – everything sparkled and the air had the same crisp feel. There is little new to be said of the return of the sun in Polar regions, yet it is such a very real and important event that one cannot pass it in silence. It changes the outlook on life of every individual, foul weather is robbed of its terrors; if it is stormy today it will be fine tomorrow or the next day, and each day's delay will mean a brighter outlook when the sky is clear.

Climbed the Ramp in the afternoon, the shouts and songs of men and the neighing of horses borne to my ears as I clambered over its kopjes.

We are now pretty well convinced that the Ramp is a moraine resting on a platform of ice.

The sun rested on the sunshine recorder for a few minutes, but made no visible impression. We did not get our first record in the *Discovery* until September. It is surprising that so little heat should be associated with such a flood of light.

Sunday 27 August Overcast sky and chill south-easterly wind. Sunday routine, no one very active. Had a run to South Bay over 'Domain'.

Monday 28 August Ponting and Gran went round the bergs late last night. On returning they saw a dog coming over the floe from the north. The animal rushed towards and leapt about them with every sign of intense joy. Then they realised that it was our long lost Julick.

His mane was crusted with blood and he smelt strongly of seal blubber – his stomach was full, but the sharpness of back-bone showed that this condition had only been temporary.

By daylight he looks very fit and strong, and he is evidently very pleased to be home again.

We are absolutely at a loss to account for his adventures. It is exactly a month since he was missed – what on earth can have happened to him all this time? One would give a great deal to hear his tale. Everything is against the theory that he was a wilful absentee – his previous habits and his joy at getting back. If he wished to get back, he cannot have been lost anywhere in the neighbourhood, for, as Meares says, the barking of the station dogs can be heard at least 7 or 8 miles away in calm weather, besides which there are tracks everywhere and unmistakable landmarks to guide man or beast. I cannot but think the animal has been cut off, but this can only have happened by his being carried away on broken sea-ice, and as far as we know the open water has never been nearer than 10 or 12 miles at the least. It is another enigma.

On Saturday last a balloon was sent up. The thread was found broken a mile away. Bowers and Simpson walked many miles in search of the instrument, but could find no trace of it. The theory now propounded is that if there is strong differential movement in air currents, the thread is not strong enough to stand the strain as the balloon passes from one current to another. It is amazing, and forces the employment of a new system. It is now proposed to discard the thread and attach the instrument to a flag and staff, which it is hoped will plant itself in the snow on falling.

The sun is shining into the hut windows – already sunbeams rest on the opposite walls.

I have mentioned the curious cones which are the conspicuous feature of our Ramp scenery – they stand from 8 to 20 feet in height, some irregular, but a number quite perfectly conical in outline. Today Taylor and Gran took pick and crowbar and started to dig into one of the smaller ones. After removing a certain amount of loose rubble they came on solid rock, kenyte, having two or three irregular cracks traversing the exposed surface. It was only with great trouble they removed one or two of the smallest fragments severed by these cracks. There was no sign of ice. This gives a great 'leg up' to the 'debris' cone theory.

Demetri and Clissold took two small teams of dogs to Cape Royds today. They found some dog footprints near the hut, but think these were not made by Julick. Demetri points far to the west as the scene of that animal's adventures. Parties from C. Royds always bring a number of illustrated papers which must have been brought down by the *Nimrod* on her last visit. The ostensible object is to provide amusement for our Russian companions, but as a matter of fact everyone finds them interesting.

Tuesday 29 August I find that the card of the sunshine recorder showed an hour and a half's burn yesterday and was very faintly marked on Saturday; already, therefore, the sun has given us warmth, even if it can only be measured instrumentally.

Last night Meares told us of his adventures in and about Lolo land, a wild Central Asian country nominally tributary to Lhassa. He had no pictures and very makeshift maps, yet he held us really entranced for nearly two hours by the sheer interest of his adventures. The spirit of the wanderer is in Meares' blood: he has no happiness but in the wild places of the earth. I have never met so extreme a type. Even now he is looking forward to getting away by himself to Hut Point, tired already of our scant measure of civilisation.

He has keen natural powers of observation for all practical facts and a quite prodigious memory for such things, but a lack of scientific training causes the acceptance of exaggerated appearances, which so often present themselves to travellers when unfamiliar objects are first seen. For instance, when the spoor of some unknown beast is described as 6 inches across, one shrewdly guesses that a cold scientific measurement would have reduced this figure by nearly a half; so it is with mountains, cliffs, waterfalls, etc. With all deduction on this account the lecture was extraordinarily interesting. Meares lost his companion and leader, poor Brook, on the expedition which he described to us. The party started up the Yangtse, travelling from Shanghai to Hankow and thence to Ichang by steamer – then by houseboat towed by coolies through wonderful gorges and one dangerous rapid to Chunking and Chengtu. In those parts the travellers always took the three principal rooms of the inn they patronised, the cost 150 cash, something less than fourpence – oranges twenty a penny – the coolies with 100 lb. loads would cover 30 to 40 miles a day – salt is got in bores sunk with bamboos to nearly a mile in depth; it takes two or three generations to sink a bore. The lecturer described the Chinese frontier town Quanchin, its people, its products, chiefly medicinal musk pods from musk deer. Here also the wonderful ancient damming of the river, and a temple to the constructor, who wrote, twenty centuries ago, 'dig out your ditches, but keep your banks low'. On we were taken along mountain trails over high snow-filled passes and across rivers on bamboo bridges to Wassoo, a timber centre from which great rafts of lumber are shot down the river, over fearsome rapids, freighted with Chinamen. 'They generally come through all right,' said the lecturer.

Higher up the river (Min) live the peaceful Ching Ming people, an ancient aboriginal stock, and beyond these the wild tribes, the Lolo themselves. They made doubtful friends with a chief preparing for war. Meares described a feast given to them in a barbaric hall hung with skins and weapons, the men clad in buckskin dyed red, and bristling with arms; barbaric dishes, barbaric music. Then the hunt for new animals; the Chinese Tarkin, the parti-coloured bear, blue mountain sheep, the golden-haired monkey, and talk of new fruits and flowers and a host of little-known birds.

More adventures among the wild tribes of the mountains; the white lamas, the black lamas and phallic worship. Curious prehistoric caves with ancient terracotta figures resembling only others found in Japan and supplying a curious link. A feudal system running with well-oiled wheels, the happiest of communities. A separation (temporary) from Brook, who wrote in his diary that tribes were very friendly and seemed anxious to help him, and was killed on the day following – the truth hard to gather – the recovery of his body, etc.

As he left the country the Nepaulese ambassador arrives, returning from Pekin with large escort and bound for Lhassa: the ambassador half demented and Meares, who speaks many languages, is begged by ambassador and escort to accompany the party. He is obliged to miss this chance of a lifetime.

This is the meagrest outline of the tale which Meares adorned with a hundred incidental facts – for instance, he told us of the Lolo trade in green waxfly – the insect is propagated seasonally by thousands of Chinese who subsist on the sale of the wax produced, but all insects die between seasons. At the commencement of each season there is a market to which the wild hill Lolos bring countless tiny bamboo boxes, each containing a male and female insect, the breeding of which is their share in the industry.

We are all adventurers here, I suppose, and wild doings in wild countries appeal to us as nothing else could do. It is good to know that there remain wild corners of this dreadfully civilised world.

We have had a bright fine day. This morning a balloon was sent up without thread and with the flag device to which I have alluded. It went slowly but steadily to the north and so over the Barne Glacier. It was difficult to follow with glasses frequently clouding with the breath, but we saw the instrument detached when the slow match burned out. I'm afraid there is no doubt it fell on the glacier and there is little hope of recovering it. We have now decided to use a thread again, but to send the bobbin up with the balloon, so that it unwinds from that end and there will be no friction where it touches the snow or rock.

This investigation of upper air conditions is proving a very difficult matter, but we are not beaten yet.

Wednesday 30 August Fine bright day. The thread of the balloon sent up today broke very short off through some fault in the cage holding the bobbin. By good luck the instrument was found in the North Bay, and held a record.

This is the fifth record showing a constant inversion of temperature for a few hundred feet and then a gradual fall, so that the temperature of the surface is not reached again for 2000 or 3000 feet. The establishment of this fact repays much of the trouble caused by the ascents.

Thursday 31 August Went round about the Domain and Ramp with Wilson. We are now pretty well decided as to certain matters that puzzled us at first. The Ramp is undoubtedly a moraine supported on the decaying end of the glacier. A great deal of the underlying ice is exposed, but we had doubts as to whether this ice was not the result of winter drifting and summer thawing. We have a little difference of opinion as to whether this morainic material has been brought down in surface layers or pushed up from the bottom ice layers, as in Alpine glaciers. There is no doubt that the glacier is retreating with comparative rapidity, and this leads us to account for the various ice slabs about the hut as remains of the glacier, but a puzzling fact confronts this proposition in the discovery of penguin feathers in the lower strata of ice in both ice caves. The shifting of levels in the morainic material would account for the drying up of some lakes and the terrace formations in others, whilst curious trenches in the ground are obviously due to cracks in the ice beneath. We are now quite convinced that the queer cones on the Ramp are merely the result of the weathering of big blocks of agglomerate. As weathering results they appear unique. We have not yet a satisfactory explanation of the broad roadway faults that traverse every small eminence in our immediate region. They must originate from the unequal weathering of lava flows, but it is difficult to imagine the process. The dip of the lavas on our Cape corresponds with that of the lavas of Inaccessible Island, and points to an eruptive centre to the south and not towards Erebus. Here is food for reflection for the geologists.

The wind blew quite hard from the N.N.W. on Wednesday night, fell calm in the day, and came from the S.E. with snow as we started to return from our walk; there was a full blizzard by the time we reached the hut.

14
PREPARATIONS, THE SPRING JOURNEY:
1 SEPTEMBER 1911 – 3 OCTOBER 1911

Friday 1 September A very windy night, dropping to gusts in morning, preceding beautifully calm, bright day. If September holds as good as August we shall not have cause of complaint. Meares and Demetri started for Hut Point just before noon. The dogs were in fine form. Demetri's team came over the hummocky tide crack at full gallop, depositing the driver on the snow. Luckily some of us were standing on the floe. I made a dash at the bow of the sledge as it dashed past and happily landed on top; Atkinson grasped at the same object, but fell, and was dragged merrily over the ice. The weight reduced the pace, and others soon came up and stopped the team. Demetri was very crestfallen. He is extremely active and it's the first time he's been unseated.

There is no real reason for Meares' departure yet awhile, but he chose to go and probably hopes to train the animals better when he has them by themselves. As things are, this seems like throwing out the advance guard for the summer campaign.

I have been working very hard at sledging figures with Bowers' able assistance. The scheme develops itself in the light of these figures, and I feel that our organisation will not be found wanting, yet there is an immense amount of detail, and every arrangement has to be more than usually elastic to admit of extreme possibilities of the full success or complete failure of the motors.

I think our plan will carry us through without the motors (though in that case nothing else must fail), and will take full advantage of such help as the motors may give. Our spring travelling is to be limited order. E. Evans, Gran, and Forde will go out to find and re-mark 'Corner Camp'. Meares will then carry out as much fodder as possible with the dogs. Simpson, Bowers, and I are going to stretch our legs across to the Western Mountains. There is no choice but to keep the rest at home to exercise the ponies. It's not going to be a light task to keep all these frisky little beasts in order, as their food is increased. Today the change in masters has taken place. By the new arrangement:

Wilson takes Nobby
Cherry-Garrard takes Michael
Wright takes Chinaman
Atkinson takes Jehu.

The new comers seem very pleased with their animals, though they are by no means the pick of the bunch.

Sunday 3 September The weather still remains fine, the temperature down in the minus thirties. All going well and everyone in splendid spirits. Last night Bowers lectured on Polar clothing. He had worked the subject up from our Polar library with critical and humorous ability, and since his recent journey he must be considered as entitled to an authoritative opinion of his own. The points in our clothing problems are too technical and too frequently discussed to need special notice at present, but as a result of a new study of Arctic precedents it is satisfactory to find it becomes more and more evident that our equipment is the best that has been devised for the purpose, always excepting the possible alternative of skins for spring journeys, an alternative we have no power to adopt. In spite of this we are making minor improvements all the time.

Sunday 10 September A whole week since the last entry in my diary. I feel very negligent of duty, but my whole time has been occupied in making detailed plans for the Southern journey. These are finished at last, I am glad to say; every figure has been checked by Bowers, who has been an enormous help to me. If the motors are successful, we shall have no difficulty in getting to the Glacier, and if they fail, we shall still get there with any ordinary degree of good fortune. To work three units of four men from that point onwards requires no small provision, but with the proper provision it should take a good deal to stop the attainment of our object. I have tried to take every reasonable possibility of misfortune into consideration, and to so organise the parties as to be prepared to meet them. I fear to be too sanguine, yet taking everything into consideration I feel that our chances ought to be good. The animals are in splendid form. Day by day the ponies get fitter as their exercise increases, and the stronger, harder food toughens their muscles. They are very different animals from those which we took south last year, and with another month of training I feel there is not one of them but will make light of the loads we shall ask them to draw. But we cannot spare any of the ten, and so there must always be anxiety of the disablement of one or more before their work is done.

E. R. Evans, Forde, and Gran left early on Saturday for Corner Camp. I hope they will have no difficulty in finding it. Meares and Demetri came back from Hut Point the same afternoon – the dogs are wonderfully fit and strong, but Meares reports no seals up in the region, and as he went to make seal pemmican, there was little object in his staying. I leave him to come and go as he pleases, merely setting out the work he has to do in the simplest form. I want him to take fourteen bags of forage (130 lbs. each) to Corner Camp before the end of October and to be ready to start for his supporting work soon after the pony party – a light task for his healthy teams. Of hopeful signs for the future none are more remarkable than the health and spirit of our people. It would be impossible to imagine a more vigorous community, and there does not seem to be a single weak spot in the twelve good men and true who are chosen for the Southern advance. All are now experienced sledge travellers, knit together with a bond of friendship that has never been equalled under such circumstances. Thanks to these people, and more especially to Bowers and Petty Officer Evans, there is not a single detail of our equipment which is not arranged with the utmost care and in accordance with the tests of experience.

It is good to have arrived at a point where one can run over facts and figures again and again without detecting a flaw or foreseeing a difficulty.

I do not count on the motors – that is a strong point in our case – but should they work well our earlier task of reaching the Glacier will be made quite easy. Apart from such help I am anxious that these machines should enjoy some measure of success and justify the time, money, and thought which have been given to their construction. I am still very confident of the possibility of motor traction, whilst realising that reliance cannot be placed on it in its present untried evolutionary state – it is satisfactory to add that my own view is the most cautious one held in our party. Day is quite convinced he will go a long way and is prepared to accept much heavier weights than I have given him. Lashly's opinion is perhaps more doubtful, but on the whole hopeful. Clissold is to make the fourth man of the motor party. I have already mentioned his mechanical capabilities. He has had a great deal of experience with motors, and Day is delighted to have his assistance.

We had two lectures last week – the first from Debenham dealing with General Geology and having special reference to the structures of our region. It cleared up a good many points in my mind concerning the gneissic base rocks, the Beacon sandstone, and the dolerite intrusions. I think we shall be in a position to make fairly good field observations when we reach the southern land.

The scientific people have taken keen interest in making their lectures interesting, and the custom has grown of illustrating them with lantern slides made from our own photographs, from books, or from drawings of the lecturer. The custom adds to the interest of the subject, but robs the reporter of notes. The second weekly lecture was given by Ponting. His store of pictures seems unending and has been an immense source of entertainment to us during the winter. His lectures appeal to all and are fully attended. This time we had pictures of the Great Wall and other stupendous monuments of North China. Ponting always manages to work in detail concerning the manners and customs of the peoples in the countries of his travels; on Friday he told us of Chinese farms and industries, of hawking and other sports, most curious of all, of the pretty amusement of flying pigeons with æolian whistling pipes attached to their tail feathers.

Ponting would have been a great asset to our party if only on account of his lectures, but his value as pictorial recorder of events becomes daily more apparent. No expedition has ever been illustrated so extensively, and the only difficulty will be to select from the countless subjects that have been recorded by his camera – and yet not a single subject is treated with haste; the first picture is rarely counted good enough, and in some cases five or six plates are exposed before our very critical artist is satisfied.

This way of going to work would perhaps be more striking if it were not common to all our workers here; a very demon of unrest seems to stir them to effort and there is now not a single man who is not striving his utmost to get good results in his own particular department.

It is a really satisfactory state of affairs all round. If the Southern journey comes off, nothing, not even priority at the Pole, can prevent the Expedition ranking as one of the most important that ever entered the Polar regions.

On Friday Cherry-Garrard produced the second volume of the *S.P.T.* – on the whole an improvement on the first. Poor Cherry perspired over the editorial, and it bears the signs of labour – the letterpress otherwise is in the lighter strain: Taylor again the most important contributor, but now at rather too great a length; Nelson has supplied a very humorous trifle; the illustrations are quite delightful, the highwater mark of Wilson's ability. The humour is local, of course, but I've come to the conclusion that there can be no other form of popular journal.

The weather has not been good of late, but not sufficiently bad to interfere with exercise, etc.

Thursday 14 September Another interregnum. I have been exceedingly busy finishing up the Southern plans, getting instruction in photographing, and preparing for our jaunt to the west. I held forth on the 'Southern Plans' yesterday; everyone was enthusiastic, and the feeling is general that our arrangements are calculated to make the best of our resources. Although people have given a good deal of thought to various branches of the subject, there was not a suggestion offered for improvement. The scheme seems to have earned full confidence: it remains to play the game out.

The last lectures of the season have been given. On Monday Nelson gave us an interesting little résumé of biological questions, tracing the evolutionary development of forms from the simplest single-cell animals.

Tonight Wright tackled 'The Constitution of Matter' with the latest ideas from the Cavendish Laboratory: it was a tough subject, yet one carries away ideas of the trend of the work of the great physicists, of the ends they achieve and the means they employ. Wright is inclined to explain matter as velocity; Simpson claims to be with J. J. Thomson in stressing the fact that gravity is not explained.

These lectures have been a real amusement and one would be sorry enough that they should end, were it not for so good a reason.

I am determined to make some better show of our photographic work on the Southern trip than has yet been accomplished – with Ponting as a teacher it should be easy. He is prepared to take any pains to ensure good results, not only with his own work but with that of others – showing indeed what a very good chap he is.

Today I have been trying a colour screen – it is an extraordinary addition to one's powers.

Tomorrow Bowers, Simpson, Petty Officer Evans, and I are off to the west. I want to have another look at the Ferrar Glacier, to measure the stakes put out by Wright last year, to bring my sledging impressions up to date (one loses details of technique very easily), and finally to see what we can do with our cameras. I haven't decided how long we shall stay away or precisely where we shall go; such vague arrangements have an attractive side.

We have had a fine week, but the temperature remains low in the twenties, and today has dropped to -35°. I shouldn't wonder if we get a cold snap.

Sunday 1 October Returned on Thursday from a remarkably pleasant and instructive little spring journey, after an absence of thirteen days from 15 September. We covered 152 geographical miles by sledging (175 statute miles) in 10 marching days. It took us 2½ days to reach Butter Point (28½ miles geog.), carrying a part of the Western Party stores which brought our load to 180 lbs. a man. Everything very comfortable; double tent great asset. The 16th: a most glorious day till 4 p.m., then cold southerly wind. We captured many frostbites. Surface only fairly good; a good many heaps of loose snow which brought sledge up standing. There seems a good deal more snow this side of the Strait; query, less wind.

Bowers insists on doing all camp work; he is a positive wonder. I never met such a sledge traveller.

The sastrugi all across the strait have been across, the main S. by E. and the other E.S.E., but these are a great study here; the hard snow is striated with long wavy lines crossed with lighter wavy lines. It gives a sort of herringbone effect.

After depositing this extra load we proceeded up the Ferrar Glacier; curious low ice foot on left, no tide crack, sea-ice very thinly covered with snow. We are getting delightfully fit. Bowers treasure all round, Evans much the same. Simpson learning fast. Find the camp life suits me well except the turning out at night! three times last night. We were trying nose nips and face guards, marching head to wind all day.

We reached Cathedral Rocks on the 19th. Here we found the stakes placed by Wright across the glacier, and spent the remainder of the day and the whole of the 20th in plotting their position accurately. (Very cold wind down glacier increasing. In spite of this Bowers wrestled with theodolite. He is really wonderful. I have never seen anyone who could go on so long with bare fingers. My own fingers went every few moments.) We saw that there had been movement and roughly measured it as about 30 feet. (The old Ferrar Glacier is more lively than we thought.) After plotting the figures it turns out that the movement varies from 24 to 32 feet at different stakes – this is 7½ months. This is an extremely important observation, the first made on the movement of the coastal glaciers; it is more than I expected to find, but small enough to show that the idea of comparative stagnation was correct. Bowers and I exposed a number of plates and films in the glacier which have turned out very well, auguring well for the management of the camera on the Southern journey.

On the 21st we came down the glacier and camped at the northern end of the foot. (There appeared to be a storm in the Strait; cumulus cloud over Erebus and the whalebacks. Very stormy look over Lister occasionally and drift from peaks; but all smiling in our Happy Valley. Evidently this is a very favoured spot.) From thence we jogged up the coast on the following days, dipping into New Harbour and climbing the moraine, taking angles and collecting rock specimens. At Cape Bernacchi we found a quantity of pure quartz *in situ*, and in it veins of copper ore. I got a specimen with two or three large lumps of copper included. This is the first find of minerals suggestive of the possibility of working.

The next day we sighted a long, low ice wall, and took it at first for a long glacier tongue stretching seaward from the land. As we approached we saw a dark mark on it. Suddenly it dawned on us that the tongue was detached from the land, and we turned towards it half recognising familiar features. As we got close we saw similarity to our old Erebus Glacier Tongue, and finally caught sight of a flag on it, and suddenly realised that it might be the piece broken off our old Erebus Glacier Tongue. Sure enough it was; we camped near the outer end, and climbing on to it soon found the depot of fodder left by Campbell and the line of stakes planted to guide our ponies in the autumn. So here firmly anchored was the huge piece broken from the Glacier Tongue in March, a huge tract about 2 miles long, which has turned through half a circle, so that the old western end is now towards the east. Considering the many cracks in the ice mass it is most astonishing that it should have remained intact throughout its sea voyage.

At one time it was suggested that the hut should be placed on this Tongue. What an adventurous voyage the occupants would have had! The Tongue which was 5 miles south of C. Evans is now 40 miles W.N.W. of it.

From the Glacier Tongue we still pushed north. We reached Dunlop Island on the 24th just before the fog descended on us, and got a view along the stretch of coast to the north which turns at this point.

Dunlop Island has undoubtedly been under the sea. We found regular terrace beaches with rounded water-worn stones all over it; its height is 65 feet. After visiting the island it was easy for us to trace the same terrace formation on the coast; in one place we found water-worn stones over 100 feet above sea-level. Nearly all these stones are erratic and, unlike ordinary beach pebbles, the under sides which lie buried have remained angular.

Unlike the region of the Ferrar Glacier and New Harbour, the coast to the north of C. Bernacchi runs on in a succession of rounded bays fringed with low ice walls. At the headlands and in irregular spots the gneissic base rock and portions of moraines lie exposed, offering a succession of interesting spots for a visit in search of geological specimens. Behind this fringe there is a long undulating plateau of snow rounding down to the coast; behind this again are a succession of mountain ranges with deep-cut valleys between. As far as we went, these valleys seem to radiate from the region of the summit reached at the head of the Ferrar Glacier.

As one approaches the coast, the 'tablecloth' of snow in the foreground cuts off more and more of the inland peaks, and even at a distance it is impossible to get a good view of the inland valleys. To explore these over the ice cap is one of the objects of the Western Party.

So far, I never imagined a spring journey could be so pleasant.

On the afternoon of the 24th we turned back, and covering nearly eleven miles, camped inside the Glacier Tongue. After noon on the 25th we made a direct course for C. Evans, and in the evening camped well out in the Sound. Bowers got angles from our lunch camp and I took a photographic panorama, which is a good deal over exposed.

We only got 2½ miles on the 26th when a heavy blizzard descended on us. We went on against it, the first time I have ever attempted to march into a blizzard; it was quite possible, but progress very slow owing to wind resistance. Decided to camp after we had done two miles. Quite a job getting up the tent, but we managed to do so, and get everything inside clear of snow with the help of much sweeping.

With care and extra fuel we have managed to get through the snowy part of the blizzard with less accumulation of snow than I ever remember, and so everywhere all-round experience is helping us. It continued to blow hard throughout the 27th, and the 28th proved the most unpleasant day of the trip. We started facing a very keen, frostbiting wind. Although this slowly increased in force, we pushed doggedly on, halting now and again to bring our frozen features round. It was 2 o'clock before we could find a decent site for a lunch camp under a pressure ridge. The fatigue of the prolonged march told on Simpson, whose whole face was frostbitten at one time – it is still much blistered. It came on to drift as we sat in our tent, and again we were weather-bound. At 3 the drift ceased, and we marched on, wind as bad as ever; then I saw an ominous yellow fuzzy appearance on the southern ridges of Erebus, and knew that another snowstorm approached. Foolishly hoping it would pass us by I kept on until Inaccessible Island was suddenly blotted out. Then we rushed for a camp site, but the blizzard was on us. In the driving snow we found it impossible to set up the inner tent, and were obliged to unbend it. It was a long job getting the outer tent set, but thanks to Evans and Bowers it was done at last. We had to risk frostbitten fingers and hang on to the tent with all our energy: got it secured inch by inch, and not such a bad speed all things considered. We had some cocoa and waited. At 9 p.m. the snow drift again took off, and we were now so snowed up, we decided to push on in spite of the wind.

We arrived in at 1.15 a.m., pretty well done. The wind never let up for an instant; the temperature remained about -16°, and the 21 statute miles which we marched in the day must be remembered amongst the most strenuous in my memory.

Except for the last few days, we enjoyed a degree of comfort which I had not imagined impossible on a spring journey. The temperature was not particularly high, at the mouth of the Ferrar it was -40°, and it varied between -15° and -40° throughout. Of course this is much higher than it would be on the Barrier, but it does not in itself promise much comfort. The amelioration of such conditions we owe to experience. We used one-third more than the summer allowance of fuel. This, with our double tent, allowed a cosy hour after breakfast and supper in which we could dry our socks, etc., and put them on in comfort. We shifted our footgear immediately after the camp was pitched, and by this means kept our feet glowingly warm throughout the night. Nearly all the time we carried our sleeping-bags open on the sledges. Although the sun does not appear to have much effect, I believe this device is of great benefit even in the coldest weather – certainly by this means our bags were kept much freer of moisture than they would have been had they been rolled up in the daytime. The inner tent gets a good deal of ice on it, and I don't see any easy way to prevent this.

The journey enables me to advise the Geological Party on their best route to Granite Harbour: this is along the shore, where for the main part the protection of a chain of grounded bergs has preserved the ice from all pressure. Outside these, and occasionally reaching to the headlands, there is a good deal of pressed up ice of this season, together with the latest of the old broken pack. Travelling through this is difficult, as we found on our return journey. Beyond this belt we passed through irregular patches where the ice, freezing at later intervals in the season, has been much screwed. The whole shows the general tendency of the ice to pack along the coast.

The objects of our little journey were satisfactorily accomplished, but the greatest source of pleasure to me is to realise that I have such men as Bowers and P.O. Evans for the Southern journey. I do not think that harder men or better sledge travellers ever took the trail. Bowers is a little wonder. I realised all that he must have done for the C. Crozier Party in their far severer experience.

In spite of the late hour of our return everyone was soon afoot, and I learned the news at once. E. R. Evans, Gran, and Forde had returned from the Corner Camp journey the day after we left. They were away six nights, four spent on the Barrier under very severe conditions – the minimum for one night registered -73°.

I am glad to find that Corner Camp showed up well; in fact, in more than one place remains of last year's pony walls were seen. This removes all anxiety as to the chance of finding the One Ton Camp.

On this journey Forde got his hand badly frostbitten. I am annoyed at this, as it argues want of care; moreover there is a good chance that the tip of one of the fingers will be lost, and if this happens or if the hand is slow in recovery, Forde cannot take part in the Western Party. I have no one to replace him.

E. R. Evans looks remarkably well, as also Gran.

The ponies look very well and all are reported to be very buckish.

Wednesday 3 October We have had a very bad weather spell. Friday, the day after we returned, was gloriously fine – it might have been a December day, and an inexperienced visitor might have wondered why on earth we had not started to the South. Saturday supplied a reason; the wind blew cold and cheerless; on Sunday it grew worse, with very thick snow, which continued to fall and drift throughout the whole of Monday. The hut is more drifted up than it has ever been, huge piles of snow behind every heap of boxes, etc., all our paths a foot higher; yet in spite of this the rocks are rather freer of snow. This is due to melting, which is now quite considerable. Wilson tells me the first signs of thaw were seen on the 17th.

Yesterday the weather gradually improved, and today has been fine and warm again. One fine day in eight is the record immediately previous to this morning.

E. R. Evans, Debenham, and Gran set off to the Turk's Head on Friday morning, Evans to take angles and Debenham to geologise; they have been in their tent pretty well all the time since, but have managed to get through some work. Gran returned last night for more provisions and set off again this morning, Taylor going with him for the day. Debenham has just returned for food. He is immensely pleased at having discovered a huge slicken-sided fault in the lavas of the Turk's Head. This appears to be an unusual occurrence in volcanic rocks, and argues that they are of considerable age. He has taken a heap of photographs and is greatly pleased with all his geological observations. He is building up much evidence to show volcanic disturbance independent of Erebus and perhaps prior to its first upheaval.

Meares has been at Hut Point for more than a week; seals seem to be plentiful there now. Demetri was back with letters on Friday and left on Sunday. He is an excellent boy, full of intelligence.

Ponting has been doing some wonderfully fine cinematograph work. My incursion into photography has brought me in close touch with him and I realise what a very good fellow he is; no pains are too great for him to take to help and instruct others, whilst his enthusiasm for his own work is unlimited.

His results are wonderfully good, and if he is able to carry out the whole of his programme, we shall have a cinematograph and photographic record which will be absolutely new in expeditionary work.

A very serious bit of news today. Atkinson says that Jehu is still too weak to pull a load. The pony was bad on the ship and almost died after swimming ashore from the ship – he was one of the ponies returned by Campbell. He has been improving the whole of the winter and Oates has been surprised at the apparent recovery; he looks well and feeds well, though a very weedily built animal compared with the others. I had not expected him to last long, but it will be a bad blow if he fails at the start. I'm afraid there is much pony trouble in store for us.

Oates is having great trouble with Christopher, who didn't at all appreciate being harnessed on Sunday, and again today he broke away and galloped off over the floe.

On such occasions Oates trudges manfully after him, rounds him up to within a few hundred yards of the stable and approaches cautiously; the animal looks at him for a minute or two and canters off over the floe again. When Christopher and indeed both of them have had enough of the game, the pony calmly stops at the stable door. If not too late he is then put into the sledge, but this can only be done by tying up one of his forelegs; when harnessed and after he has hopped along on three legs for a few paces, he is again allowed to use the fourth. He is going to be a trial, but he is a good strong pony and should do yeoman service.

Day is increasingly hopeful about the motors. He is an ingenious person and has been turning up new rollers out of a baulk of oak supplied by Meares, and with Simpson's small motor as a lathe. The motors *may* save the situation. I have been busy drawing up instructions and making arrangements for the ship, shore station, and sledge parties in the coming season. There is still much work to be done and much, far too much, writing before me.

Time simply flies and the sun steadily climbs the heavens. Breakfast, lunch, and supper are now all enjoyed by sunlight, whilst the night is no longer dark.

NOTES AT END OF VOLUME

'When they after their headstrong manner, conclude that it is their duty to rush on their journey all weathers ...' – 'Pilgrim's Progress'

'Has any grasped the low grey mist which stands
Ghostlike at eve above the sheeted lands.'

A bad attack of integrity!!

'Who is man and what his place,
Anxious asks the heart perplext,
In the recklessness of space,
Worlds with worlds thus intermixt,
What has he, this atom creature,
In the infinitude of nature?'
F. T. PALGRAVE.

It is a good lesson – though it may be a hard one – for a man who had dreamed of a special (literary) fame and of making for himself a rank among the world's dignitaries by such means, to slip aside out of the narrow circle in which his claims are recognised, and to find how utterly devoid of significance beyond that circle is all he achieves and all he aims at.

He might fail from want of skill or strength, but deep in his sombre soul he vowed that it should never be from want of heart.

'Every durable bond between human beings is founded in or heightened by some element of competition.' – R. L. STEVENSON.

'All natural talk is a festival of ostentation.' – R. L. STEVENSON.

'No human being ever spoke of scenery for two minutes together, which makes me suspect we have too much of it in literature. The weather is regarded as the very nadir and scoff of conversational topics.' – R. L. STEVENSON.

15
THE LAST WEEKS AT CAPE EVANS:
6 OCTOBER 1911 – 31 OCTOBER 1911

Friday 6 October With the rise of temperature there has been a slight thaw in the hut; the drips come down the walls and one has found my diary, as its pages show. The drips are already decreasing, and if they represent the whole accumulation of winter moisture it is extraordinarily little, and speaks highly for the design of the hut. There cannot be very much more or the stains would be more significant.

Yesterday I had a good look at Jehu and became convinced that he is useless; he is much too weak to pull a load, and three weeks can make no difference. It is necessary to face the facts and I've decided to leave him behind – we must do with nine ponies. Chinaman is rather a doubtful quantity and James Pigg is not a tower of strength, but the other seven are in fine form and must bear the brunt of the work somehow.

If we suffer more loss we shall depend on the motor, and then! ... well, one must face the bad as well as the good.

It is some comfort to know that six of the animals at least are in splendid condition – Victor, Snippets, Christopher, Nobby, Bones are as fit as ponies could well be and are naturally strong, well-shaped beasts, whilst little Michael, though not so shapely, is as strong as he will ever be.

Today Wilson, Oates, Cherry-Garrard, and Crean have gone to Hut Point with their ponies, Oates getting off with Christopher after some difficulty. At 5 o'clock the Hut Point telephone bell suddenly rang (the line was laid by Meares some time ago, but hitherto there has been no communication). In a minute or two we heard a voice, and behold! communication was established. I had quite a talk with Meares and afterwards with Oates. Not a very wonderful fact, perhaps, but it seems wonderful in this primitive land to be talking to one's fellow beings 15 miles away. Oates told me that the ponies had arrived in fine order, Christopher a little done, but carrying the heaviest load.

If we can keep the telephone going it will be a great boon, especially to Meares later in the season.

The weather is extraordinarily unsettled; the last two days have been fairly fine, but every now and again we get a burst of wind with drift, and tonight it is overcast and very gloomy in appearance.

The photography craze is in full swing. Ponting's mastery is ever more impressive, and his pupils improve day by day; nearly all of us have produced good negatives. Debenham and Wright are the most promising, but Taylor, Bowers and I are also getting the hang of the tricky exposures.

Saturday 7 October As though to contradict the suggestion of incompetence, friend 'Jehu' pulled with a will this morning – he covered 3½ miles without a stop, the surface being much worse than it was two days ago. He was not at all distressed when he stopped. If he goes on like this he comes into practical politics again, and I am arranging to give 10-feet sledges to him and Chinaman instead of 12-feet. Probably they will not do much, but if they go on as at present we shall get something out of them.

Long and cheerful conversations with Hut Point and of course an opportunity for the exchange of witticisms. We are told it was blowing and drifting at Hut Point last night, whereas here it was calm and snowing; the wind only reached us this afternoon.

Sunday 8 October A very beautiful day. Everyone out and about after Service, all ponies going well. Went to Pressure Ridge with Ponting and took a number of photographs.

So far good, but the afternoon has brought much worry. About five a telephone message from Nelson's igloo reported that Clissold had fallen from a berg and hurt his back. Bowers organised a sledge party in three minutes, and fortunately Atkinson was on the spot and able to join it. I posted out over the land and found Ponting much distressed and Clissold practically insensible. At this moment the Hut Point ponies were approaching and I ran over to intercept one in case of necessity. But the man party was on the spot first, and after putting the patient in a sleeping-bag, quickly brought him home to the hut. It appears that Clissold was acting as Ponting's 'model' and that the two had been climbing about the berg to get pictures. As far as I can make out Ponting did his best to keep Clissold in safety by lending him his crampons and ice axe, but the latter seems to have missed his footing after one of his 'poses'; he slid over a rounded surface of ice for some 12 feet, then dropped 6 feet on to a sharp angle in the wall of the berg.

He must have struck his back and head; the latter is contused and he is certainly suffering from slight concussion. He complained of his back before he grew unconscious and groaned a good deal when moved in the hut. He came to about an hour after getting to the hut, and was evidently in a good deal of pain; neither Atkinson nor Wilson thinks there is anything very serious, but he has not yet been properly examined and has had a fearful shock at the least. I still feel very anxious. Tonight Atkinson has injected morphia and will watch by his patient.

Troubles rarely come singly, and it occurred to me after Clissold had been brought in that Taylor, who had been bicycling to the Turk's Head, was overdue. We were relieved to hear that with glasses two figures could be seen approaching in South Bay, but at supper Wright appeared very hot and said that Taylor was exhausted in South Bay – he wanted brandy and hot drink. I thought it best to despatch another relief party, but before they were well round the point Taylor was seen coming over the land. He was fearfully done. He must have pressed on towards his objective long after his reason should have warned him that it was time to turn; with this and a good deal of anxiety about Clissold, the day terminates very unpleasantly.

Tuesday 10 October Still anxious about Clissold. He has passed two fairly good nights but is barely able to move. He is unnaturally irritable, but I am told this is a symptom of concussion. This morning he asked for food, which is a good sign, and he was anxious to know if his sledging gear was being got ready. In order not to disappoint him he was assured that all would be ready, but there is scarce a slender chance that he can fill his place in the programme.

Meares came from Hut Point yesterday at the front end of a blizzard. Half an hour after his arrival it was as thick as a hedge. He reports another loss – Deek, one of the best pulling dogs, developed the same symptoms which have so unaccountably robbed us before, spent a night in pain, and died in the morning. Wilson thinks the cause is a worm which gets into the blood and thence to the brain. It is trying, but I am past despondency. Things must take their course.

Forde's fingers improve, but not very rapidly; it is hard to have two sick men after all the care which has been taken.

The weather is very poor – I had hoped for better things this month. So far we have had more days with wind and drift than without. It interferes badly with the ponies' exercise.

Friday 13 October The past three days have seen a marked improvement in both our invalids. Clissold's inside has been got into working order after a good deal of difficulty; he improves rapidly in spirits as well as towards immunity from pain. The fiction of his preparation to join the motor sledge party is still kept up, but Atkinson says there is not the smallest chance of his being ready. I shall have to be satisfied if he practically recovers by the time we leave with the ponies.

Forde's hand took a turn for the better two days ago and he maintains this progress. Atkinson thinks he will be ready to start in ten days' time, but the hand must be carefully nursed till the weather becomes really summery.

The weather has continued bad till today, which has been perfectly beautiful. A fine warm sun all day – so warm that one could sit about outside in the afternoon, and photographic work was a real pleasure.

The ponies have been behaving well, with exceptions. Victor is now quite easy to manage, thanks to Bowers' patience. Chinaman goes along very steadily and is not going to be the crock we expected. He has a slow pace which may be troublesome, but when the weather is fine that won't matter if he can get along steadily.

The most troublesome animal is Christopher. He is only a source of amusement as long as there is no accident, but I am always a little anxious that he will kick or bite someone. The curious thing is that he is quiet enough to handle for walking or riding exercise or in the stable, but as soon as a sledge comes into the programme he is seized with a very demon of viciousness, and bites and kicks with every intent to do injury. It seems to be getting harder rather than easier to get him into the traces; the last two turns, he has had to be thrown, as he is unmanageable even on three legs. Oates, Bowers, and Anton gather round the beast and lash up one foreleg, then with his head held on both sides Oates gathers back the traces; quick as lightning the little beast flashes round with heels flying aloft. This goes on till some degree of exhaustion gives the men a better chance. But, as I have mentioned, during the last two days the period has been so prolonged that Oates has had to hasten matters by tying a short line to the other foreleg and throwing the beast when he lashes out. Even when on his knees he continues to struggle, and one of those nimble hind legs may fly out at any time. Once in the sledge and started on three legs all is well and the fourth leg can be released. At least, all has been well until today, when quite a comedy was enacted. He was going along quietly with Oates when a dog frightened him: he flung up his head, twitched the rope out of Oates' hands and dashed away. It was not a question of blind fright, as immediately after gaining freedom he set about most systematically to get rid of his load. At first he gave sudden twists, and in this manner succeeded in dislodging two bales of hay; then he caught sight of other sledges and dashed for them. They could scarcely get out of his way in time; the fell intention was evident all through, to dash his load against some other pony and sledge and so free himself of it. He ran for Bowers two or three times with this design, then made for Keohane, never going off far and dashing inward with teeth bared and heels flying all over the place. By this time people were gathering round, and first one and then another succeeded in clambering on to the sledge as it flew by, till Oates, Bowers, Nelson, and Atkinson were all sitting on it. He tried to rid himself of this human burden as he had of the hay bales, and succeeded in dislodging Atkinson with violence, but the remainder dug their heels into the snow and finally the little brute was tired out. Even then he tried to savage anyone approaching his leading line, and it was some time before Oates could get hold of it. Such is the tale of Christopher. I am exceedingly glad there are not other ponies like him. These capers promise trouble, but I think a little soft snow on the Barrier may effectually cure them.

E. R. Evans and Gran return tonight. We received notice of their departure from Hut Point through the telephone, which also informed us that Meares had departed for his first trip to Corner Camp. Evans says he carried eight bags of forage and that the dogs went away at a great pace.

In spite of the weather Evans has managed to complete his survey to Hut Point. He has evidently been very careful with it and has therefore done a very useful bit of work.

Sunday 15 October Both of our invalids progress favourably. Clissold has had two good nights without the aid of drugs and has recovered his good spirits; pains have departed from his back.

The weather is very decidedly warmer and for the past three days has been fine. The thermometer stands but a degree or two below zero and the air feels delightfully mild. Everything of importance is now ready for our start and the ponies improve daily.

Clissold's work of cooking has fallen on Hooper and Lashly, and it is satisfactory to find that the various dishes and bread bakings maintain their excellence. It is splendid to have people who refuse to recognise difficulties.

Tuesday 17 October Things not going very well; with ponies all pretty well. Animals are improving in form rapidly, even Jehu, though I have ceased to count on that animal. Tonight the motors were to be taken on to the floe. The drifts make the road very uneven, and the first and best motor overrode its chain; the chain was replaced and the machine proceeded, but just short of the floe was thrust to a steep inclination by a ridge, and the chain again overrode the sprockets; this time by ill fortune Day slipped at the critical moment and without intention jammed the throttle full on. The engine brought up, but there was an ominous trickle of oil under the back axle, and investigation showed that the axle casing (aluminium) had split. The casing has been stripped and brought into the hut; we may be able to do something to it, but time presses. It all goes to show that we want more experience and workshops.

I am secretly convinced that we shall not get much help from the motors, yet nothing has ever happened to them that was unavoidable. A little more care and foresight would make them splendid allies. The trouble is that if they fail, no one will ever believe this.

Meares got back from Corner Camp at 8 a.m. Sunday morning – he got through on the telephone to report in the afternoon. He must have made the pace, which is promising for the dogs. Sixty geographical miles in two days and a night is good going – about as good as can be.

I have had to tell Clissold that he cannot go out with the Motor Party, to his great disappointment. He improves very steadily, however, and I trust will be fit before we leave with the ponies. Hooper replaces him with the motors. I am kept very busy writing and preparing details.

We have had two days of northerly wind, a very unusual occurrence; yesterday it was blowing S.E., force 8, temp. -16°, whilst here the wind was north, force 4, temp. -6°. This continued for some hours – a curious meteorological combination. We are pretty certain of a southerly blizzard to follow, I should think.

Wednesday 18 October The southerly blizzard has burst on us. The air is thick with snow.

A close investigation of the motor axle case shows that repair is possible. It looks as though a good strong job could be made of it. Yesterday Taylor and Debenham went to Cape Royds with the object of staying a night or two.

Sunday 22 October The motor axle case was completed by Thursday morning, and, as far as one can see, Day made a very excellent job of it. Since that the Motor Party has been steadily preparing for its departure. Today everything is ready. The loads are ranged on the sea-ice, the motors are having a trial run, and, all remaining well with the weather, the party will get away tomorrow.

Meares and Demetri came down on Thursday through the last of the blizzard. At one time they were running without sight of the leading dogs

– they did not see Tent Island at all, but burst into sunshine and comparative calm a mile from the station. Another of the best of the dogs, 'Czigane', was smitten with the unaccountable sickness; he was given laxative medicine and appears to be a little better, but we are still anxious. If he really has the disease, whatever it may be, the rally is probably only temporary and the end will be swift.

The teams left on Friday afternoon, Czigane included; today Meares telephones that he is setting out for his second journey to Corner Camp without him. On the whole the weather continues wretchedly bad; the ponies could not be exercised either on Thursday or Friday; they were very fresh yesterday and today in consequence. When unexercised, their allowance of oats has to be cut down. This is annoying, as just at present they ought to be doing a moderate amount of work and getting into condition on full rations.

The temperature is up to zero about; this probably means about -20° on the Barrier. I wonder how the motors will face the drop if and when they encounter it. Day and Lashly are both hopeful of the machines, and they really ought to do something after all the trouble that has been taken.

The wretched state of the weather has prevented the transport of emergency stores to Hut Point. These stores are for the returning depots and to provision the *Discovery* hut in case the *Terra Nova* does not arrive. The most important stores have been taken to the Glacier Tongue by the ponies today.

In the transport department, in spite of all the care I have taken to make the details of my plan clear by lucid explanation, I find that Bowers is the only man on whom I can thoroughly rely to carry out the work without mistake, with its arrays of figures. For the practical consistent work of pony training Oates is especially capable, and his heart is very much in the business.

'*October 1911* I don't know what to think of Amundsen's chances. If he gets to the Pole, it must be before we do, as he is bound to travel fast with dogs and pretty certain to start early. On this account I decided at a very early date to act exactly as I should have done had he not existed. Any attempt to race must have wrecked my plan, besides which it doesn't appear the sort of thing one is out for.

'Possibly you will have heard something before this reaches you. Oh! and there are all sorts of possibilities. In any case you can rely on my not doing or saying anything foolish – only I'm afraid you must be prepared for the chance of finding our venture much belittled.

'After all, it is the work that counts, not the applause that follows.

'Words must always fail me when I talk of Bill Wilson. I believe he really is the finest character I ever met – the closer one gets to him the more there is to admire. Every quality is so solid and dependable; cannot you imagine how that counts down here? Whatever the matter, one knows Bill will be sound, shrewdly practical, intensely loyal and quite unselfish. Add to this a wider knowledge of persons and things than is at first guessable, a quiet vein of humour and really consummate tact, and you have some idea of his values. I think he is the most popular member of the party, and that is saying much.

'Bowers is all and more than I ever expected of him. He is a positive treasure, absolutely trustworthy and prodigiously energetic. He is about the hardest man amongst us, and that is saying a good deal – nothing seems to hurt his tough little body and certainly no hardship daunts his spirit. I shall have a hundred little tales to tell you of his indefatigable zeal, his unselfishness, and his inextinguishable good humour. He surprises always, for his intelligence is of quite a high order and his memory for details most exceptional. You can imagine him, as he is, an indispensable assistant to me in every detail concerning the management and organisation of our sledging work and a delightful companion on the march.

'One of the greatest successes is Wright. He is very thorough and absolutely ready for anything. Like Bowers he has taken to sledging like a duck to water, and although he hasn't had such severe testing, I believe he would stand it pretty nearly as well. Nothing ever seems to worry him, and I can't imagine he ever complained of anything in his life.

'I don't think I will give such long descriptions of the others, though most of them deserve equally high praise. Taken all round they are a perfectly excellent lot.'

The Soldier is very popular with all – a delightfully humorous cheery old pessimist – striving with the ponies night and day and bringing woeful accounts of their small ailments into the hut.

'X ... has a positive passion for helping others – it is extraordinary what pains he will take to do a kind thing unobtrusively.

'One sees the need of having one's heart in one's work. Results can only be got down here by a man desperately eager to get them.

'Y ... works hard at his own work, taking extraordinary pains with it, but with an astonishing lack of initiative he makes not the smallest effort to grasp the work of others; it is a sort of character which plants itself in a corner and will stop there.

'The men are equally fine. Edgar Evans has proved a useful member of our party; he looks after our sledges and sledge equipment with a care of management and a fertility of resource which is truly astonishing – on 'trek' he is just as sound and hard as ever and has an inexhaustible store of anecdote.

'Crean is perfectly happy, ready to do anything and go anywhere, the harder the work, the better. Evans and Crean are great friends. Lashly is his old self in every respect, hard working to the limit, quiet, abstemious, and determined. You see altogether I have a good set of people with me, and it will go hard if we don't achieve something.

'The study of individual character is a pleasant pastime in such a mixed community of thoroughly nice people, and the study of relationships and interactions is fascinating – men of the most diverse upbringings and experience are really pals with one another, and the subjects which would be delicate ground of discussion between acquaintances are just those which are most freely used for jests. For instance the Soldier is never tired of girding at Australia, its people and institutions, and the Australians retaliate by attacking the hide-bound prejudices of the British army. I have never seen a temper lost in these discussions. So as I sit here I am very satisfied with these things. I think that it would have been difficult to better the organisation of the party – every man has his work and is especially adapted for it; there is no gap and no overlap – it is all that I desired, and the same might be said of the men selected to do the work.'

It promised to be very fine today, but the wind has already sprung up and clouds are gathering again. There was a very beautiful curved 'banner' cloud south of Erebus this morning, perhaps a warning of what is to come.

Another accident! At one o'clock 'Snatcher', one of the three ponies laying the depot, arrived with single trace and dangling sledge in a welter of sweat. Forty minutes after P.O. Evans, his driver, came in almost as hot; simultaneously Wilson arrived with Nobby and a tale of events not complete. He said that after the loads were removed Bowers had been holding the three ponies, who appeared to be quiet; suddenly one had tossed his head and all three had stampeded – Snatcher making for home, Nobby for the Western Mountains, Victor, with Bowers still hanging to him, in an indefinite direction. Running for two miles, he eventually rounded up Nobby west of Tent Island and brought him in.[20] Half an hour after Wilson's return, Bowers came in with Victor distressed, bleeding at the nose, from which a considerable fragment hung semi-detached. Bowers himself was covered with blood and supplied the missing link – the cause of the incident. It appears that the ponies were fairly quiet when Victor tossed his head and caught his nostril in the trace hook on the hame of Snatcher's harness. The hook tore skin and flesh and of course the animal got out of hand. Bowers hung to him, but couldn't possibly keep hold of the other two as well. Victor had bled a good deal, and the blood congealing on the detached skin not only gave the wound a dismal appearance but greatly increased its irritation. I don't know how Bowers managed to hang on to the frightened animal; I don't believe anyone else would have done so. On the way back the dangling weight on the poor creature's nose would get on the swing and make him increasingly restive; it was necessary to stop him repeatedly. Since his return the piece of skin has been snipped off and proves the wound not so serious as it looked. The animal is still trembling, but quite on his feed, which is a good sign. I don't know why our Sundays should always bring these excitements.

Two lessons arise. Firstly, however quiet the animals appear, they must not be left by their drivers; no chance must be taken; secondly, the hooks on the hames of the harness must be altered in shape.

I suppose such incidents as this were to be expected, one cannot have ponies very fresh and vigorous and expect them to behave like lambs, but I shall be glad when we are off and can know more definitely what resources we can count on.

Another trying incident has occurred. We have avoided football this season especially to keep clear of accidents, but on Friday afternoon a match was got up for the cinematograph and Debenham developed a football knee (an old hurt, I have since learnt, or he should not have played). Wilson thinks it will be a week before he is fit to travel, so here we have the Western Party on our hands and wasting the precious hours for that period. The only single compensation is that it gives Forde's hand a better chance. If this waiting were to continue it looks as though we should become a regular party of 'crocks'. Clissold was out of the hut for the first time today; he is better but still suffers in his back.

THE START OF THE MOTOR SLEDGES

Tuesday 24 October Two fine days for a wonder. Yesterday the motors seemed ready to start and we all went out on the floe to give them a 'send off'. But the inevitable little defects cropped up, and the machines only got as far as the Cape. A change made by Day in the exhaust arrangements had neglected the heating jackets of the carburetters; one float valve was bent and one clutch troublesome. Day and Lashly spent the afternoon making good these defects in a satisfactory manner.

This morning the engines were set going again, and shortly after 10 a.m. a fresh start was made. At first there were a good many stops, but on the whole the engines seemed to be improving all the time. They are not by any means working up to full power yet, and so the pace is very slow. The weights seem to me a good deal heavier than we bargained for. Day sets his motor going, climbs off the car, and walks alongside with an occasional finger on the throttle. Lashly hasn't yet quite got hold of the nice adjustments of his control levers, but I hope will have done so after a day's practice.

The only alarming incident was the slipping of the chains when Day tried to start on some ice very thinly covered with snow. The starting effort on such heavily laden sledges is very heavy, but I thought the grip of the pattens and studs would have been good enough on any surface. Looking at the place afterwards I found that the studs had grooved the ice.

Now as I write at 12.30 the machines are about a mile out in the South Bay; both can be seen still under weigh, progressing steadily if slowly.

I find myself immensely eager that these tractors should succeed, even though they may not be of great help to our southern advance. A small measure of success will be enough to show their possibilities, their ability to revolutionise Polar transport. Seeing the machines at work today, and remembering that every defect so far shown is purely mechanical, it is impossible not to be convinced of their value. But the trifling mechanical defects and lack of experience show the risk of cutting out trials. A season of experiment with a small workshop at hand may be all that stands between success and failure.

At any rate before we start we shall certainly know if the worst has happened, or if some measure of success attends this unique effort.

The ponies are in fine form. Victor, practically recovered from his wound, has been rushing round with a sledge at a great rate. Even Jehu has been buckish, kicking up his heels and gambolling awkwardly. The invalids progress, Clissold a little alarmed about his back, but without cause.

Atkinson and Keohane have turned cooks, and do the job splendidly.

This morning Meares announced his return from Corner Camp, so that all stores are now out there. The run occupied the same time as the first, when the routine was: first day 17 miles out; second day 13 out, and 13 home; early third day run in. If only one could trust the dogs to keep going like this it would be splendid. On the whole things look hopeful.

1 p.m. Motors reported off Razor Back Island, nearly 3 miles out – come, come!

Thursday 26 October Couldn't see the motors yesterday till I walked well out on the South Bay, when I discovered them with glasses off the Glacier Tongue. There had been a strong wind in the forenoon, but it seemed to me they ought to have got further – annoyingly the telephone gave no news from Hut Point, evidently something was wrong. After dinner Simpson and Gran started for Hut Point.

This morning Simpson has just rung up. He says the motors are in difficulties with the surface. The trouble is just that which I noted as alarming on Monday – the chains slip on the very light snow covering of hard ice. The engines are working well, and all goes well when the machines get on to snow.

I have organised a party of eight men including myself, and we are just off to see what can be done to help.

Friday 27 October We were away by 10.30 yesterday. Walked to the Glacier Tongue with gloomy forebodings; but for one gust a beautifully bright inspiriting day. Seals were about and were frequently mistaken for the motors. As we approached the Glacier Tongue, however, and became more alive to such mistakes, we realised that the motors were not in sight. At first I thought they must have sought better surface on the other side of the Tongue, but this theory was soon demolished and we were puzzled to know what had happened. At length walking onward they were descried far away over the floe towards Hut Point; soon after we saw good firm tracks over a snow surface, a pleasant change from the double tracks and slipper places we had seen on the bare ice. Our spirits went up at once, for it was not only evident that the machines were going, but that they were negotiating a very rough surface without difficulty. We marched on and overtook them about 2½ miles from Hut Point, passing Simpson and Gran returning to Cape Evans. From the motors we learnt that things were going pretty well. The engines were working well when once in tune, but the cylinders, especially the two after ones, tended to get too hot, whilst the fan or wind playing on the carburettor tended to make it too cold. The trouble was to get a balance between the two, and this is effected by starting up the engines, then stopping and covering them and allowing the heat to spread by conductivity – of course, a rather clumsy device. We camped ahead of the motors as they camped for lunch. Directly after, Lashly brought his machine along on low gear and without difficulty ran it on to Cape Armitage. Meanwhile Day was having trouble with some bad surface; we had offered help and been refused, and with Evans alone his difficulties grew, whilst the wind sprang up and the snow started to drift. We had walked into the hut and found Meares, but now we all came out again. I sent for Lashly and Hooper and went back to help Day along. We had exasperating delays and false starts for an hour and then suddenly the machine tuned up, and off she went faster than one could walk, reaching

Cape Armitage without further hitch. It was blizzing by this time; the snow flew by. We all went back to the hut; Meares and Demetri have been busy, the hut is tidy and comfortable and a splendid brick fireplace had just been built with a brand-new stove-pipe leading from it directly upward through the roof. This is really a most creditable bit of work. Instead of the ramshackle temporary structures of last season we have now a solid permanent fireplace which should last for many a year. We spent a most comfortable night.

This morning we were away over the floe about 9 a.m. I was anxious to see how the motors started up and agreeably surprised to find that neither driver took more than 20 to 30 minutes to get his machine going, in spite of the difficulties of working a blow lamp in a keen cold wind.

Lashly got away very soon, made a short run of about ½ mile, and then after a short halt to cool, a long non-stop for quite 3 miles. The Barrier, five geographical miles from Cape Armitage, now looked very close, but Lashly had overdone matters a bit, run out of lubricant and got his engine too hot. The next run yielded a little over a mile, and he was forced to stop within a few hundred yards of the snow slope leading to the Barrier and wait for more lubricant, as well as for the heat balance in his engine to be restored.

This motor was going on second gear, and this gives a nice easy walking speed, 2½ to 3 miles an hour; it would be a splendid rate of progress if it was not necessary to halt for cooling. This is the old motor which was used in Norway; the other machine has modified gears. [This form of motor traction had been tested on several occasions; in 1908 at Lauteret in the Alps, with Dr. Charcot the Polar explorer: in 1909 and again 1910 in Norway. After each trial the sledges were brought back and improved.]

Meanwhile Day had had the usual balancing trouble and had dropped to a speck, but towards the end of our second run it was evident he had overcome these and was coming along at a fine speed. One soon saw that the men beside the sledges were running. To make a long story short, he stopped to hand over lubricating oil, started at a gallop again, and dashed up the slope without a hitch on his top speed – the first man to run a motor on the Great Barrier! There was great cheering from all assembled, but the motor party was not wasting time on jubilation. On dashed the motor, and it and the running men beside it soon grew small in the distance. We went back to help Lashly, who had restarted his engine. If not so dashingly, on account of his slower speed, he also now took the slope without hitch and got a last handshake as he clattered forward. His engine was not working so well as the other, but I think mainly owing to the first overheating and a want of adjustment resulting therefrom.

Thus the motors left us, travelling on the best surface they have yet encountered – hard windswept snow without sastrugi – a surface which Meares reports to extend to Corner Camp at least.

Providing there is no serious accident, the engine troubles will gradually be got over; of that I feel pretty confident. Every day will see improvement as it has done to date, every day the men will get greater confidence with larger experience of the machines and the conditions. But it is not easy to foretell the extent of the result of older and earlier troubles with the rollers. The new rollers turned up by Day are already splitting, and one of Lashly's chains is in a bad way; it may be possible to make temporary repairs good enough to cope with the improved surface, but it seems probable that Lashly's car will not get very far.

It is already evident that had the rollers been metal cased and the runners metal covered, they would now be as good as new. I cannot think why we had not the sense to have this done. As things are I am satisfied we have the right men to deal with the difficulties of the situation.

The motor programme is not of vital importance to our plan and it is possible the machines will do little to help us, but already they have vindicated themselves. Even the seamen, who have remained very sceptical of them, have been profoundly impressed. Evans said, 'Lord, sir, I reckon if them things can go on like that you wouldn't want nothing else' – but like everything else of a novel nature, it is the actual sight of them at work that is impressive, and nothing short of a hundred miles over the Barrier will carry conviction to outsiders.

Parting with the motors, we made haste back to Hut Point and had tea there. My feet had got very sore with the unaccustomed soft foot-gear and crinkly surface, but we decided to get back to Cape Evans. We came along in splendid weather, and after stopping for a cup of tea at Razor Back, reached the hut at 9 p.m., averaging 3½ stat. miles an hour. During the day we walked 26½ stat. miles, not a bad day's work considering condition, but I'm afraid my feet are going to suffer for it.

Saturday 28 October My feet sore and one 'tendon Achillis' strained (synovitis); shall be right in a day or so, however. Last night tremendous row in the stables. Christopher and Chinaman discovered fighting. Gran nearly got kicked. These ponies are getting above themselves with their high feeding. Oates says that Snippets is still lame and has one leg a little 'heated'; not a pleasant item of news. Debenham is progressing but not very fast; the Western Party will leave after us, of that there is no doubt now. It is trying that they should be wasting the season in this way. All things considered, I shall be glad to get away and put our fortune to the test.

Monday 30 October We had another beautiful day yesterday, and one began to feel that the summer really had come; but today, after a fine morning, we have a return to blizzard conditions. It is blowing a howling gale as I write. Yesterday Wilson, Crean, P.O. Evans, and I donned our sledging kit and camped by the bergs for the benefit of Ponting and his cinematograph; he got a series of films which should be about the most interesting of all his collection. I imagine nothing will take so well as these scenes of camp life.

On our return we found Meares had returned; he and the dogs well. He told us that (Lieut.) Evans had come into Hut Point on Saturday to fetch a personal bag left behind there. Evans reported that Lashly's motor had broken down near Safety Camp; they found the big end smashed up in one cylinder and traced it to a faulty casting; they luckily had spare parts, and Day and Lashly worked all night on repairs in a temperature of -25°. By the morning repairs were completed and they had a satisfactory trial run, dragging on loads with both motors. Then Evans found out his loss and returned on ski, whilst, as I gather, the motors proceeded; I don't quite know how, but I suppose they ran one on at a time.

On account of this accident and because some of our hardest worked people were badly hit by the two days' absence helping the machines, I have decided to start on Wednesday instead of tomorrow. If the blizzard should blow out, Atkinson and Keohane will set off tomorrow for Hut Point, so that we may see how far Jehu is to be counted on.

Tuesday 31 October The blizzard has blown itself out this morning, and this afternoon it has cleared; the sun is shining and the wind dropping. Meares and Ponting are just off to Hut Point. Atkinson and Keohane will probably leave in an hour or so as arranged, and if the weather holds, we shall all get off tomorrow. So here end the entries in this diary with the first chapter of our History. The future is in the lap of the gods; I can think of nothing left undone to deserve success.

16
SOUTHERN JOURNEY, THE BARRIER STAGE:
1 NOVEMBER 1911 – 9 DECEMBER 1911

1 November Last night we heard that Jehu had reached Hut Point in about 5½ hours. This morning we got away in detachments – Michael, Nobby, Chinaman were first to get away about 11 a.m. The little devil Christopher was harnessed with the usual difficulty and started in kicking mood, Oates holding on for all he was worth.

Bones ambled off gently with Crean, and I led Snippets in his wake. Ten minutes after Evans and Snatcher passed at the usual full speed.

The wind blew very strong at the Razor Back and the sky was threatening – the ponies hate the wind. A mile south of this island Bowers and Victor passed me, leaving me where I best wished to be – at the tail of the line.

About this place I saw that one of the animals ahead had stopped and was obstinately refusing to go forward again. I had a great fear it was Chinaman, the unknown quantity, but to my relief found it was my old friend 'Nobby' in obstinate mood. As he is very strong and fit the matter was soon adjusted with a little persuasion from Anton behind. Poor little Anton found it difficult to keep the pace with short legs.

Snatcher soon led the party and covered the distance in four hours. Evans said he could see no difference at the end from the start – the little animal simply romped in. Bones and Christopher arrived almost equally fresh, in fact the latter had been bucking and kicking the whole way. For the present there is no end to his devilment, and the great consideration is how to safeguard Oates. Some quiet ponies should always be near him, a difficult matter to arrange with such varying rates of walking. A little later I came up to a batch, Bowers, Wilson, Cherry, and Wright, and was happy to see Chinaman going very strong. He is not fast, but very steady, and I think should go a long way.

Victor and Michael forged ahead again, and the remaining three of us came in after taking a little under five hours to cover the distance.

We were none too soon, as the weather had been steadily getting worse, and soon after our arrival it was blowing a gale.

Thursday 2 November Hut Point. The march teaches a good deal as to the paces of the ponies. It reminded me of a regatta or a somewhat disorganised fleet with ships of very unequal speed. The plan of further advance has now been evolved. We shall start in three parties – the very slow ponies, the medium paced, and the fliers. Snatcher starting last will probably overtake the leading unit. All this requires a good deal of arranging. We have decided to begin night marching, and shall get away after supper, I hope. The weather is hourly improving, but at this season that does not count for much. At present our ponies are very comfortably stabled. Michael, Chinaman and James Pigg are actually in the hut. Chinaman kept us alive last night by stamping on the floor. Meares and Demetri are here with the dog team, and Ponting with a great photographic outfit. I fear he won't get much chance to get results.

Friday 3 November Camp 1. A keen wind with some drift at Hut Point, but we sailed away in detachments. Atkinson's party, Jehu, Chinaman and Jimmy Pigg led off at eight. Just before ten Wilson, Cherry-Garrard and I left. Our ponies marched steadily and well together over the sea-ice. The wind dropped a good deal, but the temperature with it, so that the little remaining was very cutting. We found Atkinson at Safety Camp. He had lunched and was just ready to march out again; he reports Chinaman and Jehu tired. Ponting arrived soon after we had camped with Demetri and a small dog team. The cinematograph was up in time to catch the flying rearguard which came along in fine form, Snatcher leading and being stopped every now and again – a wonderful little beast. Christopher had given the usual trouble when harnessed, but was evidently subdued by the Barrier Surface. However, it was not thought advisable to halt him, and so the party fled through in the wake of the advance guard.

After lunch we packed up and marched on steadily as before. I don't like these midnight lunches, but for man the march that follows is pleasant when,. as today, the wind falls and the sun steadily increases its heat. The two parties in front of us camped 5 miles beyond Safety Camp, and we reached their camp some half or three-quarters of an hour later. All the ponies are tethered in good order, but most of them are tired – Chinaman and Jehu *very tired*. Nearly all are inclined to be off feed, but this is very temporary, I think. We have built walls, but there is no wind and the sun gets warmer every minute.

Mirage Very marked waving effect to east. Small objects greatly exaggerated and showing as dark vertical lines.

1 p.m. Feeding time. Woke the party, and Oates served out the rations – all ponies feeding well. It is a sweltering day, the air breathless, the glare intense – one loses sight of the fact that the temperature is low (-22°) – one's mind seeks comparison in hot sunlit streets and scorching pavements, yet six hours ago my thumb was frostbitten. All the inconveniences of frozen footwear and damp clothes and sleeping-bags have vanished entirely.

A petrol tin is near the camp and a note stating that the motor passed at 9 p.m. 28th, going strong – they have 4 to 5 days' lead and should surely keep it.

'Bones has eaten Christopher's goggles.'

This announcement by Crean, meaning that Bones had demolished the protecting fringe on Christopher's bridle. These fringes promise very well – Christopher without his is blinking in the hot sun.

Saturday 4 November Camp 2. Led march – started in what I think will now become the settled order. Atkinson went at 8, ours at 10, Bowers, Oates and Co. at 11.15. Just after starting picked up cheerful note and saw cheerful notices saying all well with motors, both going excellently. Day wrote 'Hope to meet in 80° 30′ (Lat.).' Poor chap, within 2 miles he must have had to sing a different tale. It appears they had a bad ground on the morning of the 29th. I suppose the surface was bad and everything seemed to be going wrong. They 'dumped' a good deal of petrol and lubricant. Worse was to follow. Some 4 miles out we met a tin pathetically inscribed, 'Big end Day's motor No. 2 cylinder broken.' Half a mile beyond, as I expected, we found the motor, its tracking sledges and all. Notes from Evans and Day told the tale. The only spare had been used for Lashly's machine, and it would have taken a long time to strip Day's engine so that it could run on three cylinders. They had decided to abandon it and push on with the other alone. They had taken the six bags of forage and some odds and ends, besides their petrol and lubricant. So the dream of great help from the machines is at an end! The track of the remaining motor goes steadily forward, but now, of course, I shall expect to see it every hour of the march.

The ponies did pretty well – a cruel soft surface most of the time, but light loads, of course. Jehu is better than I expected to find him, Chinaman not so well. They are bad crocks both of them.

It was pretty cold during the night, -7° when we camped, with a crisp breeze blowing. The ponies don't like it, but now, as I write, the sun is shining through a white haze, the wind has dropped, and the picketing line is comfortable for the poor beasts.

This, 1 p.m., is the feeding hour – the animals are not yet on feed, but they are coming on.

The wind vane left here in the spring shows a predominance of wind from the S.W. quarter. Maximum scratching, about S.W. by W.

Sunday 5 November Camp 3. 'Corner Camp'. We came over the last lap of the first journey in good order – ponies doing well in soft surface, but, of course, lightly loaded. Tonight will show what we can do with the heavier weights. A very troubled note from Evans (with motor) written on morning of 2nd, saying maximum speed was about 7 miles per day. They have taken on nine bags of forage, but there are three black dots to the south which we can only imagine are the deserted motor with its loaded sledges. The men have gone on as a supporting party, as directed. It is a disappointment. I had hoped better of the machines once they got away on the Barrier Surface.

The appetites of the ponies are very fanciful. They do not like the oil cake, but for the moment seem to take to some fodder left here. However, they are off that again today. It is a sad pity they won't eat well now, because later on one can imagine how ravenous they will become. Chinaman and Jehu will not go far I fear.

Monday 6 November Camp 4. We started in the usual order, arranging so that full loads should be carried if the black dots to the south prove to be the motor. On arrival at these we found our fears confirmed. A note from

Evans stated a recurrence of the old trouble. The big end of No. 1 cylinder had cracked, the machine otherwise in good order. Evidently the engines are not fitted for working in this climate, a fact that should be certainly capable of correction. One thing is proved; the system of propulsion is altogether satisfactory. The motor party has proceeded as a man-hauling party as arranged.

With their full loads the ponies did splendidly, even Jehu and Chinaman with loads over 450 lbs. stepped out well and have finished as fit as when they started. Atkinson and Wright both think that these animals are improving.

The better ponies made nothing of their loads, and my own Snippets had over 700 lbs., sledge included. Of course, the surface is greatly improved; it is that over which we came well last year. We are all much cheered by this performance. It shows a hardening up of ponies which have been well trained; even Oates is pleased!

As we came to camp a blizzard threatened, and we built snow walls. One hour after our arrival the wind was pretty strong, but there was not much snow. This state of affairs has continued, but the ponies seem very comfortable. Their new rugs cover them well and the sheltering walls are as high as the animals, so that the wind is practically unfelt behind them. The protection is a direct result of our experience of last year, and it is good to feel that we reaped some reward for that disastrous journey. I am writing late in the day and the wind is still strong. I fear we shall not be able to go on tonight. Christopher gave great trouble again last night – the four men had great difficulty in getting him into his sledge; this is a nuisance which I fear must be endured for some time to come.

The temperature, -5°, is lower than I like in a blizzard. It feels chilly in the tent, but the ponies don't seem to mind the wind much.

The incidence of this blizzard had certain characters worthy of note:

Before we started from Corner Camp there was a heavy collection of cloud about Cape Crozier and Mount Terror, and a black line of stratus low on the western slopes of Erebus. With us the sun was shining and it was particularly warm and pleasant. Shortly after we started mist formed about us, waxing and waning in density; a slight southerly breeze sprang up, cumulo-stratus cloud formed overhead with a rather windy appearance (radial E. and W.).

At the first halt (5 miles S.) Atkinson called my attention to a curious phenomenon. Across the face of the low sun the strata of mist could be seen rising rapidly, lines of shadow appearing to be travelling upwards against the light. Presumably this was sun-warmed air. The accumulation of this gradually overspread the sky with a layer of stratus, which, however, never seemed to be very dense; the position of the sun could always be seen. Two or three hours later the wind steadily increased in force, with the usual gusty characteristic. A noticeable fact was that the sky was clear and blue above the southern horizon, and the clouds seemed to be closing down on this from time to time. At intervals since, it has lifted, showing quite an expanse of clear sky. The general appearance is that the disturbance is created by conditions about us, and is rather spreading from north to south than coming up with the wind, and this seems rather typical. On the other hand, this is not a bad snow blizzard; although the wind holds, the land, obscured last night, is now quite clear and the Bluff has no mantle.

[*Added in another hand, probably dictated*: Before we felt any air moving, during our a.m. march and the greater part of the previous march, there was dark cloud over Ross Sea off the Barrier, which continued over the Eastern Barrier to the S.E. as a heavy stratus, with here and there an appearance of wind. At the same time, due south of us, dark lines of stratus were appearing, miraged on the horizon, and while we were camping after our a.m. march, these were obscured by banks of white fog (or drift?), and the wind increasing the whole time. My general impression was that the storm came up from the south, but swept round over the eastern part of the Barrier before it became general and included the western part where we were.]

Tuesday 7 November Camp 4. The blizzard has continued throughout last night and up to this time of writing, late in the afternoon. Starting mildly, with broken clouds, little snow, and gleams of sunshine, it grew in intensity until this forenoon, when there was heavy snowfall and the sky overspread with low nimbus cloud. In the early afternoon the snow and wind took off, and the wind is dropping now, but the sky looks very lowering and unsettled.

Last night the sky was so broken that I made certain the end of the blow had come. Towards morning the sky overhead and far to the north was quite clear. More cloud obscured the sun to the south and low heavy banks hung over Ross Island. All seemed hopeful, except that I noted with misgiving that the mantle on the Bluff was beginning to form. Two hours later the whole sky was overcast and the blizzard had fully developed.

This Tuesday evening it remains overcast, but one cannot see that the clouds are travelling fast. The Bluff mantle is a wide low bank of stratus not particularly windy in appearance; the wind is falling, but the sky still looks lowering to the south and there is a general appearance of unrest. The temperature has been -10° all day.

The ponies, which had been so comparatively comfortable in the earlier stages, were hit as usual when the snow began to fall.

We have done everything possible to shelter and protect them, but there seems no way of keeping them comfortable when the snow is thick and driving fast. We men are snug and comfortable enough, but it is very evil to lie here and know that the weather is steadily sapping the strength of the beasts on which so much depends. It requires much philosophy to be cheerful on such occasions.

In the midst of the drift this forenoon the dog party came up and camped about a quarter of a mile to leeward. Meares has played too much for safety in catching us so soon, but it is satisfactory to find the dogs will pull the loads and can be driven to face such a wind as we have had. It shows that they ought to be able to help us a good deal.

The tents and sledges are badly drifted up, and the drifts behind the pony walls have been dug out several times. I shall be glad indeed to be on the march again, and oh! for a little sun. The ponies are all quite warm when covered by their rugs. Some of the fine drift snow finds its way under the rugs, and especially under the broad belly straps; this melts and makes the coat wet if allowed to remain. It is not easy to understand at first why the blizzard should have such a withering effect on the poor beasts. I think it is mainly due to the exceeding fineness of the snow particles, which, like finely divided powder, penetrate the hair of the coat and lodge in the inner warmths. Here it melts, and as water carries off the animal heat. Also, no doubt, it harasses the animals by the bombardment of the fine flying particles on tender places such as nostrils, eyes, and to lesser extent ears. In this way it continually bothers them, preventing rest. Of all things the most important for horses is that conditions should be placid whilst they stand tethered.

Wednesday 8 November Camp 5. Wind with overcast threatening sky continued to a late hour last night. The question of starting was open for a long time, and many were unfavourable. I decided we must go, and soon after midnight the advance guard got away. To my surprise, when the rugs were stripped from the 'crocks' they appeared quite fresh and fit. Both Jehu and Chinaman had a skittish little run. When their heads were loose Chinaman indulged in a playful buck. All three started with their loads at a brisk pace. It was a great relief to find that they had not suffered at all from the blizzard. They went out six geographical miles, and our section going at a good round pace found them encamped as usual. After they had gone, we waited for the rearguard to come up and joined with them. For the next 5 miles the bunch of seven kept together in fine style, and with wind dropping, sun gaining in power, and ponies going well, the march was a real pleasure. One gained confidence every moment in the animals; they brought along their heavy loads without a hint of tiredness. All take the patches of soft snow with an easy stride, not bothering themselves at all. The majority halt now and again to get a mouthful of snow, but little Christopher goes through with a non-stop run. He gives as much trouble as ever at the start, showing all sorts of ingenious tricks to escape his harness. Yesterday when brought to his knees and held, he lay down, but this served no end, for before he jumped to his feet and dashed off the traces had been fixed and he was in for the 13 miles of steady work. Oates holds like grim death to his bridle until the first freshness is worn off, and this is no little time, for even after 10 miles he seized a slight opportunity to kick up. Some four miles from this camp Evans loosed Snatcher momentarily. The little beast was off at a canter at once and on slippery snow; it was all Evans could do to hold to the bridle. As it was he dashed across the line, somewhat to its danger.

Six hundred yards from this camp there was a bale of forage. Bowers stopped and loaded it on his sledge, bringing his weights to nearly 800 lbs. His pony Victor stepped out again as though nothing had been added. Such incidents are very inspiriting. Of course, the surface is very good; the animals rarely sink to the fetlock joint, and for a good part of the time are borne up on hard snow patches without sinking at all. In passing I mention that there are practically no places where ponies sink to their hocks as described by Shackleton. On the only occasion last year when our ponies sank to their hocks in one soft patch, they were unable to get their loads on at all. The feathering of the fetlock joint is borne up on the snow crust and its upward bend is indicative of the depth of the hole made by the hoof; one sees that an extra inch makes a tremendous difference.

We are picking up last year's cairns with great ease, and all show up very distinctly. This is extremely satisfactory for the homeward march. What with pony walls, camp sites and cairns, our track should be easily followed the whole way. Everyone is as fit as can be. It was wonderfully warm as we camped this morning at 11 o'clock; the wind has dropped completely and the sun shines gloriously. Men and ponies revel in such weather. One devoutly hopes for a good spell of it as we recede from the windy northern region. The dogs came up soon after we had camped, travelling easily.

Thursday 9 November Camp 6. Sticking to programme, we are going a little over the 10 miles (geo.) nightly. Atkinson started his party at 11 and went on for 7 miles to escape a cold little night breeze which quickly dropped. He was some time at his lunch camp, so that starting to join the rearguard we came in together the last 2 miles. The experience showed that the slow advance guard ponies are forced out of their place by joining with the others, whilst the fast rearguard is reduced in speed. Obviously it is not an advantage to be together, yet all the ponies are doing well. An amusing incident happened when Wright left his pony to examine his sledgemeter. Chinaman evidently didn't like being left behind and set off at a canter to rejoin the main body. Wright's long legs barely carried him fast enough to stop this fatal stampede, but the ridiculous sight was due to the fact that old Jehu caught the infection and set off at a sprawling canter in Chinaman's wake. As this is the pony we thought scarcely capable of a single march at start, one is agreeably surprised to find him still displaying such commendable spirit. Christopher is troublesome as ever at the start; I fear that signs of tameness will only indicate absence of strength. The dogs followed us so easily over the 10 miles that Meares thought of going on again, but finally decided that the present easy work is best.

Things look hopeful. The weather is beautiful – temp. -12°, with a bright sun. Some stratus cloud about Discovery and over White Island. The sastrugi about here are very various in direction and the surface a good deal ploughed up, showing that the Bluff influences the wind direction even out as far as this camp. The surface is hard; I take it about as good as we shall get.

There is an annoying little southerly wind blowing now, and this serves to show the beauty of our snow walls. The ponies are standing under their lee in the bright sun as comfortable as can possibly be.

Friday 10 November Camp 7. A very horrid march. A strong head wind during the first part – 5 miles (geo.) – then a snowstorm. Wright leading found steering so difficult after three miles (geo.) that the party decided to camp. Luckily just before camping he rediscovered Evans' track (motor party) so that, given decent weather, we shall be able to follow this. The ponies did excellently as usual, but the surface is good distinctly. The wind has dropped and the weather is clearing now that we have camped. It is disappointing to miss even 1½ miles.

Christopher was started today by a ruse. He was harnessed behind his wall and was in the sledge before he realised. Then he tried to bolt, but Titus hung on.

Saturday 11 November Camp 8. It cleared somewhat just before the start of our march, but the snow which had fallen in the day remained soft and flocculent on the surface. Added to this we entered on an area of soft crust between a few scattered hard sastrugi. In pits between these in places the snow lay in sandy heaps. A worse set of conditions for the ponies could scarcely be imagined. Nevertheless they came through pretty well, the strong ones excellently, but the crocks had had enough at 9½ miles. Such a surface makes one anxious in spite of the rapidity with which changes take place. I expected these marches to be a little difficult, but not near so bad as today. It is snowing again as we camp, with a slight north-easterly breeze. It is difficult to make out what is happening to the weather – it is all part of the general warming up, but I wish the sky would clear. In spite of the surface, the dogs ran up from the camp before last, over 20 miles, in the night. They are working splendidly so far.

Sunday 12 November Camp 9. Our marches are uniformly horrid just at present. The surface remains wretched, not quite so heavy as yesterday, perhaps, but very near it at times. Five miles out the advance party came straight and true on our last year's Bluff depot marked with a flagstaff. Here following I found a note from Evans, cheerful in tone, dated 7 a.m. 7th inst. He is, therefore, the best part of five days ahead of us, which is good. Atkinson camped a mile beyond this cairn and had a very gloomy account of Chinaman. Said he couldn't last more than a mile or two. The weather was horrid, overcast, gloomy, snowy. One's spirits became very low. However, the crocks set off again, the rearguard came up, passed us in camp, and then on the march about 3 miles on, so that they camped about the same time. The Soldier thinks Chinaman will last for a good many days yet, an extraordinary confession of hope for him. The rest of the animals are as well as can be expected – Jehu rather better. These weather appearances change every minute. When we camped there was a chill northerly breeze, a black sky, and light falling snow. Now the sky is clearing and the sun shining an hour later. The temperature remains about +10° in the daytime.

Monday 13 November Camp 10. Another horrid march in a terrible light, surface very bad. Ponies came through all well, but they are being tried hard by the surface conditions. We followed tracks most of the way, neither party seeing the other except towards camping time. The crocks did well, all things considered; Jehu is doing extremely well for him. As we camped the sun came out and the cold chilly conditions of the march passed away, leaving everything peaceful, calm, and pleasant. We shall be in a better position to know how we stand when we get to One Ton Camp, now only 17 or 18 miles, but I am anxious about these beasts very anxious, they are not the ponies they ought to have been, and if they pull through well, all the thanks will be due to Gates. I trust the weather and surface conditions will improve; both are rank bad at present.

3 p.m. It has been snowing consistently for some hours, adding to the soft surface accumulation inch upon inch. What can such weather mean? Arguing it out, it is clearly necessary to derive this superfluity of deposition from some outside source such as the open sea. The wind and spread of cloud from the N.E. and the exceptionally warm temperature seem to point to this. If this should come as an exception, our luck will be truly awful. The camp is very silent and cheerless, signs that things are going awry. The temperature in the middle of our tent this morning when the sun was shining on it was +50°! outside +10°.

Tuesday 14 November Camp 11. The surface little improved, but a slightly better and much more cheerful march. The sun shone out midway, and although obscured for a time, it is now quite bright again. Now it is thoroughly warm, the air breathlessly still, and the ponies resting in great comfort. If the snow has finished, the surface deposit, which is three to four inches thick, ought to diminish rapidly. Yet it is painful struggling on through this snow, though the ponies carry it gallantly enough. Christopher has now been harnessed three times without difficulty. After One Ton Camp it ought to be possible to stop him for a midnight halt and so get through the easier on long marches. Nearly 12 statute miles without a stop must be a big strain on the rearguard animals. One Ton Camp is only about 7 miles farther. Meanwhile we passed two of Evans' cairns today and one old cairn of last year, so that we ought to have little difficulty in finding our depot.

Although we have been passing the black land of the Bluff I have not seen a sign of the land for four days. I had not thought it possible that misty conditions could continue for so long a time in this region; always before we have seen the land repeatedly. Either the whole sky has been clear, or the overhanging cloud has lifted from time to time to show the lower rocks. Had we been dependent on land marks we should have fared ill. Evidently a good system of cairns is the best possible travelling arrangement on this great snow plain. Meares and Demetri up with the dogs as usual very soon after we camped.

This inpouring of warm moist air, which gives rise to this heavy surface deposit at this season, is certainly an interesting meteorological fact, accounting as it does for the very sudden change in Barrier conditions from spring to summer.

Wednesday 15 November Camp 12. Found our One Ton Camp without any difficulty [130 geographical miles from Cape Evans]. About 7 or 8 miles. After 5½ miles to lunch camp, Chinaman was pretty tired, but went on again in good form after the rest. All the other ponies made nothing of the march, which, however, was over a distinctly better surface. After a discussion we had decided to give the animals a day's rest here, and then to push forward at the rate of 13 geographical miles a day. Oates thinks the ponies will get through, but that they have lost condition quicker than he expected. Considering his usually pessimistic attitude this must be thought a hopeful view. Personally I am much more hopeful. I think that a good many of the beasts are actually in better form than when they started, and that there is no need to be alarmed about the remainder, always excepting the weak ones which we have always regarded with doubt. Well, we must wait and see how things go.

A note from Evans dated the 9th, stating his party has gone on to 80° 30', carrying four boxes of biscuit. He has done something over 30 miles (geo.) in 2½ days – exceedingly good going. I only hope he has built lots of good cairns.

It was a very beautiful day yesterday, bright sun, but as we marched, towards midnight, the sky gradually became overcast; very beautiful *halo rings* formed around the sun. Four separate rings were very distinct. Wilson descried a fifth – the orange colour with blue interspace formed very fine contrasts. We now clearly see the corona ring on the snow surface. The spread of stratus cloud overhead was very remarkable. The sky was blue all around the horizon, but overhead a cumulo-stratus grew early; it seemed to be drifting to the south and later to the east. The broken cumulus slowly changed to a uniform stratus, which seems to be thinning as the sun gains power. There is a very thin light fall of snow crystals, but the surface deposit seems to be abating the evaporation for the moment, outpacing the light snowfall. The crystals barely exist a moment when they light on our equipment, so that everything on and about the sledges is drying rapidly. When the sky was clear above the horizon we got a good view of the distant land all around to the west; white patches of mountains to the W.S.W. must be 120 miles distant. During the night we saw Discovery and the Royal Society Range, the first view for many days, but we have not seen Erebus for a week, and in that direction the clouds seem ever to concentrate. It is very interesting to watch the weather phenomena of the Barrier, but one prefers the sunshine to days such as this, when everything is blankly white and a sense of oppression is inevitable.

The temperature fell to -15° last night, with a clear sky; it rose to 0° directly the sky covered and is now just +16° to +20°. Most of us are using goggles with glass of light green tint. We find this colour very grateful to the eyes, and as a rule it is possible to see everything through them even more clearly than with naked vision.

The hard sastrugi are now all from the W.S.W. and our cairns are drifted up by winds from that direction; mostly, though, there has evidently been a range of snow-bearing winds round to south. This observation holds from Corner Camp to this camp, showing that apparently all along the coast the wind comes from the land. The minimum thermometer left here shows -73°, rather less than expected; it has been excellently exposed and evidently not at all drifted up with snow at any time. I cannot find the oats I scattered here – rather fear the drift has covered them, but other evidences show that the snow deposit has been very small.

Thursday 16 November Camp 12. Resting. A stiff little southerly breeze all day, dropping towards evening. The temperature -15°. Ponies pretty comfortable in rugs and behind good walls. We have reorganised the loads, taking on about 580 lbs. with the stronger ponies, 400 odd with the others.

Friday 17 November Camp 13. Atkinson started about 8.30. We came on about 11, the whole of the remainder. The lunch camp was 7½ miles. Atkinson left as we came in. He was an hour before us at the final camp, 13¼ (geo.) miles. On the whole, and considering the weights, the ponies did very well, but the surface was comparatively good. Christopher showed signs of trouble at start, but was coaxed into position for the traces to be hooked. There was some ice on his runner and he had a very heavy drag, therefore a good deal done on arrival; also his load seems heavier and deader than the others. It is early days to wonder whether the little beasts will last; one can only hope they will, but the weakness of breeding and age is showing itself already.

The crocks have done wonderfully, so there is really no saying how long or well the fitter animals may go. We had a horribly cold wind on the march. Temp. -18°, force 3. The sun was shining but seemed to make little difference. It is still shining brightly, temp. 11°. Behind the pony walls it is wonderfully warm and the animals look as snug as possible.

Saturday 18 November Camp 14. The ponies are not pulling well. The surface is, if anything, a little worse than yesterday, but I should think about the sort of thing we shall have to expect henceforward. I had a panic that we were carrying too much food and this morning we have discussed the matter and decided we can leave a sack. We have done the usual 13 miles (geog.) with a few hundred yards to make the 15 statute. The temperature was -21° when we camped last night, now it is -3°. The crocks are going on, very wonderfully. Oates gives Chinaman at least three days, and Wright says he may go for a week. This is slightly inspiriting, but how much better would it have been to have had ten really reliable beasts. It's touch and go whether we scrape up to the Glacier; meanwhile we get along somehow. At any rate the bright sunshine makes everything look more hopeful.

Sunday 19 November Camp 15. We have struck a real bad surface, sledges pulling well over it, but ponies sinking very deep. The result is to about finish Jehu. He was terribly done on getting in tonight. He may go another march, but not more, I think. Considering the surface the other ponies did well. The ponies occasionally sink halfway to the hock, little Michael once or twice almost to the hock itself. Luckily the weather now is glorious for resting the animals, which are very placid and quiet in the brilliant sun. The sastrugi are confused, the underlying hard patches appear as before to have been formed by a W.S.W. wind, but there are some surface waves pointing to a recent south-easterly wind. Have been taking some photographs, Bowers also.

Monday 20 November Camp 16. The surface a little better. Sastrugi becoming more and more definite from S.E. Struck a few hard patches which made me hopeful of much better things, but these did not last long. The crocks still go. Jehu seems even a little better than yesterday, and will certainly go another march. Chinaman reported bad the first half march, but bucked up the second. The dogs found the surface heavy. Tomorrow I propose to relieve them of a forage bag. The sky was slightly overcast during the march, with radiating cirro-stratus S.S.W.–N.N.E. Now very clear and bright again. Temp, at night -14°, now +4°. A very slight southerly breeze, from which the walls protect the animals well. I feel sure that the long day's rest in the sun is very good for all of them.

Our ponies marched very steadily last night. They seem to take the soft crusts and difficult plodding surface more easily. The loss of condition is not so rapid as noticed to One Ton Camp, except perhaps in Victor, who is getting to look very gaunt. Nobby seems fitter and stronger than when he started; he alone is ready to go all his feed at any time and as much more as he can get. The rest feel fairly well, but they are getting a very big strong ration. I am beginning to feel more hopeful about them. Christopher kicked the bow of his sledge in towards the end of the march. He must have a lot left in him though.

Tuesday 21 November Camp 17. Lat. 80° 35'. The surface decidedly better and the ponies very steady on the march. None seem overtired, and now it is impossible not to take a hopeful view of their prospect of pulling through. (Temp. -14°, night.) The only circumstance to be feared is a reversion to bad surfaces, and that ought not to happen on this course. We marched to the usual lunch camp and saw a large cairn ahead. Two miles beyond we came on the Motor Party in Lat. 80° 32'. We learned that they had been waiting for six days. They all look very fit, but declare themselves to be very hungry. This is interesting as showing conclusively that a ration amply sufficient for the needs of men leading ponies is quite insufficient for men doing hard pulling work; it therefore fully justifies the provision which we have made for the Summit work. Even on that I have little doubt we shall soon get hungry. Day looks very thin, almost gaunt, but fit. The weather is beautiful – long may it so continue. (Temp. +6°, 11 a.m.)

It is decided to take on the Motor Party in advance for three days, then Day and Hooper return. We hope Jehu will last three days; he will then be finished in any case and fed to the dogs. It is amusing to see Meares looking eagerly for the chance of a feed for his animals; he has been expecting it daily. On the other hand, Atkinson and Oates are eager to get the poor animal beyond the point at which Shackleton killed his first beast. Reports on Chinaman are very favourable, and it really looks as though the ponies are going to do what is hoped of them.

Wednesday 22 November Camp 18. Everything much the same. The ponies thinner but not much weaker. The crocks still going along. Jehu is now called 'The Barrier Wonder' and Chinaman 'The Thunderbolt'. Two days more and they will be well past the spot at which Shackleton killed his first animal. Nobby keeps his pre-eminence of condition and has now the heaviest load by some 50 lbs.; most of the others are under 500 lbs. load, and I hope will be eased further yet. The dogs are in good form still, and came up well with their loads this morning (night temp. -14°). It looks as though we ought to get through to the Glacier without great difficulty. The weather is glorious and the ponies can make the most of their rest during the warmest hours, but they certainly lose in one way by marching at night. The surface is much easier for the sledges when the sun is warm, and for about three hours before and after midnight the friction noticeably increases. It is just a question whether this extra weight on the loads is compensated by the resting temperature. We are quite steady on the march now, and though not fast yet get through with few stops. The animals seem to be getting accustomed to the steady, heavy plod and take the deep places less fussily. There is rather an increased condition of false crust, that is, a crust which appears firm till the whole weight of the animal is put upon it, when it suddenly gives some three or four inches. This is very trying for the poor beasts. There are also more patches in which the men sink, so that walking is getting more troublesome, but, speaking broadly, the crusts are not comparatively bad and the surface is rather better than it was. If the hot sun continues this should still further improve. One cannot see any reason why the crust should change in the next 100 miles (Temp. + 2°).

The land is visible along the western horizon in patches. Bowers points out a continuous dark band. Is this the dolerite sill?

Thursday 23 November Camp 19. Getting along. I think the ponies will get through; we are now 150 geographical miles from the Glacier. But it is still rather touch and go. If one or more ponies were to go rapidly down hill we might be in queer street. The surface is much the same I think; before lunch there seemed to be a marked improvement, and after lunch the ponies marched much better, so that one supposed a betterment of the friction. It is banking up to the south (T. +9°) and I'm afraid we may get a blizzard. I hope to goodness it is not going to stop one marching; forage won't allow that.

Friday 24 November Camp 20. There was a cold wind changing from S. to S.E. and overcast sky all day yesterday. A gloomy start to our march, but the cloud rapidly lifted, bands of clear sky broke through from east to west, and the remnants of cloud dissipated. Now the sun is very bright and warm. We did the usual march very easily over a fairly good surface, the ponies now quite steady and regular. Since the junction with the Motor Party the procedure has been for the man-hauling people to go forward just ahead of the crocks, the other party following 2 or 3 hours later. Today we closed less than usual, so that the crocks must have been going very well. However, the fiat had already gone forth, and this morning after the march poor old Jehu was led back on the track and shot. After our doubts as to his reaching Hut Point, it is wonderful to think that he has actually got eight marches beyond our last year limit and could have gone more. However, towards the end he was pulling very little, and on the whole it is merciful to have ended his life. Chinaman seems to improve and will certainly last a good many days yet. The rest show no signs of flagging and are only moderately hungry. The surface is tiring for walking, as one sinks two or three inches nearly all the time. I feel we ought to get through now. Day and Hooper leave us tonight.

Saturday 25 November Camp 21. The surface during the first march was very heavy owing to a liberal coating of ice crystals; it improved during the second march becoming quite good towards the end (T. +2°). Now that it is pretty warm at night it is obviously desirable to work towards day marching. We shall start 2 hours later tonight and again tomorrow night.

Last night we bade farewell to Day and Hooper and set out with the new organisation (T. -8°). All started together, the man-haulers, Evans, Lashly, and Atkinson, going ahead with their gear on the 10-ft. sledge. Chinaman and James Pigg next, and the rest some ten minutes behind. We reached the lunch camp together and started therefrom in the same order, the two crocks somewhat behind, but not more than 300 yards at the finish, so we all got into camp very satisfactorily together. The men said the first march was extremely heavy (T. +2°).

The sun has been shining all night, but towards midnight light mist clouds arose, half obscuring the leading parties. Land can be dimly discerned nearly ahead. The ponies are slowly tiring, but we lighten loads again tomorrow by making another depot. Meares has just come up to report that Jehu made four feeds for the dogs. He cut up very well and had quite a lot of fat on him. Meares says another pony will carry him to the Glacier. This is very good hearing. The men are pulling with ski sticks and say that they are a great assistance. I think of taking them up the Glacier. Jehu has certainly come up trumps after all, and Chinaman bids fair to be even more valuable. Only a few more marches to feel safe in getting to our first goal.

Sunday 26 November Camp 22. Lunch camp. Marched here fairly easily, comparatively good surface. Started at 1 a.m. (midnight, local time). We now keep a steady pace of 2 miles an hour, very good going. The sky was slightly overcast at start and between two and three it grew very misty. Before we camped we lost sight of the men-haulers only 300 yards ahead. The sun is piercing the mist. Here in Lat. 81° 35′ we are leaving our 'Middle Barrier Depot', one week for each returning unit as at Mount Hooper.

Camp 22. Snow began falling during the second march; it is blowing from the W.S.W., force 2 to 3, with snow pattering on the tent, a kind of summery blizzard that reminds one of April showers at home. The ponies came well on the second march and we shall start 2 hours later again tomorrow, i.e. at 3 a.m. (T. +13°). From this it will be a very short step to day routine when the time comes for man-haulage. The sastrugi seem to be gradually coming more to the south and a little more confused; now and again they are crossed with hard westerly sastrugi. The walking is tiring for the men, one's feet sinking 2 or 3 inches at each step. Chinaman and Jimmy Pigg kept up splendidly with the other ponies. It is always rather dismal work walking over the great snow plain when sky and surface merge in one pall of dead whiteness, but it is cheering to be in such good company with everything going on steadily and well. The dogs came up as we camped. Meares says the best surface he has had yet.

Monday 27 November Camp 23. (T. +8°, 12 p.m.; +2°, 3 a.m.; +13°, 11 a.m.; +17°, 3 p.m.) Quite the most trying march we have had. The surface very poor at start. The advance party got away in front but made heavy weather of it, and we caught them up several times. This threw the ponies out of their regular work and prolonged the march. It grew overcast again, although after a summery blizzard all yesterday there was promise of better things. Starting at 3 a.m. we did not get to lunch camp much before 9. The second march was even worse. The advance party started on ski, the leading marks failed altogether, and they had the greatest difficulty in keeping a course. At the midcairn building halt the snow suddenly came down heavily, with a rise of temperature, and the ski became hopelessly clogged (bad fahrer, as the Norwegians say). At this time the surface was unspeakably heavy for pulling, but in a few minutes a south wind sprang up and a beneficial result was immediately felt. Pulling on foot, the advance had even greater difficulty in going straight until the last half mile, when the sky broke slightly. We got off our march, but under the most harassing circumstances and with the animals very tired. It is snowing hard again now, and heaven only knows when it will stop.

If it were not for the surface and bad light, things would not be so bad. There are few sastrugi and little deep snow. For the most part men and ponies sink to a hard crust some 3 or 4 inches beneath the soft upper snow. Tiring for the men, but in itself more even, and therefore less tiring for the animals. Meares just come up and reporting very bad surface. We shall start 1 hour later tomorrow, i.e. at 4 a.m., making 5 hours' delay on the conditions of three days ago. Our forage supply necessitates that we should plug on the 13 (geographical) miles daily under all conditions, so that we can only hope for better things. It is several days since we had a glimpse of land, which makes conditions especially gloomy. A tired animal makes a tired man, I find, and none of us are very bright now after the day's march, though we have had ample sleep of late.

Tuesday 28 November Camp 24. The most dismal start imaginable. Thick as a hedge, snow falling and drifting with keen southerly wind. The men pulled out at 3.15 with Chinaman and James Pigg. We followed at 4.20, just catching the party at the lunch camp at 8.30. Things got better half way; the sky showed signs of clearing and the steering improved. Now, at lunch, it is getting thick again. When will the wretched blizzard be over? The walking is better for ponies, worse for men; there is nearly everywhere a hard crust some 3 to 6 inches down. Towards the end of the march we crossed a succession of high hard south-easterly sastrugi, widely dispersed. I don't know what to make of these.

Second march almost as horrid as the first. Wind blowing strong from the south, shifting to S.E. as the snowstorms fell on us, when we could see little or nothing, and the driving snow hit us stingingly in the face. The general impression of all this dirty weather is that it spreads in from the S.E. We started at 4 a.m., and I think I shall stick to that custom for the present. These last four marches have been fought for, but completed without hitch, and, though we camped in a snowstorm, there is a more promising look in the sky, and if only for a time the wind has dropped and the sun shines brightly, dispelling some of the gloomy results of the distressing marching.

Chinaman, 'The Thunderbolt', has been shot tonight. Plucky little chap, he has stuck it out well and leaves the stage but a few days before his fellows. We have only four bags of forage (each one 30 lbs.) left, but these should give seven marches with all the remaining animals, and we are less than 90 miles from the Glacier. Bowers tells me that the barometer was phenomenally low both during this blizzard and the last. This has certainly been the most unexpected and trying summer blizzard yet experienced in this region. I only trust it is over. There is not much to choose between the remaining ponies. Nobby and Bones are the strongest, Victor and Christopher the weakest, but all should get through. The land doesn't show up yet.

Wednesday 29 November Camp 25. Lat. 82° 21′. Things much better. The land showed up late yesterday; Mount Markham, a magnificent triple peak, appearing wonderfully close, Cape Lyttelton and Cape Goldie. We did our march in good time, leaving about 4.20, and getting into this camp at 1.15. About 7½ hours on the march. I suppose our speed throughout averages 2 stat. miles an hour.

. The land showed hazily on the march, at times looking remarkably near. Sheety white snowy stratus cloud hung about overhead during the first march, but now the sky is clearing, the sun very warm and bright. Land shows up almost ahead now, our pony goal less than 70 miles away. The ponies are tired, but I believe all have five days' work left in them, and some a great deal more. Chinaman made four feeds for the dogs, and I suppose we can count every other pony as a similar asset. It follows that the dogs can be employed, rested, and fed well on the homeward track. We could really get though now with their help and without much delay, yet every consideration makes it desirable to save the men from heavy hauling as long as possible. So I devoutly hope the 70 miles will come in the present order of things. Snippets and Nobby now walk by themselves, following in the tracks well. Both have a continually cunning eye on their driver, ready to stop the moment he pauses. They eat snow every few minutes. It's a relief not having to lead an animal; such trifles annoy one on these marches, the animal's vagaries, his everlasting attempts to eat his head rope, etc. Yet all these animals are very full of character. Some day I must write of them and their individualities.

The men-haulers started 1½ hours before us and got here a good hour ahead, travelling easily throughout. Such is the surface with the sun on it, justifying my decision to work towards day marching. Evans has suggested the word 'glide' for the quality of surface indicated. 'Surface' is more comprehensive, and includes the crusts and liability to sink in them. From this point of view the surface is distinctly bad. The ponies plough deep all the time, and the men most of the time. The sastrugi are rather more clearly S.E.; this would be from winds sweeping along the coast. We have a recurrence of 'sinking crusts' – areas which give way with a report. There has been little of this since we left One Ton Camp until yesterday and today, when it is again very marked. Certainly the open Barrier conditions are different from those near the coast. Altogether things look much better and everyone is in excellent spirits. Meares has been measuring the holes made by ponies' hooves and finds an average of about 8 inches since we left One Ton Camp. He finds many holes a foot deep. This gives a good indication of the nature of the work. In Bowers' tent they had some of Chinaman's undercut in their hoosh yesterday, and say it was excellent. I am cook for the present. Have been discussing pony snowshoes. I wish to goodness the animals would wear them – it would save them any amount of labour in such surfaces as this.

Thursday 30 November Camp 26. A very pleasant day for marching, but a very tiring march for the poor animals, which, with the exception of Nobby, are showing signs of failure all round. We were slower by half an hour or more than yesterday. Except that the loads are light now and there are still eight animals left, things don't look too pleasant, but we should be less than 60 miles from our first point of aim. The surface was much worse today, the ponies sinking to their knees very often. There were a few harder patches towards the end of the march. In spite of the sun there was not much 'glide' on the snow. The dogs are reported as doing very well. They are going to be a great standby, no doubt. The land has been veiled in thin white mist; it appeared at intervals after we camped and I had taken a couple of photographs.

Friday 1 December Camp 27. Lat. 82° 47'. The ponies are tiring pretty rapidly. It is a question of days with all except Nobby. Yet they are outlasting the forage, and tonight against some opinion I decided Christopher must go. He has been shot; less regret goes with him than the others, in remembrance of all the trouble he gave at the outset, and the unsatisfactory way he has gone of late. Here we leave a depot [the Southern Barrier Depot] so that no extra weight is brought on the other ponies; in fact there is a slight diminution. Three more marches ought to bring us through. With the seven crocks and the dog teams we *must* get through I think. The men alone ought not to have heavy loads on the surface, which is extremely trying.

Nobby was tried in snowshoes this morning, and came along splendidly on them for about four miles, then the wretched affairs racked and had to be taken off. There is no doubt that these snowshoes are *the* thing for ponies, and had ours been able to use them from the beginning they would have been very different in appearance at this moment. I think the sight of land has helped the animals, but not much. We started in bright warm sunshine and with the mountains wonderfully clear on our right hand, but towards the end of the march clouds worked up from the east and a thin broken cumulo-stratus now overspreads the sky, leaving the land still visible but dull. A fine glacier descends from Mount Longstaff. It has cut very deep and the walls stand at an angle of at least 50°. Otherwise, although there are many cwms on the lower ranges, the mountains themselves seem little carved. They are rounded massive structures. A cliff of light yellow-brown rock appears opposite us, flanked with black or dark brown rock, which also appears under the lighter colour. One would be glad to know what nature of rock these represent. There is a good deal of exposed rock on the next range also.

Saturday 2 December Camp 28. Lat. 83°. Started under very bad weather conditions. The stratus spreading over from the S.E. last night meant mischief, and all day we marched in falling snow with a horrible light. The ponies went poorly on the first march, when there was little or no wind and a high temperature. They were sinking deep on a wretched surface. I suggested to Oates that he should have a roving commission to watch the animals, but he much preferred to lead one, so I handed over Snippets very willingly and went on ski myself. It was very easy work for me and I took several photographs of the ponies plunging along – the light very strong at 3 (Watkins actinometer).

The ponies did much better on the second march, both surface and glide improved; I went ahead and found myself obliged to take a very steady pace to keep the lead, so we arrived in camp in flourishing condition. Sad to have to order Victor's end – poor Bowers feels it. He is in excellent condition and will provide five feeds for the dogs (Temp. +17°). We must kill now as the forage is so short, but we have reached the 83rd parallel and are practically safe to get through. Tonight the sky is breaking and conditions generally more promising – it is dreadfully dismal work marching through the blank wall of white, and we should have very great difficulty if we had not a party to go ahead and show the course. The dogs are doing splendidly and will take a heavier load from tomorrow. We kill another pony tomorrow night if we get our march off, and shall then have nearly three days' food for the other five. In fact everything looks well if the weather will only give us a chance to see our way to the Glacier. Wild, in his Diary of Shackleton's Journey, remarks on 15 December, that it is the first day for a month that he could not record splendid weather. With us a fine day has been the exception so far. However, we have not lost a march yet. It was so warm when we camped that the snow melted as it fell, and everything got sopping wet. Oates came into my tent yesterday, exchanging with Cherry-Garrard.

The tents now: Self, Wilson, Oates, and Keohane. Bowers, P.O. Evans, Cherry, and Crean.

Man-haulers: E. R. Evans, Atkinson, Wright, and Lashly. We have all taken to horse meat and are so well fed that hunger isn't thought of.

Sunday 3 December Camp 29. Our luck in weather is preposterous. I roused the hands at 2.30 a.m., intending to get away at 5. It was thick and snowy, yet we could have got on; but at breakfast the wind increased, and by 4.30 it was blowing a full gale from the south. The pony wall blew down, huge drifts collected, and the sledges were quickly buried. It was the strongest wind I have known here in summer. At 11 it began to take off. At 12.30 we got up and had lunch and got ready to start. The land appeared, the clouds broke, and by 1.30 we were in bright sunshine. We were off at 2 p.m., the land showing all round, and, but for some cloud to the S.E., everything promising. At 2.15 I saw the south-easterly cloud spreading up; it blotted out the land 30 miles away at 2.30 and was on us before 3. The sun went out, snow fell thickly, and marching conditions became horrible. The wind increased from the S.E., changed to S.W., where it hung for a time, and suddenly shifted to W.N.W. and then N.N.W., from which direction it is now blowing with falling and drifting snow. The changes of conditions are inconceivably rapid, perfectly bewildering. In spite of all these difficulties we have managed to get 11½ miles south and to this camp at 7 p.m. – the conditions of marching simply horrible.

The man-haulers led out 6 miles (geo.) and then camped. I think they had had enough of leading. We passed them, Bowers and I ahead on ski. We steered with compass, the drifting snow across our ski, and occasional glimpse of south-easterly sastrugi under them, till the sun showed dimly for the last hour or so. The whole weather conditions seem thoroughly disturbed, and if they continue so when we are on the Glacier, we shall be very awkwardly placed. It is really time the luck turned in our favour – we have had all too little of it. Every mile seems to have been hardly won under such conditions. The ponies did splendidly and the forage is lasting a little better than expected. Victor was found to have quite a lot of fat on him and the others are pretty certain to have more, so that we should have no difficulty whatever as regards transport if only the weather was kind.

Monday 4 December Camp 29, 9 a.m. I roused the party at 6. During the night the wind had changed from N.N.W. to S.S.E.; it was not strong, but the sun was obscured and the sky looked heavy; patches of land could be faintly seen and we thought that at any rate we could get on, but during breakfast the wind suddenly increased in force and afterwards a glance outside was sufficient to show a regular white floury blizzard. We have all been out building fresh walls for the ponies – an uninviting task, but one which greatly adds to the comfort of the animals, who look sleepy and bored, but not at all cold. The dogs came up with us as we camped last night and the man-haulers arrived this morning as we finished the pony wall. So we are all together again. The latter had great difficulty in following our tracks, and say they could not have steered a course without them. It is utterly impossible to push ahead in this weather, and one is at a complete loss to account for it. The barometer rose from 29.4 to 29.9 last night, a phenomenal rise. Evidently there is very great disturbance of atmospheric conditions. Well, one must stick it out, that is all, and hope for better things, but it makes me feel a little bitter to contrast such weather with that experienced by our predecessors.

Camp 30. The wind fell in the forenoon, at 12.30 the sky began to clear, by 1 the sun shone, by 2 p.m. we were away, and by 8 p.m. camped here with 13 miles to the good. The land was quite clear throughout the march and the features easily recognised. There are several uncharted glaciers of large dimensions, a confluence of three under Mount Reid. The mountains are rounded in outline, very massive, with small excrescent peaks and undeveloped 'cwms' (T. +18°). The cwms are very fine in the lower foot-hills and the glaciers have carved deep channels between walls at very high angles; one or two peaks on the foot-hills stand bare and almost perpendicular, probably granite; we should know later. Ahead of us is the ice-rounded, boulder-strewn Mount Hope and the gateway to the Glacier. We should reach it easily enough on tomorrow's march if we can compass 12 miles. The ponies marched splendidly today, crossing the deep snow in the undulations without difficulty. They must be in very much better condition than Shackleton's animals, and indeed there isn't a doubt they would go many miles yet if food allowed. The dogs are simply splendid, but came in wanting food, so we had to sacrifice poor little Michael, who, like the rest, had lots of fat on him. All the tents are consuming pony flesh and thoroughly enjoying it.

We have only lost 5 or 6 miles on these two wretched days, but the disturbed condition of the weather makes me anxious with regard to the Glacier, where more than anywhere we shall need fine days. One has a horrid feeling that this is a real bad season. However, sufficient for the day is the evil thereof. We are practically through with the first stage of our journey. Looking from the last camp towards the S.S.E., where the farthest land can be seen, it seemed more than probable that a very high latitude could be reached on the Barrier, and if Amundsen journeying that way has a stroke of luck, he may well find his summit journey reduced to 100 miles or so. In any case it is a fascinating direction for next year's work if only fresh transport arrives. The dips between undulations seem to be about 12 to 15 feet. Tonight we get puffs of wind from the gateway, which for the moment looks uninviting.

FOUR DAYS' DELAY

Tuesday 5 December Camp 30. Noon. We awoke this morning to a raging, howling blizzard. The blows we have had hitherto have lacked the very fine powdery snow – that especial feature of the blizzard. Today we have it fully developed. After a minute or two in the open one is covered from head to foot. The temperature is high, so that what falls or drives against one sticks. The ponies – head, tails, legs, and all parts not protected by their rugs – are covered with ice; the animals are standing deep in snow, the sledges are almost covered, and huge drifts above the tents. We have had breakfast, rebuilt the walls, and are now again in our bags. One cannot see the next tent, let alone the land. What on earth does such weather mean at this time of year? It is more than our share of ill-fortune, I think, but the luck may turn yet. I doubt if any party could travel in such weather even with the wind, certainly no one could travel against it.

Is there some widespread atmospheric disturbance which will be felt everywhere in this region as a bad season, or are we merely the victims of exceptional local conditions? If the latter, there is food for thought in picturing our small party struggling against adversity in one place whilst others go smilingly forward in the sunshine. How great may be the element of luck! No foresight – no procedure – could have prepared us for this state of affairs. Had we been ten times as experienced or certain of our aim we should not have expected such rebuffs.

11 p.m. It has blown hard all day with quite the greatest snowfall I remember. The drifts about the tents are simply huge. The temperature was +27° this forenoon, and rose to +31° in the afternoon, at which time the snow melted as it fell on anything but the snow, and, as a consequence, there are pools of water on everything, the tents are wet through, also the wind clothes, night boots, etc.; water drips from the tent poles and door, lies on the floorcloth, soaks the sleeping-bags, and makes everything pretty wretched. If a cold snap follows before we have had time to dry our things, we shall be mighty uncomfortable. Yet after all it would be humorous enough if it were not for the seriousness of delay – we can't afford that, and it's real hard luck that it should come at such a time. The wind shows signs of easing down, but the temperature does not fall and the snow is as wet as ever – not promising signs of abatement.

Keohane's rhyme!
The snow is all melting and everything's afloat,
If this goes on much longer we shall have to turn the *tent*
upside down and use it as a boat.

Wednesday 6 December Camp 30. Noon. Miserable, utterly miserable. We have camped in the 'Slough of Despond'. The tempest rages with unabated violence. The temperature has gone to +33°; everything in the tent is soaking. People returning from the outside look exactly as though they had been in a heavy shower of rain. They drip pools on the floorcloth. The snow is steadily climbing higher about walls, ponies, tents, and sledges. The ponies look utterly desolate. Oh! but this is too crushing, and we are only 12 miles from the Glacier. A hopeless feeling descends on one and is hard to fight off. What immense patience is needed for such occasions!

11 p.m. At 5 there came signs of a break at last, and now one can see the land, but the sky is still overcast and there is a lot of snow about. The wind also remains fairly strong and the temperature high. It is not pleasant, but if no worse in the morning we can get on at last. We are very, very wet.

Thursday 7 December Camp 30. The storm continues and the situation is now serious. One small feed remains for the ponies after today, so that we must either march tomorrow or sacrifice the animals. That is not the worst; with the help of the dogs we could get on, without doubt. The serious part is that we have this morning started our summer rations, that is to say, the food calculated from the Glacier depot has been begun. The first supporting party can only go on a fortnight from this date and so forth. The storm shows no sign of abatement and its character is as unpleasant as ever. The promise of last night died away about 3 a.m., when the temperature and wind rose again, and things reverted to the old conditions. I can find no sign of an end, and all of us agree that it is utterly impossible to move. Resignation to misfortune is the only attitude, but not an easy one to adopt. It seems undeserved where plans were well laid and so nearly crowned with a first success. I cannot see that any plan would be altered if it were to do again, the margin for bad weather was ample according to all experience, and this stormy December – our finest month – is a thing that the most cautious organiser might not have been prepared to encounter. It is very evil to lie here in a wet sleeping-bag and think of the pity of it, whilst with no break in the overcast sky things go steadily from bad to worse (T. +32°). Meares has a bad attack of snow blindness in one eye. I hope this rest will help him, but he says it has been painful for a long time. There cannot be good cheer in the camp in such weather, but it is ready to break out again. In the brief spell of hope last night one heard laughter.

Midnight Little or no improvement. The barometer is rising – perhaps there is hope in that. Surely few situations could be more exasperating than this of forced inactivity when every day and indeed one hour counts. To be here watching the mottled wet green walls of our tent, the glistening wet bamboos, the bedraggled sopping socks and loose articles dangling in the middle, the saddened countenances of my companions – to hear the everlasting patter

Meares and Demetri at the blubber stove in the *Discovery* hut.

The motor party (Left to right – Lashly, B. C. Day, Lieut. Evans, Hooper).

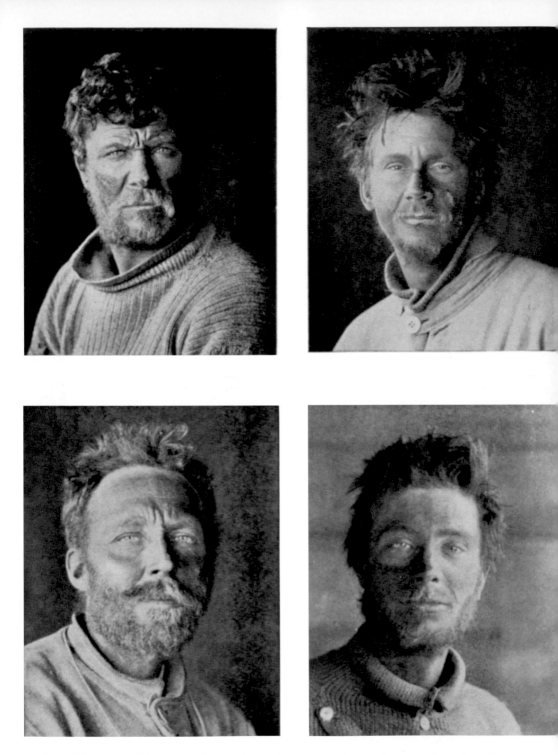

Some Members of the supporting parties as they appeared on their return from the polar journey. Top left: Petty Officer P. Keohane. Top right: C. S. Wright. Bottom left: C. H. Meares. Bottom right: B. C. Day.

Camp at three degree depot.

Above left: Chief Stoker Lashly (who received the Albert Medal).
Above right: Petty Officer Crean (who received the Albert Medal).

Pressure on the Beardmore below the Cloudmaker Mountain.

Mount Kyffin.

Camp under the wild range.

Dr. Wilson sketching on the Beardmore Glacier.

Left: H. G. Ponting and one of his
cinematograph cameras.
Above: Members of the polar party
having a meal in camp (Left to right –
P. O. Evans, Bowers, Wilson, Scott).

Members of the polar party getting into their sleeping-bags (Left to right – P. O. Evans,
Scott, Bowers, Wilson).

Ponies behind their shelter in camp on the Barrier.

Ponies on the march.

Pitching the double tent on the summit.

The polar party: On the trail.

On the way to the Pole. Some of his companions sketched by Dr. Edward A. Wilson. R. F. S. = Captain Scott. H. R. B. & B. = "Birdie" Bowers. T. O. = "Titus" Oates. A. C. G = Apsley Cherry-Garrard. P.K. = Patrick Keohane.

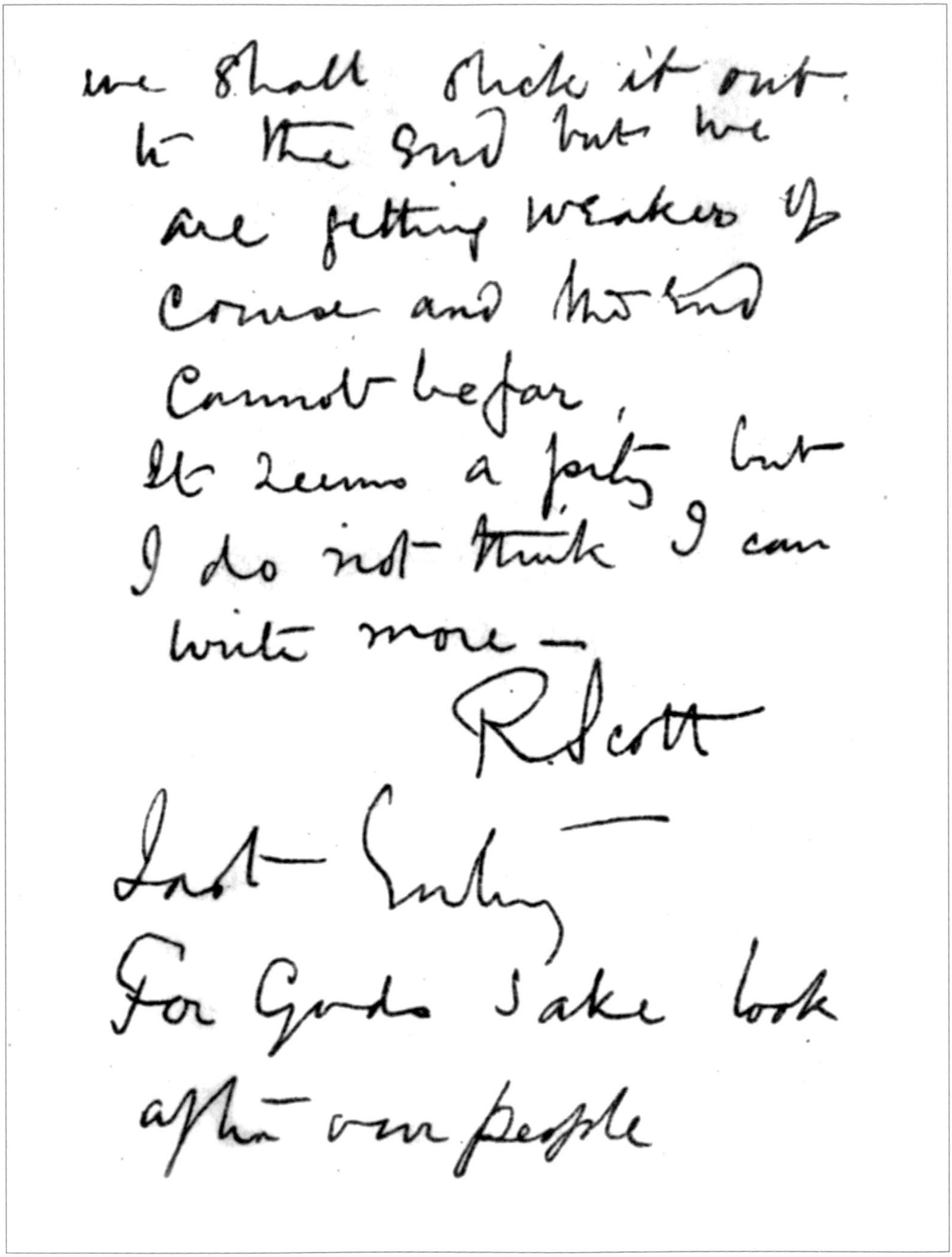

we shall stick it out
to the end but we
are getting weaker of
course and the end
cannot be far.
It seems a pity but
I do not think I can
write more —
                R. Scott
Last Entry —
For God's sake look
after our people

Diary entry March 29.

The last rest (the grave of Scott, Wilson and Bowers).

Memorial cross erected at Observation Hill to the southern party.

Amundsen's tent at the South Pole.

Mount Buckley. One of the last of many pencil sketches made by Dr. Edward A. Wilson on the return journey from the Pole under conditions of snow blindness.

Above: The Cloudmaker Mountain.
Right: Petty Officer Edgar Evans, R.N.

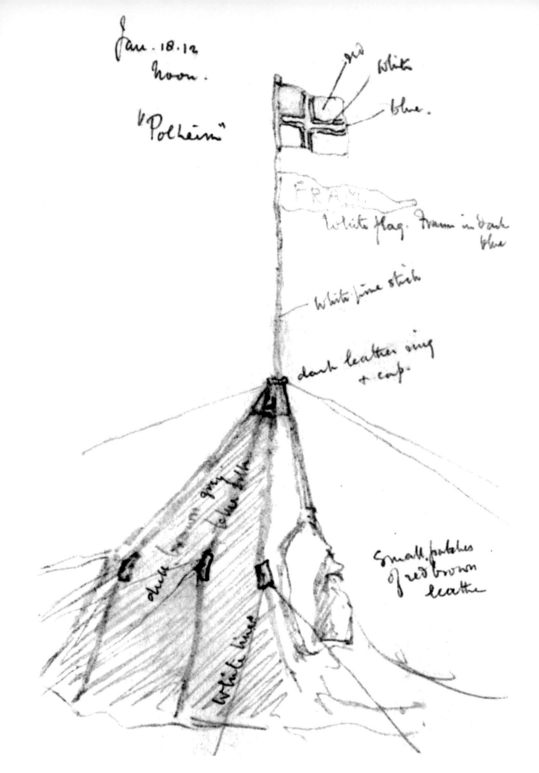

Amundsen's tent at the South Pole. Sketched by Dr. Edward A. Wilson while "it was blowing very cold -22 degrees."

Jan. 16. 1912.

Above: Black Flag Camp:
Amundsen's black flag within a
few miles of the South Pole.
Right: Cairn left by the
Norwegians S.S.W. from Black
Flag Camp and Amundsen's
South Pole mark. Sketched but
Dr. Edward A. Wilson with wind
blowing at a temperature of -22
degrees.

Cairn left by Norwegians. S.SW from Black Flag Camp
Jan. 16. 1912.

Amundsen's South Pole mark.   Jan. 18. 1912.

Bowers, Wilson, and Cherry-Garrard about to leave for Cape Crozier.

Emperor penguins.

Wilson, Bowers, and Cherry-Garrard on their return from Cape Crozier.

The last boat leaves for the ship.

Above left: Lieut. E. R. G. R. Evans surveying the four-inch theodolite which was used to locate the South Pole.
Above right: Demetri Geroff.
Below: Mount Erebus.

The hut after the winter.

Officers and scientists in the wardroom of *Terra Nova*.

The second western party at Cape Geology, Granite Harbour, on Christmas day, 1911 (Forde and Gran standing, Debenham and Taylor sitting).

The first western party in a natural ice-tunnel amid the pinnacles of the Koettlitz Glacier (Edgar Evans standing).

The second western party the day they were picked up by the ship. Taylor, Debenham, Gran and Forde.

Forde cooking seal-fry on the blubber stove at Cape Roberts.

Penguins promenade.

The northern party at Cape Adare. Left to right, top – Abbott, Dickason, Browning. Bottom – Priestley, Campbell, Levick.

The Hut at Cape Adare.

A weddell seal on the beach.

Some of the crew of the *Terra Nova*.
Deck of the *Terra Nova* from the poop.

Top left: Lieut. Bruce leading a chanty.
Top right: Mr. Williams, Chief Engineer.
Below left: The Helmsman at the wheel.
Below right: The Bo'sun with an ice anchor.

Penguins diving

Lieut. Campbell's party on their return to Cape Evans. Left to right – Dickason, Abbott, Browning, Campbell, Priestly, Levick.

Dr. Simpson in his laboratory.

Left: Captain Robert F. Scott, R.N., C.V.O. *Below*: Launch of the pram.

A pressure ridge in the sea-ice running towards Cape Barne.

Campbell and Priestley afloat on pancake ice.

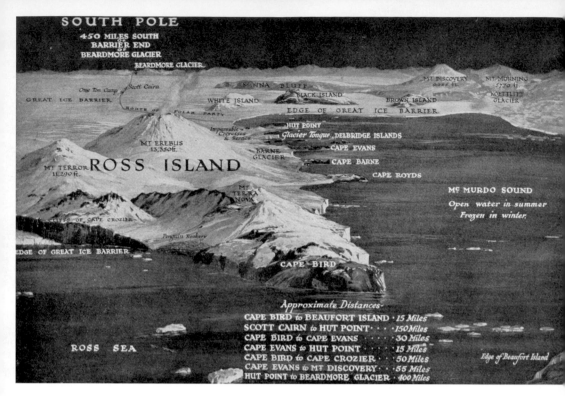

Drawing illustrating the locality of Ross Island.

Petty Officers Crean and Evans mending sleeping-bags.

Ponting attacked by killer whales.

F. Debenham.

D. G. Lille, with some of the siliceous sponges of which he secured a record haul with the dredge.

of the falling snow and the ceaseless rattle of the fluttering canvas – to feel the wet clinging dampness of clothes and everything touched, and to know that without there is but a blank wall of white on every side – these are the physical surroundings. Add the stress of sighted failure of our whole plan, and anyone must find the circumstances unenviable. But yet, after all, one can go on striving, endeavouring to find a stimulation in the difficulties that arise.

Friday 8 December Camp 30. Hoped against hope for better conditions, to wake to the mournfullest snow and wind as usual. We had breakfast at 10, and at noon the wind dropped. We set about digging out the sledges, no light task. We then shifted our tent sites. All tents had been reduced to the smallest volume by the gradual pressure of snow. The old sites are deep pits with hollowed-in wet centres. The re-setting of the tent has at least given us comfort, especially since the wind has dropped. About 4 the sky showed signs of breaking, the sun and a few patches of land could be dimly discerned. The wind shifted in light airs and a little hope revived. Alas! as I write the sun has disappeared and snow is again falling.

Our case is growing desperate. Evans and his man-haulers tried to pull a load this afternoon. They managed to move a sledge with four people on it, pulling in ski. Pulling on foot they sank to the knees. The snow all about us is terribly deep. We tried Nobby and he plunged to his belly in it. Wilson thinks the ponies finished,[21] but Oates thinks they will get another march in spite of the surface, *if it comes tomorrow*. If it should not, we must kill the ponies tomorrow and get on as best we can with the men on ski and the dogs. But one wonders what the dogs can do on such a surface. I much fear they also will prove inadequate. Oh! for fine weather, if only to the Glacier. The temperature remains +33°, and everything is disgustingly wet.

11 p.m. The wind has gone to the north, the sky is really breaking at last, the sun showing less sparingly, and the land appearing out of the haze. The temperature has fallen to +26°, and the water nuisance is already bating. With so fair a promise of improvement it would be too cruel to have to face bad weather tomorrow. There is good cheer in the camp tonight in the prospect of action. The poor ponies look wistfully for the food of which so very little remains, yet they are not hungry, as recent savings have resulted from food left in their nosebags. They look wonderfully fit, all things considered. Everything looks more hopeful tonight, but nothing can recall four lost days.

Saturday 9 December Camp 31. I turned out two or three times in the night to find the weather slowly improving; at 5.30 we all got up, and at 8 got away with the ponies – a most painful day. The tremendous snowfall of the late storm had made the surface intolerably soft, and after the first hour there was no glide. We pressed on the poor half-rationed animals, but could get none to lead for more than a few minutes; following, the animals would do fairly well. It looked as we could never make headway; the man-haulers were pressed into the service to aid matters. Bowers and Cherry-Garrard went ahead with one 10-foot sledge – thus most painfully we made about a mile. The situation was saved by P.O. Evans, who put the last pair of snowshoes on Snatcher. From this he went on without much pressing, the other ponies followed, and one by one were worn out in the second place. We went on all day without lunch. Three or four miles (T. +23°) found us engulfed in pressures, but free from difficulty except the awful softness of the snow. By 8 p.m. we had reached within a mile or so of the slope ascending to the gap which Shackleton called the Gateway.[22] I had hoped to be through the Gateway with the ponies still in hand at a very much earlier date and, but for the devastating storm, we should have been. It has been a most serious blow to us, but things are not yet desperate, if only the storm has not hopelessly spoilt the surface. The man-haulers are not up yet, in spite of their light load. I think they have stopped for tea, or something, but under ordinary conditions they would have passed us with ease.

At 8 p.m. the ponies were quite done, one and all. They came on painfully slowly a few hundred yards at a time. By this time I was hauling ahead, a ridiculously light load, and yet finding the pulling heavy enough. We camped, and the ponies have been shot. [Camp 31 received the name of Shambles Camp.] Poor beasts! they have done wonderfully well considering the terrible circumstances under which they worked, but yet it is hard to have to kill them so early. The dogs are going well in spite of the surface, but here again one cannot get the help one would wish. (T. +19°.) I cannot load the animals heavily on such snow. The scenery is most impressive; three huge pillars of granite form the right buttress of the Gateway, and a sharp spur of Mount Hope the left. The land is much more snow-covered than when we saw it before the storm. In spite of some doubt in our outlook, everyone is very cheerful tonight and jokes are flying freely around.

17
ON THE BEARDMORE GLACIER:
10 DECEMBER 1911 – 21 DECEMBER 1911

Sunday 10 December Camp 32. [While Day and Hooper, of the ex-motor party, had turned back on 24 November, and Meares and Demetri with the dogs ascended above the Lower Glacier Depot before returning on 11 December, the Southern Party and its supports were organised successively as follows:

10 December, leaving Shambles Camp – *Sledge 1* Scott, Wilson, Oates and P.O. Evans. *Sledge 2* E. Evans, Atkinson, Wright, Lashly. *Sledge 3* Bowers, Cherry-Garrard, Crean, Keohane.

21 December at Upper Glacier Depot – *Sledge 1* Scott, Wilson, Oates, P.O. Evans. *Sledge 2* E. Evans, Bowers, Crean, Lashly; while Atkinson, Wright, Cherry-Garrard and Keohane returned.

4 January, 150 miles from the Pole – *Sledge 1* Scott, Wilson, Oates, Bowers, P.O. Evans; while E. Evans, Crean, and Lashly returned.]

I was very anxious about getting our loads forward over such an appalling surface, and that we have done so is mainly due to the ski. I roused everyone at 8, but it was noon before all the readjustments of load had been made and we were ready to start. The dogs carried 600 lbs. of our weight besides the depot (200 lbs.). It was greatly to my surprise when we – my own party – with a 'one, two, three together' started our sledge, and we found it running fairly easily behind us. We did the first mile at a rate of about 2 miles an hour, having previously very carefully scraped and dried our runners. The day was gloriously fine and we were soon perspiring. After the first mile we began to rise, and for some way on a steep slope we held to our ski and kept going. Then the slope got steeper and the surface much worse, and we had to take off our ski. The pulling after this was extraordinarily fatiguing. We sank above our finnesko everywhere, and in places nearly to our knees. The runners of the sledges got coated with a thin film of ice from which we could not free them, and the sledges themselves sank to the crossbars in soft spots. All the time they were literally ploughing the snow. We reached the top of the slope at 5, and started on after tea on the down grade. On this we had to pull almost as hard as on the upward slope, but could just manage to get along on ski. We camped at 9.15, when a heavy wind coming down the glacier suddenly fell on us; but I had decided to camp before, as Evans' party could not keep up, and Wilson told me some very alarming news concerning it. It appears that Atkinson says that Wright is getting played out and Lashly is not so fit as he was owing to the heavy pulling since the blizzard. I have not felt satisfied about this party. The finish of the march today showed clearly that something was wrong. They fell a long way behind, had to take off ski, and took nearly half an hour to come up a few hundred yards. True, the surface was awful and growing worse every moment. It is a very serious business if the men are going to crack up. As for myself, I never felt fitter and my party can easily hold its own. P.O. Evans, of course, is a tower of strength, but Oates and Wilson are doing splendidly also.

Here where we are camped the snow is worse than I have ever seen it, but we are in a hollow. Every step here one sinks to the knees and the uneven surface is obviously insufficient to support the sledges. Perhaps this wind is a blessing in disguise, already it seems to be hardening the snow. All this soft snow is an aftermath of our prolonged storm. Hereabouts Shackleton found hard blue ice. It seems an extraordinary difference in fortune, and at every step S.'s luck becomes more evident. I take the dogs on for half a day tomorrow, then send them home. We have 200 lbs. to add to each sledge load and could easily do it on a reasonable surface, but it looks very much as though we shall be forced to relay if present conditions hold. There is a strong wind down the glacier tonight.

'*Beardmore Glacier* Just a tiny note to be taken back by the dogs. Things are not so rosy as they might be, but we keep our spirits up and say the luck must turn. This is only to tell you that I find I can keep up with the rest as well as of old.'

Monday 11 December Camp 33. A very good day from one point of view, very bad from another. We started straight out over the glacier and passed through a good deal of disturbance. We pulled on ski and the dogs followed. I cautioned the drivers to keep close to their sledges and we must have passed over a good many crevasses undiscovered by us, thanks to ski, and by the dogs owing to the soft snow. In one only Seaman Evans dropped a leg, ski and all. We built our depot [The Lower Glacier Depot] before starting, made it very conspicuous, and left a good deal of gear there. The old man-hauling party made heavy weather at first, but when relieved of a little weight and having cleaned their runners and re-adjusted their load they came on in fine style, and, passing us, took the lead. Starting about 11, by 3 o'clock we were clear of the pressure, and I camped the dogs, discharged our loads, and we put them on our sledges. It was a very anxious business when we started after lunch, about 4.30. Could we pull our full loads or not? My own party got away first, and, to my joy, I found we could make fairly good headway. Every now and again the sledge sank in a soft patch, which brought us up, but we learned to treat such occasions with patience. We got sideways to the sledge and hauled it out, Evans (P.O.) getting out of his ski to get better purchase. The great thing is to keep the sledge moving, and for an hour or more there were dozens of critical moments when it all but stopped, and not a few when it brought up altogether. The latter were very trying and tiring. But suddenly the surface grew more uniform and we more accustomed to the game, for after a long stop to let the other parties come up, I started at 6 and ran on till 7, pulling easily without a halt at the rate of about 2 miles an hour. I was very jubilant; all difficulties seemed to be vanishing; but unfortunately our history was not repeated with the other parties. Bowers came up about half an hour after us. They also had done well at the last, and I'm pretty sure they will get on all right. Keohane is the only weak spot, and he only, I think, because blind (temporarily). But Evans' party didn't get up till 10. They started quite well, but got into difficulties, did just the wrong thing by straining again and again, and so, tiring themselves, went from bad to worse. Their ski shoes, too, are out of trim.

Just as I thought we were in for making a great score, this difficulty overtakes us – it is dreadfully trying. The snow around us tonight is terribly soft, one sinks to the knee at every step; it would be impossible to drag sledges on foot and very difficult for dogs. Ski are the thing, and here are my tiresome fellow-countrymen too prejudiced to have prepared themselves for the event. The dogs should get back quite easily; there is food all along the line. The glacier wind sprang up about 7; the morning was very fine and warm. Tonight there is some stratus cloud forming – a hint no more bad weather in sight. A plentiful crop of snow blindness due to incaution – the sufferers Evans, Bowers, Keohane, Lashly, Oates in various degrees.

This forenoon Wilson went over to a boulder poised on the glacier. It proved to be a very coarse granite with large crystals of quartz in it. Evidently the rock of which the pillars of the Gateway and other neighbouring hills are formed.

Tuesday 12 December Camp 34. We have had a hard day, and during the forenoon it was my team which made the heaviest weather of the work. We got bogged again and again, and, do what we would, the sledge dragged like lead. The others were working hard but nothing to be compared to us. At 2.30 I halted for lunch, pretty well cooked, and there was disclosed the secret of our trouble in a thin film with some hard knots of ice on the runners. Evans' team had been sent off in advance, and we didn't – couldn't! – catch them, but they saw us camp and break camp and followed suit. I really dreaded starting after lunch, but after some trouble to break the sledge out, we went ahead without a hitch, and in a mile or two recovered our leading place with obvious ability to keep it. At 6 I saw the other teams were flagging and so camped at 7, meaning to turn out earlier tomorrow and start a better routine. We have done about 8 or perhaps 9 miles (stat.) – the sledge-meters are hopeless on such a surface.

It is evident that what I expected has occurred. The whole of the lower valley is filled with snow from the recent storm, and if we had not had ski we should be hopelessly bogged. On foot one sinks to the knees, and if pulling on a sledge to half-way between knee and thigh. It would, therefore, be absolutely impossible to advance on foot with our loads. Considering all things, we are getting better on ski. A crust is forming over the soft snow. In a week or so I have little doubt it will be strong enough to support sledges and men. At present it carries neither properly. The sledges get bogged every now and again, sinking to the crossbars. Needless to say, the hauling is terrible when this occurs.

We steered for the Commonwealth Range during the forenoon till we reached about the middle of the glacier. This showed that the unnamed glacier to the S.W. raised great pressure. Observing this, I altered course for the 'Cloudmaker' and later still farther to the west. We must be getting a much better view of the southern side of the main glacier than Shackleton got, and consequently have observed a number of peaks which he did not notice. We are about 5 or 5½ days behind him as a result of the storm, but on this surface our sledges could not be more heavily laden than they are, in fact we have not nearly enough runner surface as it is. Moreover, the sledges are packed too high and therefore capsize too easily. I do not think the glacier can be so broad as S. shows it. Certainly the scenery is not nearly so impressive as that of the Ferrar, but there are interesting features showing up – a distinct banded structure on Mount Elizabeth, which we think may well be a recurrence of the Beacon Sandstone – more banding on the Commonwealth Range. During the three days we have been here the wind has blown down the glacier at night, or rather from the S.W., and it has been calm in the morning – a sort of nightly land-breeze. There is also a very remarkable difference in temperature between day and night. It was +33° when we started, and without hard work we were literally soaked through with perspiration. It is now +23°. Evans' party kept up much better today; we had their shoes into our tent this morning, and P.O. Evans put them into shape again.

Wednesday 13 December Camp 35. A most *damnably* dismal day. We started at eight – the pulling terribly bad, though the glide decidedly good; a new crust in patches, not sufficient to support the ski, but without possibility of hold. Therefore, as the pullers got on the hard patches they slipped back. The sledges plunged into the soft places and stopped dead. Evans' party got away first; we followed, and for some time helped them forward at their stops, but this proved altogether too much for us, so I forged ahead and camped at 1 p.m., as the others were far astern. During lunch I decided to try the 10-feet runners under the crossbars and we spent three hours in securing them. There was no delay on account of the slow progress of the other parties. Evans passed us, and for some time went forward fairly well up a decided slope. The sun was shining on the surface by this time, and the temperature high. Bowers started after Evans, and it was easy to see the really terrible state of affairs with them. They made desperate efforts to get along, but ever got more and more bogged – evidently the glide had vanished. When we got away we soon discovered how awful the surface had become; added to the forenoon difficulties the snow had become wet and sticky. We got our load along, soon passing Bowers, but the toil was simply awful. We were soaked with perspiration and thoroughly breathless with our efforts. Again and again the sledge got one runner on harder snow than the other, canted on its side, and refused to move. At the top of the rise I found Evans reduced to relay work, and Bowers followed his example soon after. We got our whole load through till 7 p.m., camping time, but only with repeated halts and labour which was altogether too strenuous. The other parties certainly cannot get a full load along on the surface, and I much doubt if we could continue to do so, but we must try again tomorrow.

I suppose we have advanced a bare 4 miles today and the aspect of things is very little changed. Our height is now about 1,500 feet; I had pinned my faith on getting better conditions as we rose, but it looks as though matters were getting worse instead of better. As far as the Cloudmaker the valley looks like a huge basin for the lodgement of such snow as this. We can but toil on, but it is woefully disheartening. I am not at all hungry, but pretty thirsty. (T. +15°.) I find our summit ration is even too filling for the present. Two skuas came round the camp at lunch, no doubt attracted by our 'Shambles' camp.

Thursday 14 December Camp 36. Indigestion and the soggy condition of my clothes kept me awake for some time last night, and the exceptional exercise gives bad attacks of cramp. Our lips are getting raw and blistered. The eyes of the party are improving, I am glad to say. We are just starting our march with no very hopeful outlook (T. +13°).

Evening (Height about 2000 feet.) Evans' party started first this morning; for an hour they found the hauling stiff, but after that, to my great surprise, they went on easily. Bowers followed without getting over the ground so easily. After the first 200 yards my own party came on with a swing that told me at once that all would be well. We soon caught the others and offered to take on more weight, but Evans' pride wouldn't allow such help. Later in the morning we exchanged sledges with Bowers, pulled theirs easily, whilst they made quite heavy work with ours. I am afraid Cherry-Garrard and Keohane are the weakness of that team, though both put their utmost into the traces. However, we all lunched together after a satisfactory morning's work. In the afternoon we did still better, and camped at 6.30 with a very marked change in the land bearings. We must have come 11 or 12 miles (stat.). We got fearfully hot on the march, sweated through everything and stripped off jerseys. The result is we are pretty cold and clammy now, but escape from the soft snow and a good march compensate every discomfort. At lunch the blue ice was about 2 feet beneath us, now it is barely a foot, so that I suppose we shall soon find it uncovered. Tonight the sky is overcast and wind has been blowing up the glacier. I think there will be another spell of gloomy weather on the Barrier, and the question is whether this part of the glacier escapes. There are crevasses about, one about eighteen inches across outside Bowers' tent, and a narrower one outside our own. I think the soft snow trouble is at an end, and I could wish nothing better than a continuance of the present surface. Towards the end of the march we were pulling our loads with the greatest ease. It is splendid to be getting along and to find some adequate return for the work we are putting into the business.

Friday 15 December Camp 37. (Height about 2500. Lat. about 84° 8'.) Got away at 8; marched till 1; the surface improving and snow covering thinner over the blue ice, but the sky overcast and glooming, the clouds ever coming lower, and Evans' is now decidedly the slowest unit, though Bowers' is not much faster. We keep up and overhaul either without difficulty. It was an enormous relief yesterday to get steady going without involuntary stops, but yesterday and this morning, once the sledge was stopped, it was very difficult to start again – the runners got temporarily stuck. This afternoon for the first time we could start by giving one good heave together, and so for the first time we are able to stop to readjust footgear or do any other desirable task. This is a second relief for which we are most grateful.

At the lunch camp the snow covering was less than a foot, and at this it is a bare nine inches; patches of ice and hard névé are showing through in places. I meant to camp at 6.30, but before 5 the sky came down on us with falling snow. We could see nothing, and the pulling grew very heavy. At 5.45 there seemed nothing to do but camp – another interrupted march. Our luck is really very bad. We should have done a good march today, as it is we have covered about 11 miles (stat.).

Since supper there are signs of clearing again, but I don't like the look of things; this weather has been working up from the S.E. with all the symptoms of our pony-wrecking storm. Pray heaven we are not going to have this wretched snow in the worst part of the glacier to come. The lower part of this glacier is not very interesting, except from an ice point of view. Except Mount Kyffen, little bare rock is visible, and its structure at this distance is impossible to determine. There are no moraines on the surface of the glacier either. The tributary glaciers are very fine and have cut very deep courses, though they do not enter at grade. The walls of this valley are extraordinarily steep; we count them at least 60° in places. The ice-falls descending over the northern sides are almost continuous one with another, but the southern steep faces are nearly bare; evidently the sun gets a good hold on them. There must be a good deal of melting and rock weathering, the talus heaps are considerable under the southern rock faces. Higher up the valley there is much more bare rock and stratification, which promises to be very interesting, but oh! for fine weather; surely we have had enough of this oppressive gloom.

Saturday 16 *December* Camp 38. A gloomy morning, clearing at noon and ending in a gloriously fine evening. Although constantly anxious in the morning, the light held good for travelling throughout the day, and we have covered 11 miles (stat.), altering the aspect of the glacier greatly. But the travelling has been very hard. We started at 7, lunched at 12.15, and marched on till 6.30 – over ten hours on the march – the limit of time to be squeezed into one day. We began on ski as usual, Evans' team hampering us a bit; the pulling very hard after yesterday's snowfall. In the afternoon we continued on ski till after two hours we struck a peculiarly difficult surface – old hard sastrugi underneath, with pits and high soft sastrugi due to very recent snowfalls. The sledges were so often brought up by this that we decided to take to our feet, and thus made better progress, but for the time with very excessive labour. The crust, brittle, held for a pace or two, then let one down with a bump some 8 or 10 inches. Now and again one's leg went down a crack in the hard ice underneath. We drew up a slope on this surface and discovered a long icefall extending right across our track, I presume the same pressure which caused Shackleton to turn towards the Cloudmaker. We made in for that mountain and soon got on hard, crevassed, undulating ice with quantities of soft snow in the hollows. The disturbance seems to increase, but the snow to diminish as we approach the rocks. We shall look for a moraine and try and follow it up tomorrow. The hills on our left have horizontally stratified rock alternating with snow. The exposed rock is very black; the brownish colour of the Cloudmaker has black horizontal streaks across it. The sides of the glacier north of the Cloudmaker have a curious cutting, the upper part less steep than the lower, suggestive of different conditions of glacier-flow in succeeding ages.

We must push on all we can, for we are now 6 days behind Shackleton, all due to that wretched storm. So far, since we got amongst the disturbances we have not seen such alarming crevasses as I had expected; certainly dogs could have come up as far as this. At present one gets terribly hot and perspiring on the march, and quickly cold when halted, but the sun makes up for all evils. It is very difficult to know what to do about the ski; their weight is considerable and yet under certain circumstances they are extraordinarily useful. Everyone is very satisfied with our summit ration. The party which has been man-hauling for so long say they are far less hungry than they used to be. It is good to think that the majority will keep up this good feeding all through.

Sunday 17 December Camp 39. Soon after starting we found ourselves in rather a mess; bad pressure ahead and long waves between us and the land. Blue ice showed on the crests of the waves; very soft snow lay in the hollows. We had to cross the waves in places 30 feet from crest to hollow, and we did it by sitting on the sledge and letting her go. Thus we went down with a rush and our impetus carried us some way up the other side; then followed a fearfully tough drag to rise the next crest. After two hours of this I saw a larger wave, the crest of which continued hard ice up the glacier; we reached this and got excellent travelling for 2 miles on it, then rose on a steep gradient, and so topped the pressure ridge. The smooth ice is again lost and we have patches of hard and soft snow with ice peeping out in places, cracks in all directions, and legs very frequently down. We have done very nearly 5 miles (geo.).

Evening Temp. -12°. Height about 3500 above Barrier. After lunch decided to take the risk of sticking to the centre of the glacier, with good result. We travelled on up the more or less rounded ridge which I had selected in the morning, and camped at 6.30 with 12½ stat. miles made good. This has put Mount Hope in the background and shows us more of the upper reaches. If we can keep up the pace, we gain on Shackleton, and I don't see any reason why we shouldn't, except that more pressure is showing up ahead. For once one can say 'sufficient for the day is the good thereof'. Our luck may be on the turn – I think we deserve it. In spite of the hard work everyone is very fit and very cheerful, feeling well fed and eager for more toil. Eyes are much better except poor Wilson's; he has caught a very bad attack. Remembering his trouble on our last Southern journey, I fear he is in for a very bad time.

We got fearfully hot this morning and marched in singlets, which became wringing wet; thus uncovered the sun gets at one's skin, and then the wind, which makes it horribly uncomfortable.

Our lips are very sore. We cover them with the soft silk plaster which seems about the best thing for the purpose.

I'm inclined to think that the summit trouble will be mostly due to the chill falling on sunburned skins. Even now one feels the cold strike directly one stops. We get fearfully thirsty and chip up ice on the march, as well as drinking a great deal of water on halting. Our fuel only just does it, but that is all we want, and we have a bit in hand for the summit.

The pulling this afternoon was fairly pleasant; at first over hard snow, and then on to pretty rough ice with surface snowfield cracks, bad for sledges, but ours promised to come through well. We have worn our crampons all day and are delighted with them. P.O. Evans, the inventor of both crampons and ski shoes, is greatly pleased, and certainly we owe him much. The weather is beginning to look dirty again, snow clouds rolling in from the east as usual. I believe it will be overcast tomorrow.

Monday 18 December Camp 40. Lunch nearly 4000 feet above Barrier. Overcast and snowing this morning as I expected, land showing on starboard hand, so, though it was gloomy and depressing, we could march, and did. We have done our 8 stat. miles between 8.20 and 1 p.m.; at first fairly good surface; then the ice got very rugged with sword-cut splits. We got on a slope which made matters worse. I then pulled up to the left, at first without much improvement, but as we topped a rise the surface got much better and things look quite promising for the moment. On our right we have now a pretty good view of the Adams Marshall and Wild Mountains and their very curious horizontal stratification. Wright has found, amongst bits of wind-blown debris, an undoubted bit of sandstone and a bit of black basalt. We must get to know more of the geology before leaving the glacier finally. This morning all our gear was fringed with ice crystals which looked very pretty.

Afternoon Camp No. 40, about 4500 above Barrier. T. -11°. Lat. about 84° 34′. After lunch got on some very rough stuff within a few hundred yards of pressure ridge. There seemed no alternative, and we went through with it. Later, the glacier opened out into a broad basin with irregular undulations, and we on to a better surface, but later on again this improvement nearly vanished, so that it has been hard going all day, but we have done a good mileage (over 14 stat.). We are less than five days behind S. now. There was a promise of a clearance about noon, but later more snow clouds drifted over from the east, and now it is snowing again. We have scarcely caught a glimpse of the eastern side of the glacier all day. The western side has not been clear enough to photograph at the halts. It is very annoying, but I suppose we must be thankful when we can get our marches off. Still sweating horribly on the march and very thirsty at the halts.

Tuesday 19 December Lunch, rise 650. Dist. 8½ geo. Camp 41. Things are looking up. Started on good surface, soon came to very annoying criss-cross cracks. I fell into two and have bad bruises on knee and thigh, but we got along all the time until we reached an admirable smooth ice surface excellent for travelling. The last mile, névé predominating and therefore the pulling a trifle harder, we have risen into the upper basin of the glacier. Seemingly close about us are the various land masses which adjoin the summit: it looks as though we might have difficulties in the last narrows. We are having a long lunch hour for angles, photographs, and sketches. The slight south-westerly wind came down the glacier as we started, and the sky, which was overcast, has rapidly cleared in consequence.

Night Height about 5800. Camp 41. We stepped off this afternoon at the rate of 2 miles or more an hour, with the very satisfactory result of 17 (stat.) miles to the good for the day. It has not been a strain, except perhaps for me with my wounds received early in the day. The wind has kept us cool on the march, which has in consequence been very much pleasanter; we are not wet in our clothes tonight, and have not suffered from the same overpowering thirst as on previous days (T. +11°. Min. +5°). Evans and Bowers are busy taking angles; as they have been all day, we shall have material for an excellent chart. Days like this put heart in one.

Wednesday 20 December Camp 42. 6500 feet about. Just got off our last best half march – 10 miles 1150 yards (geo.), over 12 miles stat. With an afternoon to follow we should do well today; the wind has been coming up the valley. Turning this book [In the pocket journal, only one side of each page had been written on. Coming to the end of it, Scott reversed the book, and continued his entries on the empty backs of the pages.] seems to have brought luck. We marched on till nearly 7 o'clock after a long lunch halt, and covered 19½ geo. miles, nearly 23 (stat.), rising 800 feet. This morning we came over a considerable extent of hard snow, then got to hard ice with patches of snow; a state of affairs which has continued all day. Pulling the sledges in crampons is no difficulty at all. At lunch Wilson and Bowers walked back 2 miles or so to try and find Bowers' broken sledgemeter, without result. During their absence a fog spread about us, carried up the valleys by easterly wind. We started the afternoon march in this fog very unpleasantly, but later it gradually lifted, and tonight it is very fine and warm. As the fog lifted we saw a huge line of pressure ahead; I steered for a place where the slope looked smoother, and we are camped beneath the spot tonight. (Lat. 84° 59' 6".) We must be ahead of Shackleton's position on the 17th. All day we have been admiring a wonderful banded structure of the rock; tonight it is beautifully clear on Mount Darwin.

I have just told off the people to return tomorrow night: Atkinson, Wright, Cherry-Garrard, and Keohane. All are disappointed – poor Wright rather bitterly, I fear. I dread this necessity of choosing – nothing could be more heartrending. I calculated our programme to start from 85° 10' with 12 units of food [a unit of food means a week's supplies for four men] and eight men. We ought to be in this position tomorrow night, less one day's food. After all our harassing trouble one cannot but be satisfied with such a prospect.

Thursday 21 December Camp 43. Lat. 85° 7'. Long. 163° 4'. Height about 8000 feet. Upon Glacier Depot. Temp. -2°. We climbed the ice slope this morning and found a very bad surface on top, as far as crevasses were concerned. We all had falls into them, Atkinson and Teddy Evans going down the length of their harness. Evans had rather a shake up. The rotten ice surface continued for a long way, though I wound to and fro towards the land, trying to get on better ground.

At 12 the wind came from the north, bringing the inevitable fog up the valley and covering us just as we were in the worst of places. We camped for lunch, and were obliged to wait two and a half hours for a clearance. Then the sun began to struggle through and we were off. We soon got out of the worst crevasses and on to a long snow slope leading on part of Mount Darwin. It was a very long stiff pull up, and I held on till 7.30, when, the other team being some way astern, I camped. We have done a good march, risen to a satisfactory altitude, and reached a good place for our depot. Tomorrow we start with our fullest summit load, and the first march should show us the possibilities of our achievement. The temperature has dropped below zero, but tonight it is so calm and bright that one feels delightfully warm and comfortable in the tent. Such weather helps greatly in all the sorting arrangements, etc., which are going on tonight. For me it is an immense relief to have the indefatigable little Bowers to see to all detail arrangements of this sort.

We have risen a great height today and I hope it will not be necessary to go down again, but it looks as though we must dip a bit even to go to the south-west.

'21 *December 1911* Lat. 85° S. We are struggling on, considering all things, against odds. The weather is a constant anxiety, otherwise arrangements are working exactly as planned.

'For your own ear also, I am exceedingly fit and can go with the best of them.

'It is a pity the luck doesn't come our way, because every detail of equipment is right.

'I write this sitting in our tent waiting for the fog to clear – an exasperating position as we are in the worst crevassed region. Teddy Evans and Atkinson were down to the length of their harness this morning, and we have all been half-way down. As first man I get first chance, and it's decidedly exciting not knowing which step will give way. Still all this is interesting enough if one could only go on.

'Since writing the above I made a dash for it, got out of the valley out of the fog and away from crevasses. So here we are practically on the summit and up to date in the provision line. We ought to get through.'

18

THE SUMMIT JOURNEY TO THE POLE: 22 DECEMBER 1911 – 18 JANUARY 1912

A FRESH MS. BOOK. 1910–11
[On the Flyleaf]

Ages: Self 43, Wilson 39, Evans (P.O.) 37, Oates 32, Bowers 28. Average 36.

Friday 22 December Camp 44, about 7100 feet. T. -1°. Bar. 22.3. This, the third stage of our journey, is opening with good promise. We made our depot this morning, then said an affecting farewell to the returning party, who have taken things very well, dear good fellows as they are.[23]

Then we started with our heavy loads about 9.20, I in some trepidation – quickly dissipated as we went off and up a slope at a smart pace. The second sledge came close behind us, showing that we have weeded the weak spots and made the proper choice for the returning party.

We came along very easily and lunched at 1, when the sledgemeter had to be repaired, and we didn't get off again till 3.20, camping at 6.45. Thus with 7 hours' marching we covered 10½ miles (geo.) (12 stat.).

Obs.: Lat. 85° 13½'; Long. 161° 55'; Var. 175° 46' E.

Tomorrow we march longer hours, about 9 I hope. Every day the loads will lighten, and so we ought to make the requisite progress. I think we have climbed about 250 feet today, but thought it more on the march. We look down on huge pressure ridges to the south and S.E., and in fact all round except in the direction in which we go, S.W. We seem to be travelling more or less parallel to a ridge which extends from Mt. Darwin. Ahead of us tonight is a stiffish incline and it looks as though there might be pressure behind it. It is very difficult to judge how matters stand, however, in such a confusion of elevations and depressions. This course doesn't work wonders in change of latitude, but I think it is the right track to clear the pressures – at any rate I shall hold it for the present.

We passed one or two very broad (30 feet) bridged crevasses with the usual gaping sides; they were running pretty well in N. and S. direction. The weather has been beautifully fine all day as it was last night. (Night Temp. -9°.) This morning there was an hour or so of haze due to clouds from the N. Now it is perfectly clear, and we get a fine view of the mountain behind which Wilson has just been sketching.

Saturday 23 December Lunch. Bar. 22.01. Rise 370? Started at 8, steering S.W. Seemed to be rising, and went on well for about 3 hours, then got amongst bad crevasses and hard waves. We pushed on to S.W., but things went from bad to worse, and we had to haul out to the north, then west. West looks clear for the present, but it is not a very satisfactory direction. We have done 8½' (geo.), a good march (T. -3°. Southerly wind, force 2). The comfort is that we are rising. On one slope we got a good view of the land and the pressure ridges to the S.E. They seem to be disposed 'en échelon' and gave me the idea of shearing cracks. They seemed to lessen as we ascend. It is rather trying having to march so far to the west, but if we keep rising we must come to the end of the obstacles some time.

Saturday night Camp 45. T. -3°. Bar. 21.61. ?Rise. Height about 7750. Great vicissitudes of fortune in the afternoon march. Started west up a slope – about the fifth we have mounted in the last two days. On top, another pressure appeared on the left, but less lofty and more snow-covered than that which had troubled us in the morning. There was temptation to try it, and I had been gradually turning in its direction. But I stuck to my principle and turned west up yet another slope. On top of this we got on the most extraordinary surface – narrow crevasses ran in all directions. They were quite invisible, being covered with a thin crust of hardened névé without a sign of a crack in it. We all fell in one after another and sometimes two together. We have had many unexpected falls before, but usually through being unable to mark the run of the surface appearances of cracks, or where such cracks are covered with soft snow. How a hardened crust can form over a crack is a real puzzle – it seems to argue extremely slow movement. Dead reckoning, 85° 22' 1" S., 159° 31' E.

In the broader crevasses this morning we noticed that it was the lower edge of the bridge which was rotten, whereas in all in the glacier the upper edge was open.

Near the narrow crevasses this afternoon we got about 10 minutes on snow which had a hard crust and loose crystals below. It was like breaking through a glass house at each step, but quite suddenly at 5 p.m. everything changed. The hard surface gave place to regular sastrugi and our horizon levelled in every direction. I hung on to the S.W. till 6 p.m., and then camped with a delightful feeling of security that we had at length reached the summit proper. I am feeling very cheerful about everything tonight. We marched 15 miles (geo.) (over 17 stat.) today, mounting nearly 800 feet and all in about 8½ hours. My determination to keep mounting irrespective of course is fully justified and I shall be indeed surprised if we have any further difficulties with crevasses or steep slopes. To me for the first time our goal seems really in sight. We can pull our loads and pull them much faster and farther than I expected in my most hopeful moments. I only pray for a fair share of good weather. There is a cold wind now as expected, but with good clothes and well fed as we are, we can stick a lot worse than we are getting. I trust this may prove the turning-point in our fortunes for which we have waited so patiently.

Sunday 24 December Lunch. Bar. 21.48. ?Rise 160 feet. Christmas Eve. 7½ miles geo. due south, and a rise, I think, more than shown by barometer. This in five hours, on the surface which ought to be a sample of what we shall have in the future. With our present clothes it is a fairly heavy plod, but we get over the ground, which is a great thing. A high pressure ridge has appeared on the 'port bow'. It seems isolated, but I shall be glad to lose sight of such disturbances. The wind is continuous from the S.S.E., very searching. We are now marching in our wind blouses and with somewhat more protection on the head.

Bar. 21.41. Camp 46. Rise for day ? about 250 ft. or 300 ft. Hypsometer, 8000 ft.

The first two hours of the afternoon march went very well. Then the sledges hung a bit, and we plodded on and covered something over 14 miles (geo.) in the day. We lost sight of the big pressure ridge, but tonight another smaller one shows fine on the 'port bow', and the surface is alternately very hard and fairly soft; dips and rises all round. It is evident we are skirting more disturbances, and I sincerely hope it will not mean altering course more to the west. 14 miles in 4 hours is not so bad considering the circumstances. The southerly wind is continuous and not at all pleasant in camp, but on the march it keeps us cool (T. -3°). The only inconvenience is the extent to which our faces get iced up. The temperature hovers about zero.

We have not struck a crevasse all day, which is a good sign. The sun continues to shine in a cloudless sky, the wind rises and falls, and about us is a scene of the wildest desolation, but we are a very cheerful party and tomorrow is Christmas Day, with something extra in the hoosh.

Monday 25 December Christmas Lunch. Bar. 21.14. Rise 240 feet. The wind was strong last night and this morning; a light snowfall in the night; a good deal of drift, subsiding when we started, but still about a foot high. I thought it might have spoilt the surface, but for the first hour and a half we went along in fine style. Then we started up a rise, and to our annoyance found ourselves amongst crevasses once more – very hard, smooth névé between high ridges at the edge of crevasses, and therefore very difficult to get foothold to pull the sledges. Got our ski sticks out, which improved matters, but we had to tack a good deal and several of us went half down. After half an hour of this I looked round and found the second sledge halted some way in rear – evidently someone had gone into a crevasse. We saw the rescue work going on, but had to wait half an hour for the party to come up, and got mighty cold. It appears that Lashly went down very suddenly, nearly dragging the crew with him. The sledge ran on and jammed the span so that the Alpine rope had to be got out and used to pull Lashly to the surface again. Lashly says the crevasse was 50 feet deep and 8 feet across, in form U, showing that the word 'unfathomable' can rarely be applied. Lashly is 44 today and as hard as nails. His fall has not even disturbed his equanimity.

After topping the crevasse ridge we got on a better surface and came along fairly well, completing over 7 miles (geo.) just before 1 o'clock. We have risen nearly 250 feet this morning; the wind was strong and therefore trying, mainly because it held the sledge; it is a little lighter now.

Night Camp No. 47. Bar. 21.18. T. -7°. I am so replete that I can scarcely write. After sundry luxuries, such as chocolate and raisins at lunch, we started off well, but soon got amongst crevasses, huge snowfields roadways running almost in our direction, and across hidden cracks into which we frequently fell. Passing for two miles or so along between two roadways, we came on a huge pit with raised sides. Is this a submerged mountain peak or a swirl in the stream? Getting clear of crevasses and on a slightly down grade, we came along at a swinging pace – splendid. I marched on till nearly 7.30, when we had covered 15 miles (geo.) (17¼ stat.). I knew that supper was to be a 'tightener', and indeed it has been – so much that I must leave description till the morning.

Dead reckoning, Lat. 85° 50′ S.; Long. 159° 8′ 2″ E. Bar. 21.22.

Towards the end of the march we seemed to get into better condition; about us the surface rises and falls on the long slopes of vast mounds or undulations – no very definite system in their disposition. We camped half-way up a long slope.

In the middle of the afternoon we got another fine view of the land. The Dominion Range ends abruptly as observed, then come two straits and two other masses of land. Similarly north of the wild mountains is another strait and another mass of land. The various straits are undoubtedly overflows, and the masses of land mark the inner fringe of the exposed coastal mountains, the general direction of which seems about S.S.E., from which it appears that one could be much closer to the Pole on the Barrier by continuing on it to the S.S.E. We ought to know more of this when Evans' observations are plotted.

I must write a word of our supper last night. We had four courses. The first, pemmican, full whack, with slices of horse meat flavoured with onion and curry powder and thickened with biscuit; then an arrowroot, cocoa and biscuit hoosh sweetened; then a plum-pudding; then cocoa with raisins, and finally a dessert of caramels and ginger. After the feast it was difficult to move. Wilson and I couldn't finish our share of plum-pudding. We have all slept splendidly and feel thoroughly warm – such is the effect of full feeding.

Tuesday 26 December Lunch. Bar. 21.11. Four and three-quarters hours, 6¾ miles (geo.). Perhaps a little slow after plum-pudding, but I think we are getting on to the surface which is likely to continue the rest of the way. There are still mild differences of elevation, but generally speaking the plain is flattening out; no doubt we are rising slowly.

Camp 48. Bar. 21.02. The first two hours of the afternoon march went well; then we got on a rough rise and the sledge came badly. Camped at 6.30, sledge coming easier again at the end.

It seems astonishing to be disappointed with a march of 15 (stat.) miles, when I had contemplated doing little more than 10 with full loads.

We are on the 86th parallel. Obs.: 86° 2′ S.; 160° 26′ E. The temperature has been pretty consistent of late, -10° to -12° at night, -3° in the day. The wind has seemed milder today – it blows anywhere from S.E. to S. I had thought to have done with pressures, but tonight a crevassed slope appears on our right. We shall pass well clear of it, but there may be others. The undulating character of the plain causes a great variety of surface, owing, of course, to the varying angles at which the wind strikes the slopes. We were half an hour late starting this morning, which accounts for some loss of distance, though I should be content to keep up an average of 13′ (geo.).

Wednesday 27 December Lunch. Bar. 21.02. The wind light this morning and the pulling heavy. Everyone sweated, especially the second team, which had great difficulty in keeping up. We have been going up and down, the up grades very tiring, especially when we get amongst sastrugi which jerk the sledge about, but we have done 7¼ miles (geo.). A very bad accident this morning. Bowers broke the only hypsometer thermometer. We have nothing to check our two aneroids.

Night Camp 49. Bar. 20.82. T. -6.3°. We marched off well after lunch on a soft, snowy surface, then came to slippery hard sastrugi and kept a good pace; but I felt this meant something wrong, and on topping a short rise we were once more in the midst of crevasses and disturbances. For an hour it was dreadfully trying – had to pick a road, tumbled into crevasses, and got jerked about abominably. At the summit of the ridge we came into another 'pit' or 'whirl', which seemed the centre of the trouble – is it a submerged mountain peak? During the last hour and a quarter we pulled out on to soft snow again and moved well. Camped at 6.45, having covered 13 1/3 miles (geo.). Steering the party is no light task. One cannot allow one's thoughts to wander as others do, and when, as this afternoon, one gets amongst disturbances, I find it is very worrying and tiring. I do trust we shall have no more of them. We have not lost sight of the sun since we came on the summit; we should get an extraordinary record of sunshine. It is monotonous work this; the sledgemeter and theodolite govern the situation.

Thursday 28 December Lunch. Bar. 20.77. I start cooking again tomorrow morning. We have had a troublesome day but have completed our 13 miles (geo.). My unit pulled away easy this morning and stretched out for two hours – the second unit made heavy weather. I changed with Evans and found the second sledge heavy – could keep up, but the team was not swinging with me as my own team swings. Then I changed P.O. Evans for Lashly. We seemed to get on better, but at the moment the surface changed and we came up over a rise with hard sastrugi. At the top we camped for lunch. What was the difficulty? One theory was that some members of the second party were stale. Another that all was due to the bad stepping and want of swing; another that the sledge pulled heavy. In the afternoon we exchanged sledges, and at first went off well, but getting into soft snow, we found a terrible drag, the second party coming quite easily with our sledge. So the sledge is the cause of the trouble, and talking it out, I found that all is due to want of care. The runners ran excellently, but the structure has been distorted by bad strapping, bad loading, etc. The party are not done, and I have told them plainly that they must wrestle with the trouble and get it right for themselves. There is no possible reason why they should not get along as easily as we do.

Night Camp 50. T. -6°. Bar. 20.66. Obs.: 86° 27′ 2″ S.; 161° 1′ 15″ E.; Var. 179° 33′ E. Bar. 20.64.

Friday 29 December Bar. 20.52. Lunch. Height 9050 about. The worst surface we have struck, very heavy pulling; but we came 6½ miles (geo.). It will be a strain to keep up distances if we get surfaces like this. We seem to be steadily but slowly rising. The satisfactory thing is that the second party now keeps up, as the faults have been discovered; they were due partly to the rigid loading of the sledge and partly to the bad pacing.

Night Camp 51. Bar. 20.49. T. -6°. Had another struggle this afternoon and only managed to get 12 miles (geo.). The very hard pulling has occurred on two rises. It appears that the loose snow is blown over the rises and rests in heaps on the north-facing slopes. It is these heaps that cause our worst troubles. The weather looks a little doubtful, a good deal of cirrus cloud in motion over us, radiating E. and W. The wind shifts from S.E. to S.S.W., rising and falling at intervals; it is annoying to the march as it retards the sledges, but it must help the surface, I think, and so hope for better things tomorrow. The marches are terribly monotonous. One's thoughts wander occasionally to pleasanter scenes and places, but the necessity to keep the course, or some hitch in the surface, quickly brings them back. There have been some hours of very steady plodding today; these are the best part of the business, they mean forgetfulness and advance.

Saturday 30 December Bar. 20.42. Lunch. Night camp 52. Bar. 20.36. Rise about 150. A very trying, tiring march, and only 11 miles (geo.) covered. Wind from the south to S.E., not quite so strong as usual; the usual clear sky.

We camped on a rise last night, and it was some time before we reached the top this morning. This took it out of us as the second party dropped. I went on 6½ miles (when the second party was some way astern) and lunched. We came on in the afternoon, the other party still dropping, camped at 6.30 – they at 7.15. We came up another rise with the usual gritty snow towards the end of the march. For us the interval between the two rises, some 8 miles, was steady plodding work which we might keep up for some time. Tomorrow I'm going to march half a day, make a depot and build the 10-feet sledges. The second party is certainly tiring; it remains to be seen how they will manage with the smaller sledge and lighter load. The surface is certainly much worse than it was 50 miles back (T. -10°). We have caught up Shackleton's dates. Everything would be cheerful if I could persuade myself that the second party were quite fit to go forward.

Sunday 31 December New Year's Eve 20.17. Height about 9126. T. -10°. [Camp 53.] Corrected aneroid. The second party depoted its ski and some other weights equivalent to about 100 lbs. I sent them off first; they marched, but not very fast. We followed and did not catch them before they camped by direction at 1.30. By this time we had covered exactly 7 miles (geo.), and we must have risen a good deal. We rose on a steep incline at the beginning of the march, and topped another at the end, showing a distance of about 5 miles between the wretched slopes which give us the hardest pulling, but as a matter of fact, we have been rising all day.

We had a good full brew of tea and then set to work stripping the sledges. That didn't take long, but the process of building up the 10-feet sledges now in operation in the other tent is a long job. Evans (P.O.) and Crean are tackling it, and it is a very remarkable piece of work. Certainly P.O. Evans is the most invaluable asset to our party. To build a sledge under these conditions is a fact for special record. Evans (Lieut.) has just found the latitude – 86° 56' S., so that we are pretty near the 87th parallel aimed at for tonight. We lose half a day, but I hope to make that up by going forward at much better speed.

This is to be called the '3 Degree Depot', and it holds a week's provisions for both units.

There is extraordinarily little mirage up here and the refraction is very small. Except for the seamen we are all sitting in a double tent – the first time we have put up the inner lining to the tent; it seems to make us much snugger.

10 p.m. The job of rebuilding is taking longer than I expected, but is now almost done. The 10-feet sledges look very handy. We had an extra drink of tea and are now turned into our bags in the double tent (five of us) as warm as toast, and just enough light to write or work with. Did not get to bed till 2 a.m.

Obs.: 86° 55' 47" S.; 165° 5' 48" E.; Var. 175° 40'E. Morning Bar. 20.08.

Monday 1 January 1912 New Year's Day. Lunch. Bar. 20.04. Roused hands about 7.30 and got away 9.30, Evans' party going ahead on foot. We followed on ski. Very stupidly we had not seen to our ski shoes beforehand, and it took a good half-hour to get them right; Wilson especially had trouble. When we did get away, to our surprise the sledge pulled very easily, and we made fine progress, rapidly gaining on the foot-haulers.

Night Camp 54. Bar. 19.98. Risen about 150 feet. Height about 9600 above Barrier. They camped for lunch at 5½ miles and went on easily, completing 11.3 (geo.) by 7.30. We were delayed again at lunch camp, Evans repairing the tent, and I the cooker. We caught the other party more easily in the afternoon and kept alongside them the last quarter of an hour. It was surprising how easily the sledge pulled; we have scarcely exerted ourselves all day.

We have been rising again all day, but the slopes are less accentuated. I had expected trouble with ski and hard patches, but we found none at all (T. -14°). The temperature is steadily falling, but it seems to fall with the wind. We are *very* comfortable in our double tent. Stick of chocolate to celebrate the New Year. The supporting party not in very high spirits, they have not managed matters well for themselves. Prospects seem to get brighter – only 170 miles to go and plenty of food left.

Tuesday 2 January T. -17°. Camp 55. Height about 9980. At lunch my aneroid reading over scale 12,250, shifted hand to read 10,250. Proposed to enter heights in future with correction as calculated at end of book (minus 340 feet). The foot party went off early, before 8, and marched till 1. Again from 2.35 to 6.30. We started more than half an hour later on each march and caught the others easy. It's been a plod for the foot people and pretty easy going for us, and we have covered 13 miles (geo.).

T. -11°: Obs. 87° 20' 8" S.; 160° 40' 53" E.; Var. 180°. The sky is slightly overcast for the first time since we left the glacier; the sun can be seen already through the veil of stratus, and blue sky round the horizon. The sastrugi have all been from the S.E. today, and likewise the wind, which has been pretty light. I hope the clouds do not mean wind or bad surface. The latter became poor towards the end of the afternoon. We have not risen much today, and the plain seems to be flattening out. Irregularities are best seen by sastrugi. A skua gull visited us on the march this afternoon – it was evidently curious, kept alighting on the snow ahead, and fluttering a few yards as we approached. It seemed to have had little food – an extraordinary visitor considering our distance from the sea.

Wednesday 3 January Height: Lunch, 10,110; Night, 10,180. [Camp 56.] T. -17°. Minimum -18.5°. Within 150 miles of our goal. Last night I decided to reorganise, and this morning told off Teddy Evans, Lashly, and Crean to return. They are disappointed, but take it well. Bowers is to come into our tent, and we proceed as a five man unit tomorrow. We have 5½ units of food – practically over a month's allowance for five people – it ought to see us through. We came along well on ski today, but the foot-haulers were slow, and so we only got a trifle over 12 miles (geo.). Very anxious to see how we shall manage tomorrow; if we can march well with the full load we shall be practically safe, I take it. The surface was very bad in patches today and the wind strong.

'Lat. 87° 32'. A last note from a hopeful position. I think it's going to be all right. We have a fine party going forward and arrangements are all going well.'

Thursday 4 January T. -17°, Lunch T. -16.5°. We were naturally late getting away this morning, the sledge having to be packed and arrangements completed for separation of parties. It is wonderful to see how neatly everything stows on a little sledge, thanks to P.O. Evans. I was anxious to see how we could pull it, and glad to find we went easy enough. Bowers on foot pulls between, but behind, Wilson and myself; he has to keep his own pace and luckily does not throw us out at all.

The second party had followed us in case of accident, but as soon as I was certain we could get along we stopped and said farewell. Teddy Evans is terribly disappointed but has taken it very well and behaved like a man. Poor old Crean wept and even Lashly was affected. I was glad to find their sledge is a mere nothing to them, and thus, no doubt, they will make a quick journey back.[24] Since leaving them we have marched on till 1.15 and covered 6.2 miles (geo.). With full marching days we ought to have no difficulty in keeping up our average.

Night Camp 57. T. -16°. Height 10,280 – We started well on the afternoon march, going a good speed for 1½ hours; then we came on a stratum covered with loose sandy snow, and the pulling became very heavy. We managed to get off 12½ miles (geo.) by 7 p.m., but it was very heavy work.

In the afternoon the wind died away, and tonight it is flat calm; the sun so warm that in spite of the temperature we can stand about outside in the greatest comfort. It is amusing to stand thus and remember the constant horrors of our situation as they were painted for us: the sun is melting the snow on the ski, etc. The plateau is now very flat, but we are still ascending slowly. The sastrugi are getting more confused, predominant from the S.E. I wonder what is in store for us. At present everything seems to be going with extraordinary smoothness, and one can scarcely believe that obstacles will not present themselves to make our task more difficult. Perhaps the surface will be the element to trouble us.

Friday 5 January Camp 58. Height: morning, 10,430; night, 10,320. T. -14.8°. Obs. 87° 57′, 159° 13′. Minimum T. -23.5; T. -21°. A dreadfully trying day. Light wind from the N.N.W. bringing detached cloud and constant fall of ice crystals. The surface, in consequence, as bad as could be after the first hour. We started at 8.15, marched solidly till 1.15, covering 7.4 miles (geo.), and again in the afternoon we plugged on; by 7 p.m. we had done 12½ miles (geo.), the hardest we have yet done on the plateau. The sastrugi seemed to increase as we advanced and they have changed direction from S.W. to S. by W. In the afternoon a good deal of confusing cross sastrugi, and tonight a very rough surface with evidences of hard southerly wind. Luckily the sledge shows no signs of capsizing yet. We sigh for a breeze to sweep the hard snow, but tonight the outlook is not promising better things. However, we are very close to the 88th parallel, little more than 120 miles from the Pole, only a march from Shackleton's final camp, and in a general way 'getting on'.

We go little over a mile and a quarter an hour now – it is a big strain as the shadows creep slowly round from our right through ahead to our left. What lots of things we think of on these monotonous marches! What castles one builds now hopefully that the Pole is ours. Bowers took sights today and will take them every third day. We feel the cold very little, the great comfort of our situation is the excellent drying effect of the sun. Our socks and finnesko are almost dry each morning. Cooking for five takes a seriously longer time than cooking for four; perhaps half an hour on the whole day. It is an item I had not considered when re-organising.

Saturday 6 January Height 10,470. T. -22.3°. Obstacles arising – last night we got amongst sastrugi – they increased in height this morning and now we are in the midst of a sea of fish-hook waves well remembered from our Northern experience. We took off our ski after the first 1½ hours and pulled on foot. It is terribly heavy in places, and, to add to our trouble, every sastrugus is covered with a beard of sharp branching crystals. We have covered 6½ miles, but we cannot keep up our average if this sort of surface continues. There is no wind.

Camp 59. Lat. 88° 7′. Height 10,430–10,510. Rise of barometer? T. -22.5°. Minimum -25.8°. Morning. Fearfully hard pull again, and when we had marched about an hour we discovered that a sleeping-bag had fallen off the sledge. We had to go back and carry it on. It cost us over an hour and disorganised our party. We have only covered 10½ miles (geo.) and it's been about the hardest pull we've had. We think of leaving our ski here, mainly because of risk of breakage. Over the sastrugi it is all up and down hill, and the covering of ice crystals prevents the sledge from gliding even on the down-grade. The sastrugi, I fear, have come to stay, and we must be prepared for heavy marching, but in two days I hope to lighten loads with a depot. We are south of Shackleton's last camp, so, I suppose, have made the most southerly camp.

Sunday 7 January Height 10,560. Lunch. Temp. -21.3°. The vicissitudes of this work are bewildering. Last night we decided to leave our ski on account of the sastrugi. This morning we marched out a mile in 40 min. and the sastrugi gradually disappeared. I kept debating the ski question and at this point stopped, and after discussion we went back and fetched the ski; it cost us 1½ hours nearly. Marching again, I found to my horror we could scarcely move the sledge on ski; the first hour was awful owing to the wretched coating of loose sandy snow. However, we persisted, and towards the latter end of our tiring march we began to make better progress, but the work is still awfully heavy. I must stick to the ski after this.

Very heavy pulling still, but did 5 miles (geo.) in over four hours. Afternoon. Camp 60°. T. -23°. Height 10,570. Obs.: Lat. 88° 18' 40" S.; Long. 157° 21' E.; Var. 179° 15' W.

This is the shortest march we have made on the summit, but there is excuse. Still, there is no doubt if things remained as they are we could not keep up the strain of such marching for long. Things, however, luckily will not remain as they are. Tomorrow we depot a week's provision, lightening altogether about 100 lbs. This afternoon the welcome southerly wind returned and is now blowing force 2 to 3. I cannot but think it will improve the surface.

The sastrugi are very much diminished, and those from the south seem to be overpowering those from the S.E. Cloud travelled rapidly over from the south this afternoon, and the surface was covered with sandy crystals; these were not so bad as the 'bearded' sastrugi, and oddly enough the wind and drift only gradually obliterate these striking formations. We have scarcely risen at all today, and the plain looks very flat. It doesn't look as though there were more rises ahead, and one could not wish for a better surface if only the crystal deposit would disappear or harden up. I am awfully glad we have hung on to the ski; hard as the marching is, it is far less tiring on ski. Bowers has a heavy time on foot, but nothing seems to tire him. Evans has a nasty cut on his hand (sledge-making). I hope it won't give trouble. Our food continues to amply satisfy. What luck to have hit on such an excellent ration. We really are an excellently found party.

Monday 8 January Camp 60. Noon. T. -19.8°. Min. for night -25°. Our first summit blizzard. We might just have started after breakfast, but the wind seemed obviously on the increase, and so has proved. The sun has not been obscured, but snow is evidently falling as well as drifting. The sun seems to be getting a little brighter as the wind increases. The whole phenomenon is very like a Barrier blizzard, only there is much less snow, as one would expect, and at present less wind, which is somewhat of a surprise.

Evans' hand was dressed this morning, and the rest ought to be good for it. I am not sure it will not do us all good as we lie so very comfortably, warmly clothed in our comfortable bags, within our double-walled tent. However, we do not want more than a day's delay at most, both on account of lost time and food and the snow accumulation of ice (Night T. -13.5°). It has grown much thicker during the day, from time to time obscuring the sun for the first time. The temperature is low for a blizzard, but we are very comfortable in our double tent and the cold snow is not sticky and not easily carried into the tent, so that the sleeping-bags remain in good condition (T. -3°). The glass is rising slightly. I hope we shall be able to start in the morning, but fear that a disturbance of this sort may last longer than our local storm.

It is quite impossible to speak too highly of my companions. Each fulfils his office to the party; Wilson, first as doctor, ever on the lookout to alleviate the small pains and troubles incidental to the work, now as cook, quick, careful and dexterous, ever thinking of some fresh expedient to help the camp life; tough as steel on the traces, never wavering from start to finish.

Evans, a giant worker with a really remarkable headpiece. It is only now I realise how much has been due to him. Our ski shoes and crampons have been absolutely indispensable, and if the original ideas were not his, the details of manufacture and design and the good workmanship are his alone. He is responsible for every sledge, every sledge fitting, tents, sleeping-bags, harness, and when one cannot recall a single expression of dissatisfaction with any one of these items, it shows what an invaluable assistant he has been. Now, besides superintending the putting up of the tent, he thinks out and arranges the packing of the sledge; it is extraordinary how neatly and handily everything is stowed, and how much study has been given to preserving the suppleness and good running qualities of the machine. On the Barrier, before the ponies were killed, he was ever roaming round, correcting faults of stowage.

Little Bowers remains a marvel – he is thoroughly enjoying himself. I leave all the provision arrangement in his hands, and at all times he knows exactly how we stand, or how each returning party should fare. It has been a complicated business to redistribute stores at various stages of re-organisation, but not one single mistake has been made. In addition to the stores, he keeps the most thorough and conscientious meteorological record, and to this he now adds the duty of observer and photographer. Nothing comes amiss to him, and no work is too hard. It is a difficulty to get him into the tent; he seems quite oblivious of the cold, and he lies coiled in his bag writing and working out sights long after the others are asleep.

Of these three it is a matter for thought and congratulation that each is sufficiently suited for his own work, but would not be capable of doing that of the others as well as it is done. Each is invaluable. Oates had his invaluable period with the ponies; now he is a foot slogger and goes hard the whole time, does his share of camp work, and stands the hardship as well as any of us. I would not like to be without him either. So our five people are perhaps as happily selected as it is possible to imagine.

Tuesday 9 January Camp 61. Record. Lat. 88° 25′. Height 10,270 ft. Bar. risen I think. T. -4°. Still blowing, and drifting when we got to breakfast, but signs of taking off. The wind had gradually shifted from south to E.S.E. After lunch we were able to break camp in a bad light, but on a good surface. We made a very steady afternoon march, covering 6½ miles (geo.). This should place us in Lat. 88° 25′, beyond the record of Shackleton's walk. All is new ahead. The barometer has risen since the blizzard, and it looks as though we were on a level plateau, not to rise much further.

Obs.: Long. 159° 17′ 45″ E.; Var. 179° 55′ W.; Min. Temp. -7.2°.

More curiously the temperature continued to rise after the blow and now, at -4°, it seems quite warm. The sun has only shown very indistinctly all the afternoon, although brighter now. Clouds are still drifting over from the east. The marching is growing terribly monotonous, but one cannot grumble as long as the distance can be kept up. It can, I think, if we leave a depot, but a very annoying thing has happened. Bowers' watch has suddenly dropped 26 minutes; it may have stopped from being frozen outside his pocket, or he may have inadvertently touched the hands. Any way it makes one more chary of leaving stores on this great plain, especially as the blizzard tended to drift up our tracks. We could only just see the back track when we started, but the light was extremely poor.

Wednesday 10 January Camp 62. T. -11°. Last depot 88° 29′ S.; 159° 33′ E.; Var. 180°. Terrible hard march in the morning; only covered 5.1 miles (geo.). Decided to leave depot at lunch camp. Built cairn and left one week's food together with sundry articles of clothing. We are down as close as we can go in the latter. We go forward with eighteen days' food. Yesterday I should have said certain to see us through, but now the surface is beyond words, and if it continues we shall have the greatest difficulty to keep our march long enough. The surface is quite covered with sandy snow, and when the sun shines it is terrible. During the early part of the afternoon it was overcast, and we started our lightened sledge with a good swing, but during the last two hours the sun cast shadows again, and the work was distressingly hard. We have covered only 10.8 miles (geo.).

Only 85 miles (geo.) from the Pole, but it's going to be a stiff pull *both ways* apparently; still we do make progress, which is something. Tonight the sky is overcast, the temperature (-11°) much higher than I anticipated; it is very difficult to imagine what is happening to the weather. The sastrugi grow more and more confused, running from S. to E. Very difficult steering in uncertain light and with rapidly moving clouds. The clouds don't seem to come from anywhere, form and disperse without visible reason. The surface seems to be growing softer. The meteorological conditions seem to point to an area of variable light winds, and that plot will thicken as we advance.

Thursday 11 January Lunch. Height 10,540. T. -15° 8′. It was heavy pulling from the beginning today, but for the first two and a half hours we could keep the sledge moving; then the sun came out (it had been overcast and snowing with light south-easterly breeze) and the rest of the forenoon was agonising. I never had such pulling; all the time the sledge rasps and creaks. We have covered 6 miles, but at fearful cost to ourselves.

Night Camp 63. Height 10,530. Temp. -16.3°. Minimum -25.8°. Another hard grind in the afternoon and five miles added. About 74 miles from the Pole – can we keep this up for seven days? It takes it out of us like anything. None of us ever had such hard work before. Cloud has been coming and going overhead all day, drifting from the S.E., but continually altering shape. Snow crystals falling all the time; a very light S. breeze at start soon dying away. The sun so bright and warm tonight that it is almost impossible to imagine a minus temperature. The snow seems to get softer as we advance; the sastrugi, though sometimes high and undercut, are not hard – no crusts, except yesterday the surface subsided once, as on the Barrier. It seems pretty certain there is no steady wind here. Our chance still holds good if we can put the work in, but it's a terribly trying time.

Friday 12 January Camp 64. T. -17.5°. Lat. 88° 57'. Another heavy march with snow getting softer all the time. Sun very bright, calm at start; first two hours terribly slow. Lunch, 4¾ hours, 5.6 miles geo.; Sight Lat. 88° 52'. Afternoon, 4 hours, 5.1 miles – total 10.7.

In the afternoon we seemed to be going better; clouds spread over from the west with light chill wind and for a few brief minutes we tasted the delight of having the sledge following free. Alas! in a few minutes it was worse than ever, in spite of the sun's eclipse. However, the short experience was salutary. I had got to fear that we were weakening badly in our pulling; those few minutes showed me that we only want a good surface to get along as merrily as of old. With the surface as it is, one gets horribly sick of the monotony and can easily imagine oneself getting played out, were it not that at the lunch and night camps one so quickly forgets all one's troubles and bucks up for a fresh effort. It is an effort to keep up the double figures, but if we can do so for another four marches we ought to get through. It is going to be a close thing.

At camping tonight everyone was chilled and we guessed a cold snap, but to our surprise the actual temperature was higher than last night, when we could dawdle in the sun. It is most unaccountable why we should suddenly feel the cold in this manner; partly the exhaustion of the march, but partly some damp quality in the air, I think. Little Bowers is wonderful; in spite of my protest he *would* take sights after we had camped tonight, after marching in the soft snow all day where we have been comparatively restful on ski.

Night Position Lat. 88° 57' 25" S.; Long. 160° 21' E.; Var. 179° 49' W. Minimum T. -23.5°.

Only 63 miles (geo.) from the Pole tonight. We ought to do the trick, but oh! for a better surface. It is quite evident this is a comparatively windless area. The sastrugi are few and far between, and all soft. I should imagine occasional blizzards sweep up from the S.E., but none with violence. We have deep tracks in the snow, which is soft as deep as you like to dig down.

Saturday 13 January Lunch. Height 10,390. Barometer low? lunch Lat. 89° 3' 18". Started on some soft snow, very heavy dragging and went slow. We could have supposed nothing but that such conditions would last from now onward, but to our surprise, after two hours we came on a sea of sastrugi, all lying from S. to E., predominant E.S.E. Have had a cold little wind from S.E. and S.S.E., where the sky is overcast. Have done 5.6 miles and are now over the 89th parallel.

Night Camp 65. Height 10,270. T. -22.5°, Minimum -23.5°. Lat. 89° 9' S. very nearly. We started very well in the afternoon. Thought we were going to make a real good march, but after the first two hours surface crystals became as sandy as ever. Still we did 5.6 miles geo., giving over 11 for the day. Well, another day with double figures and a bit over. The chance holds.

It looks as though we were descending slightly; sastrugi remain as in forenoon. It is wearisome work this tugging and straining to advance a light sledge. Still, we get along. I did manage to get my thoughts off the work for a time today, which is very restful. We should be in a poor way without our ski, though Bowers manages to struggle through the soft snow without tiring his short legs.

Only 51 miles from the Pole tonight. If we don't get to it we shall be d——d close. There is a little southerly breeze tonight; I devoutly hope it may increase in force. The alternation of soft snow and sastrugi seem to suggest that the coastal mountains are not so very far away.

Sunday 14 January Camp 66. Lunch T. -18°, Night T. -15°. Sun showing mistily through overcast sky all day. Bright southerly wind with very low drift. In consequence the surface was a little better, and we came along very steadily 6.3 miles in the morning and 5.5 in the afternoon, but the steering was awfully difficult and trying; very often I could see nothing, and Bowers on my shoulders directed me. Under such circumstances it is an immense help to be pulling on ski. Tonight it is looking very thick. The sun can barely be distinguished, the temperature has risen, and there are serious indications of a blizzard. I trust they will not come to anything; there are practically no signs of heavy wind here, so that even if it blows a little we may be able to march. Meanwhile we are less than 40 miles from the Pole.

Again we noticed the cold; at lunch today (Obs.: Lat. 89° 20′ 53″ S.) all our feet were cold, but this was mainly due to the bald state of our finnesko. I put some grease under the bare skin and found it made all the difference. Oates seems to be feeling the cold and fatigue more than the rest of us, but we are all very fit. It is a critical time, but we ought to pull through. The barometer has fallen very considerably and we cannot tell whether due to ascent of plateau or change of weather. Oh! for a few fine days! So close it seems and only the weather to baulk us.

Monday 15 January Lunch camp, Height 9,950. Last depot. During the night the air cleared entirely and the sun shone in a perfectly clear sky. The light wind had dropped and the temperature fallen to -25°, minimum -27°. I guessed this meant a hard pull, and guessed right. The surface was terrible, but for 4¾ hours yielded 6 miles (geo.). We were all pretty well done at camping, and here we leave our last depot – only four days' food and a sundry or two. The load is now very light, but I fear that the friction will not be greatly reduced.

Night Height 9920. T. -25°. The sledge came surprisingly lightly after lunch – something from loss of weight, something, I think, from stowage, and, most of all perhaps, as a result of tea. Anyhow we made a capital afternoon march of 6.3 miles, bringing the total for the day to over 12 (12.3). The sastrugi again very confused, but mostly S.E. quadrant; the heaviest now almost east, so that the sledge continually bumps over ridges. The wind is from the W.N.W. chiefly, but the weather remains fine and there are no sastrugi from that direction.

Camp 67. Lunch obs.: Lat. 89° 26′ 57″; Lat. dead reckoning, 89° 33′ 15″ S.; Long. 160° 56′ 45″ E.; Var. 179° E.

It is wonderful to think that two long marches would land us at the Pole. We left our depot today with nine days' provisions, so that it ought to be a certain thing now, and the only appalling possibility the sight of the Norwegian flag forestalling ours. Little Bowers continues his indefatigable efforts to get good sights, and it is wonderful how he works them up in his sleeping-bag in our congested tent. (Minimum for night -27.5°.) Only 27 miles from the Pole. We *ought* to do it now.

Tuesday 16 January Camp 68. Height 9760. T. -23.5°. The worst has happened, or nearly the worst. We marched well in the morning and covered 7½ miles. Noon sight showed us in Lat. 89° 42′ S., and we started off in high spirits in the afternoon, feeling that tomorrow would see us at our destination. About the second hour of the March Bowers' sharp eyes detected what he thought was a cairn; he was uneasy about it, but argued that it must be a sastrugus. Half an hour later he detected a black speck ahead. Soon we knew that this could not be a natural snow feature. We marched on, found that it was a black flag tied to a sledge bearer; near by the remains of a camp; sledge tracks and ski tracks going and coming and the clear trace of dogs' paws – many dogs. This told us the whole story. The Norwegians have forestalled us and are first at the Pole. It is a terrible disappointment, and I am very sorry for my loyal companions. Many thoughts come and much discussion have we had. Tomorrow we must march on to the Pole and then hasten home with all the speed we can compass. All the day dreams must go; it will be a wearisome return. We are descending in altitude – certainly also the Norwegians found an easy way up.

Wednesday 17 January Camp 69. T. -22° at start. Night -21°. The Pole. Yes, but under very different circumstances from those expected. We have had a horrible day – add to our disappointment a head wind 4 to 5, with a temperature -22°, and companions labouring on with cold feet and hands.

We started at 7.30, none of us having slept much after the shock of our discovery. We followed the Norwegian sledge tracks for some way; as far as we make out there are only two men. In about three miles we passed two small cairns. Then the weather overcast, and the tracks being increasingly drifted up and obviously going too far to the west, we decided to make straight for the Pole according to our calculations. At 12.30 Evans had such cold hands we camped for lunch – an excellent 'week-end one'. We had marched 7.4 miles. Lat. sight gave 89° 53′ 37″. We started out and did 6½ miles due south. Tonight little Bowers is laying himself out to get sights in terrible difficult circumstances; the wind is blowing hard, T. -21°, and there is that curious damp, cold feeling in the air which chills one to the bone in no time. We have been descending again, I think, but there looks to be a rise ahead; otherwise there is very little that is different from the awful monotony of past days. Great God! this is an awful place and terrible enough for us to have laboured to it without the reward of priority. Well, it is something to have got here, and the wind may be our friend tomorrow. We have had a fat Polar hoosh in spite of our chagrin, and feel comfortable inside – added a small stick of chocolate and the queer taste of a cigarette brought by Wilson. Now for the run home and a desperate struggle. I wonder if we can do it.

Thursday morning, 18 January Decided after summing up all observations that we were 3.5 miles away from the Pole – one mile beyond it and 3 to the right. More or less in this direction Bowers saw a cairn or tent.

We have just arrived at this tent, 2 miles from our camp, therefore about 1½ miles from the Pole. In the tent we find a record of five Norwegians having been here, as follows:

> Roald Amundsen
> Olav Olavson Bjaaland
> Hilmer Hanssen
> Sverre H. Hassel
> Oscar Wisting.
> 16 Dec. 1911.

The tent is fine – a small compact affair supported by a single bamboo. A note from Amundsen, which I keep, asks me to forward a letter to King Haakon!

The following articles have been left in the tent: 3 half bags of reindeer containing a miscellaneous assortment of mits and sleeping socks, very various in description, a sextant, a Norwegian artificial horizon and a hypsometer without boiling-point thermometers, a sextant and hypsometer of English make.

Left a note to say I had visited the tent with companions. Bowers photographing and Wilson sketching. Since lunch we have marched 6.2 miles S.S.E. by compass (i.e. northwards). Sights at lunch gave us ½ to ¾ of a mile from the Pole, so we call it the Pole Camp. (Temp. Lunch -21°.) We built a cairn, put up our poor slighted Union Jack, and photographed ourselves – mighty cold work all of it – less than ½ a mile south we saw stuck up an old underrunner of a sledge. This we commandeered as a yard for a floorcloth sail. I imagine it was intended to mark the exact spot of the Pole as near as the Norwegians could fix it (Height 9500). A note attached talked of the tent as being 2 miles from the Pole. Wilson keeps the note. There is no doubt that our predecessors have made thoroughly sure of their mark and fully carried out their programme. I think the Pole is about 9500 feet in height; this is remarkable, considering that in Lat. 88° we were about 10,500. We carried the Union Jack about ¾ of a mile north with us and left it on a piece of stick as near as we could fix it. I fancy the Norwegians arrived at the Pole on the 15th Dec. and left on the 17th, ahead of a date quoted by me in London as ideal, viz. 22 Dec. It looks as though the Norwegian party expected colder weather on the summit than they got; it could scarcely be otherwise from Shackleton's account. Well, we have turned our back now on the goal of our ambition and must face our 800 miles of solid dragging – and good-bye to most of the day-dreams!

19
THE RETURN FROM THE POLE: 19 JANUARY 1912 – 17 FEBRUARY 1912

Friday 19 January Lunch 8.1 miles, T. -20.6°. Early in the march we picked up a Norwegian cairn and our outward tracks. We followed these to the ominous black flag which had first apprised us of our predecessors' success. We have picked this flag up, using the staff for our sail, and are now camped about 1½ miles further back on our tracks. So that is the last of the Norwegians for the present. The surface undulates considerably about this latitude; it was more evident today than when we were outward bound.

Night Camp R. 2. [A number preceded by R. marks the camps on the return journey.] Height 9700. T. -18.5°, Minimum -25.6°. Came along well this afternoon for three hours, then a rather dreary finish for the last 1½. Weather very curious, snow clouds, looking very dense and spoiling the light, pass overhead from the S., dropping very minute crystals; between showers the sun shows and the wind goes to the S.W. The fine crystals absolutely spoil the surface; we had heavy dragging during the last hour in spite of the light load and a full sail. Our old tracks are drifted up, deep in places, and toothed sastrugi have formed over them. It looks as though this sandy snow was drifted about like sand from place to place. How account for the present state of our three day old tracks and the month old ones of the Norwegians?

It is warmer and pleasanter marching with the wind, but I'm not sure we don't feel the cold more when we stop and camp than we did on the outward march. We pick up our cairns easily, and ought to do so right through, I think; but, of course, one will be a bit anxious till the Three Degree Depot is reached. [Still over 150 miles away. They had marched 7 miles on the homeward track the first afternoon, 18½ the second day.] I'm afraid the return journey is going to be dreadfully tiring and monotonous.

Saturday 20 January Lunch camp, 9810. We have come along very well this morning, although the surface was terrible bad – 9.3 miles in 5 hours 20 min. This has brought us to our Southern Depot, and we pick up 4 days' food. We carry on 7 days from tonight with 55 miles to go to the Half Degree Depot made on 10 January. The same sort of weather and a little more wind, sail drawing well.

Night Camp R. 3. 9860. Temp. -18°. It was blowing quite hard and drifting when we started our afternoon march. At first with full sail we went along at a great rate; then we got on to an extraordinary surface, the drifting snow lying in heaps; it clung to the ski, which could only be pushed forward with an effort. The pulling was really awful, but we went steadily on and camped a short way beyond our cairn of the 14th. I'm afraid we are in for a bad pull again tomorrow, luckily the wind holds. I shall be very glad when Bowers gets his ski; I'm afraid he must find these long marches very trying with short legs, but he is an undefeated little sportsman. I think Oates is feeling the cold and fatigue more than most of us. It is blowing pretty hard tonight, but with a good march we have earned one good hoosh and are very comfortable in the tent. It is everything now to keep up a good marching pace; I trust we shall be able to do so and catch the ship. Total march, 18½ miles.

Sunday 21 January R. 4. 10,010. Temp, blizzard, -18° to -11°, to -14° now. Awoke to a stiff blizzard; air very thick with snow and sun very dim. We decided not to march owing to likelihood of losing track; expected at least a day of lay up, but whilst at lunch there was a sudden clearance and wind dropped to light breeze. We got ready to march, but gear was so iced up we did not get away till 3.45. Marched till 7.40 – a terribly weary four-hour drag; even with helping wind we only did 5½ miles (6¼ statute). The surface bad, horribly bad on new sastrugi, and decidedly rising again in elevation.

We are going to have a pretty hard time this next 100 miles I expect. If it was difficult to drag downhill over this belt, it will probably be a good deal more difficult to drag up. Luckily the cracks are fairly distinct, though we only see our cairns when less than a mile away; 45 miles to the next depot and 6 days' food in hand – then pick up 7 days' food (T. -22°) and 90 miles to go to the 'Three Degree' Depot. Once there we ought to be safe, but we ought to have a day or two in hand on arrival and may have difficulty with following the tracks. However, if we can get a rating sight for our watches tomorrow we shall be independent of the tracks at a pinch.

Monday 22 January 10,000. Temp. -21°. I think about the most tiring march we have had; solid pulling the whole way, in spite of the light sledge and some little helping wind at first. Then in the last part of the afternoon the sun came out, and almost immediately we had the whole surface covered with soft snow.

We got away sharp at 8 and marched a solid 9 hours, and thus we have covered 14.5 miles (geo.) but, by Jove! it has been a grind. We are just about on the 89th parallel. Tonight Bowers got a rating sight. I'm afraid we have passed out of the wind area. We are within 2½ miles of the 64th camp cairn, 30 miles from our depot, and with 5 days' food in hand. Ski boots are beginning to show signs of wear; I trust we shall have no giving out of ski or boots, since there are yet so many miles to go. I thought we were climbing today, but the barometer gives no change.

Tuesday 23 January Lowest Minimum last night -30°, Temp, at start -28°. Lunch height 10,100. Temp, with wind 6 to 7, -19°. Little wind and heavy marching at start. Then wind increased and we did 8.7 miles by lunch, when it was practically blowing a blizzard. The old tracks show so remarkably well that we can follow them without much difficulty – a great piece of luck.

In the afternoon we had to reorganise. Could carry a whole sail. Bowers hung on to the sledge, Evans and Oates had to lengthen out. We came along at a great rate and should have got within an easy march of our depot had not Wilson suddenly discovered that Evans' nose was frostbitten – it was white and hard. We thought it best to camp at 6.45. Got the tent up with some difficulty, and now pretty cosy after good hoosh.

There is no doubt Evans is a good deal run down – his fingers are badly blistered and his nose is rather seriously congested with frequent frost bites. He is very much annoyed with himself, which is not a good sign. I think Wilson, Bowers and I are as fit as possible under the circumstances. Oates gets cold feet. One way and another, I shall be glad to get off the summit! We are only about 13 miles from our 'Degree and half' Depot and should get there tomorrow. The weather seems to be breaking up. Pray God we have something of a track to follow to the Three Degree Depot – once we pick that up we ought to be right.

Wednesday 24 January Lunch Temp. -8°. Things beginning to look a little serious. A strong wind at the start has developed into a full blizzard at lunch, and we have had to get into our sleeping-bags. It was a bad march, but we covered 7 miles. At first Evans, and then Wilson went ahead to scout for tracks. Bowers guided the sledge alone for the first hour, then both Oates and he remained alongside it; they had a fearful time trying to make the pace between the soft patches. At 12.30 the sun coming ahead made it impossible to see the tracks further, and we had to stop. By this time the gale was at its height and we had the dickens of a time getting up the tent, cold fingers all round. We are only 7 miles from our depot, but I made sure we should be there tonight. This is the second full gale since we left the Pole. I don't like the look of it. Is the weather breaking up? If so, God help us, with the tremendous summit journey and scant food. Wilson and Bowers are my standby. I don't like the easy way in which Oates and Evans get frostbitten.

Thursday 25 January Temp. Lunch -11°, Temp. Night -16°. Thank God we found our Half Degree Depot. After lying in our bags yesterday afternoon and all night, we debated breakfast; decided to have it later and go without lunch. At the time the gale seemed as bad as ever, but during breakfast the sun showed and there was light enough to see the old track. It was a long and terribly cold job digging out our sledge and breaking camp, but we got through and on the march without sail, all pulling. This was about 11, and at about 2.30, to our joy, we saw the red depot flag. We had lunch and left with 9½ days' provisions, still following the track – marched till 8 and covered over 5 miles, over 12 in the day. Only 89 miles (geo.) to the next depot, but it's time we cleared off this plateau. We are not without ailments: Oates suffers from a very cold foot; Evans' fingers and nose are in a bad state, and tonight Wilson is suffering tortures from his eyes. Bowers and I are the only members of the party without troubles just at present. The weather still looks unsettled, and I fear a succession of blizzards at this time of year; the wind is strong from the south, and this afternoon has been very helpful with the full sail. Needless to say I shall sleep much better with our provision bag full again. The only real anxiety now is the finding of the Three Degree Depot. The tracks seem as good as ever so far, sometimes for 30 or 40 yards we lose them under drifts, but then they reappear quite clearly raised above the surface. If the light is good there is not the least difficulty in following. Blizzards are our bugbear, not only stopping our marches, but the cold damp air takes it out of us. Bowers got another rating sight tonight – it was wonderful how he managed to observe in such a horribly cold wind. He has been on ski today whilst Wilson walked by the sledge or pulled ahead of it.

Friday 26 January Temp. -17°. Height 9700, must be high barometer. Started late, 8.50 – for no reason, as I called the hands rather early. We must have fewer delays. There was a good stiff breeze and plenty of drift, but the tracks held. To our old blizzard camp of the 7th we got on well, 7 miles. But beyond the camp we found the tracks completely wiped out. We searched for some time, then marched on a short way and lunched, the weather gradually clearing, though the wind holding. Knowing there were two cairns at four mile intervals, we had little anxiety till we picked up the first far on our right, then steering right by a stroke of fortune, and Bowers' sharp eyes caught a glimpse of the second far on the left. Evidently we made a bad course outward at this part. There is not a sign of our tracks between these cairns, but the last, marking our night camp of the 6th, No. 59, is in the belt of hard sastrugi, and I was comforted to see signs of the track reappearing as we camped. I hope to goodness we can follow it tomorrow. We marched 16 miles (geo.) today, but made good only 15.4.

Saturday 27 January R. 10. Temp. -16° (lunch), -14.3° (evening). Minimum -19°. Height 9900. Barometer low? Called the hands half an hour late, but we got away in good time. The forenoon march was over the belt of storm-tossed sastrugi; it looked like a rough sea. Wilson and I pulled in front on ski, the remainder on foot. It was very tricky work following the track, which pretty constantly disappeared, and in fact only showed itself by faint signs anywhere – a foot or two of raised sledge-track, a dozen yards of the trail of the sledge-meter wheel, or a spatter of hard snow-flicks where feet had trodden. Sometimes none of these were distinct, but one got an impression of lines which guided. The trouble was that on the outward track one had to shape course constantly to avoid the heaviest mounds, and consequently there were many zig-zags. We lost a good deal over a mile by these halts, in which we unharnessed and went on the search for signs. However, by hook or crook, we managed to stick on the old track. Came on the cairn quite suddenly, marched past it, and camped for lunch at 7 miles. In the afternoon the sastrugi gradually diminished in size and now we are on fairly level ground today, the obstruction practically at an end, and, to our joy, the tracks showing up much plainer again. For the last two hours we had no difficulty at all in following them. There has been a nice helpful southerly breeze all day, a clear sky and comparatively warm temperature. The air is dry again, so that tents and equipment are gradually losing their icy condition imposed by the blizzard conditions of the past week.

Our sleeping-bags are slowly but surely getting wetter and I'm afraid it will take a lot of this weather to put them right. However, we all sleep well enough in them, the hours allowed being now on the short side. We are slowly getting more hungry, and it would be an advantage to have a little more food, especially for lunch. If we get to the next depot in a few marches (it is now less than 60 miles and we have a full week's food) we ought to be able to open out a little, but we can't look for a real feed till we get to the pony food depot. A long way to go, and, by Jove, this is tremendous labour.

Sunday 28 January Lunch, -20°. Height, night, 10,130. R. 11. Supper Temp. -18°. Little wind and heavy going in forenoon. We just ran out 8 miles in 5 hours and added another 8 in 3 hours 40 mins. in the afternoon with a good wind and better surface. It is very difficult to say if we are going up or down hill; the barometer is quite different from outward readings. We are 43 miles from the depot, with six days' food in hand. We are camped opposite our lunch cairn of the 4th, only half a day's march from the point at which the last supporting party left us.

Three articles were dropped on our outward march – (Oates' pipe, Bowers' fur mits, and Evans' night boots. We picked up the boots and mits on the track, and tonight we found the pipe lying placidly in sight on the snow. The sledge tracks were very easy to follow today; they are becoming more and more raised, giving a good line shadow often visible half a mile ahead. If this goes on and the weather holds we shall get our depot without trouble. I shall indeed be glad to get it on the sledge. We are getting more hungry, there is no doubt. The lunch meal is beginning to seem inadequate. We are pretty thin, especially Evans, but none of us are feeling worked out. I doubt if we could drag heavy loads, but we can keep going well with our light one. We talk of food a good deal more, and shall be glad to open out on it.

Monday 29 January R. 12. Lunch Temp. -23°. Supper Temp. -25°. Height 10,000. Excellent march of 19½ miles, 10.5 before lunch. Wind helping greatly, considerable drift; tracks for the most part very plain. Some time before lunch we picked up the return track of the supporting party, so that there are now three distinct sledge impressions. We are only 24 miles from our depot – an easy day and a half. Given a fine day tomorrow we ought to get it without difficulty. The wind and sastrugi are S.S.E. and S.E. If the weather holds we ought to do the rest of the inland ice journey in little over a week. The surface is very much altered since we passed out. The loose snow has been swept into heaps, hard and wind-tossed. The rest has a glazed appearance, the loose drifting snow no doubt acting on it, polishing it like a sand blast. The sledge with our good wind behind runs splendidly on it; it is all soft and sandy beneath the glaze. We are certainly getting hungrier every day. The day after tomorrow we should be able to increase allowances. It is monotonous work, but, thank God, the miles are coming fast at last. We ought not to be delayed much now with the down-grade in front of us.

Tuesday 30 January R. 13. 9860. Lunch Temp.-25°, Supper Temp. -24.5°. Thank the Lord, another fine march – 19 miles. We have passed the last cairn before the depot, the track is clear ahead, the weather fair, the wind helpful, the gradient down – with any luck we should pick up our depot in the middle of the morning march. This is the bright side; the reverse of the medal is serious. Wilson has strained a tendon in his leg; it has given pain all day and is swollen tonight. Of course, he is full of pluck over it, but I don't like the idea of such an accident here. To add to the trouble Evans has dislodged two finger-nails tonight; his hands are really bad, and to my surprise he shows signs of losing heart over it. He hasn't been cheerful since the accident. The wind shifted from S.E. to S. and back again all day, but luckily it keeps strong. We can get along with bad fingers, but it [will be] a mighty serious thing if Wilson's leg doesn't improve.

Wednesday 31 January 9800. Lunch Temp. -20°, Supper Temp. -20°. The day opened fine with a fair breeze; we marched on the depot [Three Degree Depot], picked it up, and lunched an hour later. In the afternoon the surface became fearfully bad, the wind dropped to light southerly air. Ill luck that this should happen just when we have only four men to pull. Wilson rested his leg as much as possible by walking quietly beside the sledge; the result has been good, and tonight there is much less inflammation. I hope he will be all right again soon, but it is trying to have an injured limb in the party. I see we had a very heavy surface here on our outward march. There is no doubt we are travelling over undulations, but the inequality of level does not make a great difference to our pace; it is the sandy crystals that hold us up. There has been very great alteration of the surface since we were last here – the sledge tracks stand high. This afternoon we picked up Bowers' ski [left on 31 December] – the last thing we have to find on the summit, thank Heaven! Now we have only to go north and so shall welcome strong winds.

Thursday 1 February R. 15. 9778. Lunch Temp. -20°, Supper Temp. -19.8°. Heavy collar work most of the day. Wind light. Did 8 miles, 4¾ hours. Started well in the afternoon and came down a steep slope in quick time; then the surface turned real bad – sandy drifts – very heavy pulling. Working on past 8 p.m. we just fetched a lunch cairn of 29 December, when we were only a week out from the depot. [The Upper Glacier Depot, under Mount Darwin, where the first supporting party turned back.] It ought to be easy to get in with a margin, having 8 days' food in hand (full feeding). We have opened out on the 1/7th increase and it makes a lot of difference. Wilson's leg much better. Evans' fingers now very bad, two nails coming off, blisters burst.

Friday 2 February 9340. R. 16. Temp.: Lunch -19°, Supper -17°. We started well on a strong southerly wind. Soon got to a steep grade, when the sledge overran and upset us one after another. We got off our ski, and pulling on foot reeled off 9 miles by lunch at 1.30. Started in the afternoon on foot, going very strong. We noticed a curious circumstance towards the end of the forenoon. The tracks were drifted over, but the drifts formed a sort of causeway along which we pulled. In the afternoon we soon came to a steep slope – the same on which we exchanged sledges on 28 December. All went well till, in trying to keep the track at the same time as my feet, on a very slippery surface, I came an awful 'purler' on my shoulder. It is horribly sore tonight and another sick person added to our tent – three out of five injured, and the most troublesome surfaces to come. We shall be lucky if we get through without serious injury. Wilson's leg is better, but might easily get bad again, and Evans' fingers.

At the bottom of the slope this afternoon we came on a confused sea of sastrugi. We lost the track. Later, on soft snow, we picked up E. Evans' return track, which we are now following. We have managed to get off 17 miles. The extra food is certainly helping us, but we are getting pretty hungry. The weather is already a trifle warmer and the altitude lower, and only 80 miles or so to Mount Darwin. It is time we were off the summit – Pray God another four days will see us pretty well clear of it. Our bags are getting very wet and we ought to have more sleep.

Saturday 3 February R. 17. Temp.: Lunch -20°; Supper -20°. Height 9040 feet. Started pretty well on foot; came to steep slope with crevasses (few). I went on ski to avoid another fall, and we took the slope gently with our sail, constantly losing the track, but picked up a much weathered cairn on our right. Vexatious delays, searching for tracks, etc., reduced morning march to 8.1 miles. Afternoon, came along a little better, but again lost tracks on hard slope. Tonight we are near camp of 26 December, but cannot see cairn. Have decided it is waste of time looking for tracks and cairn, and shall push on due north as fast as we can.

The surface is greatly changed since we passed outward, in most places polished smooth, but with heaps of new toothed sastrugi which are disagreeable obstacles. Evans' fingers are going on as well as can be expected, but it will be long before he will be able to help properly with the work. Wilson's leg much better, and my shoulder also, though it gives bad twinges. The extra food is doing us all good, but we ought to have more sleep. Very few more days on the plateau I hope.

Sunday 4 February R. 18. 8620 feet. Temp.: Lunch -22°; Supper -23°. Pulled on foot in the morning over good hard surface and covered 9.7 miles. Just before lunch unexpectedly fell into crevasses, Evans and I together – a second fall for Evans, and I camped. After lunch saw disturbance ahead, and what I took for disturbance (land) to the right. We went on ski over hard shiny descending surface. Did very well, especially towards end of march, covering in all 18.1. We have come down some hundreds of feet. Half way in the march the land showed up splendidly, and I decided to make straight for Mt. Darwin, which we are rounding. Every sign points to getting away off this plateau. The temperature is 20° lower than when we were here before; the party is not improving in condition, especially Evans, who is becoming rather dull and incapable [the result of concussion in the morning's fall]. Thank the Lord we have good food at each meal, but we get hungrier in spite of it. Bowers is splendid, full of energy and bustle all the time. I hope we are not going to have trouble with ice-falls.

Monday 5 February R. 19. Lunch, 8320 ft., Temp. -17°; Supper, 8120 ft, Temp.-17.2°. A good forenoon, few crevasses; we covered 10.2 miles. In the afternoon we soon got into difficulties. We saw the land very clearly, but the difficulty is to get at it. An hour after starting we came on huge pressures and great street crevasses partly open. We had to steer more and more to the west, so that our course was very erratic. Late in the march we turned more to the north and again encountered open crevasses across our track. It is very difficult manoeuvring amongst these and I should not like to do it without ski.

We are camped in a very disturbed region, but the wind has fallen very light here, and our camp is comfortable for the first time for many weeks. We may be anything from 25 to 30 miles from our depot, but I wish to goodness we could see a way through the disturbances ahead. Our faces are much cut up by all the winds we have had, mine least of all; the others tell me they feel their noses more going with than against the wind. Evans' nose is almost as bad as his fingers. He is a good deal crocked up.

Tuesday 6 February Lunch 7900; Supper 7210. Temp. -15° [R. 20]. We've had a horrid day and not covered good mileage. On turning out found sky overcast; a beastly position amidst crevasses. Luckily it cleared just before we started. We went straight for Mt. Darwin, but in half an hour found ourselves amongst huge open chasms, unbridged, but not very deep, I think. We turned to the north between two, but to our chagrin they converged into chaotic disturbance. We had to retrace our steps for a mile or so, then struck to the west and got on to a confused sea of sastrugi, pulling very hard; we put up the sail, Evans' nose suffered, Wilson very cold, everything horrid. Camped for lunch in the sastrugi; the only comfort, things looked clearer to the west and we were obviously going downhill. In the afternoon we struggled on, got out of sastrugi and turned over on glazed surface, crossing many crevasses – very easy work on ski. Towards the end of the march we realised the certainty of maintaining a more or less straight course to the depot, and estimate distance 10 to 15 miles.

Food is low and weather uncertain, so that many hours of the day were anxious; but this evening, though we are not as far advanced as I expected, the outlook is much more promising. Evans is the chief anxiety now; his cuts and wounds suppurate, his nose looks very bad, and altogether he shows considerable signs of being played out. Things may mend for him on the glacier, and his wounds get some respite under warmer conditions. I am indeed glad to think we shall so soon have done with plateau conditions. It took us 27 days to reach the Pole and 21 days back – in all 48 days – nearly 7 weeks in low temperature with almost incessant wind.

END OF THE SUMMIT JOURNEY

Wednesday 7 February Mount Darwin [or Upper Glacier] Depot, R. 21. Height 7100. Lunch Temp. -9°; Supper Temp, [a blank here]. A wretched day with satisfactory ending. First panic, certainty that biscuit-box was short. Great doubt as to how this has come about, as we certainly haven't over-issued allowances. Bowers is dreadfully disturbed about it. The shortage is a full day's allowance. We started our march at 8.30, and travelled down slopes and over terraces covered with hard sastrugi – very tiresome work – and the land didn't seem to come any nearer. At lunch the wind increased, and what with hot tea and good food, we started the afternoon in a better frame of mind, and it soon became obvious we were nearing our mark. Soon after 6.30 we saw our depot easily and camped next it at 7.30.

Found note from Evans to say the second return party passed through safely at 2.30 on 14 January – half a day longer between depots than we have been. The temperature is higher, but there is a cold wind tonight.

Well, we have come through our 7 weeks' ice camp journey and most of us are fit, but I think another week might have had a very bad effect on Evans, who is going steadily downhill.

It is satisfactory to recall that these facts give absolute proof of both expeditions having reached the Pole and placed the question of priority beyond discussion.

RETURN FROM FIRST SUMMIT DEPOT

Thursday 8 February R. 22. Height 6260. Start Temp. -11°; Lunch Temp. -5°; Supper, zero. 9.2 miles. Started from the depot rather late owing to weighing biscuit, etc., and rearranging matters. Had a beastly morning. Wind very strong and cold. Steered in for Mt. Darwin to visit rock. Sent Bowers on, on ski, as Wilson can't wear his at present. He obtained several specimens, all of much the same type, a close-grained granite rock which weathers red. Hence the pink limestone. After he rejoined we skidded downhill pretty fast, leaders on ski, Oates and Wilson on foot alongside sledge – Evans detached. We lunched at 2 well down towards Mt. Buckley, the wind half a gale and everybody very cold and cheerless. However, better things were to follow. We decided to steer for the moraine under Mt. Buckley and, pulling with crampons, we crossed some very irregular steep slopes with big crevasses and slid down towards the rocks. The moraine was obviously so interesting that when we had advanced some miles and got out of the wind, I decided to camp and spend the rest of the day geologising. It has been extremely interesting. We found ourselves under perpendicular cliffs of Beacon sandstone, weathering rapidly and carrying veritable coal seams. From the last Wilson, with his sharp eyes, has picked several plant impressions, the last a piece of coal with beautifully traced leaves in layers, also some excellently preserved impressions of thick stems, showing cellular structure. In one place we saw the cast of small waves on the sand. Tonight Bill has got a specimen of limestone with archeo-cyathus – the trouble is one cannot imagine where the stone comes from; it is evidently rare, as few specimens occur in the moraine. There is a good deal of pure white quartz. Altogether we have had a most interesting afternoon, and the relief of being out of the wind and in a warmer temperature is inexpressible. I hope and trust we shall all buck up again now that the conditions are more favourable. We have been in shadow all the afternoon, but the sun has just reached us, a little obscured by night haze. A lot could be written on the delight of setting foot on rock after 14 weeks of snow and ice and nearly 7 out of sight of aught else. It is like going ashore after a sea voyage. We deserve a little good bright weather after all our trials, and hope to get a chance to dry our sleeping-bags and generally make our gear more comfortable.

Friday 9 February R. 23. Height 5,210 ft. Lunch Temp. +10°; Supper Temp. +12.5°. About 13 miles. Kept along the edge of moraine to the end of Mt. Buckley. Stopped and geologised. Wilson got great find of vegetable impression in piece of limestone. Too tired to write geological notes. We all felt very slack this morning, partly rise of temperature, partly reaction, no doubt. Ought to have kept close in to glacier north of Mt. Buckley, but in bad light the descent looked steep and we kept out. Evidently we got amongst bad ice pressure and had to come down over an ice-fall. The crevasses were much firmer than expected and we got down with some difficulty, found our night camp of 20 December, and lunched an hour after. Did pretty well in the afternoon, marching 3¾ hours; the sledgemeter is unshipped, so cannot tell distance traversed. Very warm on march and we are all pretty tired. Tonight it is wonderfully calm and warm, though it has been overcast all the afternoon. It is remarkable to be able to stand outside the tent and sun oneself. Our food satisfies now, but we must march to keep in the full ration, and we want rest, yet we shall pull through all right, D.V. We are by no means worn out.

Saturday 10 February R. 24. Lunch Temp. +12°; Supper Temp. +10°. Got off a good morning march in spite of keeping too far east and getting in rough, cracked ice. Had a splendid night's sleep, showing great change in all faces, so didn't get away till 10 a.m. Lunched just before 3. After lunch the land began to be obscured. We held a course for 2½ hours with difficulty, then the sun disappeared, and snow drove in our faces with northerly wind – very warm and impossible to steer, so camped. After supper, still very thick all round, but sun showing and less snow falling. The fallen snow crystals are quite feathery like thistledown. We have two full days' food left, and though our position is uncertain, we are certainly within two outward marches from the middle glacier depot. However, if the weather doesn't clear by tomorrow, we must either march blindly on or reduce food. It is very trying. Another night to make up arrears of sleep. The ice crystals that first fell this afternoon were very large. Now the sky is clearer overhead, the temperature has fallen slightly, and the crystals are minute.

Sunday 11 February R. 25. Lunch Temp. +6.5°; Supper +3.5°. The worst day we have had during the trip and greatly owing to our own fault. We started on a wretched surface with light S.W. wind, sail set, and pulling on ski – horrible light, which made everything look fantastic. As we went on light got worse, and suddenly we found ourselves in pressure. Then came the fatal decision to steer east. We went on for 6 hours, hoping to do a good distance, which in fact I suppose we did, but for the last hour or two we pressed on into a regular trap. Getting on to a good surface we did not reduce our lunch meal, and thought all going well, but half an hour after lunch we got into the worst ice mess I have ever been in. For three hours we plunged on on ski, first thinking we were too much to the right, then too much to the left; meanwhile the disturbance got worse and my spirits received a very rude shock. There were times when it seemed almost impossible to find a way out of the awful turmoil in which we found ourselves. At length, arguing that there must be a way on our left, we plunged in that direction. It got worse, harder, more icy and crevassed. We could not manage our ski and pulled on foot, falling into crevasses every minute – most luckily no bad accident. At length we saw a smoother slope towards the land, pushed for it, but knew it was a woefully long way from us. The turmoil changed in character, irregular crevassed surface giving way to huge chasms, closely packed and most difficult to cross. It was very heavy work, but we had grown desperate. We won through at 10 p.m. and I write after 12 hours on the march. I *think* we are on or about the right track now, but we are still a good number of miles from the depot, so we reduced rations tonight. We had three pemmican meals left and decided to make them into four. Tomorrow's lunch must serve for two if we do not make big progress. It was a test of our endurance on the march and our fitness with small supper. We have come through well. A good wind has come down the glacier which is clearing the sky and surface. Pray God the wind holds tomorrow. Short sleep tonight and off first thing, I hope.

Monday 12 February R. 26. In a very critical situation. All went well in the forenoon, and we did a good long march over a fair surface. Two hours before lunch we were cheered by the sight of our night camp of the 18th December, the day after we made our depot – this showed we were on the right track. In the afternoon, refreshed by tea, we went forward, confident of covering the remaining distance, but by a fatal chance we kept too far to the left, and then we struck uphill and, tired and despondent, arrived in a horrid maze of crevasses and fissures. Divided councils caused our course to be erratic after this, and finally, at 9 p.m. we landed in the worst place of all. After discussion we decided to camp, and here we are, after a very short supper and one meal only remaining in the food bag; the depot doubtful in locality. We must get there tomorrow. Meanwhile we are cheerful with an effort. It's a tight place, but luckily we've been well fed up to the present. Pray God we have fine weather tomorrow.

[At this point the bearings of the mid-glacier depot are given, but need not be quoted.]

Tuesday 13 February Camp R. 27, beside Cloudmaker. Temp. +10°. Last night we all slept well in spite of our grave anxieties. For my part these were increased by my visits outside the tent, when I saw the sky gradually closing over and snow beginning to fall. By our ordinary time for getting up it was dense all around us. We could see nothing, and we could only remain in our sleeping-bags. At 8.30 I dimly made out the land of the Cloudmaker. At 9 we got up, deciding to have tea, and with one biscuit, no pemmican, so as to leave our scanty remaining meal for eventualities. We started marching, and at first had to wind our way through an awful turmoil of broken ice, but in about an hour we hit an old moraine track, brown with dirt. Here the surface was much smoother and improved rapidly. The fog still hung over all and we went on for an hour, checking our bearings. Then the whole place got smoother and we turned outward a little. Evans raised our hopes with a shout of depot ahead, but it proved to be a shadow on the ice. Then suddenly Wilson saw the actual depot flag. It was an immense relief, and we were soon in possession of our 3½ days' food. The relief to all is inexpressible; needless to say, we camped and had a meal.

Marching in the afternoon, I kept more to the left, and closed the mountain till we fell on the stone moraines. Here Wilson detached himself and made a collection, whilst we pulled the sledge on. We camped late, abreast the lower end of the mountain, and had nearly our usual satisfying supper. Yesterday was the worst experience of the trip and gave a horrid feeling of insecurity. Now we are right up, we must march. In future food must be worked so that we do not run so short if the weather fails us. We mustn't get into a hole like this again. Greatly relieved to find that both the other parties got through safely. Evans seems to have got mixed up with pressures like ourselves. It promises to be a very fine day tomorrow. The valley is gradually clearing. Bowers has had a very bad attack of snow blindness, and Wilson another almost as bad. Evans has no power to assist with camping work.

Wednesday 14 February Lunch Temp. 0°; Supper Temp. +1°. A fine day with wind on and off down the glacier, and we have done a fairly good march. We started a little late and pulled on down the moraine. At first I thought of going right, but soon, luckily, changed my mind and decided to follow the curving lines of the moraines. This course has brought us well out on the glacier. Started on crampons; one hour after, hoisted sail; the combined efforts produced only slow speed, partly due to the sandy snowdrifts similar to those on summit, partly to our torn sledge runners. At lunch these were scraped and sand-papered. After lunch we got on snow, with ice only occasionally showing through. A poor start, but the gradient and wind improving, we did 6½ miles before night camp.

There is no getting away from the fact that we are not going strong. Probably none of us: Wilson's leg still troubles him and he doesn't like to trust himself on ski; but the worst case is Evans, who is giving us serious anxiety. This morning he suddenly disclosed a huge blister on his foot. It delayed us on the march, when he had to have his crampon readjusted. Sometimes I fear he is going from bad to worse, but I trust he will pick up again when we come to steady work on ski like this afternoon. He is hungry and so is Wilson. We can't risk opening out our food again, and as cook at present I am serving something under full allowance. We are inclined to get slack and slow with our camping arrangements, and small delays increase. I have talked of the matter tonight and hope for improvement. We cannot do distance without the ponies. The next depot [the Lower Glacier Depot] some 30 miles away and nearly 3 days' food in hand.

Thursday 15 February R. 29. Lunch Temp. -10°; Supper Temp. -4°. 13.5 miles. Again we are running short of provision. We don't know our distance from the depot, but imagine about 20 miles. Heavy march – did 13¾ (geo.). We are pulling for food and not very strong evidently. In the afternoon it was overcast; land blotted out for a considerable interval. We have reduced food, also sleep; feeling rather done. Trust 1½ days or 2 at most will see us at depot.

Friday 16 February 12.5 m. Lunch Temp. -6.1°; Supper Temp. +7°. A rather trying position. Evans has nearly broken down in brain, we think. He is absolutely changed from his normal self-reliant self. This morning and this afternoon he stopped the march on some trivial excuse. We are on short rations but not very short, food spins out till tomorrow night. We cannot be more than 10 or 12 miles from the depot, but the weather is all against us. After lunch we were enveloped in a snow sheet, land just looming. Memory should hold the events of a very troublesome march with more troubles ahead. Perhaps all will be well if we can get to our depot tomorrow fairly early, but it is anxious work with the sick man. But it's no use meeting troubles half way, and our sleep is all too short to write more.

Saturday 17 February A very terrible day. Evans looked a little better after a good sleep, and declared, as he always did, that he was quite well. He started in his place on the traces, but half an hour later worked his ski shoes adrift, and had to leave the sledge. The surface was awful, the soft recently fallen snow clogging the ski and runners at every step, the sledge groaning, the sky overcast, and the land hazy. We stopped after about one hour, and Evans came up again, but very slowly. Half an hour later he dropped out again on the same plea. He asked Bowers to lend him a piece of string. I cautioned him to come on as quickly as he could, and he answered cheerfully as I thought. We had to push on, and the remainder of us were forced to pull very hard, sweating heavily. Abreast the Monument Rock we stopped, and seeing Evans a long way astern, I camped for lunch. There was no alarm at first, and we prepared tea and our own meal, consuming the latter. After lunch, and Evans still not appearing, we looked out, to see him still afar off. By this time we were alarmed, and all four started back on ski. I was first to reach the poor man and shocked at his appearance; he was on his knees with clothing disarranged, hands uncovered and frostbitten, and a wild look in his eyes. Asked what was the matter, he replied with a slow speech that he didn't know, but thought he must have fainted. We got him on his feet, but after two or three steps he sank down again. He showed every sign of complete collapse. Wilson, Bowers, and I went back for the sledge, whilst Oates remained with him. When we returned he was practically unconscious, and when we got him into the tent quite comatose. He died quietly at 12.30 a.m.

On discussing the symptoms we think he began to get weaker just before we reached the Pole, and that his downward path was accelerated first by the shock of his frostbitten fingers, and later by falls during rough travelling on the glacier, further by his loss of all confidence in himself. Wilson thinks it certain he must have injured his brain by a fall. It is a terrible thing to lose a companion in this way, but calm reflection shows that there could not have been a better ending to the terrible anxieties of the past week. Discussion of the situation at lunch yesterday shows us what a desperate pass we were in with a sick man on our hands at such a distance from home.

At 1 a.m. we packed up and came down over the pressure ridges, finding our depot easily.

THE LAST MARCH: 18 FEBRUARY 1912
– 29 MARCH 1912[25]

Sunday 18 February R. 32. Temp. -5.5°. At Shambles Camp. We gave ourselves 5 hours' sleep at the lower glacier depot after the horrible night, and came on at about 3 today to this camp, coming fairly easily over the divide. Here with plenty of horsemeat we have had a fine supper, to be followed by others such, and so continue a more plentiful era if we can keep good marches up. New life seems to come with greater food almost immediately, but I am anxious about the Barrier surfaces.

Monday 19 February Lunch T. -16°. It was late (past noon) before we got away today, as I gave nearly 8 hours' sleep, and much camp work was done shifting sledges [sledges were left at the chief depots to replace damaged ones] and fitting up new one with mast, etc., packing horsemeat and personal effects. The surface was every bit as bad as I expected, the sun shining brightly on it and its covering of soft loose sandy snow. We have come out about 2' on the old tracks. Perhaps lucky to have a fine day for this and our camp work, but we shall want wind or change of sliding conditions to do anything on such a surface as we have got. I fear there will not be much change for the next 3 or 4 days.

R. 33. Temp. -17°. We have struggled out 4.6 miles in a short day over a really terrible surface – it has been like pulling over desert sand, not the least glide in the world. If this goes on we shall have a bad time, but I sincerely trust it is only the result of this windless area close to the coast and that, as we are making steadily outwards, we shall shortly escape it. It is perhaps premature to be anxious about covering distance. In all other respects things are improving. We have our sleeping-bags spread on the sledge and they are drying, but, above all, we have our full measure of food again. Tonight we had a sort of stew fry of pemmican and horseflesh, and voted it the best hoosh we had ever had on a sledge journey. The absence of poor Evans is a help to the commissariat, but if he had been here in a fit state we might have got along faster. I wonder what is in store for us, with some little alarm at the lateness of the season.

Monday 20 February R. 34. Lunch Temp. -13°; Supper Temp. -15°. Same terrible surface; four hours' hard plodding in morning brought us to our Desolation Camp, where we had the four-day blizzard. We looked for more pony meat, but found none. After lunch we took to ski with some improvement of comfort. Total mileage for day 7 – the ski tracks pretty plain and easily followed this afternoon. We have left another cairn behind. Terribly slow progress, but we hope for better things as we clear the land. There is a tendency to cloud over in the S.E. tonight, which may turn to our advantage. At present our sledge and ski leave deeply ploughed tracks which can be seen winding for miles behind. It is distressing, but as usual trials are forgotten when we camp, and good food is our lot. Pray God we get better travelling as we are not fit as we were, and the season is advancing apace.

Tuesday 21 February R. 35. Lunch Temp. +9½°; Supper Temp. -11°. Gloomy and overcast when we started; a good deal warmer. The marching almost as bad as yesterday. Heavy toiling all day, inspiring gloomiest thoughts at times. Rays of comfort when we picked up tracks and cairns. At lunch we seemed to have missed the way, but an hour or two after we passed the last pony walls, and since, we struck a tent ring, ending the march actually on our old pony-tracks. There is a critical spot here with a long stretch between cairns. If we can tide that over we get on the regular cairn route, and with luck should stick to it; but everything depends on the weather. We never won a march of 8½ miles with greater difficulty, but we can't go on like this. We are drawing away from the land and perhaps may get better things in a day or two. I devoutly hope so.

Wednesday 22 February R. 36. Supper Temp. -2°. There is little doubt we are in for a rotten critical time going home, and the lateness of the season may make it really serious. Shortly after starting today the wind grew very fresh from the S.E. with strong surface drift. We lost the faint track immediately, though covering ground fairly rapidly. Lunch came without sight of the cairn we had hoped to pass. In the afternoon, Bowers being sure we were too far to the west, steered out. Result, we have passed another pony camp without seeing it. Looking at the map tonight there is no doubt we are too far to the east. With clear weather we ought to be able to correct the mistake, but will the weather get clear? It's a gloomy position, more especially as one sees the same difficulty returning even when we have corrected the error. The wind is dying down tonight and the sky clearing in the south, which is hopeful. Meanwhile it is satisfactory to note that such untoward events fail to damp the spirit of the party. Tonight we had a pony hoosh so excellent and filling that one feels really strong and vigorous again.

Thursday 23 February R. 37. Lunch Temp.-9.8°; Supper Temp.-12°. Started in sunshine, wind almost dropped. Luckily Bowers took a round of angles and with help of the chart we fogged out that we must be inside rather than outside tracks. The data were so meagre that it seemed a great responsibility to march out and we were none of us happy about it. But just as we decided to lunch, Bowers' wonderful sharp eyes detected an old double lunch cairn, the theodolite telescope confirmed it, and our spirits rose accordingly. This afternoon we marched on and picked up another cairn; then on and camped only 2½ miles from the depot. We cannot see it, but, given fine weather, we cannot miss it. We are, therefore, extraordinarily relieved. Covered 8.2 miles in 7 hours, showing we can do 10 to 12 on this surface. Things are again looking up, as we are on the regular line of cairns, with no gaps right home, I hope.

Friday 24 February Lunch. Beautiful day – too beautiful – an hour after starting loose ice crystals spoiling surface. Saw depot and reached it middle forenoon. Found store in order except shortage oil[26] – shall have to be *very* saving with fuel – otherwise have ten full days' provision from tonight and shall have less than 70 miles to go. Note from Meares who passed through 15 December, saying surface bad; from Atkinson, after fine marching (2¼ days from pony depot), reporting Keohane better after sickness. Short note from Evans, not very cheerful, saying surface bad, temperature high. Think he must have been a little anxious. [It will be remembered that he was already stricken with scurvy.] It is an immense relief to have picked up this depot and, for the time, anxieties are thrust aside. There is no doubt we have been rising steadily since leaving the Shambles Camp. The coastal Barrier descends except where glaciers press out. Undulation still but flattening out. Surface soft on top, curiously hard below. Great difference now between night and day temperatures. Quite warm as I write in tent. We are on tracks with half-march cairn ahead; have covered 4½ miles. Poor Wilson has a fearful attack snow-blindness consequent on yesterday's efforts. Wish we had more fuel.

Night Camp R. 38. Temp. -17°. A little despondent again. We had a really terrible surface this afternoon and only covered 4 miles. We are on the track just beyond a lunch cairn. It really will be a bad business if we are to have this pulling all through. I don't know what to think, but the rapid closing of the season is ominous. It is great luck having the horsemeat to add to our ration. Tonight we have had a real fine 'hoosh'. It is a race between the season and hard conditions and our fitness and good food.

Saturday 25 February Lunch Temp. -12°. Managed just 6 miles this morning. Started somewhat despondent; not relieved when pulling seemed to show no improvement. Bit by bit surface grew better, less sastrugi, more glide, slight following wind for a time. Then we began to travel a little faster. But the pulling is still *very* hard; undulations disappearing but inequalities remain.

Twenty-six Camp walls about 2 miles ahead, all tracks in sight – Evans' track very conspicuous. This is something in favour, but the pulling is tiring us, though we are getting into better ski drawing again. Bowers hasn't quite the trick and is a little hurt at my criticisms, but I never doubted his heart. Very much easier – write diary at lunch – excellent meal – now one pannikin very strong tea – four biscuits and butter.

Hope for better things this afternoon, but no improvement apparent. Oh! for a little wind – E. Evans evidently had plenty.

R. 39. Temp. -20°. Better march in afternoon. Day yields 11.4 miles – the first double figure of steady dragging for a long time, but it meant and will mean hard work if we can't get a wind to help us. Evans evidently had a strong wind here, S.E. I should think. The temperature goes very low at night now when the sky is clear as at present. As a matter of fact this is wonderfully fair weather – the only drawback the spoiling of the surface and absence of wind.

We see all tracks very plain, but the pony-walls have evidently been badly drifted up. Some kind people had substituted a cairn at last camp 27. The old cairns do not seem to have suffered much.

Sunday 26 February Lunch Temp. -17°. Sky overcast at start, but able see tracks and cairn distinct at long distance. Did a little better, 6½ miles to date. Bowers and Wilson now in front. Find great relief pulling behind with no necessity to keep attention on track. Very cold nights now and cold feet starting march, as day footgear doesn't dry at all. We are doing well on our food, but we ought to have yet more. I hope the next depot, now only 50 miles, will find us with enough surplus to open out. The fuel shortage still an anxiety.

R. 40. Temp. -21° Nine hours' solid marching has given us 11½ miles. Only 43 miles from the next depot. Wonderfully fine weather but cold, very cold. Nothing dries and we get our feet cold too often. We want more food yet and especially more fat. Fuel is woefully short. We can scarcely hope to get a better surface at this season, but I wish we could have some help from the wind, though it might shake us badly if the temp. didn't rise.

Monday 27 February Desperately cold last night: -33° when we got up, with -37° minimum. Some suffering from cold feet, but all got good rest. We *must* open out on food soon. But we have done 7 miles this morning and hope for some 5 this afternoon. Overcast sky and good surface till now, when sun shows again. It is good to be marching the cairns up, but there is still much to be anxious about. We talk of little but food, except after meals. Land disappearing in satisfactory manner. Pray God we have no further set-backs. We are naturally always discussing possibility of meeting dogs, where and when, etc. It is a critical position. We may find ourselves in safety at next depot, but there is a horrid element of doubt.

Camp R. 41. Temp. -32°. Still fine clear weather but very cold – absolutely calm tonight. We have got off an excellent march for these days (12.2) and are much earlier than usual in our bags. 31 miles to depot, 3 days' fuel at a pinch, and 6 days' food. Things begin to look a little better; we can open out a little on food from tomorrow night, I think.

Very curious surface – soft recent sastrugi which sink underfoot, and between, a sort of flaky crust with large crystals beneath.

Tuesday 28 February Lunch. Thermometer went below -40° last night; it was desperately cold for us, but we had a fair night. I decided to slightly increase food; the effect is undoubtedly good. Started marching in -32° with a slight north-westerly breeze – blighting. Many cold feet this morning; long time over foot gear, but we are earlier. Shall camp earlier and get the chance of a good night, if not the reality. Things must be critical till we reach the depot, and the more I think of matters, the more I anticipate their remaining so after that event. Only 24½ miles from the depot. The sun shines brightly, but there is little warmth in it. There is no doubt the middle of the Barrier is a pretty awful locality.

Camp R. 42. Splendid pony hoosh sent us to bed and sleep happily after a horrid day, wind continuing; did 11½ miles. Temp. not quite so low, but expect we are in for cold night (Temp. -27°).

Wednesday 29 February Lunch. Cold night. Minimum Temp. -37.5°; -30° with north-west wind, force 4, when we got up. Frightfully cold starting; luckily Bowers and Oates in their last new finnesko; keeping my old ones for present. Expected awful march and for first hour got it. Then things improved and we camped after 5½ hours marching close to lunch camp – 22½. Next camp is our depot and it is exactly 13 miles. It ought not to take more than 1½ days; we pray for another fine one. The oil will just about spin out in that event, and we arrive 3 clear days' food in hand. The increase of ration has had an enormously beneficial result. Mountains now looking small. Wind still very light from west – cannot understand this wind.

Thursday 1 March Lunch. Very cold last night – minimum -41.5°. Cold start to march, too, as usual now. Got away at 8 and have marched within sight of depot; flag something under 3 miles away. We did 11½ yesterday and marched 6 this morning. Heavy dragging yesterday and *very* heavy this morning. Apart from sledging considerations the weather is wonderful. Cloudless days and nights and the wind trifling. Worse luck, the light airs come from the north and keep us horribly cold. For this lunch hour the exception has come. There is a bright and comparatively warm sun. All our gear is out drying.

Friday 2 March Lunch. Misfortunes rarely come singly. We marched to the [Middle Barrier] depot fairly easily yesterday afternoon, and since that have suffered three distinct blows which have placed us in a bad position. First we found a shortage of oil; with most rigid economy it can scarce carry us to the next depot on this surface (71 miles away). Second, Titus Oates disclosed his feet, the toes showing very bad indeed, evidently bitten by the late temperatures. The third blow came in the night, when the wind, which we had hailed with some joy, brought dark overcast weather. It fell below -40° in the night, and this morning it took 1½ hours to get our foot gear on, but we got away before eight. We lost cairn and tracks together and made as steady as we could N. by W., but have seen nothing. Worse was to come – the surface is simply awful. In spite of strong wind and full sail we have only done 5½ miles. We are in a very queer street since there is no doubt we cannot do the extra marches and feel the cold horribly.

Saturday 3 March Lunch. We picked up the track again yesterday, finding ourselves to the eastward. Did close on 10 miles and things looked a trifle better; but this morning the outlook is blacker than ever. Started well and with good breeze; for an hour made good headway; then the surface grew awful beyond words. The wind drew forward; every circumstance was against us. After 4¼ hours things so bad that we camped, having covered 4½ miles. [R. 46.] One cannot consider this a fault of our own – certainly we were pulling hard this morning – it was more than three parts surface which held us back – the wind at strongest, powerless to move the sledge. When the light is good it is easy to see the reason. The surface, lately a very good hard one, is coated with a thin layer of woolly crystals, formed by radiation no doubt. These are too firmly fixed to be removed by the wind and cause impossible friction on the runners. God help us, we can't keep up this pulling, that is certain. Amongst ourselves we are unendingly cheerful, but what each man feels in his heart I can only guess. Pulling on foot gear in the morning is getter slower and slower, therefore every day more dangerous.

Sunday 4 March Lunch. Things looking *very* black indeed. As usual we forgot our trouble last night, got into our bags, slept splendidly on good hoosh, woke and had another, and started marching. Sun shining brightly, tracks clear, but surface covered with sandy frost-rime. All the morning we had to pull with all our strength, and in 4½ hours we covered 3½ miles. Last night it was overcast and thick, surface bad; this morning sun shining and surface as bad as ever. One has little to hope for except perhaps strong dry wind – an unlikely contingency at this time of year. Under the immediate surface crystals is a hard sustrugi surface, which must have been excellent for pulling a week or two ago. We are about 42 miles from the next depot and have a week's food, but only about 3 to 4 days' fuel – we are as economical of the latter as one can possibly be, and we cannot afford to save food and pull as we are pulling. We are in a very tight place indeed, but none of us despondent *yet*, or at least we preserve every semblance of good cheer, but one's heart sinks as the sledge stops dead at some sastrugi behind which the surface sand lies thickly heaped. For the moment the temperature is in the -20° – an improvement which makes us much more comfortable, but a colder snap is bound to come again soon. I fear that Oates at least will weather such an event very poorly. Providence to our aid! We can expect little from man now except the possibility of extra food at the next depot. It will be real bad if we get there and find the same shortage of oil. Shall we get there? Such a short distance it would have appeared to us on the summit! I don't know what I should do if Wilson and Bowers weren't so determinedly cheerful over things.

Monday 5 March Lunch. Regret to say going from bad to worse. We got a slant of wind yesterday afternoon, and going on 5 hours we converted our wretched morning run of 3½ miles into something over 9. We went to bed on a cup of cocoa and pemmican solid with the chill off. (R. 47.) The result is telling on all, but mainly on Oates, whose feet are in a wretched condition. One swelled up tremendously last night and he is very lame this morning. We started march on tea and pemmican as last night – we pretend to prefer the pemmican this way. Marched for 5 hours this morning over a slightly better surface covered with high moundy sastrugi. Sledge capsized twice; we pulled on foot, covering about 5½ miles. We are two pony marches and 4 miles about from our depot. Our fuel dreadfully low and the poor Soldier nearly done. It is pathetic enough because we can do nothing for him; more hot food might do a little, but only a little, I fear. We none of us expected these terribly low temperatures, and of the rest of us Wilson is feeling them most; mainly, I fear, from his self-sacrificing devotion in doctoring Oates' feet. We cannot help each other, each has enough to do to take care of himself. We get cold on the march when the trudging is heavy, and the wind pierces our warm garments. The others, all of them, are unendingly cheerful when in the tent. We mean to see the game through with a proper spirit, but it's tough work to be pulling harder than we ever pulled in our lives for long hours, and to feel that the progress is so slow. One can only say 'God help us!' and plod on our weary way, cold and very miserable, though outwardly cheerful. We talk of all sorts of subjects in the tent, not much of food now, since we decided to take the risk of running a full ration. We simply couldn't go hungry at this time.

Tuesday 6 March Lunch. We did a little better with help of wind yesterday afternoon, finishing 9½ miles for the day, and 27 miles from depot. [R. 48.] But this morning things have been awful. It was warm in the night and for the first time during the journey I overslept myself by more than an hour; then we were slow with foot gear; then, pulling with all our might (for our lives) we could scarcely advance at rate of a mile an hour; then it grew thick and three times we had to get out of harness to search for tracks. The result is something less than 3½ miles for the forenoon. The sun is shining now and the wind gone. Poor Oates is unable to pull, sits on the sledge when we are track-searching – he is wonderfully plucky, as his feet must be giving him great pain. He makes no complaint, but his spirits only come up in spurts now, and he grows more silent in the tent. We are making a spirit lamp to try and replace the primus when our oil is exhausted. It will be a very poor substitute and we've not got much spirit. If we could have kept up our 9-mile days we might have got within reasonable distance of the depot before running out, but nothing but a strong wind and good surface can help us now, and though we had quite a good breeze this morning, the sledge came as heavy as lead. If we were all fit I should have hopes of getting through, but the poor Soldier has become a terrible hindrance, though he does his utmost and suffers much I fear.

Wednesday 7 March A little worse I fear. One of Oates' feet *very* bad this morning; he is wonderfully brave. We still talk of what we will do together at home.

We only made 6½ miles yesterday. [R. 49.] This morning in 4½ hours we did just over 4 miles. We are 16 from our depot. If we only find the correct proportion of food there and this surface continues, we may get to the next depot [Mt. Hooper, 72 miles farther] but not to One Ton Camp. We hope against hope that the dogs have been to Mt. Hooper; then we might pull through. If there is a shortage of oil again we can have little hope. One feels that for poor Oates the crisis is near, but none of us are improving, though we are wonderfully fit considering the really excessive work we are doing. We are only kept going by good food. No wind this morning till a chill northerly air came ahead. Sun bright and cairns showing up well. I should like to keep the track to the end.

Thursday 8 March Lunch. Worse and worse in morning; poor Oates' left foot can never last out, and time over foot gear something awful. Have to wait in night foot gear for nearly an hour before I start changing, and then am generally first to be ready. Wilson's feet giving trouble now, but this mainly because he gives so much help to others. We did 4½ miles this morning and are now 8½ miles from the depot – a ridiculously small distance to feel in difficulties, yet on this surface we know we cannot equal half our old marches, and that for that effort we expend nearly double the energy. The great question is, What shall we find at the depot? If the dogs have visited it we may get along a good distance, but if there is another short allowance of fuel, God help us indeed. We are in a very bad way, I fear, in any case.

Saturday 10 March Things steadily downhill. Oates' foot worse. He has rare pluck and must know that he can never get through. He asked Wilson if he had a chance this morning, and of course Bill had to say he didn't know. In point of fact he has none. Apart from him, if he went under now, I doubt whether we could get through. With great care we might have a dog's chance, but no more. The weather conditions are awful, and our gear gets steadily more icy and difficult to manage. At the same time of course poor Titus is the greatest handicap. He keeps us waiting in the morning until we have partly lost the warming effect of our good breakfast, when the only wise policy is to be up and away at once; again at lunch. Poor chap! it is too pathetic to watch him; one cannot but try to cheer him up.

Yesterday we marched up the depot, Mt. Hooper. Cold comfort. Shortage on our allowance all round. I don't know that anyone is to blame. The dogs which would have been our salvation have evidently failed. [For the last six days the dogs had been waiting at One Ton Camp under Cherry-Garrard and Demetri. The supporting party had come out as arranged on the chance of hurrying the Pole travellers back over the last stages of their journey in time to catch the ship. Scott had dated his probable return to Hut Point anywhere between mid-March and early April. Calculating from the speed of the other return parties, Dr. Atkinson looked for him to reach One Ton Camp between 3 and 10 March. Here Cherry-Garrard met four days of blizzard; then there remained little more than enough dog food to bring the teams home. He could either push south one more march and back, at imminent risk of missing Scott on the way, or stay two days at the Camp where Scott was bound to come, if he came at all.] Meares had a bad trip home I suppose.

This morning it was calm when we breakfasted, but the wind came from W.N.W. as we broke camp. It rapidly grew in strength. After travelling for half an hour I saw that none of us could go on facing such conditions. We were forced to camp and are spending the rest of the day in a comfortless blizzard camp, wind quite foul. [R. 52.]

Sunday 11 March Titus Oates is very near the end, one feels. What we or he will do, God only knows. We discussed the matter after breakfast; he is a brave fine fellow and understands the situation, but he practically asked for advice. Nothing could be said but to urge him to march as long as he could. One satisfactory result to the discussion; I practically ordered Wilson to hand over the means of ending our troubles to us, so that anyone of us may know how to do so. Wilson had no choice between doing so and our ransacking the medicine case. We have 30 opium tabloids apiece and he is left with a tube of morphine. So far the tragical side of our story. [R. 53.]

The sky completely overcast when we started this morning. We could see nothing, lost the tracks, and doubtless have been swaying a good deal since

– 3.1 miles for the forenoon – terribly heavy dragging – expected it. Know that 6 miles is about the limit of our endurance now, if we get no help from wind or surfaces. We have 7 days' food and should be about 55 miles from One Ton Camp tonight, 6 × 7 = 42, leaving us 13 miles short of our distance, even if things get no worse. Meanwhile the season rapidly advances.

Monday 12 March We did 6.9 miles yesterday, under our necessary average. Things are left much the same, Oates not pulling much, and now with hands as well as feet pretty well useless. We did 4 miles this morning in 4 hours 20 min. – we may hope for 3 this afternoon, 7 × 6 = 42. We shall be 47 miles from the depot. I doubt if we can possibly do it. The surface remains awful, the cold intense, and our physical condition running down. God help us! Not a breath of favourable wind for more than a week, and apparently liable to head winds at any moment.

Wednesday 14 March No doubt about the going downhill, but everything going wrong for us. Yesterday we woke to a strong northerly wind with temp. -37°. Couldn't face it, so remained in camp [R. 54] till 2, then did 5¼ miles. Wanted to march later, but party feeling the cold badly as the breeze (N.) never took off entirely, and as the sun sank the temp. fell. Long time getting supper in dark. [R. 55.]

This morning started with southerly breeze, set sail and passed another cairn at good speed; half-way, however, the wind shifted to W. by S. or W.S.W., blew through our wind clothes and into our mits. Poor Wilson horribly cold, could not get off ski for some time. Bowers and I practically made camp, and when we got into the tent at last we were all deadly cold. Then temp, now midday down -43° and the wind strong. We *must* go on, but now the making of every camp must be more difficult and dangerous. It must be near the end, but a pretty merciful end. Poor Oates got it again in the foot. I shudder to think what it will be like tomorrow. It is only with greatest pains rest of us keep off frostbites. No idea there could be temperatures like this at this time of year with such winds. Truly awful outside the tent. Must fight it out to the last biscuit, but can't reduce rations.

Friday 16 or Saturday 17 March Lost track of dates, but think the last correct. Tragedy all along the line. At lunch, the day before yesterday, poor Titus Oates said he couldn't go on; he proposed we should leave him in his sleeping-bag. That we could not do, and induced him to come on, on the afternoon march. In spite of its awful nature for him he struggled on and we made a few miles. At night he was worse and we knew the end had come.

Should this be found I want these facts recorded. Oates' last thoughts were of his Mother, but immediately before he took pride in thinking that his regiment would be pleased with the bold way in which he met his death. We can testify to his bravery. He has borne intense suffering for weeks without complaint, and to the very last was able and willing to discuss outside subjects. He did not – would not – give up hope to the very end. He was a brave soul. This was the end. He slept through the night before last, hoping not to wake; but he woke in the morning – yesterday. It was blowing a blizzard. He said, 'I am just going outside and may be some time.' He went out into the blizzard and we have not seen him since.

I take this opportunity of saying that we have stuck to our sick companions to the last. In case of Edgar Evans, when absolutely out of food and he lay insensible, the safety of the remainder seemed to demand his abandonment, but Providence mercifully removed him at this critical moment. He died a natural death, and we did not leave him till two hours after his death. We knew that poor Oates was walking to his death, but though we tried to dissuade him, we knew it was the act of a brave man and an English gentleman. We all hope to meet the end with a similar spirit, and assuredly the end is not far.

I can only write at lunch and then only occasionally. The cold is intense, -40° at midday. My companions are unendingly cheerful, but we are all on the verge of serious frostbites, and though we constantly talk of fetching through I don't think anyone of us believes it in his heart.

We are cold on the march now, and at all times except meals. Yesterday we had to lay up for a blizzard and today we move dreadfully slowly. We are at No. 14 pony camp, only two pony marches from One Ton Depot. We leave here our theodolite, a camera, and Oates' sleeping-bags. Diaries, etc., and geological specimens carried at Wilson's special request, will be found with us or on our sledge.

Sunday 18 March Today, lunch, we are 21 miles from the depot. Ill fortune presses, but better may come. We have had more wind and drift from ahead yesterday; had to stop marching; wind N.W., force 4, temp. -35°. No human being could face it, and we are worn out *nearly*.

My right foot has gone, nearly all the toes – two days ago I was proud possessor of best feet. These are the steps of my downfall. Like an ass I mixed a small spoonful of curry powder with my melted pemmican – it gave me violent indigestion. I lay awake and in pain all night; woke and felt done on the march; foot went and I didn't know it. A very small measure of neglect and have a foot which is not pleasant to contemplate. Bowers takes first place in condition, but there is not much to choose after all. The others are still confident of getting through – or pretend to be – I don't know! We have the last *half* fill of oil in our primus and a very small quantity of spirit – this alone between us and thirst. The wind is fair for the moment, and that is perhaps a fact to help. The mileage would have seemed ridiculously small on our outward journey.

Monday 19 March Lunch. We camped with difficulty last night, and were dreadfully cold till after our supper of cold pemmican and biscuit and a half a pannikin of cocoa cooked over the spirit. Then, contrary to expectation, we got warm and all slept well. Today we started in the usual dragging manner. Sledge dreadfully heavy. We are 15½ miles from the depot and ought to get there in three days. What progress! We have two days' food but barely a day's fuel. All our feet are getting bad – Wilson's best, my right foot worst, left all right. There is no chance to nurse one's feet till we can get hot food into us. Amputation is the least I can hope for now, but will the trouble spread? That is the serious question. The weather doesn't give us a chance – the wind from N. to N.W. and -40° temp, today.

Wednesday 21 March Got within 11 miles of depot Monday night [the 60th camp from the Pole]; had to lay up all yesterday in severe blizzard.²⁷ Today forlorn hope, Wilson and Bowers going to depot for fuel.

22 and 23 Blizzard bad as ever – Wilson and Bowers unable to start – tomorrow last chance – no fuel and only one or two of food left – must be near the end. Have decided it shall be natural – we shall march for the depot with or without our effects and die in our tracks.

[Thursday] 29 March Since the 21st we have had a continuous gale from W.S.W. and S.W. We had fuel to make two cups of tea apiece and bare food for two days on the 20th. Every day we have been ready to start for our depot *11 miles* away, but outside the door of the tent it remains a scene of whirling drift. I do not think we can hope for any better things now. We shall stick it out to the end, but we are getting weaker, of course, and the end cannot be far.

It seems a pity, but I do not think I can write more.

R. Scott

Last entry.
For God's sake look after our people.

FAREWELL LETTERS

Wilson and Bowers were found in the attitude of sleep, their sleeping-bags closed over their heads as they would naturally close them.

Scott died later. He had thrown back the flaps of his sleeping-bag and opened his coat. The little wallet containing the three notebooks was under his shoulders and his arm flung across Wilson. So they were found eight months later.

With the diaries in the tent were found the following letters:

TO MRS. E. A. WILSON

My dear Mrs. Wilson,

If this letter reaches you Bill and I will have gone out together. We are very near it now and I should like you to know how splendid he was at the end – everlastingly cheerful and ready to sacrifice himself for others, never a word of blame to me for leading him into this mess. He is not suffering, luckily, at least only minor discomforts.

His eyes have a comfortable blue look of hope and his mind is peaceful with the satisfaction of his faith in regarding himself as part of the great scheme of the Almighty. I can do no more to comfort you than to tell you that he died as he lived, a brave, true man – the best of comrades and staunchest of friends. My whole heart goes out to you in pity,

Yours,

R. Scott.

TO MRS. BOWERS

My dear Mrs. Bowers,

I am afraid this will reach you after one of the heaviest blows of your life.

I write when we are very near the end of our journey, and I am finishing it in company with two gallant, noble gentlemen. One of these is your son. He had come to be one of my closest and soundest friends, and I appreciate his wonderful upright nature, his ability and energy. As the troubles have thickened his dauntless spirit ever shone brighter and he has remained cheerful, hopeful, and indomitable to the end.

The ways of Providence are inscrutable, but there must be some reason why such a young, vigorous and promising life is taken.

My whole heart goes out in pity for you.

Yours,
R. Scott.

To the end he has talked of you and his sisters. One sees what a happy home he must have had and perhaps it is well to look back on nothing but happiness.

He remains unselfish, self-reliant and splendidly hopeful to the end, believing in God's mercy to you.

TO SIR J. M. BARRIE

My dear Barrie,

We are pegging out in a very comfortless spot. Hoping this letter may be found and sent to you, I write a word of farewell ... More practically I want you to help my widow and my boy – your godson. We are showing that Englishmen can still die with a bold spirit, fighting it out to the end. It will be known that we have accomplished our object in reaching the Pole, and that we have done everything possible, even to sacrificing ourselves in order to save sick companions. I think this makes an example for Englishmen of the future, and that the country ought to help those who are left behind to mourn us. I leave my poor girl and your godson, Wilson leaves a widow, and Edgar Evans also a widow in humble circumstances. Do what you can to get their claims recognised. Goodbye. I am not at all afraid of the end, but sad to miss many a humble pleasure which I had planned for the future on our long marches. I may not have proved a great explorer, but we have done the greatest march ever made and come very near to great success. Goodbye, my dear friend,

Yours ever,
R. Scott.

We are in a desperate state, feet frozen, etc. No fuel and a long way from food, but it would do your heart good to be in our tent, to hear our songs and the cheery conversation as to what we will do when we get to Hut Point.

Later We are very near the end, but have not and will not lose our good cheer. We have four days of storm in our tent and nowhere's food or fuel. We did intend to finish ourselves when things proved like this, but we have decided to die naturally in the track.

As a dying man, my dear friend, be good to my wife and child. Give the boy a chance in life if the State won't do it. He ought to have good stuff in him ... I never met a man in my life whom I admired and loved more than you, but I never could show you how much your friendship meant to me, for you had much to give and I nothing.

TO THE RIGHT HON. SIR EDGAR SPEYER, BART.

Dated 16 March 1912. Lat. 79.5°.

My dear Sir Edgar,

I hope this may reach you. I fear we must go and that it leaves the Expedition in a bad muddle. But we have been to the Pole and we shall die like gentlemen. I regret only for the women we leave behind.

I thank you a thousand times for your help and support and your generous kindness. If this diary is found it will show how we stuck by dying companions and fought the thing out well to the end. I think this will show that the Spirit of pluck and power to endure has not passed out of our race ...

Wilson, the best fellow that ever stepped, has sacrificed himself again and again to the sick men of the party ...

I write to many friends hoping the letters will reach them some time after we are found next year.

We very nearly came through, and it's a pity to have missed it, but lately I have felt that we have overshot our mark. No one is to blame and I hope no attempt will be made to suggest that we have lacked support.

Good-bye to you and your dear kind wife.

Yours ever sincerely,

R. Scott.

TO VICE-ADMIRAL SIR FRANCIS CHARLES BRIDGEMAN, K.C.V.O., K.C.B.

My dear Sir Francis,

I fear we have shipped up; a close shave; I am writing a few letters which I hope will be delivered some day. I want to thank you for the friendship you gave me of late years, and to tell you how extraordinarily pleasant I found it to serve under you. I want to tell you that I was not too old for this job. It was the younger men that went under first ... After all we are setting a good example to our countrymen, if not by getting into a tight place, by facing it like men when we were there. We could have come through had we neglected the sick.

Good-bye, and good-bye to dear Lady Bridgeman.

Yours ever,

R. Scott.

Excuse writing – it is -40°, and has been for nigh a month.

TO VICE-ADMIRAL SIR GEORGE LE CLEARC EGERTON, K.C.B.

My dear Sir George,

I fear we have shot our bolt – but we have been to Pole and done the longest journey on record.

I hope these letters may find their destination some day.

Subsidiary reasons of our failure to return are due to the sickness of different members of the party, but the real thing that has stopped us is the awful weather and unexpected cold towards the end of the journey.

This traverse of the Barrier has been quite three times as severe as any experience we had on the summit.

There is no accounting for it, but the result has thrown out my calculations, and here we are little more than 100 miles from the base and petering out.

Good-bye. Please see my widow is looked after as far as Admiralty is concerned.

R. SCOTT.

My kindest regards to Lady Egerton. I can never forget all your kindness.

TO MR. J. J. KINSEY – CHRISTCHURCH

24 March 1912

MY DEAR KINSEY,

I'm afraid we are pretty well done – four days of blizzard just as we were getting to the last depot. My thoughts have been with you often. You have been a brick. You will pull the expedition through, I'm sure.

My thoughts are for my wife and boy. Will you do what you can for them if the country won't.

I want the boy to have a good chance in the world, but you know the circumstances well enough.

If I knew the wife and boy were in safe keeping I should have little regret in leaving the world, for I feel that the country need not be ashamed of us – our journey has been the biggest on record, and nothing but the most exceptional hard luck at the end would have caused us to fail to return. We have been to the S. pole as we set out. God bless you and dear Mrs. Kinsey. It is good to remember you and your kindness.

Your friend,
R. SCOTT.

Letters to his Mother, his Wife, his Brother-in-law (Sir William Ellison Macartney), Admiral Sir Lewis Beaumont, and Mr. and Mrs. Reginald Smith were also found, from which come the following extracts:

The Great God has called me and I feel it will add a fearful blow to the heavy ones that have fallen on you in life. But take comfort in that I die at peace with the world and myself – not afraid.

Indeed it has been most singularly unfortunate, for the risks I have taken never seemed excessive.

… I want to tell you that we have missed getting through by a narrow margin which was justifiably within the risk of such a journey … After all, we have given our lives for our country – we have actually made the longest journey on record, and we have been the first Englishmen at the South Pole.

You must understand that it is too cold to write much.

… It's a pity the luck doesn't come our way, because every detail of equipment is right.

I shall not have suffered any pain, but leave the world fresh from harness and full of good health and vigour.

Since writing the above we got to within 11 miles of our depot, with one hot meal and two days' cold food. We should have got through but have been held for *four* days by a frightful storm. I think the best chance has gone. We have decided not to kill ourselves, but to fight to the last for that depot, but in the fighting there is a painless end.

Make the boy interested in natural history if you can; it is better than games; they encourage it at some schools. I know you will keep him in the open air.

Above all, he must guard and you must guard him against indolence. Make him a strenuous man. I had to force myself into being strenuous as you know – had always an inclination to be idle.

There is a piece of the Union Jack I put up at the South Pole in my private kit bag, together with Amundsen's black flag and other trifles. Send a small piece of the Union Jack to the King and a small piece to Queen Alexandra.

What lots and lots I could tell you of this journey. How much better has it been than lounging in too great comfort at home. What tales you would have for the boys. But what a price to pay.

Tell Sir Clements – I thought much of him and never regretted him putting me in command of the *Discovery*.

MESSAGE TO THE PUBLIC

The causes of the disaster are not due to faulty organisation, but to misfortune in all risks which had to be undertaken.

1. The loss of pony transport in March 1911 obliged me to start later than I had intended, and obliged the limits of stuff transported to be narrowed.

2. The weather throughout the outward journey, and especially the long gale in 83° S., stopped us.

3. The soft snow in lower reaches of glacier again reduced pace.

We fought these untoward events with a will and conquered, but it cut into our provision reserve.

Every detail of our food supplies, clothing and depots made on the interior ice-sheet and over that long stretch of 700 miles to the Pole and back, worked out to perfection. The advance party would have returned to the glacier in fine form and with surplus of food, but for the astonishing failure of the man whom we had least expected to fail. Edgar Evans was thought the strongest man of the party.

The Beardmore Glacier is not difficult in fine weather, but on our return we did not get a single completely fine day; this with a sick companion enormously increased our anxieties.

As I have said elsewhere we got into frightfully rough ice and Edgar Evans received a concussion of the brain – he died a natural death, but left us a shaken party with the season unduly advanced.

But all the facts above enumerated were as nothing to the surprise which awaited us on the Barrier. I maintain that our arrangements for returning were quite adequate, and that no one in the world would have expected the temperatures and surfaces which we encountered at this time of the year.

On the summit in lat. 85° 86° we had -20°, -30°. On the Barrier in lat. 82°, 10,000 feet lower, we had -30° in the day, -47° at night pretty regularly, with continuous head wind during our day marches. It is clear that these circumstances come on very suddenly, and our wreck is certainly due to this sudden advent of severe weather, which does not seem to have any satisfactory cause. I do not think human beings ever came through such a month as we have come through, and we should have got through in spite of the weather but for the sickening of a second companion, Captain Oates, and a shortage of fuel in our depots for which I cannot account, and finally, but for the storm which has fallen on us within 11 miles of the depot at which we hoped to secure our final supplies. Surely misfortune could scarcely have exceeded this last blow. We arrived within 11 miles of our old One Ton Camp with fuel for one last meal and food for two days. For four days we have been unable to leave the tent – the gale howling about us. We are weak, writing is difficult, but for my own sake I do not regret this journey, which has shown that Englishmen can endure hardships, help one another, and meet death with as great a fortitude as ever in the past. We took risks, we knew we took them; things have come out against us, and therefore we have no cause for complaint, but bow to the will of Providence, determined still to do our best to the last. But if we have been willing to give our lives to this enterprise, which is for the honour of our country, I appeal to our countrymen to see that those who depend on us are properly cared for.

Had we lived, I should have had a tale to tell of the hardihood, endurance, and courage of my companions which would have stirred the heart of every Englishman. These rough notes and our dead bodies must tell the tale, but surely, surely, a great rich country like ours will see that those who are dependent on us are properly provided for.

R. Scott.

THE FINDING OF THE POLAR PARTY, 29 OCTOBER 1912 – 25 NOVEMBER 1912 BY E. L. ATKINSON

On 29 October the mules all came down with their leaders to Hut Point and everything was ready for a start on the journey south. It was decided to march at night as we had done in the previous season, so that the mules would be moving during this cold time and camp during the warm portion of the day.

At 7.30 p.m. on 30 October the seven mules and eight men making up the Pony Party started south. C. S. Wright was in command, as he was a skilled navigator. The mules and their leaders were as follows:

E. W. Nelson, leading Khan Sahib; T. Gran, leading Lai Khan; W. Lashly, leading Pyaree; T. Crean, leading Rani; T. Williamson, leading Gulab; P. Keohane, leading Begum; F. J. Hooper, leading Abdullah.

Wright was in command and went ahead, setting the course and standing by to give any help he could. The mules' weights up to Corner Camp would not exceed 500 lbs. This was because of the deep and bad surface usually occurring over this area. The tents were under Wright and Nelson. It was proposed to march twelve geographical miles every night, but, as their progress was uncertain, the question of this distance was left entirely to Wright's judgment.

Pyaree started lame, but within a few days had lost any slight trouble which she had. Gulab had proved that he would chafe easily with the breast harness, and in his case a collar was taken as well. Their first day they did twelve miles, camping about six miles to the S.E. of Safety Camp. Where the sea-ice joined the Barrier there was a wide tide-crack, and Khan Sahib unluckily fell partially into this; he was a very quiet animal, and with the aid of an Alpine rope and hauling on his fore-legs they got him up and over on to the surface.

The next day they made good another twelve miles over a slightly worse surface, camping within six miles of Corner Camp. Owing to the dogs' experience in the earlier part of the year, we realised that this area was more crevassed than it had been previously. I had left it to Wright's judgment as to whether the leaders of the mules were to be linked up by the Alpine rope in going over these last six miles. He thought it fit to do this and they proceeded in that order. The surface they encountered was exceedingly deep and heavy, and only two of the mules struck crevasses and these, luckily, without any mishap. The mules were so tired when they had finished the six miles to Corner Camp that Wright decided to remain there for half a day.

On 1 November the two dog-teams, with Cherry-Garrard, Demetri, and myself, started to follow the mules. The dogs' loads, which had been made out to allow about 75 lbs. per dog, proved to be heavy from the start; the progress was exceedingly slow and we completed fifteen miles for the first day. The next day, again over a very bad surface, we completed another fifteen miles and reached Corner Camp. There we had a very reassuring note from Wright. He said that the mules were going well together and, instead of having to be split up into fast and slow mules, they broke camp and pitched camp, with one exception, all together, for Khan Sahib, Nelson's mule, was peculiarly slow, and in the temperature we were encountering on the march Nelson found it of the greatest difficulty to keep himself at all warm. This mule would usually lose ¾ of a mile on the others while they were completing two miles. Nelson invented a method of walking two steps forward and lumping one back, in order to keep his circulation up to the mark.

They proceeded, building cairns of snow at intervals of from two to four miles in order that we might follow their tracks.

I saw from the way that the dogs were going that we should have great difficulty, with their present weights, in catching the mules before they reached One Ton Depot. On Wright's satisfactory report I decided to entrust everything to the mules and to use the dogs as a means of lightening their heavy loads. The mules' weights had increased from Corner Camp up to nearly 700 lbs. per mule.

This was far in excess of any weights hauled by the ponies in the previous season, and here we saw the advantage of having tapered runners to our sledges. The beasts, with comparative ease, were able to move these heavy loads on the sledges, where they would have been unable to do so with the broad runners of the previous 12-foot sledge.

Wright proceeded the next day to Demetri Depot, twelve miles south from Corner Camp. The mules here took on their full loads and proceeded south before we could get up to them. Here the remainder of the surplus weights of the dogs was left.

Kasoi, one of the dogs, had refused for that day to work; no amount of beating would induce him to do so. We therefore took him off the trace and tied him with the harness to the rear of the sledge. Demetri's team, who were following, realised that something was wrong with this dog: they pulled their very hardest with the idea of getting up to him and finishing him. Kasoi realised what this meant, and it decided him in favour of work as nothing else could have done. He resumed his pulling, and never slackened his trace afterwards.

On the night of the 4th and the morning of the 5th of November we had got on to a very good surface; we started early and light, in order to reach the mules before they had started, and this we eventually did after we had made our twelve miles. In view of their condition and

the tired dogs I decided to give animals and men a day's rest at this place. The weather, which had been windy and drifting up to now, had begun to clear and would give the animals some chance of drying off, as well as having a good night's rest.

Gulab, Williamson's mule, had been badly chafed by the breast harness on his shoulder. Williamson had changed him to his collar and almost immediately after the first day of this he chafed again. Throughout the whole of his journey Williamson took the very greatest care of his animal and invented various new and clever designs for taking the weight of his draught off his chafed shoulder. Eventually Gulab's tail was brought as an aid to this. By means of a back strap connecting his collar and his tail most of the drag was taken off his shoulder and, under these conditions, the chafe began to heal.

About this time, as the lights were very strong, the mules began to show signs of snow-blindness. It was then that their snow-goggles were tried for the first time. We found that they were of the greatest use and generally stayed on while the mules were on their lines; they were of the greatest comfort to the animals.

The mules would not eat their ration of oil cake and oats at all. They showed a liking for everything except their ration. They would eat man or dog biscuits, tea-leaves and tobacco, ash and various portions of garments, with the greatest of relish, but they needed the utmost care and coaxing to be induced to touch their ration at all. They were picketed by their fore-legs, as the ponies had been in the previous year, and they showed the greatest ingenuity in getting themselves free and strolling about the camp, testing various articles of the store goods.

The same routine was kept by this party. The morning march was seven miles in length; they then camped and had tea, which lasted for about one hour and a half. When camp was struck, they marched on for five miles more, completing the twelve geographical miles for the day. Their speed on march was favourable compared with that of the ponies of the previous year. Our surfaces were so hard and good that the mules did not with their small hooves sink appreciably into the snow.

The dogs' weights here having been much reduced, they were able to relieve the mules to a large extent. The routine of the march was now changed: from one to two hours after the mules had started, the dogs followed them. The change in the dogs and in their rate of progress was now wonderful: when they had something to follow, and especially when the mules came into view, they proceeded during the whole of the day at a full gallop.

Abdullah, Hooper's mule, had constituted himself leader throughout, and continued so until his return from the Barrier towards the end of November. This was a difficult feat, as the first mule has always the added hardship of having to break the track.

The surface was extremely good, hard, and almost marbled, and the sledges followed the animals easily.

Each night, on camping, a wall was built for the mules, consisting of large slabs of hard snow dug in the Barrier; they were a considerable amount of trouble, but afforded shelter to the beasts from the wind and drift. The mules had so eaten their covers that it required much ingenuity to make these useful for protecting the beasts.

The day's rest had done everyone good, and on a glorious day we proceeded and soon finished the twelve miles for the day.

On the night of the 6th and 7th we started at 10.30, and, on a slightly worse surface, did seven miles up to lunch. All along this way we had been building cairns of snow at intervals of from two to four miles apart. The day, which was cloudy, cleared towards morning, and was much colder. During this time we were marching in temperature which ranged from -20 to the lowest of -29. In the daytime, when the sun had reached its full height, the temperature would rise almost to zero.

On the night of the 7th and morning of the 8th of November we made the old Bluff Depot in 79° South and re-built it, placing a new flag of black bunting on the pole. Here we left two boxes of dog biscuit for the dogs returning on their journey back from the south. The surface again continued good, and never in any previous experience had it been so hard and good as far south as this.

On the night of the 8th and 9th we continued over this same good surface, before a slight north-easterly wind and a cold day. The dogs had now again begun to fail. They seemed to lack enthusiasm and spirit; I believe that in their case they had had too much work upon the Barrier and were spiritless and easily depressed by the lack of anything to see. In the previous year we had had certain 'cuts' of land for the Bluff Depot and Corner Camp. It was quite easy to see from these that both camps had changed their positions owing to the gradual movement of the Barrier, year by year. Approximately, and judging very roughly, the movement in either case had been about half a mile for the year.

On the night of the 9th and 10th we came again to a curious phenomenon of the Barrier surface. As the mules proceeded ahead of us loud crackling roars could be heard from time to time. These were caused by a subsidence of the surface over a large area, as an animal or man trod upon it. The depth of the subsidence was only a fraction of an inch, but the resulting report was exceedingly loud and startling, if unexpected. The mules soon settled down to the roars and became accustomed to them, but it was always a source of great interest to the dogs.

As soon as one of these subsidences with its roar came to them they started off at full gallop, expecting at any moment some animal to appear. They had been accustomed in Siberia to dig out animals lying up snowed in. These subsidences were a great help and kept the dogs interested, and they ran very well.

On the night of the 10th and morning of the 11th we made One Ton Depot, coming up 5¾ miles to it. I decided to give men and animals a half-day's rest here. It was a beautiful sunny and bright day but with some wind. Here we found the stores which had been left by Demetri and Cherry-Garrard. One of the tins of paraffin on top of the cairns had leaked and spoilt some of the stores placed at the foot of the camp. There was no hole of any kind in this tin.

Our progress up to this point had been made in a day and a half less time than it had taken us on the previous year, and that was with the mules drawing full loads for the whole of the time. There was no doubt that our surface had been infinitely better than in the previous season. Everything was favourable and the health of men and animals was splendid.

On the night of the 11th and morning of the 12th, after we had marched eleven miles due south of One Ton, we found the tent. It was an object partially snowed up and looking like a cairn. Before it were the ski sticks and in front of them a bamboo which probably was the mast of the sledge. The tent was practically on the line of cairns which we had built in the previous season. It was within a quarter of a mile of the remains of the cairn, which showed as a small hummock beneath the snow.

Inside the tent were the bodies of Captain Scott, Doctor Wilson, and Lieutenant Bowers. They had pitched their tent well, and it had withstood all the blizzards of an exceptionally hard winter. Each man of the Expedition recognised the bodies. From Captain Scott's diary I found his reasons for this disaster. When the men had been assembled I read to them these reasons, the place of death of Petty Officer Evans, and the story of Captain Oates' heroic end.

We recovered all their gear and dug out the sledge with their belongings on it. Amongst these were 35 lbs. of very important geological specimens which had been collected on the moraines of the Beardmore Glacier; at Doctor Wilson's request they had stuck to these up to the very end, even when disaster stared them in the face and they knew that the specimens were so much weight added to what they had to pull.

When everything had been gathered up, we covered them with the outer tent and read the Burial Service. From this time until well into the next day we started to build a mighty cairn above them. This cairn was finished the next morning, and upon it a rough cross was placed, made from the greater portion of two skis, and on either side were up-ended two sledges, and they were fixed firmly in the snow, to be an added mark. Between the eastern sledge and the cairn a bamboo was placed, containing a metal cylinder, and in this the following record was left:

'12 November 1912, lat. 79 degrees, 50 mins. South. This cross and cairn are erected over the bodies of Captain Scott, C.V.O., R.N., Doctor E. A. Wilson, M.B., B.C., Cantab., and Lieutenant H. R. Bowers, Royal Indian Marine – a slight token to perpetuate their successful and gallant attempt to reach the Pole. This they did on 17 January 1912, after the Norwegian Expedition had already done so. Inclement weather with lack of fuel was the cause of their death. Also to commemorate their two gallant comrades, Captain L. E. G. Oates of the Inniskilling Dragoons, who walked to his death in a blizzard to save his comrades about eighteen miles south of this position; also of Seaman Edgar Evans, who died at the foot of the Beardmore Glacier. "The Lord gave and the Lord taketh away; blessed be the name of the Lord."'

This was signed by all the members of the party. I decided then to march twenty miles south with the whole of the Expedition and try to find the body of Captain Oates.

For half that day we proceeded south, as far as possible along the line of the previous season's march. On one of the old pony walls, which was simply marked by a ridge of the surface of the snow, we found Oates' sleeping-bag, which they had brought along with them after he had left.

The next day we proceeded thirteen more miles south, hoping and searching to find his body. When we arrived at the place where he had left them, we saw that there was no chance of doing so. The kindly snow had covered his body, giving him a fitting burial. Here, again, as near to the site of the death as we could judge, we built another cairn to his memory, and placed thereon a small cross and the following record: 'Hereabouts died a very gallant gentleman, Captain L. E. G. Oates of the Inniskilling Dragoons. In March 1912, returning from the Pole, he walked willingly to his death in a blizzard, to try and save his comrades, beset by hardships. This note is left by the Relief Expedition of 1912.'

It was signed by Cherry and myself.

From here I decided to turn back and to take, as far as possible, all the stores to Hut Point. I then thought that by any means that lay within our power we should try to reach Lieutenant Campbell and his party. As the sea-ice would in all likelihood be impossible, we should probably have to take the route along the plateau, ascending the first Ferrar Glacier and making our way along the plateau as far as we were able.

On the second day we came again to the resting-place of the three and bade them there a final farewell. There alone in their greatness they will lie without change or bodily decay, with the most fitting tomb in the world above them.

Our journey back was uneventful. Two of the mules had to be killed because of their condition and to give food to the dogs. Five returned from the Barrier, and for the remainder of their days had as good a time as we could give them.

On the morning of 25 November two dog teams, with Cherry-Garrard, Demetri, and myself, having pushed ahead of the mules, reached Hut Point. Cherry went into the hut and returned with a letter and his face transformed. I think we had then the best news that any men could wish for many, many a long weary day. Campbell and his party, having all survived the winter, had made their way down, arriving at Hut Point on 6 November.

We proceeded in all haste to Cape Evans, there to have the goodly sight of their rounding countenances. They had filled out wonderfully on the good and unusual food, and each and every one was now heavier than he had ever been in his life. It was a sad home-coming for them after their hard time.

I can only here say that I can never be sufficiently grateful to all the members of the Expedition who were with me during this bad season, for their entire loyalty and good-fellowship; never one moment's trouble and always cheerful and willing.

NOTES

1. Dogs. These included thirty-three sledging dogs and a collie bitch, 'Lassie'. The thirty-three, all Siberian dogs excepting the Esquimaux 'Peary' and 'Borup', were collected by Mr. Meares, who drove them across Siberia to Vladivostok with the help of the dog-driver Demetri Gerof, whom he had engaged for the expedition. From Vladivostok, where he was joined by Lieutenant Wilfred Bruce, he brought them by steamer to Sydney, and thence to Lyttelton.

The dogs were the gift of various schools, as shown by the following list:

DOGS PRESENTED BY SCHOOLS, &C.

School's, &c., name for Dog.	Russian name of Dog.	Translation, description, or nickname of Dog.	Name of School, &c., that presented Dog.
Beaumont	Kumgai	Isle off Vladivostok	Beaumont College.
Bengeo	Mannike Noogis	LittleLeader	Bengeo, Herts.
Bluecoat	Giliak	Indian tribe	Christ's Hospital.
Bristol	LappaUki	Lop Ears	Grammar, Bristol.
Bromsgrove	'Peary'	'Peary'	Bromsgrove School (cost of transport).
Colston's	Bullet	Bullet	Colston's School.
Danum	Rabchick	Grouse	Doncaster Grammar Sch.
Derby I.	Suka	Lassie	Girls' Secondary School, Derby.
Derby II.	Silni	Stocky	Secondary Technical School, Derby.
Devon	Jolti	Yellowboy	Devonshire House Branch of Navy League.
Duns	Brodiaga	Robber	Berwickshire High School.

School's, &c., name for Dog.	Russian name of Dog.	Translation, description, or nickname of Dog.	Name of School, &c., that presented Dog.
Falcon	Seri	Grey	High School, Winchester
Felsted	Visoli	Jollyboy	Felsted School.
Glebe	Pestry	Piebald	Glebe House School.
Grassendale	Suhoi II.	Lanky	Grassendale School.
Hal	Krisravitsa	Beauty	Colchester Royal Grammar School.
Hampstead	Ishak	Jackass	South Hampstead High School (Girls).
Hughie	Gerachi	Ginger	Master H. Gethin Lewis.
Ilkley	Wolk	Wolf	Ilkley Grammar.
Innie	Suhoi I.	Lanky	Liverpool Institute.
Jersey	Bear	Bear	Victoria College, Jersey
John Bright	Seri Uki	Grey Ears	Bootham.
Laleham	Biela Noogis	White Leader	Laleham.
Leighton	Pudil	Poodle	Leighton Park, Reading.
Lyon	Trésor	Treasure	Lower School of J. Lyon.
Mac	Deek I.	Wild One	Wells House.
Manor	Colonel	Colonel	Manor House.
Mount	Vesoi	One Eye	Mount, York.
Mundella	Bulli	Bullet	Mundella Secondary.
Oakfield	Ruggiola Sabaka	' Gun Dog ' (Hound)	Oakfield School, Rugby.
Oldham	Vaida	Christian name	Hulme Grammar School, Oldham.
Perse	Vaska	Lady's name	Perse Grammar.
Poacher	Malchick Chorney Stareek	Black Old Man	Grammar School, Lincoln.
Price Llewelyn	Hohol	Little Russian	Intermediate, Llandudno Wells.
Radlyn	Czigane	Gipsy	Radlyn, Harrogate.
Richmond	Osman	Christian name	Richmond, Yorks.
Regent	Marakas seri	Grey	Regent Street Polytechnic.
Steyne	Petichka	Little Bird	Steyne, Worthing.
Sir Andrew	Deek II.	Wild One	Sir Andrew Judd's Commercial School.
Somerset	Churnie kesoi	One eye	Somerset School, 13 Somerset Street, W.
Tiger	Mukáka	Monkey	Bournemouth School.
Tom	Stareek	Old Man	Woodbridge.
Tua r Golleniai	Julik	Scamp	Intermediate School, Cardiff.
Vic	Glinie	Long Nose	Modern, Southport.
Whitgift	Mamuke Rabchick	Little Grouse	Whitgift Grammar.
Winston	Borup	Borup	Winston Higher Grade School (cost of transport).
	Meduate	Lion	N.Z. Girls' School.

2. Those who are named in these opening pages were all keen supporters of the Expedition. Sir George Clifford, Bart., and Messrs. Arthur and George Rhodes were friends from Christchurch. Mr. M. J. Miller, Mayor of Lyttelton, was a master shipwright and contractor, who took great interest in both the *Discovery* and the *Terra Nova*, and stopped the leak in the latter vessel which had been so troublesome on the voyage out. Mr. Anderson belonged to the firm of John Anderson & Sons, engineers, who own Lyttelton Foundry. Mr. Kinsey was the trusted friend and representative who acted as the representative of Captain Scott in New Zealand during his absence in the South. Mr. Wyatt was business manager to the Expedition.

3. Dr. Wilson writes: I must say I enjoyed it all from beginning to end, and as one bunk became unbearable after another, owing to the wet, and the comments became more and more to the point as people searched out dry spots here and there to finish the night in oilskins and greatcoats on the cabin or ward-room seats, I thought things were becoming interesting.

Some of the staff were like dead men with sea-sickness. Even so Cherry-Garrard and Wright and Day turned out with the rest of us and alternately worked and were sick.

I have no sea-sickness on these ships myself under any conditions, so I enjoyed it all, and as I have the run of the bridge and can ask as many questions as I choose, I knew all that was going on.

All Friday and Friday night we worked in two parties, two hours on and two hours off; it was heavy work filling and handing up huge buckets of water as fast as they could be given from one to the other from the very bottom of the stokehold to the upper deck, up little metal ladders all the way. One was of course wet through the whole time in a sweater and trousers and sea boots, and every two hours one took these off and hurried in for a rest in a greatcoat, to turn out again in two hours and put in the same cold sopping clothes, and so on until 4 a.m. on Saturday, when we had baled out between four and five tons of water and had so lowered it that it was once more possible to light fires and try the engines and the steam pump again and to clear the valves and the inlet which was once more within reach. The fires had been put out at 11.40 a.m. and were then out for twenty-two hours while we baled. It was a weird night's work with the howling gale and the darkness and the immense seas running over the ship every few minutes and no engines and no sail, and we all in the engine-room, black as ink with the engine-room oil and bilge water, singing chanties as we passed up slopping buckets full of bilge, each man above slopping a little over the heads of all below him; wet through to the skin, so much so that some of the party worked altogether naked like Chinese coolies; and the rush of the wave backwards and forwards at the bottom grew hourly less in the dim light of a couple of engine-room oil lamps whose light just made the darkness visible, the ship all the time rolling like a sodden lifeless log, her lee gunwale under water every time.

3 December We were all at work till 4 a.m. and then were all told off to sleep till 8 a.m. At 9.30 a.m. we were all on to the main hand pump, and, lo and behold! it worked, and we pumped and pumped till 12.30, when the ship was once more only as full of bilge water as she always is and the position was practically solved.

There was one thrilling moment in the midst of the worst hour on Friday when we were realising that the fires must be drawn, and when every pump had failed to act, and when the bulwarks began to go to pieces and the petrol cases were all afloat and going overboard, and the word was suddenly passed in a shout from the hands at work in the waist of the ship trying to save petrol cases that smoke was coming up through the seams in the after hold. As this was full of coal and patent fuel and was next the engine-room, and as it had not been opened for the airing, it required to get rid of gas on account of the flood of water on deck making it impossible to open the hatchways; the possibility of a fire there was patent to everyone and it could not possibly have been dealt with in any way short of opening the hatches and flooding the ship, when she must have floundered. It was therefore a thrilling moment or two until it was discovered that the smoke was really steam, arising from the bilge at the bottom having risen to the heated coal.

4. *26 December* We watched two or three immense blue whales at fairly short distance; this is *Balænoptera Sibbaldi*. One sees first a small dark hump appear and then immediately a jet of grey fog squirted upwards fifteen to eighteen feet, gradually spreading as it rises vertically into the frosty air. I have been nearly in these blows once or twice and had the moisture in my face with a sickening smell of shrimpy oil. Then the bump elongates and up rolls an immense blue-grey or blackish grey round back with a faint ridge along the top, on which presently appears a small hook-like dorsal fin, and then the whole sinks and disappears. [Dr. Wilson's Journal]

5. *18 December* Watered ship at a tumbled floe. Sea-ice when pressed up into large hummocks gradually loses all its salt. Even when sea water freezes it squeezes out the great bulk of its salt as a solid, but the sea water gets into it by soaking again, and yet when held out of the water, as it is in a hummock, the salt all drains out and the melted ice is blue and quite good for drinking, engines, etc. [Dr. Wilson's Journal]

6. It may be added that in contradistinction to the nicknames of Skipper conferred upon Evans, and Mate on Campbell, Scott himself was known among the afterguard as The Owner.

7. *Penguins* They have lost none of their attractiveness, and are most comical and interesting; as curious as ever, they will always come up at a trot when we sing to them, and you may often see a group of explorers on the poop singing 'For she's got bells on her fingers and rings on her toes, elephants to ride upon wherever she goes,' and so on at the top of their voices to an admiring group of Adélie penguins. Meares is the greatest attraction; he has a full voice which is musical but always very flat. He declares that 'God save the King' will always send them to the water, and certainly it is often successful. [Dr. Wilson's Journal]

8. We were to examine the possibilities of landing, but the swell was so heavy in its break among the floating blocks of ice along the actual beach and ice foot that a landing was out of the question. We should have broken up the boat and have all been in the water together. But I assure you it was tantalising to me, for there about 6 feet above us on a small dirty piece of the old bay ice about ten feet square one living Emperor penguin chick was standing disconsolately stranded, and close by stood one faithful old Emperor parent asleep. This young Emperor was still in the down, a most interesting fact in the bird's life history at which we had rightly guessed, but which no one had actually observed before. It was in a stage never yet seen or collected, for the wings were already quite clean of down and feathered as in the adult, also a line down the breast was shed of down, and part of the head. This bird would have been a treasure to me, but we could not risk life for it, so it had to remain where it was. It was a curious fact that with as much clean ice to live on as they could have wished for, these destitute derelicts of a flourishing colony now gone north to sea on floating bay ice should have preferred to remain standing on the only piece of bay ice left, a piece about ten feet square and now pressed up six feet above water level, evidently wondering why it was so long in starting north with the general exodus which must have taken place just a month ago. The whole incident was most interesting and full of suggestion as to the slow working of the brain of these queer people. Another point was most weird to see, that on the under side of this very dirty piece of sea-ice, which was about two feet thick and which hung over the water as a sort of cave, we could see the legs and lower halves of dead Emperor chicks hanging through, and even in one place a dead adult. I hope to make a picture of the whole quaint incident, for it was a corner crammed full of Imperial history in the light of what we already knew, and it would otherwise have been about as unintelligible as any group of animate or inanimate nature could possibly have been. As it is, it throws more light on the life history of this strangely primitive bird ...

We were joking in the boat as we rowed under these cliffs and saying it would be a short-lived amusement to see the overhanging cliff part company and fall over us. So we were glad to find that we were rowing back to the ship and already 200 or 300 yards away from the place and in open water when there was a noise like crackling thunder and a huge plunge into the sea and a smother of rock dust like the smoke of an explosion, and we realised that the very thing had happened which we had just been talking about. Altogether it was a very exciting row, for before we got on board we had the pleasure of seeing the ship shoved in so close to these cliffs by a belt of heavy pack ice that to us it appeared a toss-up whether she got out again or got forced in against the rocks. She had no time or room to turn and get clear by backing out through the belt of pack stern first, getting heavy bumps under the counter and on the rudder as she did so, for the ice was heavy and the swell considerable. [Dr. Wilson's Journal]

9. Dr. Wilson writes in his Journal: *14 January* He also told me the plans for our depot journey on which we shall be starting in about ten days' time. He wants me to be a dog driver with himself, Meares, and Teddie Evans, and this is what I would have chosen had I had a free choice at all. The dogs run in two teams and each team wants two men. It means a lot of running as they are being driven now, but it is the fastest and most interesting work of all, and we go ahead of the whole caravan with lighter loads and at a faster rate; moreover, if any traction except ourselves can reach the top of Beardmore Glacier, it will be the dogs, and the dog drivers are therefore the people who will have the best chance of doing the top piece of the ice cap at 10,000 feet to the Pole. May I be there! About this time next year may I be there or thereabouts! With so many young bloods in the heyday of youth and strength beyond my own I feel there will be a most difficult task in making choice towards the end and a most keen competition – and a universal lack of selfishness and self-seeking with a complete absence of any jealous feeling in any single one of the comparatively large number who at present stand a chance of being on the last piece next summer.

It will be an exciting time and the excitement has already begun in the healthiest possible manner. I have never been thrown in with a more unselfish lot of men – each one doing his utmost fair and square in the most cheery manner possible.

As late as 15 October he writes further: 'No one yet knows who will be on the Summit party: it is to depend on condition, and fitness when we get there.' It is told of Scott, while still in New Zealand, that being pressed on the point, he playfully said, 'Well, I should like to have Bill to hold my hand when we get to the Pole'; but the Diary shows how the actual choice was made on the march. [Dr. Wilson's Journal]

10. Campbell, Levick, and Priestly set off to the old *Nimrod* hut eight miles away to see if they could find a stove of convenient size for their own hut, as well as any additional paraffin, and in default of the latter, to kill some seals for oil.

11. The management of stores and transport was finally entrusted to Bowers. Rennick therefore remained with the ship. A story told by Lady Scott illustrates the spirit of these men – the expedition first, personal distinctions nowhere. It was in New Zealand and the very day on which the order had been given for Bowers to exchange with Rennick. In the afternoon Captain Scott and his wife were returning from the ship to the house where they were staying; on the hill they saw the two men coming down with arms on each other's shoulders – a fine testimony to both. 'Upon my word,' exclaimed Scott, 'that shows Rennick in a good light!'

12. *29 January* The seals have been giving a lot of trouble, that is just to Meares and myself with our dogs. The whole teams go absolutely crazy when they sight them or get wind of them, and there are literally hundreds along some of the cracks. Occasionally when one pictures oneself quite away from trouble of that kind, an old seal will pop his head up at a blowhole a few yards ahead of the team, and they are all on top of him

before one can say 'Knife!' Then one has to rush in with the whip – and every one of the team of eleven jumps over the harness of the dog next to him and the harnesses become a muddle that takes much patience to unravel, not to mention care lest the whole team should get away with the sledge and its load and leave one behind to follow on foot at leisure. I never did get left the whole of this depot journey, but I was often very near it and several times had only time to seize a strap or a part of the sledge and be dragged along helter-skelter over everything that came in the way till the team got sick of galloping and one could struggle to one's feet again. One gets very wary and wide awake when one has to manage a team of eleven dogs and a sledge load by oneself, but it was a most interesting experience, and I had a delightful leader, 'Stareek' by name – Russian for 'Old Man', and he was the most wise old man. We have to use Russian terms with all our dogs. 'Ki Ki' means go to the right, 'Chui' means go to the left, 'Esh to' means lie down – and the remainder are mostly swear words which mean everything else which one has to say to a dog team. Dog driving like this in the orthodox manner is a very different thing to the beastly dog driving we perpetrated in the *Discovery* days. I got to love all my team and they got to know me well, and my old leader even now, six months after I have had anything to do with him, never fails to come and speak to me whenever he sees me, and he knows me and my voice ever so far off. He is quite a ridiculous 'old man' and quite the nicest, quietest, cleverest old dog I have ever come across. He looks in face as if he knew all the wickedness of all the world and all its cares and as if he were bored to death by them. [Dr. Wilson's Journal]

13. *15 February* There were also innumerable subsidences of the surface – the breaking of crusts over air spaces under them, large areas of dropping ¼ inch or so with a hushing sort of noise or muffled report. My leader Stareek, the nicest and wisest old dog in both teams, thought there was a rabbit under the crust every time one gave way close by him and he would jump sideways with both feet on the spot and his nose in the snow. The action was like a flash and never checked the team – it was most amusing. I have another funny little dog, Mukáka, small but very game and a good worker. He is paired with a fat, lazy and very greedy black dog, Nugis by name, and in every march this sprightly little Mukáka will once or twice notice that Nugis is not pulling and will jump over the trace, bite Nugis like a snap, and be back again in his own place before the fat dog knows what has happened. [Dr. Wilson's Journal]

13a. Taking up the story from the point where eleven of the thirteen dogs had been brought to the surface, Mr. Cherry-Garrard's Diary records:

This left the two at the bottom. Scott had several times wanted to go down. Bill said to me that he hoped he wouldn't, but now he insisted. We found the Alpine rope would reach, and then lowered Scott down to the platform, sixty feet below. I thought it very plucky. We then hauled the two dogs up on the rope, leaving Scott below. Scott said the dogs were very glad to see him; they had curled up asleep – it was wonderful they had no bones broken.

Then Meares' dogs, which were all wandering about loose, started fighting our team, and we all had to leave Scott and go and separate them, which took some time. They fixed on Noogis (I.) badly. We then hauled Scott up: it was all three of us could do – fingers a good deal frost-bitten at the end. That was all the dogs. Scott has just said that at one time he never hoped to get back the thirteen or even half of them. When he was down in the crevasse he wanted to go off exploring, but we dissuaded him. Of course it was a great opportunity. He kept on saying, 'I wonder why this is running the way it is – you expect to find them at right angles.'

Scott found inside crevasse warmer than above, but had no thermometer. It is a great wonder the whole sledge did not drop through: the inside was like the cliff of Dover.

14. *28 February* Meares and I led off with a dog team each, and leaving the Barrier we managed to negotiate the first long pressure ridge of the sea-ice where the seals all lie, without much trouble – the dogs were running well and fast and we kept on the old tracks, still visible, by which we had come out in January, heading a long way out to make a wide detour round the open water off Cape Armitage, from which a very wide extent of thick black fog, 'frost smoke' as we call it, was rising on our right. This completely obscured our view of the open water, and the only suggestion it gave me was that the thaw pool off the Cape was much bigger than when we passed it in January and that we should probably have to make a detour of three or four miles round it to reach Hut Point instead of one or two. I still thought it was not impossible to reach Hut Point this way, so we went on, but before we had run two miles on the sea-ice we noticed that we were coming on to an area broken up by fine thread-like cracks evidently quite fresh, and as I ran along by the sledge I paced them and found they curved regularly at every 30 paces, which could only mean that they were caused by a swell. This suggested to me that the thaw pool off Cape Armitage was even bigger than I thought and that we were getting on to ice which was breaking up, to flow north into it. We stopped to consider, and found that the cracks in the ice we were on were the rise and fall of a swell. Knowing that the ice might remain like this with each piece tight against the next only until the tide turned, I knew that we must get off it at once in case the tide did turn in the next half-hour, when each crack would open up into a wide lead of open water and we should find ourselves on an isolated floe. So we at once turned and went back as fast as possible to the unbroken sea-ice. Obviously it was now unsafe to go round to Hut Point by Cape Armitage and we therefore made for the Gap. It was between eight and nine in the evening when we turned, and we soon came in sight of the pony party, led as we thought by Captain Scott. We were within ½ a mile of them when we hurried right across their bows and headed straight for the Gap, making a course more than a right angle off the course we had been on. There was the seals' pressure ridge of sea-ice between us and them, but as I could see them quite distinctly I had no doubt they could see us, and we were occupied more than once just then in beating the teams

off stray seals, so that we didn't go by either vary quickly or very silently. From here we ran into the Gap, where there was some nasty pressed-up ice to cross and large gaps and cracks by the ice foot; but with the Alpine rope and a rush we got first one team over and then the other without mishap on to the land ice, and were then practically at Hut Point. However, expecting that the pony party was following us, we ran our teams up on to level ice, picketed them, and pitched our tent, to remain there for the night, as we had a half-mile of rock to cross to reach the hut and the sledges would have to be carried over this and the dogs led by hand in couples – a very long job. Having done this we returned to the ice foot with a pick and a shovel to improve the road up for horse party, as they would have to come over the same bad ice we had found difficult with the dogs; but they were nowhere to be seen close at hand as we had expected, for they were miles out, as we soon saw, still trying to reach Hut Point by the sea-ice round Cape Armitage thaw pool, and on the ice which was showing a working crack at thirty paces. I couldn't understand how Scott could do such a thing, and it was only the next day that I found out that Scott had remained behind and had sent Bowers in charge of this pony party. Bowers, having had no experience of the kind, did not grasp the situation for some time, and as we watched him and his party – or as we thought Captain Scott and his party – of ponies we saw them all suddenly realise that they were getting into trouble and the whole party turned back; but instead of coming back towards the Gap as we had, we saw them go due south towards the Barrier edge and White Island. Then I thought they were all right, for I knew they would get on to safe ice and camp for the night. We therefore had our supper in the tent and were turning in between eleven and twelve when I had a last look to see where they were and found they had camped as it appeared to me on safe Barrier ice, the only safe thing they could have done. They were now about six miles away from us, and it was lucky that I had my Goerz glasses with me so that we could follow their movements. Now as everything looked all right, Meares and I turned in and slept. At 5 a.m. I awoke, and as I felt uneasy about the party I went out and along the Gap to where we could see their camp, and I was horrified to see that the whole of the sea-ice was now on the move and that it had broken up for miles further than when we turned in and right back past where they had camped, and that the pony party was now, as we could see, adrift on a floe and separated by open water and a lot of drifting ice from the edge of the fast Barrier ice. We could see with our glasses that they were running the ponies and sledges over as quickly as possible from floe to floe whenever they could, trying to draw nearer to the safe Barrier ice again. The whole Strait was now open water to the N. of Cape Armitage, with the frost smoke rising everywhere from it, and full of pieces of floating ice, all going up N. to Ross Sea.

  1 March, Ash Wednesday The question for us was whether we could do anything to help them. There was no boat anywhere and there was no one to consult with, for everyone was on the floating floe as we believed, except Teddie Evans, Forde, and Keohane, who with one pony were on their way

back from Corner Camp. So we searched the Barrier for signs of their tent and then saw that there was a tent at Safety Camp, which meant evidently to us that they had returned. The obvious thing was to join up with them and go round to where the pony party was adrift, and see if we could help them to reach the safe ice. So without waiting for breakfast we went off six miles to this tent. We couldn't go now by the Gap, for the ice by which we had reached land yesterday was now broken up in every direction and all on the move up the Strait. We had no choice now but to cross up by Crater Hill and down by Pram Point and over the pressure ridges and so on to the Barrier and off to Safety Camp. We couldn't possibly take a dog sledge this way, so we walked, taking the Alpine rope to cross the pressure ridges, which are full of crevasses.

We got to this tent soon after noon and were astonished to find that not Teddie Evans and his two seamen were here, but that Scott and Oates and Gran were in it and no pony with them. Teddie Evans was still on his way back from Corner Camp and had not arrived. It was now for the first time that we understood how the accident had happened. When we had left Safety Camp yesterday with the dogs, the ponies began their march to follow us, but one of the ponies was so weak after the last blizzard and so obviously about to die that Bowers, Cherry-Garrard, and Crean were sent on with the four capable ponies, while Scott, Oates, and Gran remained at Safety Camp till the sick pony died, which happened apparently that night. He was dead and buried when we got there. We found that Scott had that morning seen the open water up to the Barrier edge and had been in a dreadful state of mind, thinking that Meares and I, as well as the whole pony party, had gone out into the Strait on floating ice. He was therefore much relieved when we arrived and he learned for the first time where the pony party was trying to get to fast ice again. We were now given some food, which we badly wanted, and while we were eating we saw in the far distance a single man coming hurriedly along the edge of the Barrier ice from the direction of the catastrophe party and towards our camp. Gran went off on ski to meet him, and when he arrived we found it was Crean, who had been sent off by Bowers with a note, unencumbered otherwise, to jump from one piece of floating ice to another until he reached the fast edge of the Barrier in order to let Capt. Scott know what had happened. This he did, of course not knowing that we or anyone else had seen him go adrift, and being unable to leave the ponies and all his loaded sledges himself. Crean had considerable difficulty and ran a pretty good risk in doing this, but succeeded all right. There were now Scott, Oates, Crean, Gran, Meares, and myself here and only three sleeping-bags, so the three first remained to see if they could help Bowers, Cherry-Garrard, and the ponies, while Meares, Gran, and I returned to look after our dogs at Hut Point. Here we had only two sleeping-bags for the three of us, so we had to take turns, and I remained up till 1 o'clock that night while Gran had six hours in my bag. It was a bitterly cold job after a long day. We had been up at 5 with nothing to eat till 1 o'clock, and walked 14 miles. The nights are now almost dark.

2 March A very bitter wind blowing and it was a cheerless job waiting for six hours to get a sleep in the bag. I walked down from our tent to the hut and watched whales blowing in the semi-darkness out in the black water of the Strait. When we turned out in the morning the pony party was still on floating ice but not any further from the Barrier ice. By a merciful providence the current was taking them rather along the Barrier edge, where they went adrift, instead of straight out to sea. We could do nothing more for them, so we set to our work with the dogs. It was blowing a bitter gale of wind from the S.E. with some drift and we made a number of journeys backwards and forwards between the Gap and the hut, carrying our tent and camp equipment down and preparing a permanent picketing line for the dogs. As the ice had all gone out of the Strait we were quite cut off from any return to Cape Evans until the sea should again freeze over, and this was not likely until the end of April. We rigged up a small fireplace in the hut and found some wood and made a fire for an hour or so at each meal, but as there was no coal and not much wood we felt we must be economical with the fuel, and so also with matches and everything else, in case Bowers should lose his sledge loads, which had most of the supplies for the whole party to last twelve men for two months. The weather had now become too thick for us to distinguish anything in the distance and we remained in ignorance as to the party adrift until Saturday. I had also lent my glasses to Captain Scott. This night I had first go in the bag, and turned out to shiver for eight hours till breakfast. There was literally nothing in the hut that one could cover oneself with to keep warm and we couldn't run to keeping the fire going. It was very cold work. There were heaps of biscuit cases here which we had left in *Discovery* days, and with these we built up a small inner hut to live in.

3 March Spent the day in transferring dogs in couples from the Gap to the hut. In the afternoon Teddie Evans and Atkinson turned up from over the hills, having returned from their Corner Camp journey with one horse and two seamen, all of which they had left encamped at Castle Rock, three miles off on the hills. They naturally expected to find Scott here and everyone else and had heard nothing of the pony party going adrift, but having found only open water ahead of them they turned back and came to land by Castle Rock slopes. We fed them and I walked half-way back to Castle Rock with them.

4 March Meares, Gran, and I walked up Ski Slope towards Castle Rock to meet Evans's party and pilot them and the dogs safely to Hut Point, but half-way we met Atkinson, who told us that they had now been joined by Scott and all the catastrophe party, who were safe, but who had lost all the ponies except one – a great blow. However, no lives were lost and the sledge loads and stores were saved, so Meares and I returned to Hut Point to make stables for the only two ponies that now remained, both in wretched condition, of the eight with which we started. [Dr. Wilson's Journal]

15. 12 *March* Thawed out some old magazines and picture papers which were left here by the *Discovery*, and gave us very good reading. [Dr. Wilson's Journal]

16. *4 April* Fun over a fry I made in my new penguin lard. It was quite a success and tasted like very bad sardine oil. [Dr. Wilson's Journal]

17. *Voyage of the Discovery*, chap. ix. 'The question of the moment is, what has become of our boats? Early in the winter they were hoisted out to give more room for the awning, and were placed in a line about one hundred yards from the ice foot on the sea-ice. The earliest gale drifted them up nearly gunwale high, and thus for two months they remained in sight whilst we congratulated ourselves on their security. The last gale brought more snow, and piling it in drifts at various places in the bay, chose to be specially generous with it in the neighbourhood of our boats, so that afterwards they were found to be buried three or four feet beneath the new surface. Although we had noted with interest the manner in which the extra weight of snow in other places was pressing down the surface of the original ice, and were even taking measurements of the effects thus produced, we remained fatuously blind to the risks our boats ran under such conditions. It was from no feeling of anxiety, but rather to provide occupation, that I directed that the snow on top of them should be removed, and it was not until we had dug down to the first boat that the true state of affairs dawned on us. She was found lying in a mass of slushy ice, with which also she was nearly filled. For the moment we had a wild hope that she could be pulled up, but by the time we could rig shears the air temperature had converted the slush into hardened ice, and she was found to be stuck fast. At present there is no hope of recovering any of the boats: as fast as one could dig out the sodden ice, more sea-water would flow in and freeze … The danger is that fresh gales bringing more snow will sink them so far beneath the surface that we shall be unable to recover them at all. Stuck solid in the floe they must go down with it, and every effort must be devoted to preventing the floe from sinking. As regards the rope, it is a familiar experience that dark objects which absorb heat will melt their way through the snow or ice on which they lie.

18.

PONIES PRESENTED BY SCHOOLS, &c.		
School's, &c., name of Pony.	Nickname of Pony.	Name of School, &c., presented by.
Floreat Etona	Snippet	Eton College.
Christ'sHospital	Hackenschmidt	Christ's Hospital.
Westminster	Blossom	Westminster.
St. Paul's	Michael	St. Paul's.
Stubbington	Weary Willie	Stubbington House, Fareham.
Bedales	Christopher	Bedales, Petersfield.
Lydney	Victor	The Institute, Lydney, Gloucester.
West Down	Jones	West Down School.
Bootham	Snatcher	Bootham.
South Hampstead	Bones	South Hampstead High School (Girls).
Altrincham	Chinaman	Seamen's Moss School, Altrincham.
Rosemark	Cuts	Captain and Mrs. Mark Kerr (H.M.S. *Invincible*).
Invincible	James Pigg	Officers and Ship's Company of H.M.S. *Invincible*.
Snooker King	Jehu	J. Foster Stackhouse and friend.
Brandon	Punch	The Bristol Savages.
Stoker	Blucher	R. Donaldson Hudson, Esq.
Manchester	Nobby	Manchester various
Cardiff	Uncle Bill	Cardiff „
Liverpool	Davy	Liverpool „

SLEEPING-BAGS PRESENTED BY SCHOOLS

School's, &c., name of Sleeping-bag.	Name of traveller using Sleeping-bag.	Name of School, &c., presenting Sleeping-bag.
Cowbridge	Commander Evans	Cowbridge
Wisk Hove	Lieutenant Campbell	The Wisk, Hove.
Taunton	Seaman Williamson	King's College, Taunton.
Bryn Derwen	Seaman Keohane	Bryn Derwen.
Grange	Dr. Simpson	The Grange, Folkestone.
Brighton	Lieutenant Bowers	Brighton Grammar School.
Cardigan	Captain Scott	The County School, Cardigan.
Carter-Eton	Mr. Cherry-Garrard	Mr. R. T. Carter, Eton College.
Radley	Mr. Ponting	Stones Social School, Radley.
Woodford	Mr. Meares	Woodford House.
Bramhall	Seaman Abbott	Bramhall Grammar School.
Louth	Dr. Atkinson	King Edward VI. Grammar School, Louth.
Twyford I.	Seaman Forde	Twyford School
Twyford II.	Mr. Day	„　　　„
Abbey House	Seaman Dickason	Mr. Carvey's House, Abbey House School.
Waverley	Mr. Wright	Waverley Road, Birmingham.
St. John's	Seaman Evans	St. John's House
Leyton	Ch. Stoker Lashly	Leyton County High School.
St. Bede's	Seaman Browning	Eastbourne.
Sexeys	Dr. Wilson	Sexeys School.
Worksop	Mr. Debenham	Worksop College.
Regent	Mr. Nelson	Regent Street Polytechnic Secondary School.
Trafalgar	Captain Oates	Trafalgar House School, Winchester.

School's, &c., name of Sleeping-bag.	Name of traveller using Sleeping-bag.	Name of School, &c., presenting Sleeping-bag.
Altrincham	Mr. Griffith Taylor	Altrincham, various.
Invincible	Dr. Levick	Ship's Company, H.M.S. *Invincible*.
Leeds	Mr. Priestley	Leeds Boys' Modern School.

SLEDGES PRESENTED BY SCHOOLS

School's, &c., name of Sledge.	Description of Sledge.	Name of School, &c., presenting Sledge.
Amesbury	Pony : Uncle Bill (Cardiff)	Amesbury, Bickley Hall, Kent.
John Bright	Dog sledge	Bootham.
Sherborne	Pony : Snippets (Floreat Etona)	Sherborne House School.
Wimbledon	Pony : Blossom (Westminster)	King's College School, Wimbledon.
Kelvinside	Northern sledge (man-hauled)	Kelvinside Academy.
Pip	Dog sledge	Copthorne.
Christ'sHospital	Dog sledge	Christ's Hospital.
Hampstead	Dog sledge	University College School, Hampstead.
Glasgow	Pony : Snatcher (Bootham)	High School, Glasgow.
George Dixon	Pony : Nobby (Manchester)	George Dixon Secondary School.
Leys	Pony : Punch (Brandon)	Leys School, Cambridge.
Northampton	Motor sledge, No. 1	Northampton County School.
Charterhouse I.	Pony : Blucher (Stoker)	Charterhouse.
Charterhouse II.	Western sledge (man-hauled)	Charterhouse.

School's, &c., name of Sledge.	Description of Sledge.	Name of School, &c., presenting Sledge.
Regent	Northern sledge (man-hauled)	Regent Street Polytechnic Secondary School.
Sidcot	Pony : Hackenschmidt (Christ's Hospital)	Sidcot, Winscombe.
Retford	Pony : Michael (St. Paul's)	Retford Grammar School.
Tottenham	Northern sledge (man-hauled)	Tottenham Grammar School.
Cheltenham	Pony : James Pigg (H.M.S. *Invincible*)	The College, Cheltenham.
Knight	First Summit sledge (man-hauled)	Sidcot School, Old Boys.
Crosby	Pony : Christopher (Bedales)	Crosby Merchant Taylors'.
Grange	Pony : Chinaman (Altrincham)	' Grange,' Buxton.
Altrincham	Pony : Victor (Lydney)	Altrincham (various).
Probus	Pony : Weary Willie (Stubbington)	Probus.
Rowntree	Second Summit sledge (man-hauled)	Workmen, Rowntree's Cocoa Works.
' Invincible ' I.	Third Summit sledge (man-hauled)	Officers and Men, H.M.S. *Invincible*.
' Invincible ' II.	Pony : Jehu (Snooker King)	Do.
Eton	Pony : Bones (South Hampstead)	Eton College.
Masonic	Motor Sledge, No. 2	Royal Masonic School, Bushey.

TENTS PRESENTED BY SCHOOLS

Name of Tent.	Party to which attached.	School presenting Tent.
Fitz Roy	Southern Party	Fitz Roy School, Crouch End.
Ashdown	Northern Party	Ashdown House, Forest Row, Sussex.
Brighton & Hove	Reserve, Cape Evans	Brighton & Hove High School, (Girls).
Bromyard	Do.	Grammar, Bromyard.
Marlborough	Do.	The College, Marlborough.
Bristol	Mr. Ponting (photographic artist)	Colchester House, Bristol.
Croydon	Reserve, Cape Evans	Croydon High School.
Broke Hall	Do.	Broke Hall, Charterhouse.
Pelham	Southern Party	Pelham House, Folkestone.
Tollington	Depôt Party	Tollington School, Muswell Hill.
St. Andrews	Southern Party	St. Andrews, Newcastle.
Richmond	Dog Party	Richmond School, Yorks.
Hymers	Depôt Party	Scientific Society, Hymers College, Hull.
King Edward	Do.	King Edward's School.
Southport	Cape Crozier Depôt	Southport Physical Training College.
Jarrow	Reserve, Cape Evans	Jarrow Secondary School.
Grange	Do.	The Grange, Buxton.
Swindon	Do.	Swindon
Sir John Deane	Motor Party	Sir. J. Deane's Grammar School.
Llandaff	Reserve, Cape Evans	Llandaff.

Name of Tent.	Party to which attached.	School presenting Tent.
Castleford	Reserve, Cape Evans	Castleford Secondary School.
Hailey	Do.	Hailey.
Uxbridge	Northern Party	Uxbridge County School.
Stubbington	Reserve, Cape Evans	Stubbington House, Fareham.

19. These hints on Polar Surveying fell on willing ears. Members of the afterguard who were not mathematically trained plunged into the very practical study of how to work out observations. Writing home on 26 October 1911, Scott remarks:

'"Cherry" has just come to me with a very anxious face to say that I must not count on his navigating powers. For the moment I didn't know what he was driving at, but then I remembered that some months ago I said that it would be a good thing for all the officers going South to have some knowledge of navigation so that in emergency they would know how to steer a sledge home. It appears that "Cherry" thereupon commenced a serious and arduous course of study of abstruse navigational problems which he found exceedingly tough and now despaired mastering. Of course there is not one chance in a hundred that he will ever have to consider navigation on our journey and in that one chance the problem must be of the simplest nature, but it makes matters much easier for me to have men who take the details of one's work so seriously and who strive so simply and honestly to make it successful.'

And in Wilson's diary for 23 October comes the entry: 'Working at latitude sights – mathematics which I hate – till bedtime. It will be wiser to know a little navigation on the Southern sledge journey.'

20. Happily I had a biscuit with me and I held it out to him a long way off. Luckily he spotted it and allowed me to come up, and I got hold of his head again. [Dr. Wilson's Journal]

21. *8 December* I have left Nobby all my biscuits tonight as he is to try and do a march tomorrow, and then happily he will be shot and all of them, as their food is quite done.

9 December Nobby had all my biscuits last night and this morning, and by the time we camped I was just ravenously hungry. It was a close cloudy day with no air and we were ploughing along knee deep ... Thank God the horses are now all done with and we begin the heavy work ourselves. [Dr. Wilson's Journal]

22. *9 December* The end of the Beardmore Glacier curved across the track of the Southern Party, thrusting itself into the mass of the Barrier with vast pressure and disturbance. So far did this ice disturbance extend, that if the travellers had taken a bee-line to the foot of the glacier itself, they must have begun to steer outwards 200 miles sooner.

The Gateway was a neck or saddle of drifted snow lying in a gap of the mountain rampart which flanked the last curve of the glacier. Under the cliffs on either hand, like a moat beneath the ramparts, lay a yawning ice-cleft or bergschrund, formed by the drawing away of the steadily moving Barrier ice from the rocks. Across this moat and leading up to the gap in the ramparts, the Gateway provided a solid causeway. To climb this and descend its reverse face gave the easiest access to the surface of the glacier.

23. Return of first Southern Party from Lat. 85° 7' S. top of the Beardmore Glacier.

Party: E. L. Atkinson, A. Cherry-Garrard, C. S. Wright, Petty Officer Keohane.

On the morning of 22 December 1911, we made a late start after saying good-bye to the eight going on, and wishing them all good luck and success. The first 11 miles was on the down-grade over the ice-falls, and at a good pace we completed this in about four hours. Lunched, and on, completing nearly 23 miles for the first day. At the end of the second day we got among very bad crevasses through keeping too far to the eastward. This delayed us slightly and we made the depot on the third day. We reached the Lower Glacier Depot three and a half days after. The lower part of the glacier was very badly crevassed. These crevasses we had never seen on the way up, as they had been covered with three to four feet of snow. All the bridges of crevasses were concave and very wide; no doubt their normal summer condition. On Christmas Day we made in to the lateral moraine of the Cloudmaker and collected geological specimens. The march across the Barrier was only remarkable for the extremely bad lights we had. For eight consecutive days we only saw an exceedingly dim sun during three hours. Up to One Ton Depot our marches had averaged 14.1 geographical miles a day. We arrived at Cape Evans on 28 January 1912, after being away for three months. [E.L.A.]

24. *3 January* Return of the second supporting party.

Under average conditions, the return party should have well fulfilled Scott's cheery anticipations. Three-man teams had done excellently on previous sledging expeditions, whether in *Discovery* days or as recently as the mid-winter visit to the Emperor penguins' rookery; and the three in this party were seasoned travellers with a skilled navigator to lead them. But a blizzard held them up for three days before reaching the head of the glacier. They had to press on at speed. By the time they reached the foot of the glacier, Lieut. Evans developed symptoms of scurvy. His spring work of surveying and sledging out to Corner Camp and the man-hauling, with Lashly, across the Barrier after the breakdown of the motors, had been successfully accomplished; this sequel to the Glacier and Summit marches was an unexpected blow.

Withal, he continued to pull, while bearing the heavy strain of guiding the course. While the hauling power thus grew less, the leader had to make up for loss of speed by lengthening the working hours. He put his watch on an hour. With the 'turning out' signal thus advanced, the actual marching period reached 12 hours. The situation was saved, and Evans flattered himself on his ingenuity. But the men knew it all the time, and no word said!

At One Ton Camp he was unable to stand without the support of his ski sticks; but with the help of his companions struggled on another 53 miles in four days. Then he could go no farther. His companions, rejecting his suggestion that he be left in his sleeping-bag with a supply of provisions while they pressed on for help, 'cached' everything that could be spared, and pulled him on the sledge with a devotion matching that of their captain years before, when he and Wilson brought their companion Shackleton, ill and helpless, safely home to the *Discovery*. Four days of this pulling, with a southerly wind to help, brought them to Corner Camp; then came a heavy snowfall: the sledge could not travel. It was a critical moment. Next day Crean set out to tramp alone to Hut Point, 34 miles away. Lashly stayed to nurse Lieut. Evans, and most certainly saved his life till help came. Crean reached Hut Point after an exhausting march of 18 hours; how the dog-team went to the rescue is told by Dr. Atkinson in the second volume. At the *Discovery* hut Evans was unremittingly tended by Dr. Atkinson, and finally sent by sledge to the *Terra Nova*. It is good to record that both Lashly and Crean have received the Albert medal.

25. At this point begins the last of Scott's notebooks. The record of the Southern Journey is written in pencil in three slim MS. books, some 8 inches long by 5 wide. These little volumes are meant for artists' notebooks, and are made of tough, soft, pliable paper which takes the pencil well. The pages, 96 in number, are perforated so as to be detachable at need.

In the Hut, large quarto MS. books were used for the journals, and some of the rough notes of the earlier expeditions were recast and written out again in them; the little books were carried on the sledge journeys, and contain the day's notes entered very regularly at the lunch halts and in the night camps. But in the last weeks of the Southern Journey, when fuel and light ran short and all grew very weary, it will be seen that Scott made his entries at lunch time alone. They tell not of the morning's run only, but of 'yesterday'.

The notes were written on the right-hand pages, and when the end of the book was reached, it was 'turned' and the blank backs of the leaves now became clean right-hand pages. The first two MS. books are thus entirely filled: the third has only part of its pages used and the Message to the Public is written at the reverse end.

Inside the front cover of No. 1 is a 'ready' table to convert the day's run of geographical miles as recorded on the sledgemeter into statute miles, a list of the depots and their latitude, and a note of the sledgemeter reading at Corner Camp.

These are followed in the first pages by a list of the outward camps and distances run as noted in the book, with special 'remarks' as to cairns, latitude, and so forth. At the end of the book is a full list of the cairns that marked the track out.

Inside the front cover of No. 2 are similar entries, together with the ages of the Polar party and a note of the error of Scott's watch.

Inside the front cover of No. 3 are the following words: 'Diary can be read by finder to ensure recording of Records, etc., but Diary should be sent to my widow.' And on the first page:

Send this diary to my widow.

R. SCOTT.

The word 'wife' had been struck out and 'widow' written in.

26. At this, the Barrier stage of the return journey, the Southern Party were in want of more oil than they found at the depots. Owing partly to the severe conditions, but still more to the delays imposed by their sick comrades, they reached the full limit of time allowed for between depots. The cold was unexpected, and at the same time the actual amount of oil found at the depots was less than they had counted on.

Under summer conditions, such as were contemplated, when there was less cold for the men to endure, and less firing needed to melt the snow for cooking, the fullest allowance of oil was 1 gallon to last a unit of four men ten days, or 1/40th of a gallon a day for each man.

The amount allotted to each unit for the return journey from the South was apparently rather less, being 2/3rd gallon for eight days, or 1/48th gallon a day for each man. But the eight days were to cover the march from depot to depot, averaging on the Barrier some 70–80 miles, which in normal conditions should not take more than six days. Thus there was a substantial margin for delay by bad weather, while if all went well the surplus afforded the fullest marching allowance.

The same proportion for a unit of five men works out at 5/6th of a gallon for the eight-day stage.

Accordingly, for the return of the two supporting parties and the Southern Party, two tins of a gallon each were left at each depot, each unit of four men being entitled to 1/48th of a gallon, and the units of three and five men in proportion.

The return journey on the Summit had been made at good speed, taking twenty-one days as against twenty-seven going out, the last part of it, from Three Degree to Upper Glacier Depot, taking nearly eight marches as against ten, showing the first slight slackening as P.O. Evans and Oates began to feel the cold; from Upper Glacier to Lower Glacier Depot ten marches as against eleven, a stage broken by the Mid Glacier Depot of three and a half day's provisions at the sixth march. Here, there was little gain, partly owing to the conditions, but more to Evans' gradual collapse.

The worst time came on the Barrier; from Lower Glacier to Southern Barrier Depot (51 miles), 6½ marches as against 5 (two of which were short marches, so that the 5 might count as an easy 4 in point of distance); from Southern Barrier to Mid Barrier Depot (82 miles), 6½ marches as against 5½; from Mid Barrier to Mt. Hooper (70 miles), 8 as against 4¾, while the last remaining 8 marches represent but 4 on the outward journey. (**See table on page 343.**)

At to the cause of the shortage, the tins of oil at the depot had been exposed to extreme conditions of heat and cold. The oil was specially volatile, and in the warmth of the sun (for the tins were regularly set in an accessible place on the top of the cairns) tended to become vapour and escape through the stoppers even without damage to the tins. This process was much accelerated by reason that the leather washers about the stoppers had perished in the great cold. Dr. Atkinson gives two striking examples of this.

1. Eight 1-gallon tins in a wooden case, intended for a depot at Cape Crozier, had been put out in September 1911. They were snowed up; and when examined in December 1912 showed three tins full, three empty, one a third full, and one two-thirds full.

2. When the search party reached One Ton Camp in November 1912 they found that some of the food, stacked in a canvas 'tank' at the foot of the cairn, was quite oily from the spontaneous leakage of the tins seven feet above it on the top of the cairn.

The tins at the depots awaiting the Southern Party had of course been opened and the due amount to be taken measured out by the supporting parties on their way back. However carefully re-stoppered, they were still liable to the unexpected evaporation and leakage already described. Hence, without any manner of doubt, the shortage which struck the Southern Party so hard.

27. The Fatal Blizzard. Mr. Frank Wild, who led one wing of Dr. Mawson's Expedition on the northern coast of the Antarctic continent, Queen Mary's Land, many miles to the west of the Ross Sea, writes that 'from March 21 for a period of nine days we were kept in camp by the same blizzard which proved fatal to Scott and his gallant companions' (*Times*, 2 June 1913). Blizzards, however, are so local that even when, as in this case, two are nearly contemporaneous, it is not safe to conclude that they are part of the same current of air.

TABLE OF DISTANCES showing the length of the Outward and Return Marches on the Barrier from and to One Ton Camp.

3 miles to each sub-division

Date	Camp No.	Outward		Return	Camp No.	Date
Nov. 15, 16	12	— One Ton Camp —				
		15				
Nov. 17	13			— The Last Camp —	R. 60	Mar. 19
				‑‑Lunch, 15½ (17½) to Depot		
		15			R. 59	Mar. 18
				····Lunch, 21 (24) to Depot	R. 58	Mar. 17
Nov. 18	14			··Lunch, 25½ (30) to Depot	Blizz'd R. 57	Mar. 15–16
		15		?6 ?5	R. 56	Mar. 14
Nov. 19	15			?7 ?6	R. 55	Mar. 13
		15		6 5¼	R. 54	Mar. 12
				— 47 (55) to Depot —		
Nov. 20	16			····Lunch ?8 ?7	R. 53	Mar. 11
		15 Mt. Hooper Depot —		8 6·9	R. 52	Mar. 9-10
Nov. 21	17			?6	R. 51	Mar. 8
		15		····Lunch, 8½ (9¾) to Depot ?8		
Nov. 22	18			···Lunch, 16 (18½) to Depot 8 7	R. 50	Mar. 7
		15		7½ 6½	R. 49	Mar. 6
				— 27 (31½) to Depot —	R. 48	Mar. 5
Nov. 23	19			11 9½		
		15			R. 47	Mar. 4
Nov. 24	20			····Lunch, 42 to Depot 10¾ 9	R. 46	Mar. 3
		15		5¼ 4½	R. 45	Mar. 2
Nov. 25	21			11½ Nearly 10		
		Mid Barrier Depot — 15			R. 44	Mar. 1
Nov. 26	22			··Lunch, under 3 to Depot 10¼ Nearly 9	R. 43	Feb. 29
		15		····Lunch, 13 to Depot		
Nov. 27	23			13¼ 11½	R. 42	Feb. 28

The figures give statute miles, excepting those on the extreme right or those in brackets, which give geographical miles.

TABLE OF DISTANCES showing the length of the Outward and Return Marches on the Barrier from and to One Ton Camp.

3 miles to each sub-division.

Outward marches

Date	Camp No.	Miles	
Nov. 27	23		
		15	
Nov. 28	24		
		15	
Nov. 29	25		
		15	
Nov. 30	26		
		15	
Dec. 1	27		Southern Barrier Depot
		15	
Dec. 2	28		
		11½	
Dec. 3	29		
		13	
Dec. 4-8	30		
		? 7	
Dec. 9	31		Shambles
		3½	
Dec. 10	32		Lower Glacier Depot
		? 6	
Dec. 11	33		
		8½	
Dec. 12	34		
		4	
Dec. 13	35		
		11½	[11 or 12]
Dec. 14	36		
		11	
Dec. 15	37		
		11	
Dec. 16	38		

Return marches

Statute miles	Geographical miles	Camp No.	Date
		R. 42	Feb. 28
....Lunch			
13¼	11½		
		R. 41	Feb. 27
14	12·2		
		R. 40	Feb. 26
13¼	11½		
		R. 39	Feb. 25
13¼	11·4		
		R. 38	Feb. 24
9¾	8½		
		R. 37	Feb. 23
9½	8¼		
		R. 36	Feb. 22
? 9¾			
		R. 35	Feb. 21
9¾	8½		
		R. 34	Feb. 20
8¼	7		
		R. 33	Feb. 19
	4·6		
		R. 32	Feb. 18
		R. 31	Feb. 17
		R. 30	Feb. 16
? 15			
		R. 29	Feb. 15
15½			
		R. 28	Feb. 14
? 13			
		R. 27	Feb. 13

The figures give statute miles, excepting those on the extreme right, which give geographical miles. The marches from Feb. 13–17 do not follow the same track as the outward marches, and must not be measured by the scale.

TABLE OF DISTANCES showing the length of the Outward and Return Marches on the Barrier from and to One Ton Camp.

3 miles to each sub-division.

Date	Camp No.				Camp No.	Date
Dec. 16	38					
		12⅓			R. 27	Feb. 13
Dec. 17	39	— Depot —	66	.... Lunch		
				? 13	R. 26	Feb. 12
		14				
Dec. 18	40			(? 16)		
				? 13 made good	R. 25	Feb. 11
		17				
Dec. 19	41		96	(? 17)		
				? 13 made good	R. 24	Feb. 10
		23		? 12		
					R. 23	Feb. 9
Dec. 20	42			15 about 13	R. 22	Feb. 8
		13				
Dec. 21	43	—Upper Glacier Depot—	132	10⅓ 9·2	R. 21	Feb. 7
		12				
Dec. 22	44			18		
					R. 20	Feb. 6
		17¼				
Dec. 23	45		162	(17) 15 made good	R. 19	Feb. 5
		16				
Dec 24	46					
				21		
		17¼			R. 18	Feb. 4
Dec. 25	47		192			
		15		21		
Dec. 26	48				R. 17	Feb. 3
		15⅓		18		
Dec. 27	49		222		R. 16	Feb. 2

The numbers give statute miles, excepting those on the extreme right, which give geographical miles. The marches after Feb. 8 are of uncertain length.

TABLE OF DISTANCES showing the length of the Outward and Return Marches on the Barrier from and to One Ton Camp.

3 miles to each sub-division.

Date	Camp No.	Outward		Return	Camp No.	Date
Dec. 27	49		222		R. 16	Feb. 2
Dec. 28	50	15	237	19½		
					R. 15	Feb. 1
Dec. 29	51	13¾	252	18		
					R. 14	Jan. 31
Dec. 30	52	12⅔				
Dec. 31	53	8 Half march to —Three Degree Depot—	273	15½ —Depot		
					R. 13	Jan. 30
Jan. 1	54	13	285			
Jan. 2	55	15	300	24	R. 12	Jan. 29
Jan. 3	56	13¾	312			
				23	R. 11	Jan. 28
Jan. 4	57	14¼ Morning; Evans returned	327			
Jan. 5	58	14¼	342	18	R. 10	Jan. 27
Jan. 6	59	12	354	16		
					R. 9	Jan. 26
Jan. 7–8	60	10½	363			
Jan. 9	61	7¼ Half-day	372	17¾		
					R. 8	Jan. 25
Jan. 10	62	12 One-and-a-half Degree Depot	384	—Depot		
				14	R. 7	Jan. 24
Jan. 11	63	12¾	396	8 Half-day; Blizzard	R. 6	Jan. 23

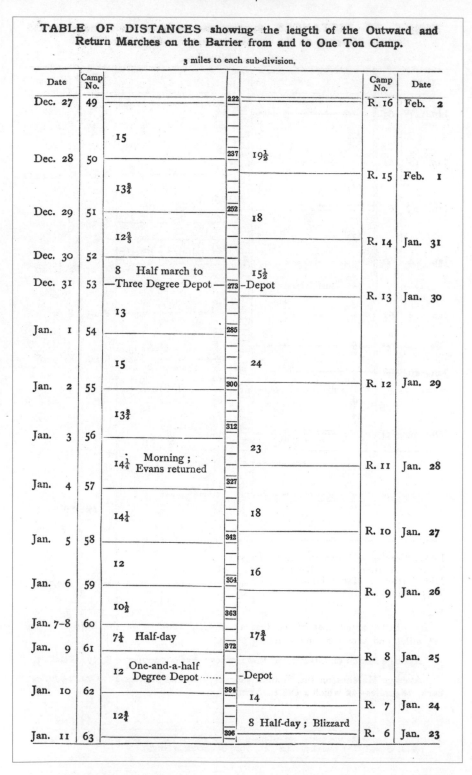

TABLE OF DISTANCES showing the length of the Outward and Return Marches on the Barrier from and to One Ton Camp.

3 miles to each sub-division.

Date	Camp No.				Camp No.	Date
Jan. 11	63		396		R. 6	Jan. 23
		12½		18		
Jan. 12	64		408		R. 5	Jan. 22
		12¾				
Jan. 13	65		420	16¾		
		13¼			R. 4	Jan. 21
Jan. 14	66		435	6¼ Half-day ; Blizzard	R. 3	Jan. 20
		14 Last Depot ⋯⋯		⋯⋯ Lunch at Depot		
Jan. 15	67		450	18⅓		
		15			R. 2	Jan. 19
Jan. 16	68		465	18½		
		16			R. 1	Jan. 18
				7		
Jan. 17	69	5 POLE	480	12 Total for the day ⋯⋯		
				5		

The figures give statute miles.

				Marches	
				Out	Return
Lower Glacier to Southern Barrier Depot	...	...	...	5	6½
Southern Barrier to Mid Barrier Depot	...	...	...	5½	8¼
Mid Barrier to Mount Hooper...	...	...	...	4¾	8
Thereafter...	...	...	...	4	8

It will be noted that of the first 15 Return Marches on the Barrier, 5 are 11⅓ miles and upwards, and 5 are 8½ to 10.

Average March on Glacier : Out, 12 miles ; Back, 13 miles.

Average Marches on the Summit Journey, omitting half-days : Out, 14 miles ; Back, 18½ miles—of which 4 exceed 20 miles.

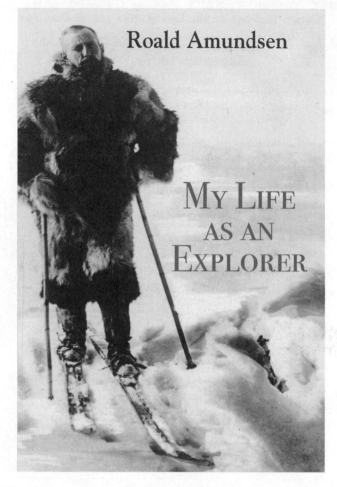

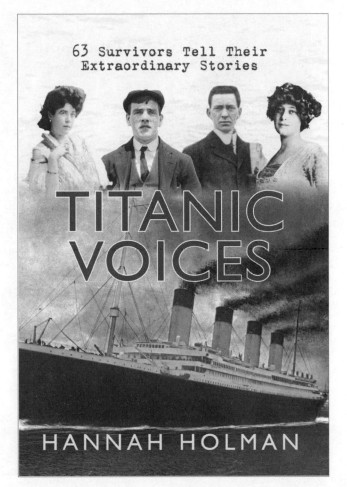

Also available from Amberley Publishing

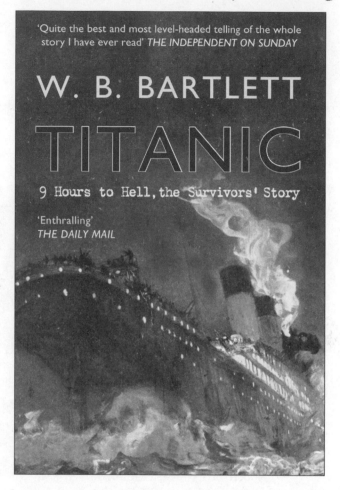

A major new history of the disaster that weaves into the narrative the first-hand accounts of those who survived

'Enthralling' THE DAILY MAIL
'Quite the best and most level-headed telling of the whole story I have ever read'
THE INDEPENDENT ON SUNDAY

It was twenty minutes to midnight on Sunday 14 April, when Jack Thayer felt the Titanic lurch to port, a motion followed by the slightest of shocks. Seven-year old Eva Hart barely noticed anything was wrong. For Stoker Fred Barrett, shovelling coal down below, it was somewhat different; the side of the ship where he was working caved in. For the next nine hours, Jack, Eva and Fred faced death and survived. 1600 people did not. This is the story told through the eyes of Jack, Eva, Fred and over a hundred others of those who survived and recorded their experiences.

£9.99 Paperback
72 illustrations (14 colour)
368 pages
978-1-4456-0482-4

Available from all good bookshops or to order direct
Please call **01453-847-800**
www.amberleybooks.com

SHIP'S PARTY

Harry L. L. Pennell, Lieutenant, R.N.

Henry E. de P. Rennick, Lieutenant, R.N.

Wilfred M. Bruce, Lieutenant, R.N.R.

Francis R. H. Drake, Asst. Paymaster, R.N. (Retired), Secretary &
Meteorologist in Ship.

Dennis G. Lillie, M.A., Biologist in Ship.

James R. Denniston, In Charge of Mules in Ship.

Alfred B. Cheetham, R.N.R., Boatswain.

William Williams, Chief Engine-room Artificer, R.N., Engineer.

William A. Horton, Eng. Rm. Art., 3rd Cl., R.N., 2nd Engineer.

Francis E. C. Davies, Leading Shipwright, R.N.

Frederick Parsons, Petty Officer, R.N.

William L. Heald, Late P.O., R.N.

Arthur S. Bailey, Petty Officer, 2nd Class, R.N.

Albert Balson, Leading Seaman, R.N.

Joseph Leese, Able Seaman, R.N.

John Hugh Mather, Petty Officer, R.N.V.R.

Robert Oliphant, Able Seaman.

Thomas F. McLeon, Able Seaman.

Mortimer McCarthy, Able Seaman.

William Knowles, Able Seaman.

Charles Williams, Able Seaman.

James Skelton, Able Seaman.

William McDonald, Able Seaman.

James Paton, Able Seaman.

Robert Brissenden, Leading Stoker, R.N.

Edward A. McKenzie, Leading Stoker, R.N.

William Burton, Leading Stoker, R.N.

Bernard J. Stone, Leading Stoker, R.N.

Angus McDonald, Fireman.

Thomas McGillon, Fireman.

Charles Lammas, Fireman.

W. H. Neale, Steward.

LIST OF EXPEDITION TEAM:
BRITISH ANTARCTIC EXPEDITION, 1910

SHORE PARTIES

Officers
Robert Falcon Scott, Captain, R.N., C.V.O.
Edward R. G. R. Evans, Commander, R.N.
Victor L. A. Campbell, Lieutenant, R.N. (Emergency List).
Henry R. Bowers, Lieutenant, R.I.M.
Lawrence E. G. Oates, Captain 6th Inniskilling Dragoons.
G. Murray Levick, Surgeon, R.N.
Edward L. Atkinson, Surgeon, R.N., Parasitologist.

Scientific Staff
Edward Adrian Wilson, M.A., M.B. (Cantab), Chief of the Scientific Staff,
and Zoologist.
George C. Simpson, D.Sc., Meteorologist.
T. Griffith Taylor, B.A., B.Sc., B.E., Geologist.
Edward W. Nelson, Biologist.
Frank Debenham, B.A., B.Sc., Geologist.
Charles S. Wright, B.A., Physicist.
Raymond E. Priestley, Geologist.
Herbert G. Ponting, F.R.G.S., Camera Artist.
Cecil H. Meares, In Charge of Dogs.
Bernard C. Day, Motor Engineer.
Apsley Cherry-Garrard, B.A., Asst. Zoologist.
Tryggve Gran, Sub-Lieutenant, Norwegian N.R., Ski Expert.

Men
W. Lashly, Chief Stoker R.N..
W. W. Archer, Chief Steward, late R.N.
Thomas Clissold, Cook, late R.N.
Edgar Evans, Petty Officer, R.N.
Robert Forde, Petty Officer, R.N.
Thomas Crean, Petty Officer, R.N.
Thomas S. Williamson, Petty Officer, R.N.
Patrick Keohane, Petty Officer, R.N.
George P. Abbott, Petty Officer, R.N.
Frank V. Browning, Petty Officer, 2nd Class, R.N.
Harry Dickason, Able Seaman, R.N.
F. J. Hooper Steward, late R.N.
Anton Omelchenko, Groom.
Demetri Gerof, Dog Driver.